A PRACTICAL GUIDE FOR PILGRIMS

THE ROAD TO SANTIAGO

MILLÁN BRAVO LOZANO

Carried out by the «Centro de Estudios del Camino de Santiago»
(Centre for Studies into the Pilgrims' Route to Santiago)

centro
estudios
camino
santiago
s a h a g ú n

EDITORIAL EVEREST, S. A.

Madrid • León • Barcelona • Sevilla • Granada • Valencia
Zaragoza • Las Palmas de Gran Canaria • La Coruña
Palma de Mallorca • Alicante • México • Lisboa

A PRACTICAL GUIDE FOR PILGRIMS
THE ROAD TO SANTIAGO

MILLÁN BRAVO LOZANO

centro
estudios
camino
santiago
s a h a g ú n

EDITORIAL EVEREST, S. A.

Collaborating team:
Director: Millán BRAVO LOZANO
Field researchers: José María ANGUITA JAÉN
Documentation: José María ANGUITA JAÉN, Ana R. PASCUAL VELÁZQUEZ
Coordination: Carmen SACEDA GARCÍA-ABAD

From Roncesvalles to Santiago: see page 248

Transalation:
Sara Keane and EURO:TEXT

Photographs:
Miguel RAURICH
With help from Agustín BERRUETA, Justino DÍEZ, ORONOZ, CIGANOVIC,
Francisco DÍEZ and the EVEREST Archives
Cover photograph courtesy of Hans-Günther KAUFMANN

Design and layout:
Gerardo RODERA

Cover design:
Alfredo ANIEVAS

FOURTH EDITION
© MILLÁN BRAVO LOZANO
© EDITORIAL EVEREST
Carretera León-La Coruña, km 5 - LEÓN
ISBN: 84-241-3833-3
Depósito legal: LE. 2-1997
Printed in Spain - Impreso en España

EDITORIAL EVERGRÁFICAS, S. L.
Carretera León-La Coruña, km 5
LEÓN (España)

CONTENTS

INTRODUCTION

Dedicated to the Pilgrims' Way to Santiago,
'European Cultural Route', 'European Cultural
Heritage', 'Heritage of Mankind'.

To all who were born along its edge.
To all who value it.
To all who travel along it.

As this book is a 'Practical guide for pilgrims', it has certain special characteristics. Rather than writing a conventional tourist guidebook or historical and artistic reference book, my intention has been to describe the route that the pilgrim on foot must take from either Somport or Roncesvalles to Santiago, following the 'Camino francés'.

Obviously, as there is a wider cultural and spiritual context beyond the physical details of the route, I have also included ample information on its historical, artistic and cultural aspects. However, my personal experience as a pilgrim —I have walked the venerable pilgrims' way from Somport and Roncesvalles to Compostela on two occasions, and have retraced my steps painstakenly over a dozen times during my research— has dictated the extent of this information: pilgrims should not be overwhelmed with too much academic discussion of history and art, but guided on their journey and offered key information on the route. For this reason, each of the 35 stages into which I have divided this 'Guide' (4 stages through Aragón and 31 from Roncesvalles) share the same regular structure, divided into three sections:

1. Description of the route (illustrated with a route map).
2. History, art and legends.
3. Historical pilgrims' accounts.

Given this uniformity of layout, at whatever stage you open this 'Guide' you will easily find the information you require. The 'Año Santo Compostelano 1993' has given new impulse and vitality to everything connected with the pilgrimage. One of the most direct consequences has been work done on the pilgrims' way itself (in certain cases, with an unfortunate lack of respect) and the restoration or construction of a considerable number of hostels. Due to the late date of going to press, all the latest developments have been carefully recorded in this 'Guide'.

The photos of the monuments are small, so as to be able to include as many as possible in each stage, and because they are merely intended to serve as a check-list: pilgrims will have the opportunity to visit and enjoy them personally.

Below are some comments on the route described, its distribution in stages and the criteria used in choosing the route.

1. The route described. I have described the route known as the 'Camino francés', while regretting the impossibility of including other ancient pilgrims' routes, such as the 'Camino de Levante', the 'Camino del Cantábrico', the 'Camino de Álava', the 'Camino asturiano', the 'Via de la Plata' or the 'Caminho portugués'. However, to do so would be an impossible task, and less useful to pilgrims than a description of the 'Camino francés'.

2. Distribution in stages. The traditional, time-honoured division of the pilgrims' route into 16 stages (3 plus 13) in Aymeric Picaud's classic 'Pilgrims' Guide' was not based on practical considerations. My division of the route, on the other hand, takes practical considerations very much into account. However, pilgrims should feel free to organise the pilgrimage in the way most suitable to their personal circumstances, using my suggestions as general guidelines. The approximately 170 km of the Aragonese stretch and the 780 km between Roncesvalles and Santiago have been divided into 4 and 31 stages respectively. Each stage is more or less the same length, with the exception of stage 2 of the Aragonese route (Jaca-Sangüesa) and stage 17 of the main route (Carrión-Sahagún), for reasons which are outlined in the text.

3. Criteria used in selecting the route described. This is undoubtedly the thorniest question for a guide of this nature. It is virtually impossible to ascertain the exact route, kilometre by kilometre, followed by pilgrims in the past, one of many reasons being that the route was never a single, unchanging entity, but underwent constant variation. What is more, new research is constantly being carried out on this subject and we would be obliged to alter the described route in the light of each new piece of data. In view of this, I have opted for a pragmatic approach to the subject and have described the generally accepted route, which is also the one marked by the various associations of 'Amigos del Camino de Santiago', who have done much excellent work in this field. By adopting this criterion, I absolve myself of blame for the not infrequent occasions when the pilgrims' way follows a capriciously zig-zagging route.

In passing, I must add that the traditional well-known yellow arrows with which the 'Amigos del Camino de Santiago' have always marked the route are a marvellous aid to pilgrims. Along the Aragonese stretch of the route, the signposting is that used by hikers or 'senderistas' (GR), and is easily identifiable and very effective.

This book is primarily directed at the foot pilgrim. However, information is included in each stage on the practicability of the pedestrian route for cyclists, although I must make it clear from the outset that as the route mainly follows country lanes and paths, it is by its very nature likely to present serious obstacles for cyclists.

I have opted not to include a detailed breakdown of distances between each and every town or village along the route, so as not to confuse pilgrims, given the enormous difficulty of calculating this correctly along lanes, footpaths and tracks. However, sufficient information is given as a guide.

I have not forgotten the motorist either, and in each stage frequent directions are given to enable them to leave the main road and meet up with the pilgrims' way. In this way, motorists can act as a back-up to pilgrims on foot, or do some of the stretches on foot themselves.

One of the most original features of this 'Guide', and one which I consider of special importance, is the section entitled 'Historical Pilgrims' Accounts'. The most interesting impressions of four of the great historical pilgrims are included in each stage:

1. Aymeric Picaud: 'Liber peregrinationis' ('Pilgrims' Guide').

This account by a Poitou priest, written in Latin around 1130, is the first European guidebook. Vividly and colourfully written, with a wealth of details, it is one of the most delightful and revealing documents on the pilgrims' way.

2. Hermann Künig von Vach: 'Das Wallfahrtsbuch des Hermann Künig von Vach' ('The Pilgrim's Notebook of Hermann Künig von Vach').

A short account consisting of 640 lines written in German, published in Strasbourg in 1495. Writing in a restrained and concise style, the author (a Servite monk from Vach) offers numerous practical suggestions for pilgrims going to Santiago to Compostela, having recently made the pilgrimage himself.

3. Arnold von Harff: 'Die Pilgerfahrt des Ritters Arnold von Harff' ('The Pilgrimage of the Horseman Arnold von Harff').

A long account (in German) of the great journey undertaken by this German knight through Italy, Syria, Egypt, Arabia..., France and Spain between the years 1496 and 1499. While in Spain, he travelled as a pilgrim to Santiago de Compostela, and this account supplies extremely interesting and lively details and comments on the journey.

4. Domenico Laffi: 'Viaggi in Ponente a San Giacomo di Galitia e Fiesterrae' ('A Journey Westwards to Santiago in Galicia and Finisterre').

In 1673, this Italian priest left his native Bologna to go as a pilgrim to Santiago de Compostela. His travel journal (written in Italian) contains a wealth of observations, facts and colourful comments on everything he encountered throughout his journey.

The work which has gone into preparing this 'Guide' has been lengthy, detailed and sometimes exhausting. However, it has been written with affection and enthusiasm, and the hope that it will be of use to the enormous number of men and women of all ages and backgrounds, from Europe and beyond, who have rediscovered the excitement of walking towards the 'limina Sancti Iacobi'. This long and arduous project would never have been finished without the generous, intelligent and unstinting collaboration of José María Anguita Jaén and Carmen Saceda García-Abad, to whom I extend my sincerest gratitude.

I would also like to thank EDITORIAL EVEREST for the whole-hearted support and enthusiasm shown towards this project, and for so generously publishing this book in four languages simultaneously: Spanish, French, German and English.

I must also express my gratitude to all those who so efficiently and charitably helped us on our way on the long journey from Somport and Roncesvalles to Compostela, namely the Cathedral chapters, parish priests, mayors, guards, guides and pilgrims.

Finally, if it were not for the enthusiastic, work-oriented atmosphere of the *Centro de Estudios del Camino de Santiago* and for the extensive resources of its library, the creation of this modest but nevertheless complex and laborious guide would simply not have been possible.

Millán Bravo Lozano
'Centro de Estudios del Camino de Santiago'
Sahagún, 12th June 1993

Preliminary remark to the Fourth Edition

This fourth edition, following on so quickly from the third (April 1996), has merely required a few light modifications in order to update certain items of «tourist» information. Owing to our professional dedication and the true vocation we feel for the pilgrimage, we have maintained frequent contact with pilgrims of all four languages (Spanish, French, German and English) as they make their way along the «Route». Consequently we are aware of the unanimous approval they have shown the «Guide». The only task that remains to be done is that of reducing somewhat its weight. In each new edition we take into account the many observations sent to us by friends and pilgrims, for which we are truly grateful.

M.B.L. October 1996

Getting prepared

If you are intending to do the pilgrimage on foot, it would be sensible to fit in some kind of training prior to setting out: short walks in the country, hiking in the hills... preferably wearing the footwear and clothing you intend to use on the journey itself. However, nothing will prevent the first few days on the road being the most difficult, and you are bound to suffer from blisters and aching muscles. After about four or five days, your body will have adjusted and the going will get much easier.

First aid kit for pilgrims

Setting aside possible accidents, the most frequent problems are those derived from the action of walking itself: blisters, aching joints and muscles... Bring scissors and needles to cut or puncture blisters and a healing product. Anti-inflammatory ointment and bandages for muscles and joints are vital. Be prepared for possible allergic reactions, and for over-exposure to sun and wind. Don't forget to use a protective sun cream, especially on your face.

Documents to carry

Valid passport or identity papers and any documents relating to health care. You should also obtain a 'pilgrim's passport' which will be stamped at various places along the route, and which shows that you have completed the pilgrimage. Don't forget to pack this guidebook: it will be a constant source of useful information.

Pilgrims' refuges

The fact that most of the refuges along the pilgrims' way are either extremely cheap or even free, does not mean that we should exploit their hospitality. Please show consideration and respect towards the premises and furnishings, and towards fellow pilgrims sharing the accommodation.

PRACTICAL ADVICE FOR PILGRIMS

Walking to Santiago

If you are accustomed to a modern, sedentary lifestyle, a journey on foot of over 800 kilometres (assuming you walk the whole way) could become quite an ordeal unless you take a series of basic precautions.

• Footwear

Your feet are going to bear the brunt of the work, so it is essential to choose suitable footwear. Look for a combination of durability and lightness: your best bets are a pair of sturdy sports shoes which let your feet breathe, or classic hiking boots. Choose your socks with care too, and always make sure they lie smooth against the skin to avoid rubbing.

• Clothing

The main consideration is the time of year you will be making the journey, although you must bear in mind the different microclimates you will pass through as you travel from the peaks of the Pyrenees, across the high Castilian plateau to the woods of Galicia. Temperature, humidity level and other factors vary enormously from region to region. Whatever clothes you choose, they should be light, comfortable and practical and made of natural fibres to allow your skin to breathe.

• Luggage

However light your bags are, after a few kilometres any load becomes a burden. Be ruthless in rejecting superfluous items of baggage and only take what you really need. A basic checklist, which you can adapt according to your personal needs, would be a sleeping bag, a change of clothes, a raincoat, headwear, something for carrying water in and a small first aid kit.

Driving to Santiago

Although motorists are not considered bona fide pilgrims, many travellers choose to drive all, or part, of the route to Santiago. No special preparations are necessary, apart from those which apply to any long car journey: make sure your vehicle is checked and serviced before setting out, respect road signs, traffic lights and speed limits, drive with care at all times and so on. The only special request to motorists travelling to Santiago is that they show special consideration to all pedestrians and cyclists they encounter on the edge of the road. We'll all meet up in Santiago...

Cycling to Santiago

Those choosing to cycle along the pilgrims' route face special conditions. Throughout this book, a special section for cyclists will be found in the description of each stage of the route, warning of possible difficulties which might be encountered. The following general advice applies:

• *Preparing the journey*

You should start getting in training at least three months before setting off, and practise over different terrain: on the flat, cross-country, mountains...
Choose a bike that is not too heavy, which means avoiding trendy mountain bikes. The ideal model is the traditional touring bike.

• *Throughout the journey*

Always carry your luggage in saddle-bags, with the weight evenly distributed on both sides and between the front and back wheels. Load your bike following its structure: for example, the crossbar would be a good place to attach tent poles.
Never carry heavy things on your back, and learn to pedal with the weight of the bike, especially up and down hills.
The bike should be well lit and extra reflectors used. You should also make sure that your clothes make you easy to spot when cycling along roads. Don't blow the tyres up too hard, otherwise they will puncture more easily on rough ground.

• *Essential clothes and equipment*

The basic checklist includes
—Hard-soled shoes or trainers.
—'Culotte' to avoid rubbing the inside of your thighs.
—Cotton T-shirts which absorb sweat well.
—Protective headgear and gloves.
—Cap and goggles to protect from the sun and mosquitoes.
—Rain jacket or cape.
—First aid kit (basically the same as for foot pilgrims, but covering possible injuries from falls and putting greater emphasis on protection from sun, wind and insects).
—Pump, spare tyres or inner tubes, patches, rubber solution, tyre lever, fine grain sandpaper, brake liners, spare spokes, brake and gear wires, chain links, adjustable spanner, torch and small pot of lubricant.

The pilgrim's staff
Pilgrims of old carried a long staff (known as a *bordón* in Spanish) to help them on their journey. It might be useful to copy them, as a stick gives you something to lean on and could be especially welcome on steep hills.

What to eat
Always start the day with a good breakfast. Light snacks during the day's travel will keep your blood sugar up, with a generous but healthy supper to look forward to in the evening. If you eat something light just before going to bed it will help you relax and sleep well. As you walk, you should nibble on things like dried fruit and raisins, which are rich in protein. Chocolate is also good, although it makes you thirsty. As for drinks, apart from water, the occasional cup of tea or coffee is a good idea.

Money
We have already warned against carrying too much weight, which means that certain items will have to be bought along the route, as and when necessary. It is therefore advisable to carry enough money to cover essential expenses, bearing in mind your likely level of spending (are you going to sleep in refuges or 5-star hotels?). Credit cards, cash dispenser cards and travellers cheques will be extremely useful.

Telephone dialling codes
The area codes for the provinces through which the pilgrims' way passes are as follows:

Huesca: 974
Zaragoza: 976
Navarra: 948
La Rioja: 941
Burgos: 947
Palencia: 979
León: 987
Lugo: 982
La Coruña: 981

HOW TO USE THIS GUIDEBOOK

I. ROUTE DESCRIPTION

After the introductory page to each stage (in which the most important places along the route are listed), this page contains a description of the route for foot pilgrims, cyclists and motorists.

- **Pilgrims' refuges**
  Number of rooms, facilities, etc...

- **Description of the route for foot pilgrims**
  Distance in kilometres, landmarks, towns and villages...

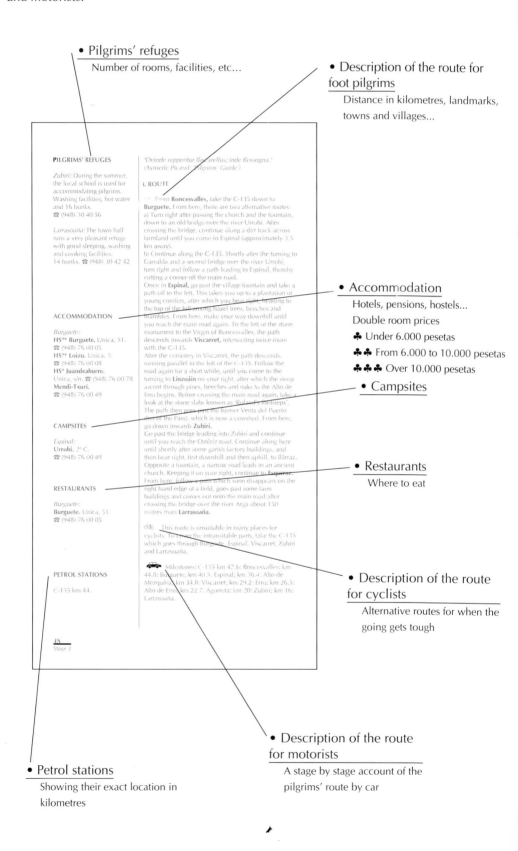

PILGRIMS' REFUGES

Zubiri: During the summer, the local school is used for accommodating pilgrims. Washing facilities, hot water and 16 bunks.
☎ (948) 30 40 56

Larrasoaña: The town hall runs a very pleasant refuge with good sleeping, washing and cooking facilities.
14 bunks. ☎ (948) 30 42 42

ACCOMMODATION

Burguete:
HS** Burguete. Unica, 51.
☎ (948) 76 00 05
HS** Loizu. Unica, 3.
☎ (948) 76 00 08
HS* Juandeaburre.
Unica, s/n. ☎ (948) 76 00 78
Mendi-Txuri.
☎ (948) 76 00 49

CAMPSITES

Espinal:
Urrobi. 2ª C.
☎ (948) 76 00 49

RESTAURANTS

Burguete:
Burguete. Unica, 51.
☎ (948) 76 00 05

PETROL STATIONS

C-135 km 44.

18
Stage 2

'Deinde repperitur Biscarellus; inde Ressogna.'
(Aymeric Picaud; *Pilgrims' Guide*)

I. ROUTE

From **Roncesvalles**, take the C-135 down to **Burguete**. From here, there are two alternative routes:
a) Turn right after passing the church and the fountain, down to an old bridge over the river Urrobi. After crossing the bridge, continue along a dirt track across farmland until you come to Espinal (approximately 3.5 km away).
b) Continue along the C-135. Shortly after the turning to Garralda and a second bridge over the river Urrobi, turn right and follow a path leading to Espinal, thereby cutting a corner off the main road.
Once in **Espinal**, go past the village fountain and take a path off to the left. This takes you up to a plantation of young conifers, after which you bear right, heading to the top of the hill among hazel trees, beeches and brambles. From here, make your way downhill until you reach the main road again. To the left of the stone monument to the Virgin of Roncesvalles, the path descends towards **Viscarret**, intersecting twice more with the C-135.
After the cemetery in Viscarret, the path descends, running parallel to the left of the C-135. Follow the road again for a short while, until you come to the turning to **Linzoáin** on your right, after which the steep ascent through pines, beeches and oaks to the Alto de Erro begins. Before crossing the main road again, take a look at the stone slabs known as 'Roland's footsteps'. The path then goes past the former Venta del Puerto (Inn of the Pass), which is now a cowshed. From here, go down towards **Zubiri**.
Go past the bridge leading into Zubiri and continue until you reach the Ostériz road. Continue along here until shortly after some garish factory buildings, and then bear right, first downhill and then uphill, to Ilárraz. Opposite a fountain, a narrow road leads to an ancient church. Keeping it on your right, continue to Esquíroz. From here, follow a path which soon disappears on the right hand edge of a field, goes past some farm buildings and comes out onto the main road after crossing the bridge over the river Arga about 150 metres from **Larrasoaña**.

This route is unsuitable in many places for cyclists. To cover the intransitable parts, take the C-135 which goes through Burguete, Espinal, Viscarret, Zubiri and Larrasoaña.

Milestones: C-135 km 47.6: Roncesvalles; km 44.8: Burguete; km 40.5: Espinal; km 36.4: Alto de Mezquíriz; km 34.8: Viscarret; km 29.2: Erro; km 26.5: Alto de Erro; km 22.7: Agorreta; km 20: Zubiri; km 16: Larrasoaña.

- **Accommodation**
  Hotels, pensions, hostels...
  Double room prices
  ♣ Under 6.000 pesetas
  ♣ ♣ From 6.000 to 10.000 pesetas
  ♣ ♣ ♣ Over 10.000 pesetas

- **Campsites**

- **Restaurants**
  Where to eat

- **Description of the route for cyclists**
  Alternative routes for when the going gets tough

- **Description of the route for motorists**
  A stage by stage account of the pilgrims' route by car

- **Petrol stations**
  Showing their exact location in kilometres

MAPS ILLUSTRATING EACH STAGE

Each stage includes a detailed route map, with the pilgrims' way plotted, geographical features, the towns and villages on or near the pilgrims' way and the services available, possible recommended detours, etc.

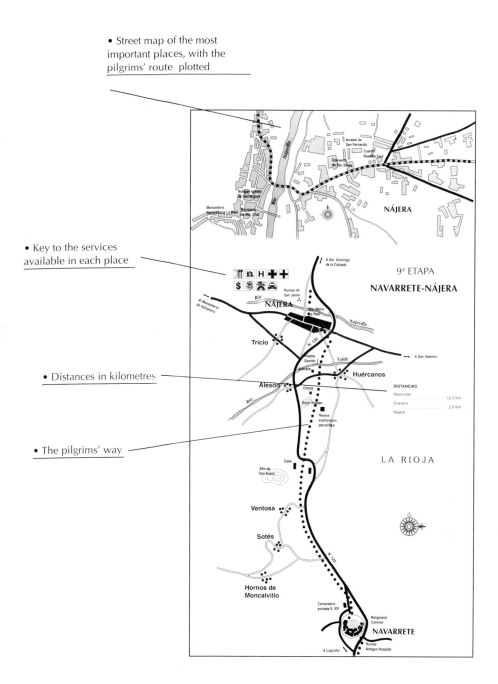

- Street map of the most important places, with the pilgrims' route plotted

- Key to the services available in each place

- Distances in kilometres

- The pilgrims' way

9ª ETAPA

NAVARRETE-NÁJERA

DISTANCIAS

Navarrete	
Gravera	12.0 Km
Nájera	2.0 Km

LA RIOJA

Street maps of the most important cities are also included, and the pilgrims' route through them is plotted.

II. HISTORY, ART AND LEGENDS

This section gives a detailed overview of the history, artistic background, folklore and anecdotes relevant to each stage of the pilgrims' way. Mention is made not only of the great monuments (cathedrals, monasteries, churches, palaces, castles...) but also of small, secluded hermitages and chapels, stone crosses, fountains, interesting corners of the different cities and all sorts of places full of history and atmosphere which the average sightseer rushes past, but which together lend the pilgrims' way its particular significance. The events and historical figures which have had an influence on the pilgrims' way are also mentioned, together with legends and traditions which have passed down by word of mouth through successive generations of pilgrims: miraculous events, tales of hermits and saints, feudal lords, wolves and bandits, terrible blizzards...

Special emphasis is given to alternative routes which add interest and enjoyment to the journey: a short detour might lead to a village where time has stood still, to a place of incredible natural beauty or to an important historical landmark.

By the same token, reference is made to the changes which the pilgrims' way has undergone over the centuries. It is explained how human activity and the action of time and the elements have changed many of the original paths, and have sometimes ruined, sometimes restored, old stretches of the pilgrims' way, its hostels and monuments...

This section endeavours to make pilgrims feel part of the pilgrims' way, to incorporate it into their personal experience as something which belongs to their history, to their centuries-old heritage. The pilgrims' way has a message for each and every one of us, whether this be on a spiritual level, an aesthetic level or in terms of personal fulfilment. The object of this section is to help pilgrims hear its call.

III. HISTORICAL PILGRIMS' ACCOUNTS

Four pilgrims from different centuries and backgrounds round off each stage with their impressions. Through their accounts, we gain an insight into the importance of the pilgrimage to Santiago throughout the centuries, and its profound social and religious impact. We will see how pilgrims of old were faced with innumerable difficulties and certain danger, and how their will and determination to reach Compostela helped them overcome the trials and tribulations of each stage of their journey. We will also meet the vast cross-section of human types that have frequented the pilgrims' way at different stages in its history: rogues, bandits, unscrupulous landlords, prostitutes who seduce virtuous pilgrims, feudal lords who send their bailiffs to fleece passers-by, hospitable monks, merchants, noblemen... A complex, multifaceted world, which is presented first hand and which allows us to soak up the past atmosphere of the route we are now travelling so much more comfortably and easily than our predecessors.

Using this book

THE ARAGÓN ROUTE STAGE I

SOMPORT • JACA

Jaca cathedral: capital depicting King David

PUERTO DE SOMPORT • CANDANCHÚ •
CANFRANC-ESTACIÓN • CANFRANC-PUEBLO •
VILLANÚA • CASTIELLO DE JACA • JACA

PILGRIMS' REFUGES

Canfranc-Estación: The pilgrims' shelter provided by the town council has a large capacity and affords good facilities.
Jaca: The Old Hospital has been fitted out for use as a pilgrims' refuge. Well-equipped.

ACCOMMODATION

Candanchú:
H* Edelweiss.**
☎ (974) 37 32 00.
76 rooms. ♣♣♣
H Candanchú.** ☎ (974) 37 30 25. 54 rooms. ♣♣
H Tobazo.** ♣♣
HS* Somport. ♣
Canfranc:
HR* Ara. ♣
HS* Casa Marraco. ♣
Canfranc-Estación:
H* Albergue de Santa Cristina de Canfranc.** ♣♣
H* Villa de Canfranc.** ♣
H Villa Anayet.** ♣
Villanúa:
H Faus-Hutte.** ♣♣
HR* Reno. ♣♣
H* Roca Nevada. ♣
Castiello de Jaca:
H* El Mesón. ♣♣
Jaca:
♣♣♣
H* Europa. H*** Gran Hotel. HA*** Oroel.**
♣♣♣
H Canfranc. H** Conde Aznar. H** La Paz.**
HR Pradas. H** Ramiro I. H* Aboira. H* Mur.**
HS* Charle.**
♣
H* Ciudad de Jaca.
HSR El Abeto. HSR* Galindo. HSR* París.**
HSR* Victoria.

CAMPSITES

Canfranc:
Canfranc. 2nd Category.
Jaca:
Peña Oroel. 1st Category.
☎ (974) 36 02 15
Victoria. 2nd Category.
☎ (974) 36 03 23

RESTAURANTS

Jaca:
La Cocina Aragonesa.
Cervantes, 5.
☎ (974) 36 10 50. Cuisine from Navarre and Aragón.
Mesón Corbacho. Ramiro I, 2.
☎ (974) 36 36 43
Gastón. ☎ (974) 36 05 31. Basque cuisine.

PETROL STATIONS

At Villanúa and Jaca.

'Inde Camfrancus; inde Iacca.' (Aymeric Picaud: *'Pilgrims' Guide'*)

I. ROUTE

🚶 This stretch of the French-Spanish border is marked by the Pic d'Aspe and the Somport Pass. The *Gave d'Aspe* rises in the former and flows along the *Vallée d'Aspe* through the French towns of Urdos and Borce to Oloron. The journey starts at the **Somport Pass** on the frontier, from where you head towards **Candanchú** on the N-330, bearing left off it after a short distance to follow the course of the river Aragón as far as the Puente de Santa Cristina, where you return briefly to the main road, leaving it almost immediately to cross a small gorge which then leads back onto the N-330. Cross the main road and then follow a dirt track as it skirts around the bottom of the hill crowned by Candanchú Castle and heads down towards the N-330 by the Puente del Ruso. However, before reaching the road, you get onto a tricky path which leads downhill following the left-hand bank of the river Aragón and comes out on an asphalted track by a campsite. You then cross the river and make your way along a disused section of the old N-330, passing a hotel complex. After a short while, bear left off the old road and cross back over the river Aragón via a footbridge. Continue for about a kilometre, before re-crossing the Aragón and returning to the N-330 which leads into **Canfranc-Estación.** Follow the N-330 out of Canfranc and, immediately after a tunnel, bear left off the road, go down some steps and cross the river. Continue along the left bank for about 4 km before crossing a stone bridge over the river which leads into **Canfranc-Pueblo.** Follow the pilgrims' route through the village and then cross back over to the left bank of the Aragón via a medieval bridge next to the cemetery. Some 2 km further on, go through a subway under a tunnelled section of the N-330, and after a further 2 km cross the river Aragón once again and enter **Villanúa.** Upon leaving the village, continue for 1.5 km along an animal path on the left-hand side of the N-330 until you come to a rest area, where you cross over to the opposite side of the road and take a path which borders a summer camp and comes out on the local road to Borau. Follow this road for a short stretch, leaving it shortly before it meets the N-330 to take a dirt track which brings you onto the Calle de Santiago in Castiello, just over 2 km away. From here, make your way down towards the N-330 and cross over, and then get onto a track heading in the direction of La Garcipollera, which leads across the river. Immediately after crossing the river, take a path on the right, cross the river Ijuez and then follow the course of the river Aragón along its left-hand bank until you reach the old N-330, which you follow for a few metres as far as the new road. You then cross the road and follow an animal path between the road and the river up to Jaca, entering the town on the N-330 (Avenida de Francia).

🚲 The pedestrian route is impracticable for cyclists in several parts, and it is therefore advisable to follow the N-330 throughout this stage.

🚗 Milestones: N-330: km 675: Somport; km 673.2: Candanchú; km 667: Canfranc-Estación; km 667: Canfranc-Pueblo; km 658: Villanúa; km 651: Castiello de Jaca; km 336: Jaca.

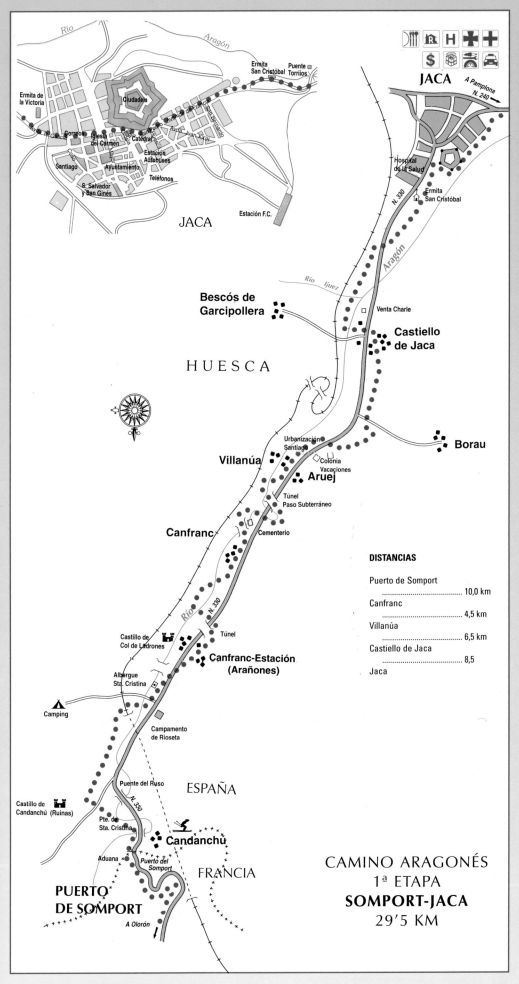

JACA

A Pampiona
N. 240

Río Aragón

Ermita San Cristóbal
Puente Torriios

Ermita de la Victoria

Ciudadela

Avenida de Franc. Sti Fernando

Correos
Iglesia del Carmen
Catedral
Estación Autobuses
Santiago
Ayuntamiento
S. Salvador y San Ginés
Teléfonos
Estación F.C.

JACA

Hospital de la Salud

Ermita San Cristóbal

N. 330

Río Aragón

Río Ijuez

Venta Charle

Bescós de Garcipollera

Castiello de Jaca

H U E S C A

Borau

Urbanización Santiago
Colonia Vacaciones
Villanúa
Aruej
Túnel Paso Subterráneo

Canfranc
Cementerio

Río N. 330

DISTANCIAS

Puerto de Somport
.... 10,0 km
Canfranc
.... 4,5 km
Villanúa
.... 6,5 km
Castiello de Jaca
.... 8,5
Jaca

Castillo de Col de Ladrones
Túnel

Canfranc-Estación (Arañones)

Albergue Sta. Cristina

Camping

Campamento de Rioseta

Puente del Ruso
ESPAÑA

Castillo de Candanchú (Ruinas)

Pte. de Sta. Cristina
Candanchú
Aduana
Puerto del Somport
FRANCIA

N. 330

PUERTO DE SOMPORT

A Olorón

CAMINO ARAGONÉS
1ª ETAPA
SOMPORT-JACA
29'5 KM

Somport

Skiing in Candanchú

The river Aragón

II. HISTORY, ART AND LEGENDS

Three of the four main pilgrim routes through France converged in Ostabat and entered Spain via the Port de Cize and Roncesvalles. The fourth and most southerly route crossed the Pyrenees at the **Somport Pass,** known to the Romans as *'Summus Portus'*. This route originated at Arles, which was also the meeting-point for pilgrims coming from Italy (who called this route the *'Via francigena'*) and pilgrims following the *'Oberstraße'* (*'High road'*) from Germany. After Arles, it passed through the cities of Saint-Gilles, Montpellier and Toulouse, and thus became known as the *'Via Tolosana'*. According to Aymeric Picaud's *Pilgrims' Guide,* this route crossed into Spain through the *'Portus Asperi',* although other contemporaneous sources refer to the *'Summus Portus',* and one must conclude that both are references to the Somport Pass, as the *'Pic d'Aspe'* (and its mountain pass, the *'Pas d'Aspe'*) are quite distinct landmarks. In any case, the Somport Pass is the more likely candidate, being the more accessible of the two.

Close to the Somport Pass are the ruins of the **Hospital de Santa Cristina,** which Aymeric Picaud described as *'one of the three pillars which the Lord placed on this earth for the succour of His poor children, namely the Hospital of Jerusalem, the Hospital of Mont-Joux and the Hospital of Santa Cristina at Somport.'* (The Hospital of Mont-Joux in the Great St. Bernard Pass in the Alps ministered to the needs of pilgrims going to Rome, and the Hospital of Jerusalem cared for pilgrims to the Holy Land.)

The modern ski-resort of **Candanchú** is close by, a town which has sprung up in the course of this century on the ancient site of the *'Camp d'Anjou',* from which it derives its name. Some scant remains can still be seen of *Candanchú Castle,* which was built for the purpose of protecting pilgrims and for collecting tolls from merchants and traders.

The modern village of **Canfranc-Estación** grew up around the international railway station, and stands on a site known as *'los Arañones',* which is the local name for the blackthorn.

The original village of **Canfranc,** the medieval *'Campus Francus'* which was founded as a frontier control post, is two kilometres further down. The villagers were assigned the task of keeping the route clear for travellers and pilgrims, and this is where the village gets its name from. After a devastating fire in 1944, practically all traces of its prosperous past were wiped out. However, it still retains the typical layout of the villages situated on the pilgrims' route, consisting of a line of buildings bordering both sides of the pilgrims' way. Records show the existence of a pilgrims' hospital in Canfranc at least as early as the 12th century, which was probably situated at the far end of the village close to the ruined Romanesque church. A perfectly preserved single-arched Romanesque bridge leads out of the village.

The area around **Villanúa** (*'Villanoua'*) is rich in archaeological remains testifying to the village's antiquity. However, the earliest records and the name of the village itself only date from the 10th century, when it was resettled after the Reconquest. As you approach the village, you will see a stretch of the old paved road leading up to the bridge over the river Aragón. In the old district, on the left bank of the river, stands the *Parish Church of San Esteban,* where a priceless Romanesque image of the Virgin and a polychromed wood figure of St. James dressed as a pilgrim are venerated.

Further down, and somewhat set back from the pilgrims' way, is the recently-restored 11th-century Romanesque **Church of San Vicente de Aruej,** a single-aisled construction with an interesting apse.

The pilgrims' route enters **Castiello de Jaca** along the Calle de Santiago. The village, which still conserves its higgledy-piggledy medieval layout, is situated on a hill which would have been the site of the castle after which it is named. The Parish Church of San Miguel is Romanesque in origin, although it has been fairly extensively restored. Lower down, on your way out of the village (after crossing a medieval bridge), you come to the Romanesque Ermita de Santa Juliana situated at the confluence of the rivers Ijuez and Aragón.

Outside Jaca

After crossing the Puente Torrijos and with Jaca visible up ahead, you pass the *Ermita de San Cristóbal,* which dates from the 18th century, although it stands on the site of a medieval chapel. A bit further up, just outside Jaca, are the gardens of the *Hospital de la Salud,* which grow on the site of the former pilgrims' leprosarium, of which only a capital survives which is displayed in the gardens. From here, pilgrims crossed the walled perimeter and entered Jaca. The walls are now practically non-existent, although as late as the mid-19th century they were intact with 23 fortified towers and 7 gates.

Jaca is one of the earliest recorded Spanish cities. The ancient capital of the Jacetanos, its name is associated with the resistance to the Roman invasion and the Iberian leaders Indibil and Mandonio. After periods of Roman and then Visigothic domination, it was captured by the Moors in about 716, although they were quickly ousted. On the death of King Sancho III 'the Great', the County of Aragón passed to his son, Ramiro, who raised it to the status of a kingdom, with Jaca as the capital. The 'fuero' or municipal charter which he granted Jaca in 1063 served as a model for cities such as Estella, Sangüesa and Puente la Reina. In common with other towns along the pilgrims' way, Jaca was divided into different areas known as 'burgos'. Outside the walls, on the present site of the citadel, was the *'Burgo Novo'* *('Burnau'),* whose inhabitants included numerous foreign pilgrims who came to settle in the city, attracted by the rights and privileges granted by the municipal charter. The Puerta de San Pedro led into the walled Burgo de San Nicolás, at the heart of which the **cathedral** was built. Sancho Ramírez (1063-1094), the great king of Navarre and Aragón, established the Bishopric of Jaca in 1076 and work commenced immediately on the cathedral, one of the earliest and most outstanding examples of Spanish Romanesque architecture, which was to exert a considerable influence on other great

General view of Jaca

Jaca: entrance to the Citadel

Jaca cathedral

Apse of Jaca cathedral

*Romanesque portal,
Jaca cathedral*

Romanesque monuments along the road to Santiago. A Latin cross shape with three apses, it is notable for the innovative use of techniques adapted from other architectural styles, particularly the Moorish style. But its most outstanding features are the sculpted decoration on the west and south portals and the varied and richly-carved capitals.

The cathedral houses the relics of San Indalecio, one of the seven apostles consecrated by St. James, and first Bishop of Urci (in Almería) and of Auca (Villafranca-Montes de Oca, in Burgos). His remains were transferred to the nearby Monastery of San Juan de la Peña in 1084, and they now rest in the High Altar in the cathedral, in a gilded silver urn crafted in 1735. The inscription reads: 'INDALETII OSSA THECA TEGIT SIDERA MENTEM' ('This urn contains the bones of Indalecio/the stars guard his soul.') Beside it is another urn containing the remains of St. Felix and St. Voto, the founders of San Juan de la Peña, which bears the following inscription: 'FELICI VOTO DICATA VOTO ET FELICI' ('With a happy wish dedicated to Voto and Felix.')

The *Diocesan Museum* houses one of the finest collection of Romanesque wall paintings in the world, and is well worth a visit.

The Santiago district grew up around the *Church of Santiago*. Largely rebuilt, it retains a Romanesque tower and a magnificent Romanesque baptismal font.

East of the cathedral and the Church of Santiago is the *Iglesia del Salvador*, which is part of the *Benedictine Convent*, where visitors can admire the magnificent tomb of Doña Sancha, the daughter of King Ramiro, as well as a Romanesque sculpture of the Saviour and a collection of medieval frescoes.

Apart from these outstanding monuments, other sights of interest in Jaca include the *Casa Consistorial*, the *Torre del Reloj*, the *Citadel* and the *Puente de San Miguel…*

III. HISTORICAL PILGRIMS' ACCOUNTS

Aymeric Picaud: *'There are three pillars which the Lord placed on this earth for the succour of His poor children, namely the Hospital of Jerusalem, the Hospital of Mont-Joux and the Hospital of Santa Cristina at Somport.'*

'A river of pure waters flows down from Somport ('Portus Asperi') across Spanish territory, called 'Aragonus' [the Aragón].'

'From Somport to Puente la Reina, these are the places through which you will pass on the pilgrims' way: the first is Borce ('Borcia') at the foot of the mountain on the Gascon side; after crossing the summit, you come to the Hospital de Santa Cristina ('Hospitalis Sante Cristine'): then, Canfranc ('Camfrancus') followed by Jaca ('Iacca').'

THE ARAGÓN ROUTE STAGE II

JACA • SANGÜESA

The façade of the Church of Santa María, Sangüesa

JACA • SAN JUAN DE LA PEÑA • SANTA CILIA
• PUENTE LA REINA DE JACA • BERDÚN •
TIERMAS • YESA • LEYRE • JAVIER • MARTES •
MIANOS • ARTEIDA • RUESTA •
UNDUÉS DE LERDA •
SANGÜESA

PILGRIMS' REFUGES

PILGRIMS' REFUGES
Sangüesa: A good refuge run by
the Sisters of Charity. Well-
equipped and has a large capacity.

In villages such as *Martes, Berdún,
Ruesta* or *Undués de Lerda,* which
have no facilities specifically
dedicated to the shelter of
pilgrims, the traveller has to rely
on the generosity of the local town
councils and that of the local
people.

CAMPSITES
Santa Cilia de Jaca:
Pirineos. 1st Category.
☎ (974) 37 73 51

PETROL STATIONS
On the N-240 at Jaca; at km 303:
Puente la Reina de Jaca.

*'Inde Osturit, inde Termas.' (Aymeric Picaud: 'Pilgrims'
Guide')*
I. ROUTE

[NOTE: The lack of suitable stopping-places and
hostel accommodation along this stage of the route, and
the fact that after Puente la Reina de Jaca there are two
long alternative routes which do not meet up again until
Sangüesa (some 50 km later), have made it necessary to
treat the long stretch between Jaca and Sangüesa as a
single stage. However, pilgrims will find it takes them
more than one day to complete.]
The Avenida de la Constitución, in the centre of **Jaca,**
leads straight out of the town onto the road to Monte
Pano (or Mocorones), from where the river Aragón is
visible in the distance. 2 km later, beside the cemetery,
you come out onto the N-240 and bear right off it after a
short distance onto an animal path running parallel to it.
After 1.5 km, you return to the road and cross the river
Gas. A few metres further on, past a factory, a side road
to the Monastery of San Juan de la Peña (11 km away)
leads off to the left. Opposite the factory, at a place
known as the *'Casa del Municionero',* you turn right off
the road onto a path running parallel to it which takes
you past a military barracks. About 800 metres further
on, the path crosses over and continues along the left-
hand side of the road. Very soon you reach the Atarés
gully, which is usually negotiable (alternatively you can
make a detour via the N-240). On the far side of the
gully, the road to Atarés drops down in the direction of
the N-240. Before reaching it, get onto a path running
parallel to the road which leads up through a pine and
oak wood and then drops down to the junction of the
old road to San Juan de la Peña with the N-240. Follow
the old road and bear right off it a few metres later onto a
path which crosses another gully and skirts around the
back of the old *'Venta de Esculabolsas'* (nowadays a
hotel and restaurant). You then cross the new road to San
Juan de la Peña and after 1.5 km reach the Binacua road
(at this point those who made the detour to San Juan de
la Peña return to the route). Continue down this road for
a few metres and then turn left off it along a path which
runs behind some houses and then crosses the road and
turns into an asphalted track leading straight into the
village of **Santa Cilia.** Carry on from there down a path
running along the right-hand side of the road, and about
1 km further on you come out onto the road leading into
Puente la Reina de Jaca, a distance of 4.5 km.
After **Puente la Reina de Jaca** there are **two alternative
routes,** which run parallel to each other to the left and
right of the river Aragón, and then on past the the Yesa
reservoir, for over 50 km. (Both routes are described
overleaf.)
🚲 This first stretch of the pedestrian route is not
always suitable for cyclists, but it runs close to the road
which can always be resorted to when necessary.
🚗 Milestones: N-240 km 294: turning to San Juan
de la Peña and Santa Cruz de los Serós; km 297: Santa
Cilia; km 303: Puente la Reina de Jaca.

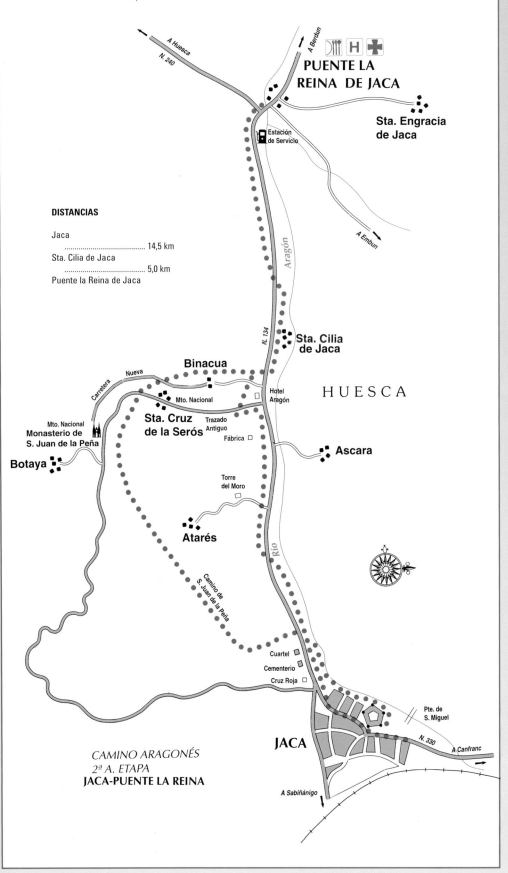

CAMINO ARAGONÉS
2ª ETAPA A
JACA-SANGÜESA
19,5 KM

A Huesca
N. 240

A Berdún

🍴 H ✚

**PUENTE LA
REINA DE JACA**

Estación
de Servicio

**Sta. Engracia
de Jaca**

A Embun

DISTANCIAS

Jaca
.... 14,5 km
Sta. Cilia de Jaca
.... 5,0 km
Puente la Reina de Jaca

Aragón

N. 134

**Sta. Cilia
de Jaca**

Nueva

Binacua

Carretera

Hotel
Aragón

H U E S C A

Mto. Nacional

**Sta. Cruz
de la Serós**

Trazado
Antiguo

Fábrica

Mto. Nacional
**Monasterio de
S. Juan de la Peña**

Ascara

Botaya

Torre
del Moro

Río

Atarés

Camino de
S. Juan de la Peña

Cuartel

Cementerio

Cruz Roja

Pte. de
S. Miguel

JACA

N. 330

A Canfranc

*CAMINO ARAGONÉS
2ª A. ETAPA*
JACA-PUENTE LA REINA

A Sabiñánigo

Puente la Reina de Jaca:
H** Anaya. National road N-240,
km 303.
☎ (974) 37 74 11.
30 rooms. ♣
HS** Del Carmen.
N-240, km 285.
☎ (974) 38 90 31.
30 rooms. ♣

Berdún:
HS* Rincón de Emilio.
Plaza Martincho, 1.
☎ (974) 37 17 15.
7 rooms. ♣
HS* La Canal. Castillo, 4.
☎ (974) 37 70 45.
3 rooms. ♣

Yesa:
HS** De Leyre.
Monasterio de Leyre.
☎ (948) 88 41 00.
29 rooms. ♣♣
HS** El Jabalí.
Leyre-Yesa.
☎ (948) 88 40 42. 21 rooms. ♣

Javier:
H*** Xavier.
Plaza del Santo, s/n.
☎ (948) 88 40 06.
46 rooms. ♣♣
H* Mesón.
Plaza de Javier, s/n.
☎ (948) 88 40 35.
8 rooms. ♣♣

Route A:

From **Puente la Reina de Jaca,** at km 303, carry on along the N-240 (Jaca-Pamplona road). After 9 km across a harsh landscape between the winding river and a series of low limestone hills, covered in dwarf oak and Aleppo pine, you reach **Berdún,** situated on a hill some 400 metres over to the right of the road. 5 km further on, across the wide cornfield plains known as the *'Canal de Berdún',* you reach the end of *'Jacetania'* (the district of Jaca) and the border between the provinces of Huesca and Zaragoza. For the next 24 km, as you follow the N-240 across the province of Zaragoza, the great Yesa reservoir dominates the landscape to the left, and the spurs of the Leyre hills rise up on the right, while the road winds its way on, hemmed between the two. Before reaching the reservoir, there is a turning off on the left to Sos and Ejea, which connects with Route B. Continuing along Route A, the village of Sigüés and the abandoned village of Esco lie on the right and, shortly afterwards on the left, the village of **Tiermas** perches up on a promontory on the banks of the reservoir, with a campsite below it. On crossing the provincial and autonomous border betwen Aragón and Navarre, the roadside kilometre numbering jumps from km 340 (the last in Aragón) to km 52 (the first on the Navarrese side). 4 km later you reach **Yesa,** where there is a turning to the **Castle of Javier** (3 km away) and **Sangüesa** (13 km) on the left, and a turning to Leyre (4 km) a little further on, on the right.

SANGÜESA

Sta. María
Iglesia Santiago
Palacio

Río Irati

A Monreal

A Pamplona

N. 240

Liédena

NAVARRA

A Sos del Rey Católico

Ermita del Socorro

Javier

Yesa

Aragón

Fuente de las Santas

Monasterio de Leyre

CAMINO ARAGONÉS
2ª B. ETAPA
PUENTE LA REINA-SANGÜESA

Undués de Lerda

Calzada Romana

Pantano de Yesa

Tiermas

ZARAGOZA

A Sos del Rey Católico

C-137

Ermita de Santiago Apóstol

Camping

Ruesta
(Abandonado)

Esco

Sigües

Estación de Servicio

A Salvatierra de Esca

DISTANCIAS

Puente la Reina de Jaca
.... 7,5 km
Martes
.... 8,5 km
Artieda
.... 10,0 km
Ruesta
.... 11,0 km
Undués
.... 10,0 km
Sangüesa

Artieda

Mianos

Río

N. 240

Martes

Conjunto Urbano Monumental
Berdun

HUESCA

Arrés

A Huesca

N. 240

A Ansó

Sta. Engracia de Jaca

PUENTE LA REINA DE JACA

N. 330

A Jaca

CAMINO ARAGONÉS
2ª ETAPA B
JACA-SANGÜESA
47 KM

ACCOMMODATION
(OPTION B)

Sangüesa:
H** Yamaguchi.
Ctra. Javier, s/n.
☎ (948) 87 01 27.
40 rooms. ♣♣
P** Las Navas.
Alfonso el Batallador, 7.
☎ (948) 87 00 77.
6 rooms. ♣

CAMPSITES
Sangüesa:
Cantolagua. 1st Category.
☎ (948) 43 03 52

RESTAURANTS
(OPTION B)
Sangüesa:
Asador Mediavilla.
Alfonso el Batallador, 17.
☎ (948) 87 02 12

Route B:

Instead of going into Puente la Reina de Jaca, continue along the N-240 in the direction of Huesca, and bear right off it about 400 metres further on, onto the road to Arrés. After about 3 km, on a long left-hand bend, take a farm track running to the left of the river Aragón as far as the Pardina del Solano farm. Less than 3 km further on, the track crosses the **Martes** road, and takes you down rutted farm paths for about 6 km until you reach **Mianos,** which is slightly off the route. By turning right off the road down a path for about 2.5 km, you reach **Artieda,** where you cross the road and join up with the C-137 about 1 km further on. Follow the C-137 in the direction of Sos for all but a short stretch for the next 7 km, until you come to **Ruesta.** Set off out of the village past the fountain and the Ermita de Santiago and, before reaching the road, turn right in a westerly direction and continue for 11 km along paths until you reach **Undués de Lerda.** Just over 2 km further on, you come to the Navarre-Aragón boundary marker, and soon afterwards cross the road to Canal de Bardenas. It is then a straight 7 km to Sangüesa.

🚲 Both alternative routes are negotiable by bicycle, but Route B is more difficult.

🚗 Milestones; N-240 km 312: turnings to Berdún (right) and Martes (left); km 316.8: Huesca-Zaragoza border; km 325.3: turning to Ruesta, Sos and Ejea; km 339: Tiermas; km 340/52: Zaragoza-Navarre border; km 47.5: turning to Javier (3 km) and Sangüesa (13 km); km 46.8: turning to Leyre.

II. HISTORY, ART AND LEGENDS

The pilgrims' way did not actually pass through the centre of Jaca, but skirted the city along the left bank of the river Aragón, down the Mocorones road, where a victory over the Saracens helped restore Jaca to the Christians. The road is also known as the 'Camino de Monte Pano' since, after crossing the Aragón, it leads up the ancient Monte Pano hill to a thick, sheltered wood where two brothers, **Voto and Felix,** fleeing from the Moors at Zaragoza, founded a hermitage which later became the *Monastery of San Juan de la Peña.* About three leagues from Jaca, slightly off the pilgrims' way and sheltering under a great rocky overhang which lends it its name, stands the Old Monastery of San Juan. Legend places its foundation as far back as the 8th century, but it was not until 1025 that Sancho the Great founded the monastery under its present name. Before long it became the most important monastery in Aragón and, as a result, the burial-site of the nobility of the kingdom. After 1071, at the height of its splendour, it became the first centre for the Cluniac reform in Spain for which, as we shall see, the pilgrims' route to Santiago was a vital vehicle. Within the split-level monastery complex, the survivors from better times are, on the lower level, the 10th-century Mozarabic church and the chamber known as the *'Sala de los Concilios'* which dates from the 11th century; and on the upper level, the Pantheon of Nobles, the Royal Pantheon (burial-site of the Kings of Navarre and Aragón), the Romanesque church and the famous open cloister, sheltered only by the great rock which dominates the whole setting. The most important relics kept here were those of its founders, St. Voto and St. Felix, and the apostle San Indalecio which, as we have already seen, rest in silver urns in Jaca Cathedral. It was also the home of one of the many purported Holy Grails, which was later taken to Valencia: this may have been the source of inspiration for Wolfram von Eschenbach's *'Parsifal'* on which Wagner based his immortal opera of the same name. It is interesting to note that the 'Eucharistic Miracle of Cebreiro', which we shall encounter in STAGE 26, might also have been a source of Wagnerian inspiration.

In the vicinity of San Juan de la Peña, on the way back to the main pilgrims' route, is the village of **Santa Cruz de la Serós** with its magnificent Romanesque *Church of Santa María,* the only remaining part of what was once the most important and famous convent in Aragón, where King Ramiro's three daughters, the *'sorores'* *('sisters'),* took their vows (this perhaps explains the toponymous use of 'Serós'). Nearby stands another Romanesque church, the *Parish Church of San Caprasio,* named after the Holy Bishop of Agen, a town on the French section of the pilgrims' way (see STAGE 11). Back on the main route, the pilgrims' way runs alongside the main road, passing the *'Venta Esculabolsas'* (Bag-swindlers Inn), where wicked inn-keepers swindled unfortunate pilgrims of the money in their purses. The village of Santa Cilia takes the name of

San Juan de la Peña: capitals

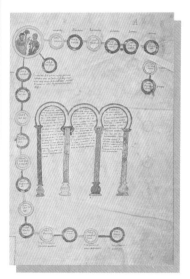

San Juan de la Peña:
Mozarabic bible

View of Santa Cruz de la Serós

Santa Cruz de la Serós: the Church of Santa María

The last inhabitant of the abandoned village of Tiermas

Leyre: the crypt

Leyre: the apses

its patron saint, St. Cecilia, after whom the parish church is also named.

Puente la Reina de Jaca (which would appear to be the village referred to as *'Osturit'* in Aymeric Picaud's *Pilgrims' Guide*) has always been an important crossroads, since both the Somport route and the important medieval route from Puerto del Palo converged there, together with the roads from Pamplona and Huesca coming from the opposite direction. Its name clearly refers to the bridge over the river Aragón, and it should not be confused with the other famous 'Puente la Reina', at the point where the Somport and the Roncesvalles branches of the pilgrims' way meet.

From here, the two alternative routes of the pilgrims' way run through the great depression of the river Aragón valley, the *'Canal de Berdún'*, which is partly taken up by the Yesa reservoir. On the northern route lie **Berdún,** a beautiful medieval-looking village set on a hill at the head of the valley which takes its name, and **Sigües, Escó** and **Tiermas,** other villages which were abandoned after the Yesa reservoir was built. Aymeric Picaud refers to Tiermas as an important point along the pilgrims' way. As its name indicates, there was once a spa there, which was built during Roman times to make use of the sulphurous hot springs found down near the river, now submerged by the waters of the reservoir. The following inscription can still be read in the ruined Church of the Holy Trinity in Tiermas:

'SANCTA TRINITAS VNVS
ET TRINVS MISERERE NOBIS'

At the end of 1992 there was one elderly, solitary inhabitant left in Tiermas, Bartolomé Torrea Orduña, who, with some difficulty, was able to recall his date of birth as 25th January, 1913.

After Yesa comes a turning off to the **Monastery of San Salvador de Leyre,** one of the most ancient and important monasteries in Spain which dates from Visigothic times, although its period of splendour coincided with the golden age of the pilgrimage (11th and 12th centuries). King Sancho 'the Great' (1000-1035) granted it many privileges, thereby enhancing its importance, which was already quite considerable in the 9th century to judge from contemporary testimonies such as that of St. Eulogius of Córdoba (died 859). Its historical significance is equalled by its exceptional artistic and monumental importance. The most ancient part is the primitive, rough, almost rudimentary pre-Romanesque crypt of San Babil, consisting of four narrow naves separated by three arches resting on disproportionately large capitals of varying sizes, which probably dates from somewhere between the 9th and 11th centuries. The church consists of three apses separated by semicircular arches, of unequal line and size, and has a particularly noteworthy west portal in the form of a splayed arch, adorned with figures, which is known as the *'Puerta Speciosa'*. One of its chapels was the Royal Pantheon of the early kings of Navarre.

Leyre's most emblematic figure is Abbot *San Virila* (870-950), who was the subject of a poetic legend about the song of a little bird which enchanted him, making him fall asleep for 300 years. The poet-king Alfonso X 'the Wise' refers to this legend, which is also to be found in other writings. The *Fountain of San Virila* just outside the Monastery is a reminder of the setting of this beautiful episode. Today, a cultured and flourishing Benedictine community occupies the monastery, dedicated to the study of the arts and to running an excellent hostelry, under the able management of the mitred Abbot, Dom Augusto Pascual of Sahagún.

Back at **Yesa,** halfway down the road leading from the village to Sangüesa, stands the Castle of **Javier,** owned by the family of the great Jesuit missionary to the Far East, San Francisco Javier. It has recently been restored and enlarged, and has become the great spiritual centre of Navarre, with the famous *'javierada'* (a mass pilgrimage to the sanctuary) held on its Saint's Day (Mars).

The Yesa Reservoir

Following Route B, the more southerly of the two, along the left bank of the river Aragón and the Yesa reservoir, the pilgrims' route passes through **Martes, Mianos, Artieda, Ruesta** and **Undués de Lerda,** all ancient villages set in the 'Canal de Berdún', but greatly undermined by the flooding of their lands.

Sangüesa, which stands on a crossroads, takes its name from the ancient pre-Roman settlement of *'Sancosa'*, which was originally located on the site of what is now Rocaforte, a hillside village on the far bank of the river Aragón. The town itself, which was an immensely important halt on the road to Santiago, owed its splendour to the pilgrimage. In 1122, Alfonso I 'the Battler' granted it the 'Fuero de Jaca' (special rights and privileges), whereupon a large number of foreign settlers moved there to set up the *'Burgo nuevo'*, which is the origin of modern Sangüesa. The late date of its foundation perhaps explains the fact that Aymeric Picaud never referred to it in his *Pilgrims' Guide* (written in about 1130). Sangüesa retains numerous exceptional vestiges of its important Jacobean past.

Castle of Javier

At the end of the Rúa Mayor, the old pilgrims' route through Sangüesa, stands the magnificent *Collegiate Church of Santa María la Real,* which has a Latin cross ground-plan and a triple-aisled, tri-apsidal interior. Its slender, majestic tower, crowned with a 13th-century spire, has become one of Sangüesa's most distinctive landmarks, together with the south portal, adorned with statuary constituting one of the most outstanding iconographic compositions of the Spanish Romanesque style (12th-13th centuries). The church houses a Gothic statue of Our Lady of Rocamadour, the famous French name so closely linked to the Santiago pilgrimage.

In addition to its slender, quadrangular tower, the *Church of Santiago* (12th-13th centuries) is also noteworthy for its west portal which displays a polychrome statue of St. James dressed as a pilgrim dating from the 16th century. During some restoration work in 1965, an enormous Gothic statue of St. James was discovered.

The Church of Santa María, Sangüesa

Sangüesa: detail of the portal of the Church of Santa María

It is also worth visiting the *Church of San Francisco,* the *Town Hall,* the *Palace of the Prince of Viana* and the *Parish House* opposite the Church of Santiago, the façade of which displays a large number of Jacobean motifs.

Another detail of the portal of the Church of Santa María at Sangüesa

Sangüesa: portal of the Church of Santiago

Sangüesa: Palace of the Prince of Viana

THE ARAGÓN ROUTE STAGE III

SANGÜESA • MONREAL

Monreal

SANGÜESA • ROCAFORTE • IZCO • ABÍNZANO •
SALINAS DE IBARGOITI • MONREAL

Monreal: The local parish owns a building equipped for the reception of pilgrims.

ACCOMMODATION

Liédena:
Hostal La Torre.
40 rooms. ♣

Lumbier:
Hostal Iru-bide.
☎ (948) 88 04 35
12 rooms.

Monreal:
HS Unzue.
Carretera, s/n.
9 rooms. ♣♣

CAMPSITES

Lumbier:
Iturbero. 2nd Category.

PETROL STATIONS

On the C-127 at Sangüesa;
On the N-240 at Liédena and Monreal.

'Inde Mons Reellus.' (Aymeric Picaud: 'Pilgrims' Guide')

I. ROUTE

🚶🚶 Leave **Sangüesa** by way of the Puente de Santa María over the river Aragón, and proceed for half a kilometre along the C-127 before bearing left onto the **Rocaforte** road, which you follow for a short stretch. A road then leads off to the right which takes you past a rather smelly paper mill and directly uphill into Rocaforte. On leaving the village, make your way back down the hill (passing the *Fuente de San Francisco*) and continue over gently rolling farmland until you reach an animal path (the *'Cañada Real'*), which you cross. At this point the climb up to the Puerto de Aibar begins. Flanked by a row of poplars, the pilgrims' way follows the course of a stream and, after just under a kilometre, passes through the ruined medieval village of Santa Cilia. Shortly afterwards, it crosses the Aibar road and descends for a short stretch parallel to it, before drawing away from it and turning left. A forest track then leads up a small hill, and descends towards the N-240 on a level with the village of Nardués, which is visible on the other side of the road. You then cross a stream and continue along the right-hand bank for about 2 km, passing a cattle farm on your right which is built on the site of the former village of Olatz. From here, the pilgrims' route enters a pine forest, reaching the village of **Izco** after just over a kilometre. A wide farm track leads to Abinzano and then to **Salinas de Ibargoiti** some 5 km further on (which you enter via the *Puente Grande*), passing Idocín, on the N-240, on the right. Directly upon leaving Salinas, cross a stream and take a path which leads to Monreal, passing first through pines and scrub and then through an oak grove, and crossing a bridge over the river Elorz. The pilgrims' route enters **Monreal** flanked by a row of poplars growing on the banks of the Elorz.

🚲 As this stage is almost exclusively covered on paths and tracks certain stretches could be difficult for cyclists, particularly the climb up to and down from Rocaforte, the ascent to the Alto de Aibar and the route out of Salinas de Ibargoiti, where there is a brook to ford. However, given the close proximity of the N-240 throughout the stage, cyclists can easily resort to the road whenever necessary.

🚗 Milestones: C-127 km 45: Sangüesa; km 40: Liédena; N-240 km 40: Liédena; km 39: La Foz de Lumbier; km 35.5: turning to Aibar, Aoiz and Lumbier; km 32: Nardués; km 27: turning to Izco; km 22: Idocín; km 20.6: Salinas de Ibargoiti; km 19.5: Monreal.

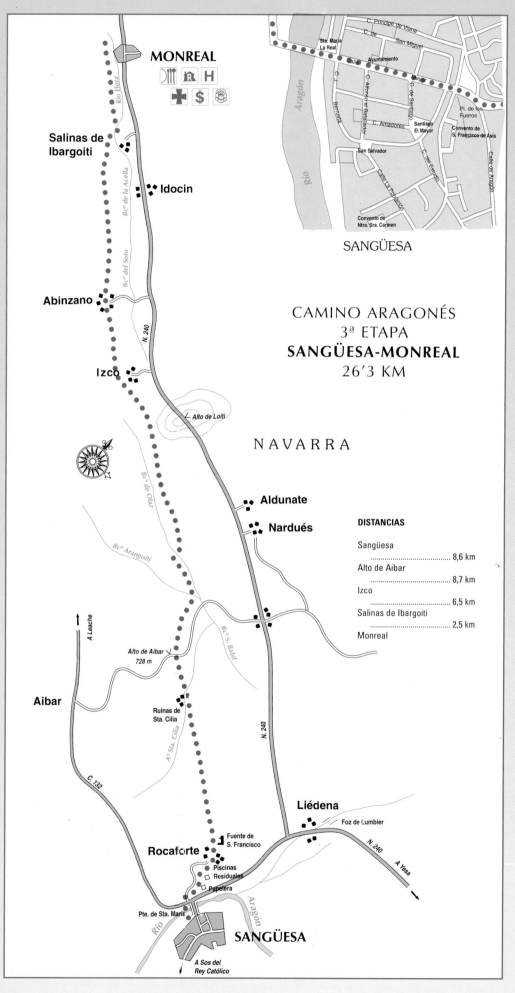

Rocaforte

Rocaforte: the parish church

II. HISTORY, ART AND LEGENDS

On their way out of the *'Burgo Nuevo'* of Sangüesa, medieval pilgrims were fortunate in being able to take one last look at the magnificent south portal of the Church of Santa María la Real, situated at the end of the main street, the Rúa Mayor, as the pilgrims' route through the new town (built by the architects of King Alfonso I) went right past it. At one time this street emerged straight onto a bridge, as does the Calle Mayor at Puente la Reina, a town created under the same conditions and with the same royal patronage as Sangüesa. Unfortunately, the magnificent Romanesque bridge over the Aragón has long since disappeared, and in its place stands the current version over which the C-127 passes.

After crossing the bridge towards Rocaforte you come to the ruined Ermita de San Miguel (next to a paper mill), the last remnant of the former Hospital de San Miguel, a dependency of the Collegiate Church of Roncesvalles. To judge by the account of a 19th-century chronicler, its Romanesque church was superb. The pre-Roman site of Sangüesa is on a nearby hilltop. Formerly known as the *'Burgo Viejo'*, its name was changed to **Rocaforte** with the flourishing of the *'Burgo Nuevo'*. The picturesque present-day village is organised around the Parish Church of the Assumption, whose origins are medieval although most of the present structure dates from the 16th century. The Chronicles of the Franciscan Order cite Rocaforte as the first place on Spanish soil where St. Francis of Assisi (probably the most illustrious pilgrim to have taken the *'Via Tolosana'* and the Aragonese branch of the pilgrims' route) rested on his way to Santiago. This claim is corroborated in part by local tradition, which is full of mementos of the saint's passage through the area. The Franciscan Order's first foundation in Spain is supposed to have been established by St. Francis himself at the *Eremitorio de San Bartolomé*, situated north-west of the town. A charming local legend has it that St. Francis planted a mulberry tree with healing properties in the monastery garden. When the monks left Rocaforte, the mulberry tree withered and only bloomed again when they returned to the town. Not far from the hermitage and close to the course of the pilgrims' way is the *'Fuente de San Francisco'* and a stone where St. Francis is supposed to have rested, the *'Piedra del descanso de San Francisco'*. As we shall see, reminders of St. Francis' passing occur time and again along the pilgrims' route, although it is impossible to say whether these are historically accurate, or whether they are later inventions to fit the tradition linking St. Francis with one of Christianity's most important and spectacular phenomena, the Santiago pilgrimage.

The route described above runs south of the N-240. Close to the right-hand side of the road are the remains of the *Roman town of Liédena*, discovered fairly recently, which dates from the Low Empire. Very close by are the remains of the *'Puente del Diablo'* ('Devil's Bridge') over the river Irati, an indication that the old

View over the countryside from Rocaforte

road probably passed this way. The bridge was built on a single arch and spanned the incredible natural gorge known as the *'Foz de Lumbier'*. A few kilometres further on, before arriving at Nardués, you come to the *Ermita de San Bartolomé* which is built in a tentative Gothic style. Opposite, on the site known as the *'Venta de Judás'*, paleolithic remains have been unearthed. Back on the pilgrims' way, between Rocaforte and the Alto de Aibar, are the remains of the medieval village of **Santa Cilia.** The medieval devotion to this Roman martyr, the patron saint of musicians, is striking in this area: there are several chapels and churches dedicated to her, and more than one village bears her name. After the Alto de Aibar, the local toponymy (a stream and a ravine) reveals the ancient presence of *San Babil,* a cult very strongly-rooted in the area. In the 15th century, the relics of this 3rd-century saint and martyr (who was Bishop of Antioch and was executed on the orders of the Emperor Decio), were brought to this area at the behest of King Juan II of Castile and his mother, Doña Catalina. After being taken to Sangüesa, a basilica was built in their honour. However, the cult of San Babil pre-dates this event, as there was already a chapel dedicated to him at Sangüesa, as was the famous pre-Romanesque crypt at the Monastery of Leyre, over which the Iglesia del Salvador is built.

Roman town of Liédena

After passing the former village of Olatz (now a farm), the pilgrims' route passes through **Izco.** The 13th-century Parish Church of San Martín is a transitional Romanesque structure, with repairs and additions dating from the 16th century. The Church of San Pedro in **Abínzano** is of the same period and style, and also has numerous later additions. Before entering Salinas de Ibargoiti, the route passes the village of Idocin on the right, which flanks the N-240. The Parish Church of San Clemente is Gothic, but was remodelled in the 16th century. This was the home of the renowned partisan, *Francisco Espoz y Mina,* the leader of the Navarrese resistance during the Napoleonic wars. **Salinas de Ibargoiti** is just under a kilometre further on, and receives its name from the local salt mines. Here there is another good specimen of the Navarrese rural Gothic style, the Church of San Miguel Arcángel, which is named after St. Michael, the defender of Christianity and the protector of pilgrims exposed to the dangers of the pilgrims' way.

River Irati

The fact that Aymeric Picaud's *Pilgrims' Guide* designates **Monreal** as the end of a stage shows that at one time it was an important halt on the pilgrims' road to Compostela. Its layout is also highly suggestive of this, being organised along a long main street which is also the pilgrims' route through the town, a layout typical of so many other places on the way to Santiago. Contemporaneous sources also mention pilgrims' hospitals in Monreal, dependent on Pamplona. At about the same time (in 1149), King García Ramírez granted Monreal a municipal charter similar to that of Estella, with the intention of creating a prosperous French settlement there. The *'Barrio de francos'* and the *'Calle del Burgo'* (the main street) are carry-overs from this

Izco: the village and the church

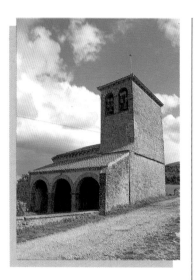

The church at Abínzano

Salinas de Ibargoiti

The church at Salinas de Ibargoiti

Monreal

time. The parish church, which is Gothic in origin but extensively remodelled, was dedicated initially to St. Martin. After the destruction of the other church in the town, the image of *Santa María del Burgo* was taken there, and this local Virgin's name was added to that of the French St. Martin. A castle once defended the town, but no trace of it remains today. A gigantic conical hill, *La Higa*, dominates Monreal, and a chapel dedicated to Santa Bárbara was recently built at the top. Of especial note is the portal, which was salvaged from the *Ermita de San Babil*.

III. HISTORICAL PILGRIMS' ACCOUNTS

Aymeric Picaud: *'Then comes Monreal ('Mons Reellus').'*

THE ARAGÓN ROUTE STAGE IV

MONREAL • PUENTE LA REINA

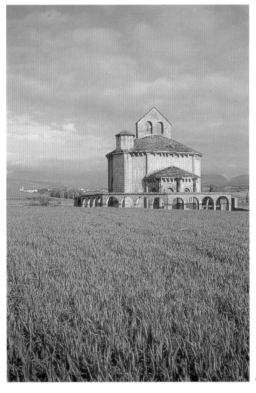

Eunate

MONREAL • YÁRNOZ • OTANO • EZPERUN •
GUERENDIÁIN • TIEBAS • CAMPANAS •
BIURRUN • UCAR • ENÉRIZ • EUNATE •
OBANOS • PUENTE LA REINA

PILGRIMS' REFUGES

Puente la Reina: This is one of the traditional refuges to be found along the Pilgrims' Route and is run by the *Padres Reparadores,* who are in charge of the Church of the Crucifix. It has good facilities, a large number of beds and comfortable, clean toilets.
☎ (948) 34 00 50

ACCOMMODATION

Tiebas:
HS** Iranzu.
Ctra. Zaragoza, km 14.
☎ (948) 36 00 67.
18 rooms. ♣♣

Puente la Reina:
H** Jakue. Irunbidea.
☎ (948) 34 10 17.
28 rooms. ♣♣
H** Mesón el Peregrino.
Ctra. Pamplona-Logroño,
km 23. ☎ (948) 34 00 75.
15 rooms. ♣♣
HS* Puente.
Cerco Nuevo, 77.
☎ (948) 34 01 46.
13 rooms. ♣♣

RESTAURANTS

Puente la Reina:
Mesón del Peregrino.
Ctra. Pamplona - Logroño, 23.
☎ (948) 34 00 75.

PETROL STATIONS

On the N-240, on leaving Monreal;
On the N-111 at Puente la Reina.

'Inde Pons Regine constat.' (Aymeric Picaud: *'Pilgrims Guide')*

I. ROUTE

🚶 Having followed the Jacobean *Calle del Burgo* out of **Monreal,** make your way along the *Camino de los Carros* which skirts the great Higa de Monreal hill (1 289 m), past buildings belonging to a publishing house on the right, and continue along the right bank of the river Elorz until you cross a bridge. (The *'St. Blase Stone'* is seen on the right.) Taking farm tracks, skirt the Sierra de Alaiz, until you cross a stream near the remains of the *Ermita de Garitoain.* You soon reach the top entrance of the hamlet of Yárnoz, 4 km from Monreal. Leave **Yárnoz** by the cemetery path and continue along the hillside to **Otano** (just over 1.5 km) and on to **Ezperun** (1.5 km) passing a quarry, until you reach **Guerendiáin** 1 km further on. After that, while still skirting the hillside, the pilgrims' route passes another quarry and then continues between a beautiful holm oak wood on the left and the cornfields of the Elorz valley on the right. Before entering **Tiebas,** the pilgrims' way comes out onto the local road which joins it from the right. After Tiebas, there are two alternative routes:
a) Continue along the secondary road until you reach the **Campanas** district. Cross the motorway and head for the Estación de Ferrocarril (train station). Go around the station and leave the town on a tarmac road which very soon turns into an unpaved track used for farming purposes. This leads on to **Biurrun**, a village situated 2 km from Campanas. After Biurrun you get back onto the road and turn straight off it again down a lane on the right which leads to **Úcar** (3.5 km away), and then to **Enériz** (1 km further on).
b) From the top of the village of Tiebas, head towards the motorway, and take a path running parallel to it, and then cross the motorway through a tunnel. You then cross the N-121 and the railway track on your way into **Muruarte de Reta.** From here, we take a path that leads through the village of **Olcoz** and, following the course of the river Robo, we reach **Enériz** itself. Make your way along the left bank of the river Robo for just over 3 km, to the Church of **Eunate.** From there, follow the river Robo and the main road to **Puente la Reina,** about 5 km further on. If you wish, you can visit Obanos, clearly visible on a hilltop on the right.

🚴 The whole of this stage is negotiable by bicycle. However, some parts could present difficulties, such as the appoach to Eunate.

🚗 Milestones: N-240 km 15.5: turning to Yárnoz, Otano, Ezperún, Tiebas and Campanas. NA-6010 km 4: turning to Ucar; km 6.2: Enériz; km 8.8: Eunate; km 10.4: turning to Obanos; km 12: exit onto the N-111 in Puente la Reina.

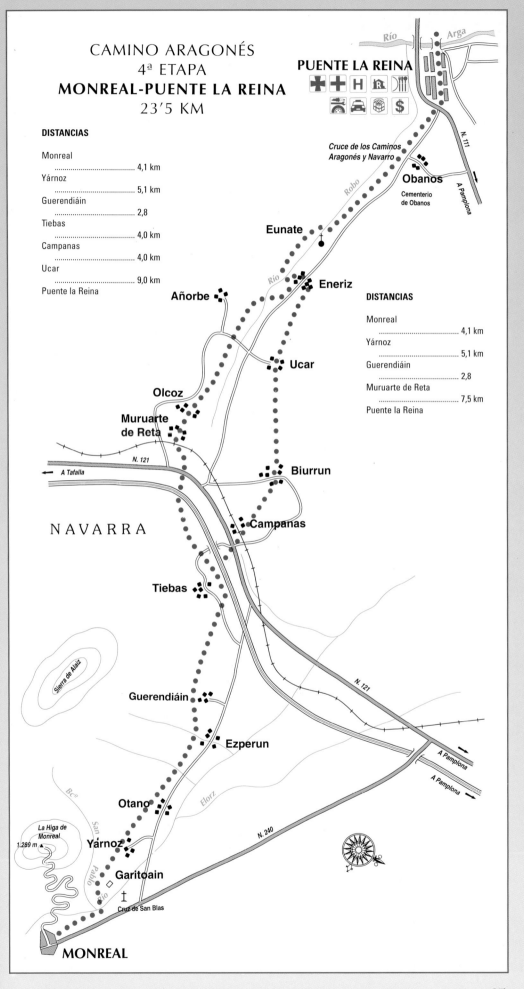

CAMINO ARAGONÉS
4ª ETAPA
MONREAL-PUENTE LA REINA
23'5 KM

PUENTE LA REINA

DISTANCIAS

Monreal
.... 4,1 km
Yárnoz
.... 5,1 km
Guerendiáin
.... 2,8
Tiebas
.... 4,0 km
Campanas
.... 4,0 km
Ucar
.... 9,0 km
Puente la Reina

Cruce de los Caminos
Aragonés y Navarro

Obanos

Cementerio
de Obanos

Eunate

Eneriz

Añorbe

Ucar

DISTANCIAS

Monreal
.... 4,1 km
Yárnoz
.... 5,1 km
Guerendiáin
.... 2,8
Muruarte de Reta
.... 7,5 km
Puente la Reina

Olcoz

Muruarte
de Reta

N. 121

← A Tafalla

Biurrun

NAVARRA

Campanas

Tiebas

N. 121

A Pamplona

Guerendiáin

Ezperun

A Pamplona

Sierra de Aláiz

Otano

Bcª

Elorz

N. 240

Pablo

La Higa de
Monreal
1.289 m ▲

Yárnoz

San

Garitoain

río

Cruz de San Blas

MONREAL

Bridge over the Elorz at Monreal

Outside Monreal

Yárnoz

Otano

II. HISTORY, ART AND LEGENDS

Before the paths were changed as a result of present-day agricultural land distribution and the introduction of modern asphalted roads, one of the exits from Monreal took pilgrims over a finely-paved double-arched medieval bridge over the river Elorz. Nowadays anyone crossing the bridge finds the way barred by a private farm.

Soon after leaving Monreal and heading down the *Camino de los Carros,* you come to a Gothic stone cross standing in the middle of a cornfield which is known as the *'Piedra de San Blas' ('St. Blase Stone')* and is possibly a vestige of an old hospital for pilgrims with contagious diseases on the outskirts of Monreal. Further on are the sites of the hospital and church of Garitoain, which were dependencies of *Sainte Foi de Conques.* The chapel which survived the rest of the hospital complex also fell to ruins and disappeared not very long ago.

Still overshadowed by the Higa mountain as it skirts the *Sierra de Alaiz,* the pilgrims' route reaches the small hillside village of **Yárnoz.** Amongst its interesting old buildings, the Church of the Nativity and a 14th-century fortified tower in the upper part of the village are of particular interest.

In **Otano,** which also conserves some of its oldest ancestral mansions (although the general impression is one of abandonment), stands the Church of the Ascension, a medieval building which was reformed at a later date. In the lower part of the village, a medieval bridge with four arches spans the Elorz river.

The next leg of this stage leads to the village of **Ezperun,** which is very similar to Yárnoz and Otanos, set between the cultivated plains of the Elorz valley and the first spurs of the rugged Sierra de Alaiz. Its ancient parish church, the Iglesia Parroquial de la Purísima Concepción, a medieval shrine reformed in the 16th-century, stands in semi-ruins, along with some of the ancient houses in this small village.

The old road from Monreal continues through **Guerendiáin** towards Tiebas and Campanas, while the river Elorz deviates from the pilgrims' route. Though small, the ancient farming community of Guerendiáin has an eventful past and lies in the foothills of the Sierra de Alaiz, somewhat set back from the road, clustered around the Church of San Juan Bautista, another medieval shrine which was reformed in the 16th century.

Although **Tiebas** also stands at the foot of the Sierra de Alaiz, it belongs to a different geographical and political district. On reaching it, the pilgrims' route enters the *'Cuenca de Pamplona'* (Pamplona basin). Its importance as a strategic point at the crossroads of several routes of communication probably dates from quite ancient times, although records and architectural remains do not date back much before the late high-medieval era. The castle, which surveys the village from a small hill and of which only a few ruins remain, was built by the troubadour king, Teobaldo I, who made the town one of his favourite haunts. His son, Teobaldo II, continued to favour it to the extent of establishing the royal residence there at one stage. The *royal archives* of the Kingdom of Navarre were once housed there. Apart from the castle, the Parish Church of Santa Eufemia, the ancient martyr of Calcedonia, still stands with much of its original Romanesque masonry intact. Nevertheless, Classical and baroque reforms, ever disrespectful of the 'barbarism' of medieval styles, are an inevitable feature.

Near Tiebas is the modern village of **Campanas,** which grew up around an inn on the pilgrims' route which, in its turn, stood on the site of an old pilgrims' hospital named after St. Nicholas of Bari, the Holy Bishop of Mira, who is to this day one of Catholicism's most popular saints when it comes to requesting a divine favour. A chapel dedicated to St. Nicholas of Bari still remains, thus perpetuating the memory of the old hospital. After Campanas you enter the Valdizarbe region, and there are two alternative routes which meet up again at Enériz.

The first, more northerly route, goes through Biurrun and Ucar, two typical villages of the Valdizarbe region. In **Biurrun,** in addition to the parish church dedicated to Nuestra Señora del Rosario, there are two chapels both dedicated to saints associated with pilgrimages, St. Martin and St. Christopher. In **Ucar,** the village church is dedicated to the Assumption. On the outskirts of the village, the Ermita de San Miguel stands on a knoll.

The other route takes you through **Muruarte de Reta,** where the Romanesque Parish Church of San Esteban, dating from the early 13th century, is the most interesting feature. The Parish Church of San Miguel Arcángel at **Olcoz** is another attractive Romanesque shrine.

The church at Guerendiáin

Tiebas

The two routes, which separated at Campanas, join up again at **Enériz,** an elegant Valdizarbe village situated near Puente la Reina, the famous town where the Aragonese and Navarrese branches of the pilgrims' way converge. The parish church, which dates entirely from the 18th century, is dedicated to Mary Magdalene, a sure sign of its connection at one time with hospital assistance to pilgrims.

By following the route along the river Robo, you reach the **Church of Santa María de Eunate,** which stands in solitary splendour among the cornfields. It is, without a doubt, one of the most precious and well-known monuments on the pilgrims' way. It is a small, octagonal Romanesque church with a pentagonal apse, surrounded by free-standing arcading in the manner of an external cloister. The octagonal building is crowned by an eight-angled pyramidal roof. The west portal is particularly impressive, being richly decorated with carvings which incorporate a wealth of symbolism. The twin capitals on one part of the 'cloister' reveal the most exquisite and refined workmanship. Anyone who is interested should take a look at the numerous 'stonemasons' marks' to be found on the church's external masonry. These architectural curiosities, and the fact that remains of pilgrim burial-sites have been

The castle at Tiebas

Biurrun

Úcar

An inn at Enériz

Eunate

One of the capitals at Eunate

found in the vicinity, have made the church a subject of controversy among art historians and other specialists. Some believe this type of building to be linked to the Knights Templar, who imported the design of these strange octagonal churches from the East, in imitation of the Church of the Holy Sepulchre in Jerusalem, which they defended from the Moors for many years. This would also explain its function as a burial place. However, there is no documentary proof to confirm the link between this church and the mysterious military order. It is nevertheless clear that it was used as a funerary chapel, similar to others found in France or, nearer still, at Torres del Río. Later documents vaguely mention that it was founded by 'a Lady' who wished to be buried there, and that a confraternity of villagers from Enériz, Muruzábal and other places was also involved. Inside the church there is a reproduction of the original Romanesque statue of Santa María de Eunate, the 'Virgin of one hundred doors'.

After this memorable visit to Eunate, the pilgrims' route continues to Puente la Reina along the river Robo, a tributary of the Arga. On one side Obanos stands majestically on a hill, from where pilgrims coming from Roncesvalles make their way down to **Puente la Reina.**

III. HISTORICAL PILGRIMS' ACCOUNTS

Aymeric Picaud: *'There are three short stages from Somport to Puente la Reina... The third leads from Monreal ('Mons Reellus') to Puente la Reina ('Pons Regine').'*

'... [the routes which converged in Ostabat] after Port de Cize join the road from Somport ('Portus Asperi') at Puente la Reina ('Pons Regine'), forming thence a single route to Santiago.'

STAGE 1

ST. JEAN-PIED-DE-PORT • RONCESVALLES

The Collegiate Church, Roncesvalles

ST. JEAN-PIED-DE-PORT • ERRECULUCH •
UNTTO • IBAÑETA • ARNEGUY •
VALCARLOS • RONCESVALLES

'Deinde repperitur uilla Runcieuallis.' (Aymeric Picaud: 'Pilgrims' Guide')

I. ROUTE

🚶 Starting out from the church of Nôtre-Dame in the old part of **St Jean-Pied-de-Port,** cross the bridge over the river Nive, go down the bustling rue d'Espagne ('Españako kalea') and leave the walled haute ville by the 'Porte d'Espagne'. You are now confronted with the first major decision of the journey: to take the so-called 'Route de Napoléon' (otherwise known as the 'Route des Ports de Cize'), or follow the road over the Valcarlos Pass.
a) If you opt for the former route, the uphill climb starts as soon as you leave St Jean-Pied-de-Port, along a narrow asphalt track. After a steep climb of just over a kilometre, you come to a small peneplain and the village of Othatzenea. Keeping to the asphalt track and climbing steadily uphill, you reach **Erreculuch** and, 1 km further along, the village of **Untto,** meeting up with the path from St Jean-le-Vieux and St Michel-Pied-de-Port. The ascent continues for two hard kilometres until you reach Arbola Azpian, and then eases off over the next 5 km as far as Biakorre, where there is a statue of the Virgin Mary. 2 km further up, bear right off the asphalt track (which continues to Urkulu) and follow a barely-marked grass path which leads up the Pic de Leizar Atheka. After reaching the summit, make your way down to the wire fence which marks the French-Spanish border, which you cross a few metres further up. The first section of the route on Spanish soil is along a paved forest path through a thick beech wood, which runs alongside the north face of Mount Txangoa. At the collado de Izandorre, shortly after the ruins of Elizarra (where there is a drinking fountain), take a wide track which begins the climb up Mount Aztobiscar as far as the 'collado de Lepoeder'. From here, either follow the asphalt track to the **Ibañeta pass,** some 2.5 km away, or the old path which runs through a beech wood and which leads directly to the **Monastery of Roncesvalles,** about 3.5 km away.
b) Take the N-133 out of **St Jean-Pied-de-Port.** Leave the road shortly afterwards and cross the 'Petite Nive'. Running alongside the river within sight of the road, the path enters deep into the narrow Valcarlos valley, crosses the Franco-Spanish border at Las Ventas and comes to **Arneguy** after about 8 km. From here, take the C-135 to **Valcarlos,** 2 km away. Follow the road for about 8 km as far as the 'Barranco de la Ortiga', when you branch off it to the left and take the path which goes to Zabaleta. After crossing a stream you begin the hard climb uphill along the left bank of the river Nive, through hazel, beech and chestnut trees, with a high-tension cable constantly overhead. After about 2 km, you come out onto the road again by the 'Casa del Guardiano', and leave it immediately at the 'Revuelta de Ferrán'. After just over 1 km you reach **Ibañeta,** from where you take the C-135 down to **Roncesvalles.**
🚴 Cyclists should follow the road (N-133 and C-135): between Arneguy and Ibañeta (20 km) there is an altitude difference of 1 000 metres.
🚗 Milestones: N-133 km 1: St Jean-Pied-de-Port; km 8: Arneguy; C-135 km 66.7: Franco-Spanish border; km 64: Valcarlos; km 52.5: 'Casa del Guardiano'; km 48.9: Alto de Ibañeta; km 47.6: Roncesvalles.

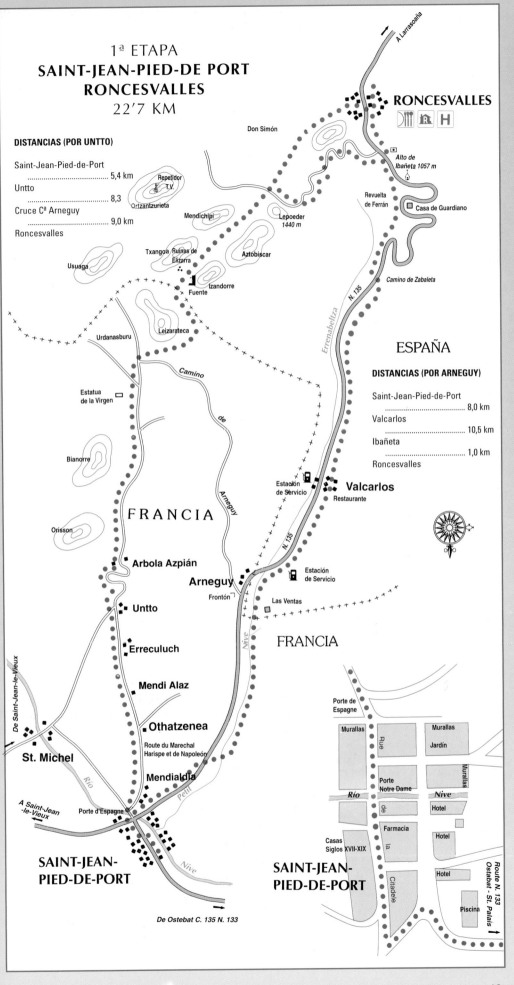

1ª ETAPA
SAINT-JEAN-PIED-DE PORT
RONCESVALLES
22'7 KM

DISTANCIAS (POR UNTTO)

Saint-Jean-Pied-de-Port
.... 5,4 km
Untto
.... 8,3
Cruce Cª Arneguy
.... 9,0 km
Roncesvalles

RONCESVALLES

A Larrasoaña

Don Simón

Alto de
Ibañeta 1057 m

Repetidor
T.V.
Ortzantzurieta

Mendichipi

Revuelta
de Ferrán

Casa de Guardiano

Lepoeder
1440 m

Txangoa Ruinas de
Elizarra

Aztobiscar

Camino de Zabaleta

Usuaga

Fuente Izandorre

Leizarateca

Errenabeltza

N. 135

ESPAÑA

Urdanasburu

Camino

DISTANCIAS (POR ARNEGUY)

Saint-Jean-Pied-de-Port
.... 8,0 km
Valcarlos
.... 10,5 km
Ibañeta
.... 1,0 km
Roncesvalles

Estatua
de la Vírgen

de

Bianorre

Arneguy

Estación
de Servicio

Valcarlos
Restaurante

FRANCIA

N. 135

Orisson

Arbola Azpián

Arneguy
Frontón

Estación
de Servicio

Las Ventas

Untto

FRANCIA

Erreculuch

Mendi Alaz

De Saint-Jean-le-Vieux

Porte de
Espagne

Othatzenea

Murallas

Murallas
Jardín

Route du Marechal
Harispe et de Napoleón

Rue

Murallas

St. Michel

Mendialdia

Río

Río

Porte
Notre Dame

Nive

Hotel

A Saint-Jean
-le-Vieux

Porte d'Espagne

Petit

de

Farmacia

Hotel

**SAINT-JEAN-
PIED-DE-PORT**

Nive

Casas
Siglos XVII-XIX

la

Hotel

Citadele

Route N. 133
Ostabat - St. Palais

De Ostebat C. 135 N. 133

**SAINT-JEAN-
PIED-DE-PORT**

Piscina

St. Jean-Pied-de-Port

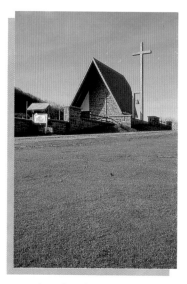

Chapel in the Ibañeta pass

Detail of the 'Las Navas' stained-glass window at Roncesvalles

II. HISTORY, ART AND LEGENDS

The *Liber peregrinationis* or *Pilgrims' Guide* written by the French monk, Aymeric Picaud, in about 1130, clearly identifies four main pilgrims' routes through France. The first is known as the 'Via Turonensis', in reference to the city of Tours ('Turones' or 'Turonensis'). This was undoubtedly the most well-trodden route, as it started in Paris and also linked up with the pilgrims' route from the Lower Rhine and Netherlands, the 'Niederstraße' or 'Low Road'. A second route, the 'Via Lemovicensis' (deriving from 'Lemovicum', the Latin name for Limoges), originated at the Abbé de la Madeleine in Vézelay, in Burgundy. Another route, the 'Via Podensis' (from the Latin word 'podium'), began at the Basilica of Notre-Dame-du-Puy, in Le Puy. The fourth route set out from Arles, and was known as the 'Via Tolosana', as it passed through the city of Toulouse. This was the route taken by Germanic pilgrims who had followed the 'Oberstraße' or 'High road', and by the majority of Italian pilgrims, who referred to it as the 'Via Francigena'.

The first three routes converged in the small, peaceful town of **Ostabat** in Lower Navarre, 21 kilometres away from the capital of the region, St Jean-Pied-de-Port. Today it has little to show for having been the 'carrefour des chemins de Saint Jacques'.

Aymeric Picaud places the starting point of this stage of the journey at **St Michel-Pied-de-Port,** from where pilgrims set off on the arduous climb up to the Port de Cize. However, he mentions the town of 'St Jean' (which is probably St Jean-Pied-de-Port rather than St Jean-le-Vieux) in the context of the extortionate taxes charged to unfortunate pilgrims by 'evil tax collectors' there, as well as in Ostabat and St Michel-Pied-de-Port. Picaud's outraged diatribe against the tax collectors' abusive methods is justified by the scenes he describes of cruel officials who 'waylay pilgrims, armed with clubs and sticks, forcing them to pay unjust tributes'. St Jean-Pied-de-Port, head of the Navarrese Merindad de Ultra Puertos from the 9th century, still retains the layout of an early medieval fortified stronghold. Its most important buildings are to be found in the rue de la Citadelle, which crosses the ancient haute ville from the Porte St-Jacques to the Porte d'Espagne, and include the 13th-century Gothic *Prison des Evêques,* the 14th-century Gothic *Eglise de Nôtre-Dame* and the Arch of St. John leading to the *Pont d'Espagne* which crosses the river Nive. At the end of the rue d'Espagne stands the Porte d'Espagne, through which travellers left the walled city bound for Spain, taking either the so-called 'Route de Napoléon et du Maréchal Harispe' which joined up with the route from St Michel-Pied-de-Port in the village of Untto, or the route over the Valcarlos Pass, the less ancient of the two routes, which is bound up with the *Charlemagne legend.*

The former route dates back at least as far as Roman times, and was part of the 'Via Traiana' which linked 'Burdegala' (Bordeaux) and 'Asturica Augusta' (Astorga). The 'Imus Pyrinaeus' in the 'Itinerarium Antonini' is usually identified as St Jean-le-Vieux, and the 'Summus Pyrinaeus' is a reference to the 'collado de Lepoeder' and Mount

Aztobiscar, known as the 'Port de Cize' in medieval times. More recently, there is evidence of the existence of pilgrims' hospitals in the villages of **Erreculuch** and **Untto**. After **Orisson,** the former site of a Priory linked to Roncesvalles, you come to Biakorre, where there is a modern statue of the Virgin Mary. From here there are panoramic views stretching as far as the Pic d'Aspe and the Somport Pass (about 70 kilometres away), the route into Spain taken by pilgrims coming from Arles on the 'Via Tolosana'.

On the Spanish side of the border, you come to a pass which runs alongside Mount Aztobiscar at the foot of the 'collado de Lepoeder', which is probably the 'Portus Cisere' mentioned by Aymeric Picaud in his *Pilgrims' Guide* (see *Historical Pilgrims' Accounts*).

Beech wood at Roncesvalles

This area was also the site of 'Charlemagne's Cross', a medieval cross mentioned by Picaud, marking the supposed place where Charlemagne fell to his knees and prayed towards Santiago after his army's long and arduous trek through the mountains. Medieval pilgrims would imitate his action, and would drive a cross into the ground in his memory. Aymeric Picaud writes that 'up to one thousand crosses can be seen there. This is why it is the first place pilgrims stop and pray to St. James on their way to Santiago.'

Collegiate Church at Roncesvalles

Ibañeta was the site of the important monastery of San Salvador. Today, all that remains of its glorious past is a modest stone monument and a chapel. The **Valcarlos** route goes through the Ibañeta pass, and is much easier than the Port de Cize route, although in Aymeric Picaud's day the latter route was most often taken. 'Valcarlos' derives from 'Valle de Carlos' and is so called because Charlemagne and his army camped there after their defeat in the Battle of Roncesvalles. The parish church of Valcarlos is dedicated to St. James and this was the site of a pilgrims' hospital dependent on the Monastery of Roncesvalles.

Roncesvalles: the inn

Roncesvalles embraces two different worlds: the Santiago pilgrimage and the French epic tradition. Together with Cebreiro, Roncesvalles is considered one of the earliest pilgrims' hospices, even though the *Pilgrims' Hospital,* founded by Sancho Larrosa, the Bishop of Pamplona, is not documented until 1127. The running of the hospital was entrusted to the Augustinians, and it soon acquired enormous importance, renown and wealth, receiving endowments from all over Europe. But it was the 'Chanson de Roland' which came to immortalise Roncesvalles, setting the famous battle scene there, when an assorted Basque and Aragonese army massacred the rearguard of Charlemagne's army as it retreated to Valcarlos. The story of the death of Roland and the Twelve Peers, the tragic wail of the enchanted horn, Olifant, summoning help... gave Roncesvalles mythical status, and pilgrims used to worship the supposed weapons of these heroes as if they were holy relics. The present day visitor to the *Real Colegiata monastery* will be more interested in the 13th-century Collegiate Church, built on the orders of the great King of Navarre, Sancho VII *the Strong,* which is dominated by the beautiful 14th-century seated statue of the Virgin of Roncesvalles. The magnificent Royal

The Virgin of Roncesvalles

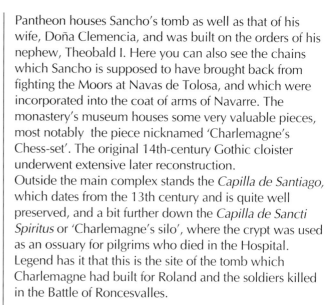

The Collegiate Church at Roncesvalles

Pantheon houses Sancho's tomb as well as that of his wife, Doña Clemencia, and was built on the orders of his nephew, Theobald I. Here you can also see the chains which Sancho is supposed to have brought back from fighting the Moors at Navas de Tolosa, and which were incorporated into the coat of arms of Navarre. The monastery's museum houses some very valuable pieces, most notably the piece nicknamed 'Charlemagne's Chess-set'. The original 14th-century Gothic cloister underwent extensive later reconstruction.

Outside the main complex stands the *Capilla de Santiago,* which dates from the 13th century and is quite well preserved, and a bit further down the *Capilla de Sancti Spiritus* or 'Charlemagne's silo', where the crypt was used as an ossuary for pilgrims who died in the Hospital. Legend has it that this is the site of the tomb which Charlemagne had built for Roland and the soldiers killed in the Battle of Roncesvalles.

Tomb of Sancho the Strong

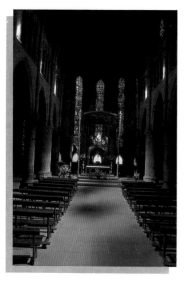

Charlemagne's Silo

III. HISTORICAL PILGRIMS' ACCOUNTS

Aymeric Picaud: *'The routes of St Faith, of St Leonard of Limoges and of St Martin of Tours join up in Ostabat ('Hostauallam'), and after the Port de Cize ('portus Cisere') they join the Somport route at Puente la Reina, forming thence a single route to Santiago.'* *'Still within the territory of the Basques, the Pilgrims' Way goes over a very high mountain which is known as the Port de Cize ('Portus Cisere'), either because it is the gateway into Spain, or because merchandise is transported from one country to another across it. It is eight miles up and eight miles down: indeed, it is so high that it seems to touch the sky.'*

Künig von Vach: *'A mile further on is the town of St Jean-Pied-de-Port ('Sant Johans')... Crossing a bridge, you come to a hospital on your right; five miles further on there is a monastery, built on a hill, in Roncesvalles ('Rontzefall').*

Arnold van Harff: *'It is three leagues from Ostabat ('Astabat') to St Jean ('Sent Johanne de pede port'), a 'villa franca' with a castle on a low hill.'*

Laffi: *'Continuing our journey, we reached St Jean-Pied-de-Port ('San Giovanni de Piedeporto')... We set off again over those vast, bleak mountains, climbing uphill for seven leagues... [At the top] there is an ancient little chapel [at Ibañeta]... After passing the chapel we began our descent and, after a quarter of a league, came to the place we had been longing to see: Roncesvalles ('Roncisvalle')... On the left is the great church, which is exceedingly ancient; Charlemagne had it built...'*

The countryside near Roncesvalles

STAGE 2

RONCESVALLES • LARRASOAÑA

Commemorative stone to the Virgen del Puerto, at Mezquíriz

RONCESVALLES • BURGUETE •
ESPINAL • VISCARRET • LINZOAIN •
ZUBIRI • ILARRAZ • ESQUIROZ •
LARRASOAÑA

PILGRIMS' REFUGES

Zubiri: During the summer months, the town council puts the local schools at the disposal of the pilgrims. Toilets. No individual beds are available, but there are 16 bunk-beds and hot water.
☎ (948) 30 40 56

Larrasoaña: This refuge is well equipped and has beds, toilets and a kitchen. It is managed with great care by the town council. 14 bunk-beds.
☎ (948) 30 42 42

ACCOMMODATION

Burguete:
HS** Burguete. Unica, 51.
☎ (948) 76 00 05.
22 rooms. ♣
HS** Loizu. Unica, 3.
☎ (948) 76 00 08.
47 rooms. ♣♣
HS* Juandeaburre. Unica, s/n.
☎ (948) 76 00 78.
4 rooms at 3.300 pesetas each.
Mendi-Txuri. ☎ (948) 76 00 49.
6 beds. ♣

Zubiri:
Enquire at the **Estanco** (state tobacco store) (☎ (948) 30 40 92) or ask a lady called **Ramona**, in the town square
(☎ (948) 30 40 56); both have rooms for rent at very economical prices.

CAMPSITES

Espinal:
Urrobi. 2nd Category.
☎ (948) 76 00 49

RESTAURANTS

Burguete:
Burguete. Unica, 51.
☎ (948) 76 00 05. In the boarding house.

Zubiri:
Gau Txori.
☎ (948) 30 40 76

PETROL STATIONS
On the C-135, at km 44.

'Deinde repperitur Biscarellus; inde Ressogna.'
(Aymeric Picaud: 'Pilgrims' Guide')

I. ROUTE

🚶🚶 From **Roncesvalles,** take the C-135 down to **Burguete.** From here, there are two alternative routes:
a) Turn right after passing the church and the fountain, down to an old bridge over the river Urrobi. After crossing the bridge, continue along a dirt track across farmland until you come to Espinal (approximately 3.5 km away).
b) Continue along the C-135. Shortly after the turning to Garralda and a second bridge over the river Urrobi, turn right and follow a path leading to Espinal, thereby cutting a corner off the main road.
Once in **Espinal,** go past the village fountain and take a path off to the left. This takes you up to a plantation of young conifers, after which you bear right, heading to the top of the hill among hazel trees, beeches and brambles. From here, make your way downhill until you reach the main road again. To the left of the stone monument to the Virgin of Roncesvalles, the path descends towards **Viscarret,** intersecting twice more with the C-135.
After the cemetery in Viscarret, the path descends, running parallel to the left of the C-135. Follow the road again for a short while, until you come to the turning to **Linzoáin** on your right, after which the steep ascent through pines, beeches and oaks to the Alto de Erro begins. Before crossing the main road again, take a look at the stone slabs known as 'Roland's footsteps'. The path then goes past the former Venta del Puerto (Inn of the Pass), which is now a cowshed. From here, go down towards **Zubiri.**
Go past the bridge leading into Zubiri and continue until you reach the Ostériz road. Continue along here until shortly after some garish factory buildings, and then bear right, first downhill and then uphill, to Ilárraz. Opposite a fountain, a narrow road leads to an ancient church. Keeping it on your right, continue to **Esquíroz.** From here, follow a path which soon disappears on the right hand edge of a field, goes past some farm buildings and comes out onto the main road after crossing the bridge over the river Arga about 150 metres from **Larrasoaña.**

🚴 This route is unsuitable in many places for cyclists. To cover the intransitable parts, take the C-135 which goes through Burguete, Espinal, Viscarret, Zubiri and Larrasoaña.

🚗 Milestones: C-135 km 47.6: Roncesvalles; km 44.8: Burguete; km 40.5: Espinal; km 36.4: Alto de Mezquíriz; km 34.8: Viscarret; km 29.2: Erro; km 26.5: Alto de Erro; km 22.7: Agorreta; km 20: Zubiri; km 16: Larrasoaña.

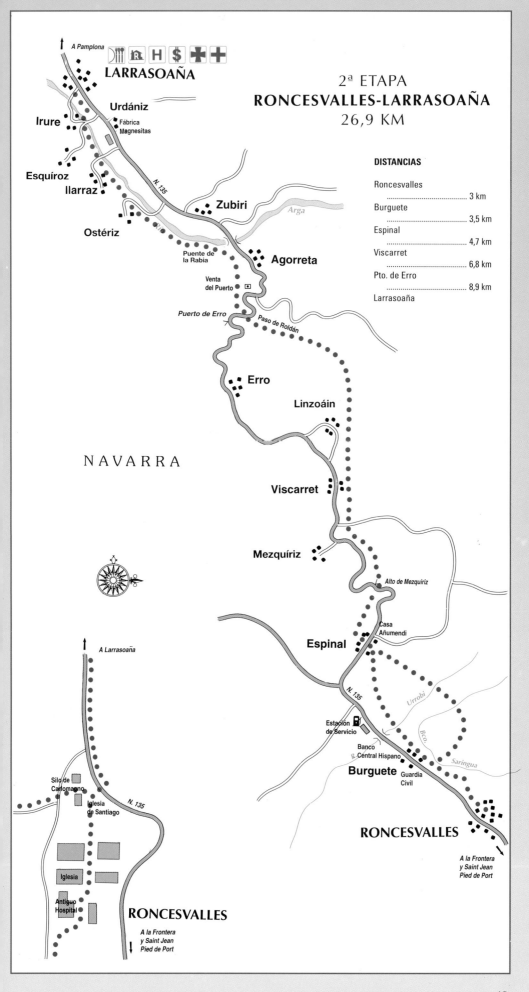

LARRASOAÑA

A Pamplona

Urdániz

Irure

Esquíroz

Ilarraz

Fábrica
Magnesitas

Ostériz

N. 135

Río

Zubiri

Arga

Puente de
la Rabia

Agorreta

Venta
del Puerto

Puerto de Erro

Paso de Roldán

Erro

Linzoáin

NAVARRA

Viscarret

Mezquíriz

Alto de Mezquíriz

Casa
Añumendi

Espinal

A Larrasoaña

N. 135

Urrobi

Bco.

Estación
de Servicio

Banco
Central Hispano

Saringua

Silo de
Carlomagno

Iglesia
de Santiago

N. 135

Burguete

Guardia
Civil

Iglesia

RONCESVALLES

Antiguo
Hospital

RONCESVALLES

*A la Frontera
y Saint Jean
Pied de Port*

*A la Frontera
y Saint Jean
Pied de Port*

2ª ETAPA
RONCESVALLES-LARRASOAÑA
26,9 KM

DISTANCIAS

Roncesvalles
.... 3 km
Burguete
.... 3,5 km
Espinal
.... 4,7 km
Viscarret
.... 6,8 km
Pto. de Erro
.... 8,9 km
Larrasoaña

The Pilgrims' Cross at Roncesvalles

Stone commemorating the 1200th anniversary of the Battle of Roncesvalles

Burguete

Espinal

II. HISTORY, ART AND LEGENDS

On the way out of Roncesvalles stands the so-called 'Pilgrims' Cross', a 14th-century Gothic cross placed there in 1880, which is referred to as 'Old Cross' in some documents. The base is inlaid with a Renaissance capital representing the Kings of Navarre, Sancho the Strong and Clemencia, his wife. Climbing the hill, the route passes through **Burguete,** once a borough of Roncesvalles ('uilla Roscidaullis'). Aymeric Picaud's *Pilgrim's Guide* and *The Pseudo-Turpin Chronicles* both place the Battle of Roncesvalles here, in which (according to legend) Roland, Oliveros and King Marsilius perished alongside 40 000 Christian and Saracen troops. The *Chronicles* recount the destruction of the main part of both armies in the following, somewhat ingenuous, manner:

'Charlemagne was crossing the pass with Ganelon, Turpin and twenty thousand Christians, with Roland and Oliveros and twenty thousand soldiers bringing up the rearguard, when Marsilius and Beligando [the Moorish caliphs] *and fifty thousand Saracens came out at dawn from the forests and hills where, at Ganelon's treacherous counsel, they had hidden themselves for two days and two nights; and divided their army into two corps, one of twenty thousand men and the other of thirty thousand. The twenty thousand ambushed our rearguard; but our men turned at once against them and after fighting from dawn until the hour of Terce* [nine o'clock in the morning] *forced them to succumb each and every one of them: not one of the twenty thousand escaped with his life. But at once, the other thirty thousand Saracens attacked our men, who were weak and exhausted after such mighty combat, and slew them all, big and small.'*

The present church of San Nicolás de Bari inherited the name and location of a much earlier one, and retains the original baroque portal. The route crosses the river Urrobi over a small single-arched Romanesque bridge.
Espinal was founded in 1269 by King Theobald II of Navarre, who is commemorated by a recently erected bust. The huge parish church is dedicated to St. Bartholomew and is of modern construction.
Until the founding of the Hospital of Roncesvalles, **Viscarret** was the resting place at the end of the first stage of the route on Spanish soil. Even in the mid-12th century, the *Pilgrim's Guide* omits to mention the recently-founded hospital, and cites 'Biscaretum' instead. However, no trace remains of the old pilgrims' hospital or of the town's important Jacobean past. The parish church, dedicated to St. Peter, is a 13th-century transitional Romanesque construction, restored in modern times.
Before beginning the climb to the Alto de Erro, you come to **Linzoáin,** a small village set back from the

C-135. Worth a visit is the small parish church, named after St. Saturninus (the popular San Cernin of Pamplona). The devotion to this French saint (who was Bishop of Toulouse) was imported by French pilgrims. The church dates from the 13th century, and is late Romanesque with later additions.

Up on the **Alto de Erro,** a great block of stone measuring two metres lies on the path. According to local tradition, it represents the footstep of the great French hero, Roland. It is but one of the countless reminders in this region of the legend surrounding the figures of Charlemagne, Roland and the Twelve Peers. According to medieval sources, these were objects of veneration in themselves for French pilgrims, who regarded Charlemagne as the discoverer of the Apostle's tomb and the founder and defender of the pilgrims' route to Santiago.

Espinal

Further along the path stands the **Venta del Puerto** (the 'Inn of the Pass'), which offered lodging to pilgrims and other wayfarers. It is now a cowshed.

Zubiri, Basque for *village of the bridge,* is reached over a great Gothic bridge, with two semicircular arches, which crosses the river Arga. It is known as the 'Bridge of Rabies' after the traditional local ritual of driving livestock three times around its central pillar to rid them of the disease. This power to ward off illness is attributed by local tradition to the relics of St. Quiteria, which are buried in the abutment of the bridge. Writing at the end of the 15th century, the German traveller, Arnold von Harff, refers to this town as 'Bridge of Paradise' ('Pont de paradijs'). The Parish Church of San Esteban dates from medieval times, but only the original walls remain. No identifiable trace remains of a leprosarium which was supposed to have existed in the village.

Viscarret

Larrasoaña is also entered via a bridge, which is 14th-century Gothic and was nicknamed *the bandits' bridge,* after the brigands who used to hold up and rob pilgrims at obligatory passing places such as this. Larrasoaña has a notable Jacobean past and figures as a port of call in Aymeric Picaud's *Pilgrims' Guide.* As far back as the 11th century there was an Augustinian monastery here, an order which has always shown great zeal in looking after Santiago pilgrims, as is evident in Roncesvalles, Pamplona and other parts of Navarre. In 1087, the monastery passed under the patronage of Leyre.

View from the Alto de Erro

Larrasoaña's links with the Santiago pilgrimage were reinforced by its declaration as a 'Villa de francos' (a community for French settlers) in 1174. The village layout, consisting of a row of houses flanking the main street (which is the pilgrims' way), dates from around this time, and is typical of many other villages which grew up along the pilgrims' route. Of a somewhat later date (13th-century) is the parish church of San Nicolás de Bari, one of the principal protectors of pilgrims and one of the most ubiquitous saints on the route. Künig von Vach refers to a hospice on the way from Roncesvalles to Pamplona, which was probably the building known as the

Bridge over the Arga, at Zubiri

The Church of San Nicolás at Larrasoaña

'Cillería de Roncesvalles' which, although somewhat altered, still retains traces of it links with the Collegiate Church. In the 18th century, a confraternity of St. Blase and a confraternity of St. James existed here, both dedicated to helping pilgrims and each with its own hospice. Today you can still visit the hermitages of San Blas and Santiago, located to the south and north of the village respectively.

Emblazoned houses, Larrasoaña

III. HISTORICAL PILGRIMS' ACCOUNTS

Aymeric Picaud: *'First you come to Viscarret ('Biscarellum') and then to Larrasoaña ('Rossogna').'*

Künig von Vach: *'After about three miles you reach a hospital* [Larrasoaña].*'*

Arnold von Harff: *'It is a league's distance from Zubiri ('Pont de paradijs') to Larrasoaña ('Raschona'), a 'villa franca'.'*

Laffi: *'...taking one last look at the tomb and all that area, we continued our journey to a place called Burguete ('Il Borghetto'), at one league's distance... from here we walked to Zubiri ('Ponte del Paradiso') which is situated at three leagues' distance... In Larrasoaña ('Risogna') we rested a while. It is a beautiful place, rich and well-populated...'*

The river Urrobi

STAGE 3

LARRASOAÑA • PAMPLONA (CIZUR)

Church bell at Zabaldica

AQUERRETA • ZURIÁIN •
IROZ • ZABALDICA •
ARLETA • VILLAVA • BURLADA •
PAMPLONA • CIZUR

PILGRIMS' REFUGES

Villava: As far as it is possible for them to do so, the Trinidad de Arre nuns still offer accommodation to pilgrims.
☎ (948) 33 29 41

Pamplona: The address of the Pamplona hostel is as follows: Ansoleaga, 2, Parroquia de San Saturnino.
☎ (948) 22 14 79

Cizur Menor: Magnificent private hostel. It is advisable to book in advance. Hot water and kitchen.
☎ (948) 18 38 85 (Mrs. Maribel Roncal).

ACCOMMODATION

NB: During the San Fermín week of festivities, you may expect to pay double the normal price for accommodation.
Burlada:
H** Green Burlada. La Fuente, 2.
☎ (948) 13 13 00.
53 rooms. ♣♣

Pamplona:
H**** Iruña Palace.
☎ (948) 22 66 00. ♣♣♣
H*** Iruña Park Hotel.
☎ (948) 17 32 00. 17.000 pesetas.
H*** Avenida. ☎ (948) 24 54 54.
♣♣♣
H*** Blanca de Navarra.
☎ (948) 17 10 10. 14.500 pesetas.
H*** Europa. ☎ (948) 22 18 00.
♣♣♣
H*** Maisonnave.
☎ (948) 22 26 00. ♣♣♣
HR*** Ciudad de Pamplona.
☎ (948) 26 60 11. ♣♣♣
H*** Ohri. ☎ (948) 22 85 00.
♣♣♣
H*** Sancho Ramírez.
☎ (948) 27 17 12. ♣♣♣
HR*** Yoldi. ☎ (948) 22 48 00.
♣♣♣
HR** Eslava. ☎ (948) 22 22 70.
♣♣♣
HR* La Perla. ☎ (948) 22 77 06.
♣♣
At a more reasonable price one can spend the night at the following hotels: **Príncipe de Viana I y II. Sarasate. Amezcua. Artazcoz. Bearán. Casa García. Velate.**

RESTAURANTS

Pamplona:
Alhambra. Hartza. Don Pablo. Josetxo. Mosquito. Sarasate. Shanti. Urdax.

PETROL STATIONS

On the C-135, at km 7.
On the C-135, at km 4.4.

'Inde urbs Pampilonia.' (Aymeric Picaud: 'Pilgrims' Guide')

I. ROUTE

🚶🚶 Set off from the church of San Nicolás and cross the bridge over the river Arga, bearing right along an asphalted lane towards **Aquerreta.** From Aquerreta, take a narrow path downhill, cross a secondary road and go through a field and a copse of beech trees. Then make your way gradually downhill towards the left bank of the river Arga and follow its course towards **Zuriáin,** where you cross the river. Next, go along the C-135 for about 500 metres, turn left off it and follow the local road which goes to Ilúrdoz. Cross the river over the bridge at **Anchoriz** and go along a path that runs between the hillside and the river Arga until you get to Iroz, where you cross the Arga again and come out onto the C-135, bearing right off it at **Zabaldica.** From here there are two alternative routes:
a) Along the top of the hill, past some electric transformers.
b) Along the hillside, through the hamlet of **Arleta.** Both routes meet up again just before an embankment, which skirt round. You then cross the main N-121-A Pamplona-Irún road through an underpass and continue parallel to it along an asphalted track which skirts Mount Miravalles. After crossing an old bridge over the river Ulzama, you come to the Basilica of the Trinidad de Arre in Villava. Continue through Villava along the Calle Mayor and the Avenida de Serapio Huici, entering **Burlada** (which is virtually a continuation of Villava) along the Calle Mayor. When you get to a Renault dealer, turn right, cross a road and make your way through the Magdalena district. From here, you enter **Pamplona** over the Magdalena bridge, which has a stone cross at the entrance on the right hand side. Follow a path skirting the city walls, go through the 'Portal de Francia' and head towards the cathedral. From this point, cross the city by the following route: calle de la Curia, calle Mercaderes, Plaza Consistorial, calle Mayor, calle Bosquecillo, Vuelta del Castillo and, after crossing Avenida de Sancho el Fuerte, Fuente del Hierro and the university campus. You then cross the river Sadar and carry straight on up to **Cizur Menor.**

🚲 Given both the hilly terrain and the state of the ground, this stage is hardly negotiable by bicycle, with the exception of the stretch from Zuriáin to Zabaldica, and of course the urban route from Arre to Cizur. Cyclists should therefore take an alternative route along the road.

🚗 Milestones: C-135 km 12: Zuriáin; km 11.5: turning to Ilúrdoz; km 10.2: Iroz; km 9.7: Zabaldica; km 9: turning to Arleta; km 7: Huarte; Pamplona; C-111 km: 5: Cizur Mayor, turning to Cizur Menor.

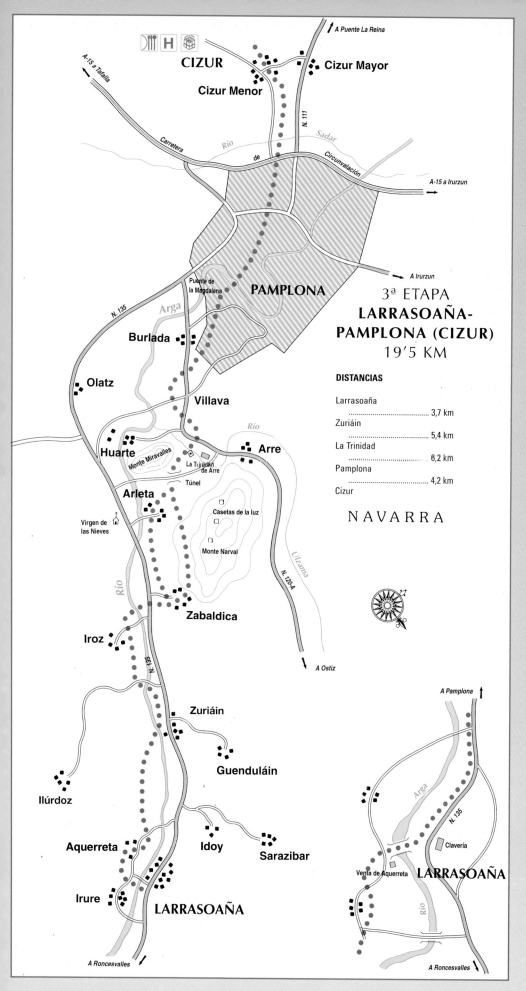

CIZUR

Cizur Mayor

Cizur Menor

A Puente La Reina

A-15 a Tafalla

N. 111

Carretera

Río

Sadar

de

Circunvalación

A-15 a Irurzun

A Irurzun

PAMPLONA

Puente de
la Magdalena

N. 135

Arga

Burlada

Olatz

Villava

Río

Arre

Huarte

Monte Miravalles

La Trinidad
de Arre

Túnel

Arleta

Virgen de
las Nieves

Casetas de la luz

Monte Narval

Ulzama

N. 120-A

Río

Zabaldica

Iroz

N. 135

A Ostiz

Zuriáin

Guenduláin

Ilúrdoz

Aquerreta

Idoy

Sarazibar

Irure

LARRASOAÑA

A Roncesvalles

3ª ETAPA
**LARRASOAÑA-
PAMPLONA (CIZUR)**
19'5 KM

DISTANCIAS

Larrasoaña
.... 3,7 km
Zuriáin
.... 5,4 km
La Trinidad
.... 6,2 km
Pamplona
.... 4,2 km
Cizur

NAVARRA

A Pamplona

Arga

N. 135

Clavería

Venta de Aquerreta

LARRASOAÑA

Río

A Roncesvalles

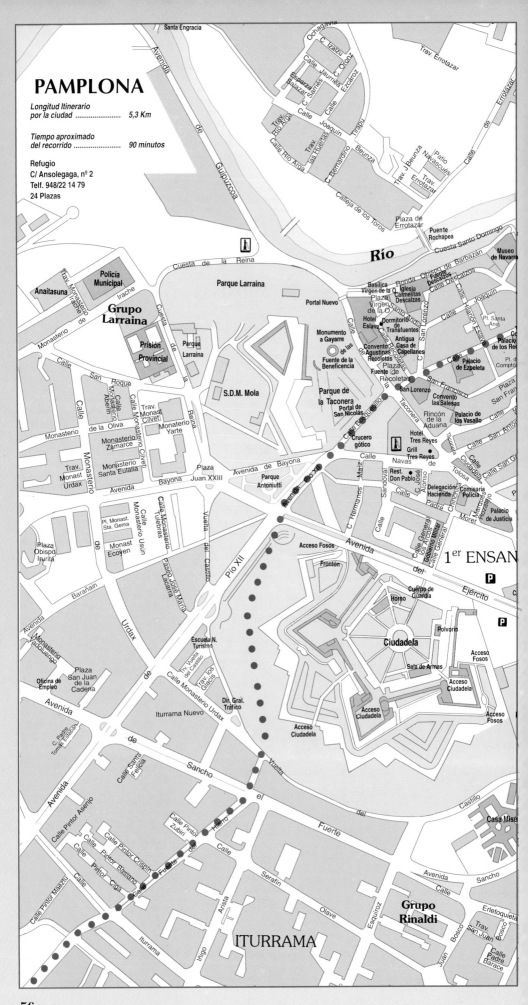

PAMPLONA

Longitud Itinerario
por la ciudad .... 5,3 Km

Tiempo aproximado
del recorrido .... 90 minutos

Refugio
C/ Ansolegaga, nº 2
Telf. 948/22 14 79
24 Plazas

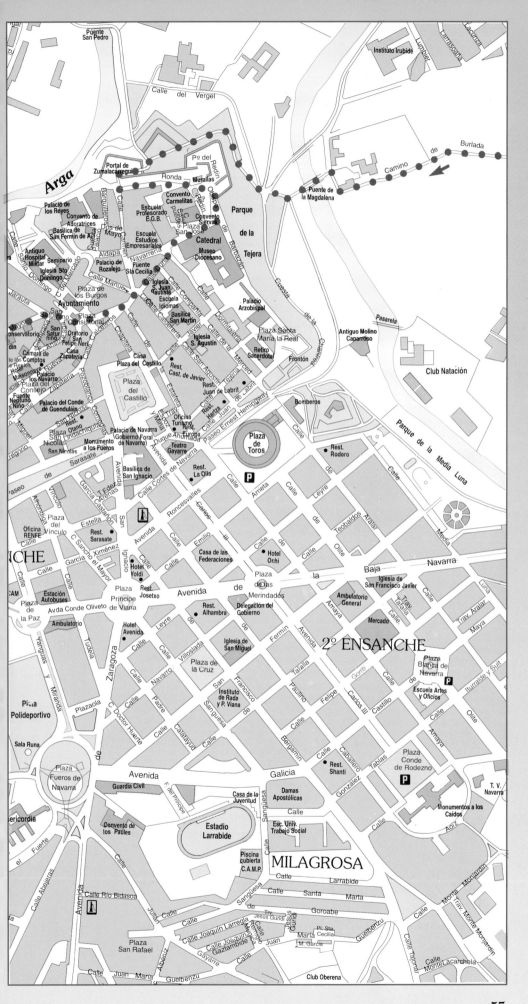

Iturgáiz: Romanesque bridge

La Trinidad de Arre

*Villava: bridge over
the river Arga*

San Fermín

II. HISTORY, ART AND LEGENDS

The pilgrims' way follows the river Arga in its descent towards Pamplona, passing through several villages as it crosses the Esteríbar valley. **Zuriáin** is about 4 kilometres from Larrasoaña, and its most eyecatching feature, given its elevated position, is the small medieval Church of San Millán, which was restored in the 16th and 17th centuries.

The village of **Iroz** is located 2 kilometres further down, on the opposite bank of the Arga, and has a modern church dedicated to St. Peter.

You cross the Arga again over the ancient Romanesque bridge of Iturgáiz (which has three arches of different sizes) on the way to **Zabaldica,** where the 12th-century Romanesque Church of San Esteban Protomártir is worth a visit.

The hamlet of **Arleta** consists of only two buildings: an elegant old manor house (where there is a remarkable geminate window in the tower), and the Church of Santa Marina, which houses a Gothic statue of the saint.

Heading away from the Esteríbar valley, the route skirts round Mount Miravalles and reaches the Ezcabarte valley, location of the famous Basilica de la **Trinidad de Arre,** which is reached by crossing a medieval bridge with six depressed arches spanning the river Ulzama. It used to house a pilgrims' hostelry, of which the 16th-century *Constitutions* survive, although the hostelry tradition goes back much further. After passing through the modern suburb of Burlada, the Romanesque Magdalena bridge takes you across the river Arga and into Pamplona. A stone cross bearing the image of St James dressed as a pilgrim stands at the entry to the bridge. Künig von Vach refers to a hospital at the far end of the bridge, and the fact that the bridge is named after Mary Magdalene is suggestive of this. Given its location outside the city, it would probably have been a leoprosarium housing those with infectious diseases.

Pamplona, allegedly founded by the Roman general Pompey *the Great* (75 B.C.?), derived its name, 'Pompaelo', from that of its founder compounded with the Ibero-Basque suffix *ili,* a variant of *iri,* meaning 'city'. An episcopal see from the 6th century and the driving force behind the evangelism of the Vascon territory, it was destroyed several times during the high Middle Ages. The city started to flourish during the reign of Sancho III (1000-1035), the great promotor of the Santiago pilgrimage, who created the 'burgos de francos' of **San Nicolás** and **San Cernín.** The 'francos' were foreign artisans and merchants, many of them former pilgrims, drawn by the financial opportunities and the privileges granted by the Crown to settlers in the recently created districts. This aroused the envy of the inhabitants of the early nucleus of Pamplona, **la Navarrería,** the district where most of the native population lived. The ensuing confrontation between the three heavily-armed and fortified districts turned the city into a bloody battleground. Despite this, the city prospered, due mainly to its position and its links with the Santiago pilgrimage, of which many traces remain.

With the amalgamation of the three original medieval districts, the interior walls were superseded by a new general enclosure, completed in the 16th century. The pilgrims' way enters the city through the appropriately-named **Portal de Francia,** before arriving at the **Cathedral,** the heart of the ancient Navarrería district. The original Romanesque construction was the work of Maestro Esteban, one of the pilgrims' way's most wimportant and famous master builders. Destroyed by a fire in 1390, it was rebuilt in the Gothic style, following the model of the beautiful cloisters which had been completed in 1356. The magnificent present-day cathedral is a Latin Cross shape, with three naves, a polygonal apse and a large ambulatory, which is characteristic of the churches along the pilgrims' way. The exterior had decayed to such an extent, that in the 18th century Ventura Rodríguez was commissioned to build the existing neoclassical façade. Inside, in front of the high altar, scene of the coronation of the Kings of Navarre, lies the *tomb of Charles III and Leonor of Trastámara,* the work of the Tournai artist Jean de Lomme and a splendid example of 15th-century French Gothic sculpture. Also of note are the *capilla de San Juan Bautista,* sacred to Christ of Caporroso; the *capilla del Santísimo,* with its marvellous Renaissance Christ; the *capilla de la Barbazana* and, above all, the *Capilla Mayor,* with its splendid 12th-century Romanesque statue of the seated Santa María del Real. The entrance to the cloisters —a quintessential example of French Gothic architecture— is presided over by 'La Puerta Preciosa', a 14th-century carving of the death of the Virgin Mary, based on the 'Golden Legend' by Jacobus de Voragine. Lastly, the Diocesan Museum houses important works of art from the Cathedral and other Navarrese churches, including sculptures, paintings, reliquaries and manuscripts.

The former district of San Saturnino is the location of the 13th-century fortified church of **San Cernin,** where the patroness of Pamplona, the *Virgen del Camino,* is venerated. Other sites of interest in this area are the **Hospital General** (now the Museum of Navarre) of which only the plateresque façade and a chapel remain, the **Cámara de Comptos** with its Gothic façade and the **Church of San Lorenzo,** which houses the 15th-century reliquary bust of **San Fermín,** the city's patron saint.

Off to the left of the pilgrims' route, in the San Nicolás district, is the Parish Church of San Nicolás, another fortified church and a reminder of the city's violent medieval past.

With the amalgamation of the three medieval districts, the outer defences of the city were reinforced and extended. In 1571, work began on the **Ciudadela,** which is now a park. The **Archivo General de Navarra,** which houses a vast wealth of documents, is next door to the neoclassical **Palacio Navarro.**

The **Church of Santo Domingo** is an unmistakable and

Pamplona. Stone cross on the puente de la Magdalena

Pamplona. the church of San Cernín

Pamplona. The walls and the cathedral

Pamplona cathedral: the cloister

outstanding reminder of the city's Jacobean past. Part of the erstwhile **Universidad de Santiago,** it is decorated with the typical scallop shell symbols, and a statue of St James dressed as a pilgrim dominates the high altar.

Leaving Pamplona, you come to Cizur Menor and the Romanesque **Church of San Miguel Arcángel,** which belonged to the ancient Hospitallers order.

The Church of San Andrés in **Cizur Mayor** features a serene Gothic Christ (circa 1 300) and a plateresque altarpiece by Juan Bustamante.

The Museum of Navarra

III. HISTORICAL PILGRIMS' ACCOUNTS

Aymeric Picaud: *'Then (comes) the city of Pamplona ('Pampilonia').'*

Künig von Vach: *'Then you reach a city called Pamplona ('Pepelonia'), and after crossing the bridge you turn towards a hospital... then you can visit the city in which the King of Navarre ('Nafern') has his residence.'*

Arnold von Harff: *'After Larrasoaña you come to Pamplona ('Pampalonia'). This is a large and beautiful city, but has neither strong walls nor moats around it.'*

Laffi: *'...we came to a beautiful plain from which we devised the great city of Pamplona, which is a beautiful sight from afar, being situated on a small hill, not more than four leagues away.'*

Pamplona town hall

STAGE 4

PAMPLONA (CIZUR) • PUENTE LA REINA

Monumen. to the Pilgrim at the entrance to Puente la Reina

PAMPLONA (CIZUR)• GUENDULAIN•
ZARIQUIEGUI• UTERGA• MURUZÁBAL•
OBANOS• PUENTE LA REINA

Puente la Reina: This is one of the traditional refuges to be found along the Pilgrims' Route and is run by the *Padres Reparadores,* who are in charge of the Church of the Crucifix. It has good facilities, a large number of beds and comfortable, clean toilets.
☎ (948) 34 00 50

ACCOMMODATION
Obanos:
HS** Hospedería Arnotegui.
San Juan, 1.
☎ (948) 34 42 08

Puente la Reina:
H** Jakue. Irunbidea.
☎ (948) 34 10 17.
28 rooms. ♣♣
H** Mesón el Peregrino.
Ctra. Pamplona-Logroño, 23. ☎ (948) 34 00 75. 15 rooms. ♣♣
HS* Puente.
Cerco Nuevo, 77
☎ (948) 34 01 46.
13 rooms. ♣

RESTAURANTS
Puente la Reina:
Mesón del Peregrino.
Ctra. Pamplona - Logroño, 23.
☎ (948) 34 00 75.
La Conrada.
Paseo de los Fueros.
☎ (948) 34 00 52

PETROL STATIONS
On the N-111, at km 11.

'Inde Pons Regine.' (Aymeric Picaud: 'Pilgrims' Guide')

I. ROUTE

🚶🚶 On your way out of **Cizur,** turn right at the 'pelota' court through some plain trees, and go down a wide dirt track through a housing estate. After a big bend to the right, leave the path, make your way across some cultivated fields and cross the road to Galar. Skirt round the outside of this little village (which is set up on a hill to the left) and follow the path until you reach a small poplar grove. Here the path disappears again across arable land, so follow the edge of the fields. You then come to a footpath which runs alongside a stream leading to the hamlet of **Guenduláin.** From this point on, the path starts to climb the first foothills of the Sierra del Perdón, the dominant feature on the horizon since Pamplona. After a gentle climb of 2 km you reach **Zariquiegui.** Go through the village, passing alongside the church, and regain the path which climbs steeply up to the Alto de Santa María de Erreniega (780 metres above sea-level), one of the highest points of the Sierra del Perdón. Shortly before reaching the summit you pass the 'Fuente de Reniega' (Fountain of Denial) on your left. From the top, in one direction, the Pamplona 'basin' lies before you against the backdrop of the Pyrenees, and in the other, the Valdizarbe valley and the villages of Uterga, Muruzábal and Obanos lining the road to Puente la Reina, with Mount Arnotegui and Mount Montejurra in the distance. After crossing a wire fence you begin the steep descent, through evergreen oaks and scrub, to **Uterga,** about 3 km away. An asphalt track then leads to **Muruzábal,** 1 km from Uterga. On your way out of the village you will see a cross: leave the road at this point and follow a path that runs parallel to the right of it, which takes you to **Obanos.** From here, you go down to a road which is part of the Somport route. This road joins the N-111 shortly afterwards, at the point where the Somport and Roncesvalles routes converge and where there is a statue of a pilgrim. Immediately after this, you enter **Puente la Reina.**

🚲 Since the path disappears at various points cyclists are advised to cover the Cizur-Alto del Perdón itinerary along the N-111, taking the turning to Uterga at km 15 and following the path to Puente la Reina.

🚗 Milestones: N-111 km 9.7: turning to Zariquiegui; km 13.7: turning to Alto del Perdón; km 15: turning to Uterga and Muruzábal; km 19: turning to Obanos; km 22: Puente la Reina.

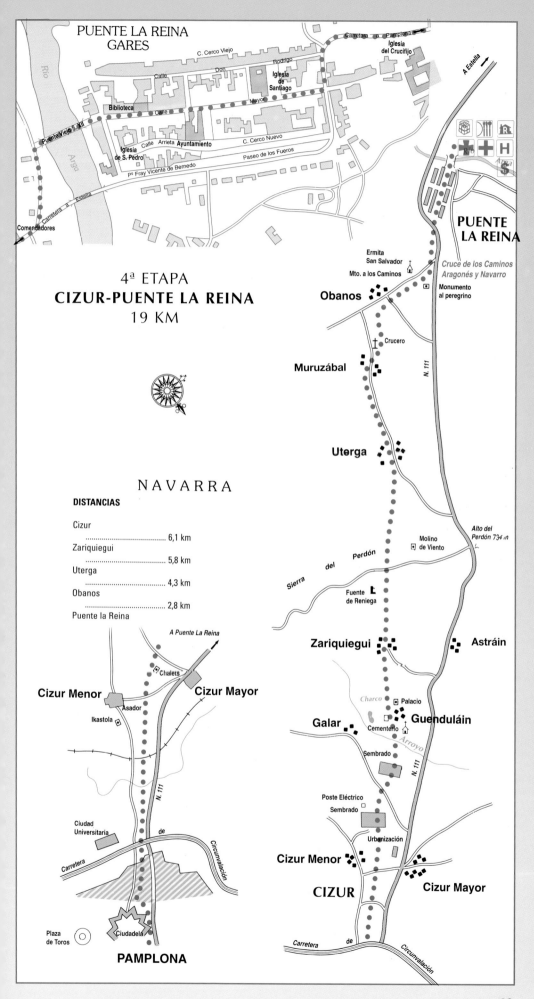

PUENTE LA REINA
GARES

C. Cerco Viejo

Calle · Don · Rodrigo

Iglesia de Santiago

Biblioteca · Calle · Mayor

Iglesia de S. Pedro · Calle · Arrieta · Ayuntamiento · C. Cerco Nuevo

Puente Viejo S. XII

Carretera a Estella

Pº Fray Vicente de Bernedo · Paseo de los Fueros

Comendadores

Río

Arga

Carretera a Pamplona

Iglesia del Crucifijo

A Estella

PUENTE LA REINA

Ermita San Salvador

Mto. a los Caminos

Cruce de los Caminos Aragonés y Navarro

Obanos

Monumento al peregrino

N. 111

Crucero

Muruzábal

Uterga

Alto del Perdón 734 m

Molino de Viento

Sierra · del · Perdón

Fuente de Reniega

Zariquiegui

Astráin

Charco

Palacio

Galar

Guenduláin

Cementerio

Arroyo

Sembrado

N. 111

Poste Eléctrico

Sembrado

Urbanización

Cizur Menor

CIZUR

Cizur Mayor

Carretera · de · Circunvalación

4ª ETAPA
CIZUR-PUENTE LA REINA
19 KM

N A V A R R A

DISTANCIAS

Cizur

.... 6,1 km

Zariquiegui

.... 5,8 km

Uterga

.... 4,3 km

Obanos

.... 2,8 km

Puente la Reina

A Puente La Reina

Chalets

Cizur Menor

Asador

Ikastola

Cizur Mayor

Ciudad Universitaria

N. 111

de

Circunvalación

Carretera

Plaza de Toros

Ciudadela

PAMPLONA

*Palace of the Counts
of Guendulain*

*View over the Pamplona basin
from the Sierra del Perdón*

Uterga

II. HISTORY, ART AND LEGENDS

This is the third stage in Aymeric Picaud's *Pilgrims' Guide.* According to *'The Pseudo-Turpin Chronicles,* the open plain (now planted with cereals) which we crossed before embarking on the climb up to the **Sierra del Perdón,** is the site of the meeting, theological disputes and the pitched battle between Charlemagne and the Moorish caliph, Aigolando, who had waited for Charlemagne in Pamplona and who was defeated and killed in the battle.

Just before the foothills of the Sierra del Perdón is the hamlet of **Guendulain,** where there was once a pilgrims' hospital run by a Confraternity of St James. The village is virtually abandonded and its most significant buildings —the 16th-century Church of San Andrés and the Palace of the Counts of Guenduláin— are in ruins.

Halfway up the hill is the village of Zariquiegui, a typical Wayside village in its layout. Here there is another church of San Andrés, which retains an original Romanesque door.

Shortly before reaching the Alto del Perdón, on the left hand side of the path, a modern fountain commemorates the traditional legend of the *Fuente Reniega,* the Fountain of Denial, the sources of which are obscure. According to the legend, an exhausted and parched pilgrim was tempted by the Devil, who offered to show him a spring to quench his thirst in return for denying his faith. The pilgrim resisted temptation and his staunchness was rewarded by the appearance of the Apostle dressed as a pilgrim, who revealed the location of the spring and gave him water from his scallop-shell.

Historically, this area has always shown great devotion to Nuestra Señora del Perdón (Our Lady of Forgiveness). Every year pilgrims from all over Navarre would visit her and there are records of the annual visit her image made to the Basilica of the Trinidad de Arre. As late as 1816, there are records here of two hermitages, the Basilica de Nuestra Señora del Perdón and a hospice opposite, with a hermitage where poor pilgrims were lodged.

On the other side of the hill you come to **Uterga,** which has a Gothic church dedicated to the Assumption of the Virgin.

The church at **Muruzábal,** a little further on, is dedicated to Saint Stephen, and has a carving of St. James dressed as a pilgrim in one of its chapels.

Obanos is the historic 'Villa de los Infanzones'. Led by the 'Infanzones', the lowest rank of nobility, the different social forces in the kingdom gathered here in 1327 and swore to put a stop to the abuses and prepotency of the foreign monarchy and aristocracy. Their proverbial motto was *'Pro libertate patriae gens libera state'* ('For a free country, be yourselves free'). Between 1965 and 1978, the play 'The Mystery of Obanos', written by the illustrious local Canon and writer Don Santos Beguiristáin, was enacted every summer. It was a dramatization of the old Jacobean legend of Saint Felicia and her brother William, Duke of Aquitaine. On her return from a pilgrimage to Santiago, Felicia decides to live as a hermit in Amocain. William, furious at her refusal to return to the court, kills her. Appalled at what he has done, he makes the pilgrimage to Santiago in penitence, and then returns to Obanos where he spends the rest of his life lamenting his sin in the odour of sanctity. A simple monument on the path which leads up to the **Ermita de Arnotegui** commemorates this legend and William's burial place at the hermitage of Santa María. (Fortunately, the 'Año Santo Compostelano 1993' has inspired the reinstatement of the annual performance of the play.)

The Church of San Juan Bautista was rebuilt on the present site between April 1911 and November 1912, in neo-Gothic style. The silver-covered skull of St. William is preserved as a relic in the sacristy and is traditionally used every Maundy Thursday to bless the wine and water served to the villagers.

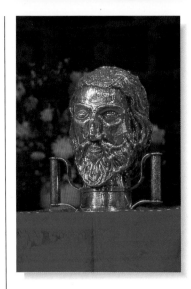

Obanos: the head of St. William

The Roncesvalles and Somport routes converge on the N-111 at the entrance to Puente la Reina, and this is the site of an intriguing iron statue of a pilgrim, done by Gerardo Brun in 1965.

Puente la Reina owed its importance to its strategic position as a bridgehead, equidistant between Pamplona and Estella. The influx of pilgrims prompted the building of the 'Puente de Arga', later renamed 'Puente la Reina' in honour of its sponsor, who was either Doña Mayor, wife of Sancho III (1000-1035), or her successor, Doña Estefanía, wife of Don García de Nájera. In the 12th century, Alfonso I 'the Battler' granted the nascent town 'fueros', or special rights and privileges, similar to those of Jaca and Estella, to stimulate its growth.

Obanos: Santa María de Arnotegui

The Templars were entrusted with the protection of pilgrims from 1142 until their suppression in the 14th century, when the Hospitallers took over the task. The *Iglesia del Crucifijo* (or 'Santa María de las Huertas' as it used to be called) was founded by the Templars, and a large hospital was built beside it. When the order was suppressed, its property and functions were transferred to the Hospitallers, whose prior, Jean de Beaumont, reformed and extended the original structure in 1447, building a new convent and hospital dedicated to the Holy Cross. The church therefore has an earlier and later part, with two apses, two naves, and so on. The church houses a Romanesque statue of Santa María de las Huertas, and a magnificent carved wooden crucified Christ of German origin, on a curious tree-shaped cross, which gives the church its name.

The route goes down the *Calle Mayor,* one of the pilgrims' way's most characteristic and perfectly-proportioned village streets. Halfway along is the *Iglesia de Santiago,* which has an impressive 12th-century Romanesque façade and a multilobed main portal, similar to those to be found at the churches of San Pedro de la Rúa at Estella and San Román at Cirauqui. The interior features an 18th-century high altar retable dedicated to St James, a 14th- century statue of St.

Puente la Reina: German crucifix in the Iglesia del Crucifijo

Portal of the Church of Santiago, Puente La Reina

Puente la Reina: the bridge over the Arga

Puente la Reina. Santiago 'Beltza'

Puente la Reina

Bartholomew and the famous Gothic statue of St. James 'the Black'. As in other Navarrese churches, one of the most distinctive features are the floor tombs marked by great slabs of chestnut.

In the Church of San Pedro Apóstol, the image of Nuestra Señora del Puy, also known as Nuestra Señora del 'Chori' (bird), is worshipped. Legend has it that when the statue was kept in a small chapel in the middle of the bridge (until the last century), a little bird used to go and clean the Virgin's face, which was seen as a good sign.

The Calle Mayor leads directly to the *Puente de los Peregrinos* which crosses the river Arga. This Romanesque construction, consisting of six semicircular arches and five pillars with spillways, is a typical hump-backed shape and is one of the most famous bridges on the road to Santiago.

III. HISTORICAL PILGRIMS' ACCOUNTS

Aymeric Picaud: '...(the routes which converged in Ostabat) *after Port de Cize join the Somport route at Puente la Reina ('Pons Regine'), forming thence a single route to Santiago.'*

Künig von Vach: *'After a distance of two miles you come to Puente la Reina ('Ponteregina') ...where you will find a beautiful bridge.'*

Arnold von Harff: *'It is three leagues from Guenduláin ('Indulay') to Puente la Reina ('la punt de regina'), a small town. You go up a mountain and down again. You must cross a stone bridge over a river called Arga ('Harga').'*

Laffi: *'...we left Pamplona and made our way over some hills, which were not very high but difficult. On the other side of the hills we went through a great wood and at last reached Puente la Reina ('Ponte della Ruvina'), five long, difficult leagues away.'*

STAGE 5

PUENTE LA REINA • ESTELLA

The Church of San Miguel at Estella

PUENTE LA REINA • MAÑERU •
CIRAUQUI • LORCA •
VILLATUERTA • ESTELLA

PILGRIMS' REFUGES

Estella: Newly constructed 50-bed municipal hostel, situated next to the San Miguel Bridge at the beginning of Calle de la Rúa.
☎ (948) 55 15 62

ACCOMMODATION

Estella:

HSR ** Cristina.**
Baja Navarra 1-1.
☎ (948) 55 07 72.
15 rooms. ♣♣
Izarra. ☎ (948) 55 00 24.
12 beds. ♣
San Andrés. ☎ (948) 55 04 48.
50 beds. ♣♣♣
Volante. (948) ☎ 55 39 57.
16 beds. ♣
Joaquín. ☎ (948) 55 06 80.
Five rooms. ♣
Maeztu. ☎ (948) 55 04 32.
10 beds. ♣

CAMPSITES

Estella:
Lizarra. 1st Category.
☎ (948) 55 17 33

RESTAURANTS

Estella:
La Cepa.
Plaza de los Fueros, 18.
☎ (948) 55 00 32. Traditional cuisine.
Casanova. Nueva, 8.
☎ (948) 55 28 09

PETROL STATIONS

On the N-111, at km 34'2 (Cirauqui);
at km 42, in Estella.

'Inde Stella.' (Aymeric Picaud: Pilgrims' Guide)

I. ROUTE

🚶 Leave **Puente la Reina** along the Calle Mayor ('Nagusia Kalea') which leads directly to the famous bridge over the river Arga. After the bridge, turn left and cross the N-111 and enter the Zubiurrutia district or 'barrio de la Monjas (Nuns)', in allusion to the Convent of the Comendadoras del Espíritu Santo. Next, go through the centre of **Eunea** and continue along a smooth dirt track, keeping the river Arga to your right and the road to your left. Further on, the path becomes narrow and winding, running over very rugged ground. Shortly before the village of **Mañeru** you come to a special 'pilgrims' footpath' (made of compacted earth) which runs parallel to the road. Only one road leads out of Mañeru: the Calle Forzosa. Passing the village cemetery on your left, you catch sight of the hill-village of **Cirauqui** about 3 kilometres away, which you reach along a dirt track running through vegetable plots and orchards. Cross the Gothic bridge which leads into Cirauqui and make your way up to the top of the village. From here, the route leads steeply downhill along a fascinating stretch of original Roman road, flanked by cypresses on either side, and crosses a gorge over a Roman bridge (fortunately recently-restored!). Cross the N-III and follow the Roman road through farmland, getting progressively further away from the main road. After just over 1.5 km you go through the ruined medieval village of Urbe, situated on a hill. From here, head downhill past a little farmhouse and, shortly afterwards, come out onto a road right by the turning to the 'Pantano de Alloz'. Follow this road for a short distance and bear left off it, after passing a modern aqueduct and an old water mill. Cross an old bridge over the river Salado and follow a dirt track up to the village of **Lorca,** having crossed the N-111 through an underpass. Leave Lorca along the N-111 and bear left off it after the turning to Lácar and Abárzuza and make your way through farmland until you come to **Villatuerta.** From the centre of the village, head towards the Ermita de San Miguel. Cross a road and a bridge over the river Ega, and follow the Ordoiz road which leads to **Estella.**

🚲 This stage has several difficult stretches for cyclists: the stretch just before Mañeru; the Urbe area, between Cirauqui and Lorca; and the stretch between Villatuerta and Estella. Cyclists are advised to cover these parts by road.

🚗 Milestones: N-111 km 26.9: Mañeru; km 30: Cirauqui; km 35: Lorca; km 30: Villatuerta; km 42: Estella.

ESTELLA

A Los Arcos

Pl. Pta.
de la Paz

Iglesia de
San Pedro
de Lizarra

San Pol

C. Caldereria

San Lorenzo

Pl. de
los Fueros

C. Estrella

Antiguo
Hospital
Imprenta

Pl. de
S. Miguel

Pl. del
Mercado
Viejo

Pl. de
Santiago

Iglesia
San Juan

Pl. de
Coronación

Calle
Mayor

Paseo de la Inmaculada

Iglesia
San Miguel

San Agustín

Correos
y Telégrafos

Puente de
la Cárcel

Ega

Pl. San
Francisco
de Asís

Rúa Curtidores

Iglesia del
Santo
Sepulcro

Estación de
Autobuses

C. Sancho El Sabio

C. Sancho El Fuerte

Pl. San
Martín

Río

Pl. de
la Coronación

Convento
Santa Clara

Iglesia de
Santa María
Jus del Castillo

Iglesia de
San Pedro
de La Rúa

Convento de
Santo Domingo

Portal
de
Castilla

Ega

Monolito
Palacio
de los Reyes
S. Pedro

ESTELLA
Verbo
Divino

H   ✚   ✚

$ 📦   🧺   🚕

Ermita
de S. Miguel

Río   Iranzu

Villatuerta

Fuente

Arandigoyen

N. 111

Lácar

Salado

A Alloz

Lorca

Fuente

Molino

Acueducto

Túnel
Puente Medieval
Ruinas

Casa

Río

Ruinas
de Urbe

Puente Romano

Calzada Romana
Cirauqui

NAVARRA

Cementerio

Mañeru

5ª ETAPA
PUENTE LA REINA-ESTELLA
19 KM

Cruz

N. 111

Merendero

Arga

Río

Eunea

Iglesia
del Crucifijo

Convento
Reparadores

Iglesia
de Santiago

PUENTE LA REINA

A Pamplona

DISTANCIAS

Puente la Reina
.... 4,5 km
Mañeru
.... 2,7 km
Cirauqui
.... 5,3 km
Lorca
.... 4,3 km
Villatuerta
.... 2,2 km
Estella

Cirauqui: portal of the Church of San Román

Cirauqui: Church of Santa Catalina

Immediately after crossing the magnificent bridge over the Arga you come to the Zubiurrutia district, otherwise known as the 'barrio de las Monjas', or Nuns District, in allusion to the *Convent of the Comendadoras del Espíritu Santo,* founded in the 13th century and with a long tradition of hospitality to pilgrims. Its beautiful, single-aisled Renaissance church, which substituted the former medieval church, is open to the public.

Not far off the path, after passing Eunea, are the ruins of the Hospital de Bargota, which was run by the Hospitallers, an order whose influence is felt all along the pilgrims' way.

The ruined Gothic church at **Mañeru** also belonged to the Hospitallers. The current parish church dates from the 18th century and is dedicated to St. Peter the Apostle. St. Barbara is a strong presence in the village: her image graces the parish church and there is a hermitage dedicated to her.

Cirauqui is Basque for 'vipers' nest', this being a reference to the rocky hill on which it is built. It is an enchanting place which retains much of its medieval character (walls, buildings, layout, etc.). One of the most outstanding buildings is the *Church of San Román,* at the top of the village, which has a 13th-century Gothic multilobed main portal, similar to the one we already encountered at the Iglesia de Santiago in Puente la Reina and to the one at San Pedro de la Rúa in Estella. The original 13th-century construction was considerably remodelled in 1692 and houses an inscribed Roman votive altar stone. The Church of Santa Catalina de Alejandría also dates from the early 13th century.

From Cirauqui the route heads downhill to a bridge, along a stretch of the old Roman path. The single-arched bridge is also of Roman origin and was partially restored not long ago. Before descending towards the Yerri valley, you pass the ruined medieval village of **Urbe** of which the foundations of a few buildings are all that remain. Just outside the village of Lorca, you cross the river **Salado** over a small double-arched medieval bridge, which was the setting for this well-known tale told by Aymeric Picaud in the *Pilgrims' Guide:*

'Take care not to drink the water here, neither yourself nor your horse, for it is a deadly river! On the way to Santiago we came across two Navarrese sitting by the bank, sharpening the knives they used to flay pilgrims' horses which had drunk the water and died. We asked them if the water was fit to drink, and they lyingly replied that it was, whereupon we gave it to our horses to drink. Two of them dropped dead at once and the Navarrese flayed them there and then.'

Lorca is another typical wayside village. The Church of San Salvador dates from the 12th century, with later modifications. The theory that a pilgrims' hospital dependent on the Collegiate monastery at Roncesvalles

Cirauqui: Roman bridge

existed in the village is borne out by the frequent references to Lorca and the Church of San Salvador in the medieval manuscripts at Roncesvalles.

Somewhere between Lorca and Villatuerta there used to be a hospital which belonged to the Hospitallers, although the exact location is unknown.

Villatuerta is reached across a double-arched Romanesque bridge which spans the river Iranzu. From the 15th century there was a monastery dependendent on Leyre here, of which only the Ermita de San Miguel remains. The parish church of the Assumption is 14th-century, with a 13th-century belfry. The high altar and the side chapels are lovely examples of Renaissance and baroque styles.

Estella grew up around the castle of Lizarra, and was granted special status by Sancho Ramírez in 1090, who created a new district for French settlers on the left bank of the river Ega. The 'burgo franco', or San Martín district, grew up at the foot of the rocky spur on which the church of San Pedro de la Rúa stands, and quickly flourished due to trade and its privileged position on the pilgrims' way. In the 12th century, the churches of San Nicolás and Santo Sepulcro were built. The town's important Jewish population built their ghetto on the side of the castle hill: the former synagogue became a church in 1145, and was dedicated to Santa María Jus del Castillo. In the second half of the 12th century, two new districts for French settlers were created: the San Miguel and San Juan districts, built around their respective churches. The San Juan district, founded by Sancho the Wise, was the first area in which the Navarrese were permitted to live alongside the French settlers and enjoy the same privileges. Other district grew up later, and was also a mixture of French settlers and native Navarrese. Each parish church had its own pilgrims' hospital until 1524, when they were all merged into one on the orders of Charles V. The Hospital de San Lázaro, for contagious patients, was built outside the town.

The pilgrims' route enters Estella through the San Miguel district, which grew up around the late Romanesque Church of *San Miguel,* interesting above all for the magnificent carvings on the north portal. Before crossing the Ega, you come to the area which used to be the original village of Lizarra, where the churches of San Pedro de Lizarra and of the Virgen del Puy are to be found. In the old San Juan quarter you should visit the Plaza de los Fueros and the *Church of San Juan Bautista,* which houses a Romanesque font and a Gothic crucifix. The Monastery of San Benito del Real and the Convent of the Order of St. Clare are also located on the right bank of the Ega. The elegant bridge known as the *Puente de la Cárcel* or *Puente de San Miguel,* fortunately restored in 1971, takes you across to the old 'burgo franco' of San Martín. The main street here is the historic Rúa de las Tiendas, location of the *Church of Santo Sepulcro,* which has a Gothic façade featuring a statue of St James dressed as a pilgrim. Nearby is the *Convento de Santo Domingo,* and below the completely ruined castle stands the Church of *Santa María Jus del*

Cirauqui: Roman road

North portal of the Church of San Miguel, Estella

Estella: Church of the Virgen del Puy

Estella: Puente de los Peregrinos over the river Ega

Estella: Church of San Pedro de la Rúa

The Cloisters of the Church of San Pedro de la Rúa, Estella

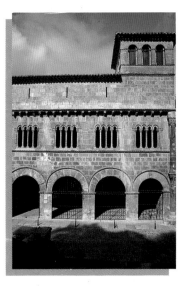

Estella: the Palace of the Kings of Navarre

Castillo, built on the site of the old synagogue. The beautiful 12th-century *Palace of the Kings of Navarre,* in the Plaza de San Martín, is built on the site of the old church of San Martín, and is a unique example of Romanesque secular architecture. Visitors are always spellbound by the wonderful capital depicting Roland's battle with the giant Ferragut. Opposite stands the *Church of San Pedro de la Rúa,* which is steeped in history and is full of artistic treasures; this where the Kings of Navarre took the oath when passing new laws and granting special privileges. This is the site of the third portal with polylobed arches, similar to those already seen at Puente la Reina and Cirauqui. The church houses many precious statues and is famous for its Romanesque cloisters, of which two parts survive. Outside the old San Martín district stands the **Ermita de Rocamador,** which has a lovely statue of its namesake as well as a 17th-century statue of St James dressed as a pilgrim.

III. HISTORICAL PILGRIMS' ACCOUNTS

Aymeric Picaud: *'...next we come to Estella ('Stella'), where the bread is good, the wine excellent, the meat and fish are abundant, and which enjoys all delights.'*

Künig von Vach: *'A mile further on* [from Puente la Reina] *you come to a village on your left. In the four miles that follow there are four bridges. Next to the third bridge is a fountain from which you can drink if necessary. After the fourth bridge, you come to the Jewish city of Los Arcos...'* [It is interesting that Künig von Vach makes no mention of Estella between Puente la Reina and Los Arcos.]

Arnold von Harff: *'It is four leagues from Puente la Reina to Estella ('La stella'), a small town. We passed through many burnt villages and ravaged cities. In the local tongue, Estella is called 'Sudat' ('ciudad' = city).'*

Laffi: *'Estella ('Lustella')... is a fine place, set on either side of a great river spanned by a bridge which, though not long, is fairly high...'*

STAGE 6

ESTELLA • LOS ARCOS

Los Arcos: the Church of Santa María

ESTELLA • AYEGUI •
AZQUETA • VILLAMAYOR DE MONJARDÍN •
LOS ARCOS

PILGRIMS' REFUGES

Los Arcos: Comfortable 40-bed municipal hostel set up in former teachers' dwellings.
☎ (948) 64 02 30

ACCOMMODATION

Ayegui:
HR* Irache.**
Ctra. Logroño, km 43.
☎ (948) 55 11 50
74 rooms. ♣♣♣
Bar Montejurra.
☎ (948) 55 00 43.
Eight beds. ♣

Los Arcos:
H Mónaco.**
Plza. del Coso, 22.
☎ (948) 64 00 00
17 rooms. ♣
HS Ezequiel.**
General Mola s/n.
☎ (948) 64 02 96.
13 rooms. ♣

PETROL STATIONS
On the N-111, at km 61, at the centre of Los Arcos.

'Inde est Arcus.' (Aymeric Picaud: 'Pilgrims' Guide')

I. ROUTE

🚶 Leave **Estella** on the N-111 in the direction of Logroño, bearing right off it to **Ayegui** shortly after a service station. From here there are two alternative routes:
a) Keep going on this side of the road, round the back of the Hotel Irache, towards Azqueta.
b) Cross the N-111 and head towards the winemakers 'Bodegas Irache', where a free-flowing 'Fuente del Vino' (Wine Fountain) was inaugurated in 1991. To the left is the Monastery of Nuestra Señora la Real de Irache. Leave the Monastery through the gardens and make your way through a residential area. Keep on going towards Azqueta through a thin grove of holm oaks, with Mount Montejurra to your left and the N-111 to your right.
Whichever route you choose, there is always a clear point of reference on the horizon, as the village of Azqueta is clearly visible on a hilltop.
From **Azqueta,** the route takes you down past a cowshed and through cornfields and vineyards to **Villamayor de Monjardín,** just over 1 km away. Before entering Villamayor you pass the exotic 'Fuente de los Moros' (Fountain of the Moors) on your right. The majestic ruins of the hilltop castle of Monjardín tower over the town and dominate the landscape.
From Villamayor, go down an asphalted road towards the N-111 and take a farm track off it to the right. There are no villages from here to Los Arcos (about 12 km away) and the route never deviates from this track, which winds through cornfields and vineyards, cutting across the municipal boundaries of La Cañada, Cogullo and Capanaldia. Go past some ramshackle farm buildings and continue along the side of a conifer-covered hill. Next, cross a stream almost hidden by reeds and make your way down towards Charconegro, location of the 'Paso de Baurín' fountain. It is then a gentle climb up the 'Portillo de las Cabras', from where **Los Arcos** is visible a short distance away.

🚲 Cyclists should follow alternative route (b) as far as Azqueta, then take the N-111 to Villamayor de Monjardín. They should then take the farm track to Los Arcos.

🚗 Milestones: N-111 km 45: Ayegui; km 49.3: Azqueta; km 51: turning to Villamayor de Monjardín; km 61: Los Arcos.

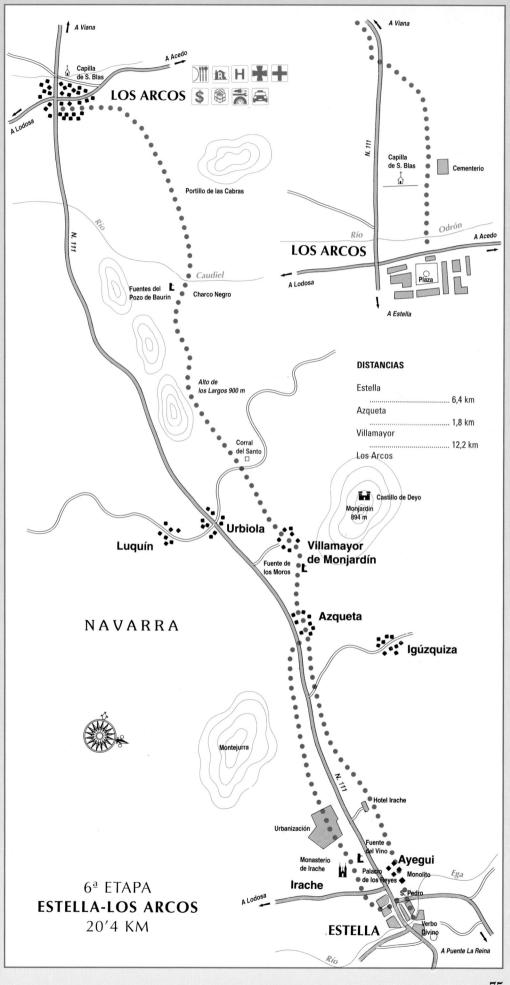

A Viana

Capilla de S. Blas

LOS ARCOS

A Acedo

A Lodosa

Portillo de las Cabras

N. 111

Río

Caudiel

Fuentes del Pozo de Baurin

Charco Negro

Alto de los Largos 900 m

Corral del Santo

A Viana

N. 111

Capilla de S. Blas

Cementerio

Río   Odrón

A Acedo

LOS ARCOS

A Lodosa

Plaza

A Estella

DISTANCIAS

Estella
.... 6,4 km

Azqueta
.... 1,8 km

Villamayor
.... 12,2 km

Los Arcos

Castillo de Deyo

Monjardín 894 m

Luquín

Urbiola

Fuente de los Moros

Villamayor de Monjardín

Azqueta

Igúzquiza

NAVARRA

Montejurra

N. 111

Hotel Irache

Urbanización

Fuente del Vino

Ayegui

Monasterio de Irache

Monolito

Palacio de los Reyes

S. Pedro

Ega

A Lodosa

Irache

ESTELLA

Verbo Divino

A Puente La Reina

Río

6ª ETAPA
ESTELLA-LOS ARCOS
20'4 KM

75
Stage 6

Montejurra from Monjardín

The Monastery of Irache

II. HISTORY, ART AND LEGENDS

In **Ayegui,** which is joined to Estella, the 17th-century baroque Church of San Martín de Tours is worth a visit. Amongst several fine pieces is a 14th-century Gothic crucifix.

On your way out of Ayegui one of the most agreeable surprises of the whole journey awaits you: a most original drinking fountain installed recently by the winery 'Bodegas Irache'. Pilgrims can either refresh themselves with water or the equally wholesome and restorative local Navarrese wine —the traditional travellers' thirst-quencher— all compliments of the house!

With restored strength, you come to the neighbouring *Monastery of Santa María la Real de Irache.* Built on the north slope of Mount Montejurra, a symbol of the Navarrese Carlists (a 19th-century movement, culminating in civil war in the north, to enthrone Carlos, brother of King Fernando VII, who died without a male heir in 1833), the monastery was receiving pilgrims before Estella even existed. Indeed, records of the Monastery of Irache and the Benedictine community it housed go back to 958, although it is possible that it dates back as far as Visigothic times. A pilgrims' hospital was founded here in 1054 by Don García de Nájera, some forty years before King Sancho Ramírez founded the town of Estella. It has always held an important place in the history of Navarre, although its period of greatest splendour came in the late 11th century under the leadership of Saint Veremundus, who considerably increased the monastery's wealth and prestige. It flourished again in the 17th century, when it was granted the status of a university, the first such establishment in Navarre. The massive monastery complex includes a superb Romanesque church, begun in the late 12th century and completed in the early 13th century. It has a large domed transept, three naves, three apses, two portals and a plateresque cloister, the work of Martín de Oyarzábal and Juan de Aguirre, which is reminiscent of the cloisters which we will encounter later on at San Zoilo in Carrión de los Condes. In the 17th century, another wing and a cloister were added to accommodate the university. The bell-tower of 1609 is inspired by Juan de Herrera's Palace and Monastery of El Escorial, near Madrid.

The most notable feature of **Azqueta** is the church of San Pedro, which has some interesting pieces, among them the high altar retable.

As you enter **Villamayor de Monjardín,** look out for the unusual 13th-century Gothic *Fuente de los Moros* (Fountain of the Moors) which stands by the roadside. This is a solid but elegant barrel-vaulted cistern which you enter through a double semi-circular arch, supported by a geminate central column with a capital. Wide stone steps lead down to the water level. Restoration work was completed in 1991, and has been carefully and tastefully done, as the stone-tiled roof attests.

The *Monjardín* hill, at the foot of which lies Villamayor,

Monastery of Irache:
the Cloisters

is crowned by the castle of St Stephen, the fortress of the kingdom of Deyo-Pamplona in the 10th century, after Sancho Garcés seized it from its previous owners, the powerful half-Spanish, half-Moorish Banu Qasi family. According to *The Pseudo-Turpin Chronicles,* which calls it 'Mons Garzini', Charlemagne took the castle from the Navarrese prince 'Furre' (a corruption, perhaps, of 'Fortún Garcés', the name of one of the kings of Navarre), after defeating him in battle and 'slaying both him and his army, consisting of 3 000 Navarrese and Saracens'. After taking this castle, continues the account in the *Chronicles,* 'Charlemagne took possession of the whole of Navarre'.

The 'Fuente del Vino' at Irache

Villamayor is dominated by the elegant baroque tower of the *Church of San Andrés,* which is a pleasing single-aisled Romanesque construction, with a semicircular apse and a barrel-vaulted roof. A capital on the south façade shows a combat scene which could be another version of Roland fighting Ferragut, similar to the one in the Palace of the Kings of Navarre in Estella and to another on the façade of the Hospital of San Juan de Acre, at Navarrete. Undoubtedly, the most valuable of the church's treasures, given the quality of the workmanship and its rarity, is the 12th-century silver Romanesque processional cross.

Urbiola lies on the N-111, and is mentioned in several pilgrims' itineraries, including those of Arnold von Harff and Laffi. It has a medieval parish church dedicated to the Saviour, which is extensively restored. At one time there was a pilgrims' hospital here run by the Hospitallers of the Order of St John of Jerusalem.

Castle of Monjardín

Los Arcos, which is called 'Urancia' in *The Pseudo-Turpin Chronicles,* is a medieval town built on the site of a Roman town, which perhaps grew up from a 'mansio' at a crossroads. Its location on the pilgrims' route to Santiago and its proximity to the border between the kingdoms of Navarre and Castille turned it into a thriving centre of foreign exchange and toll collection, although Künig von Vach ascribes this double function to Logroño, a few kilometres further on. In 1175, King Sancho the Wise granted the Navarrese the same rights and privileges as the French settlers, as he had done to the local population of Estella. A pilgrims' hospital is mentioned in King Theobald II's will at the end of the 13th century, which quite possibly had already been in existence for almost a century by then. The most notable building in Los Arcos is the magnificent *Church of Santa María,* with architectural elements spanning from the 12th century to the 18th century. It is an impressive construction, mirroring the town's different moments of splendour, and brings together a mixture of Romanesque, Gothic, plateresque and baroque architecture. The single nave is profusely decorated with a variety of baroque elements, such as the high altar retable, which is presided over by a splendid polychrome Gothic statue of Santa María de los Arcos. Other outstanding features include the richly-carved plateresque choir stalls and the great baroque organ, while the splendid plateresque north façade is as ornate as any retable. The lofty 16th-century bell-tower

Villamayor de Monjardín

Villamayor. The Fountain of the Moors.

Villamayor de Monjardín: capital depicting Roland and Ferragut in the parish church

Villamayor de Monjardín, parish Church

Portal of the Church of Santa María, Los Arcos

is a combination of Gothic and Renaissance styles, and is decorated with tracery. Finally, no visit would be complete without a look at the beautiful late Gothic cloisters.

The old pilgrims' way entered Los Arcos from the north and crossed the town along the Calle Mayor, which lead to the church of Santa María, leaving the town through the 'Portal de Castilla'. Not only was this the direction of Castile, but also the town belonged to the crown of Castile from 1463 to 1753.

III. HISTORICAL PILGRIMS' ACCOUNTS

Aymeric Picaud: *'Through the town known as Los Arcos ('Arcus') there flows a deadly river.'*

Künig von Vach: *'After the fourth* [bridge] *you come to the City of the Jews ('Juden stat'). However, pilgrims call it 'Arcus' (Los Arcos).*

Arnold von Harff: *'It is two leagues from 'Sudat'* [Estella] *to Urbiola ('Orbeola'). Likewise, it is two leagues from Urbiola to Los Arcos ('Lons zarkons').'*

Laffi: *'...Here stands the vast and beautiful convent of St Benedict* [Irache], *which is very rich and looks like a city in itself, as it has great walls around it and is so big... We then set off towards Urbiola ('Orivola')... a small place, but not lacking for anything... We continued to Los Arcos ('Il Arco del Re')... the last town in the kingdom of Navarre.'*

STAGE 7

LOS ARCOS • VIANA

Viana: high altar retable in the Church of Santa María

LOS ARCOS • SANSOL •
TORRES DEL RÍO •
VIANA

PILGRIMS' REFUGES

Viana: «Albergueria Andrés Muñoz». This comfortable and very well-equipped hostel, with capacity for about 40 guests, is located in a restored building next to the Church of *San Pedro*. It is named after Pamplona's late, great expert on the Pilgrimage to Santiago.
☎ (948) 64 50 07

ACCOMMODATION

Viana:
P** La Granja.
Navarro Villoslada, 19.
☎ (948) 64 50 78.
7 rooms. ♣
Chavarri.
☎ (948) 64 51 36.
20 beds. ♣

RESTAURANTS

Viana:
Borgia. Serapio Urra, s/n.
☎ (948) 64 57 81

PETROL STATIONS

On the N-111, at km 81, in Viana.

'Ad uillam que dicitur Turres...' (Aymeric Picaud: 'Pilgrims' Guide')

I. ROUTE

🚶 The route out of **Los Arcos** leads across the local road NA-129 and a bridge over the river Odrón. A narrow asphalted lane then takes you up past the cemetery, where a singular inscription on the gate warns: 'Yo que fui lo que tú eres, tú serás lo que yo soy.' ('I was once what you are, and you will be what I am.'). This lane soon becomes a dirt track, which runs parallel to the right of the N-111. The path disappears every now and then across farmland, but you should simply keep heading in the direction of the village of Sansol, clearly visible all the way. At the first intersection, take a path to the right, cross a stream and come out onto a secondary road which takes you into **Sansol.**

From Sansol, cross over the N-111 and follow a path which leads steeply down to the river Linares. Cross the river over a bridge and make your way up to **Torres del Río,** passing the Church of Santo Sepulcro on your right. Go through the village and come out past the cemetery on your left. From here, a dirt track leads up a slope towards the N-111, and then runs parallel to the left of the road, emerging onto it shortly before the Ermita de la Virgen de Poyo. Bear right off it about 150 metres after the hermitage and take a dirt track which soon crosses the secondary road leading to Bargota. After this, the path descends a ravine (the 'Barranco Mataburros'), with the N-111 on one side and vineyards, olive and almond groves on the other, until it reaches the river Cornava. Cross the river, go past the abandoned village of Cornava and continue parallel to the N-111 again for a short while. You then cross over to the left hand side of the N-111 and continue alongside it until you come to a track which brings you out, once and for all, onto the N-111. This will take you into **Viana,** which looms before you on the horizon.

🚲 Most of this stage is unsuitable for cyclists. Although the path from Los Arcos to Sansol is fairly decent, it disappears from view on several occasions. The descent from Sansol to Torres del Río is impracticable due to the steepness and the state of the ground, while the deep ravines that have to be negotiated between the Ermita de Bargota and the road into Viana make this stretch unpassable too. Cyclists should therefore take the N-111 from Los Arcos all the way to Viana.

🚗 Milestones: N-111 km 67.9: Sansol; km 68.2: Torres del Río; km 71.8: Ermita de la Virgen del Poyo; km 81: Viana.

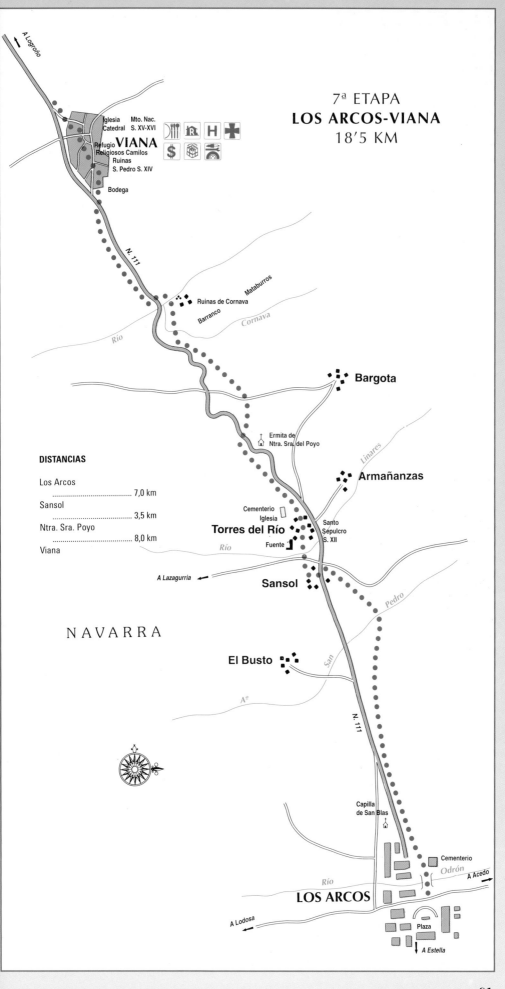

A Logroño

7ª ETAPA
LOS ARCOS-VIANA
18'5 KM

Iglesia   Mto. Nac.
Catedral   S. XV-XVI
Refugio **VIANA**
Religiosos Camilos
Ruinas
S. Pedro S. XIV

Bodega

N. 111

Ruinas de Cornava

Barranco   *Cornava*

Río

Mataburros

Bargota

Ermita de
Ntra. Sra. del Poyo

Linares

Armañanzas

Cementerio
Iglesia
Torres del Río   Santo
Sépulcro
Fuente   S. XII

Río

A Lazagurria ←

Sansol

Pedro

DISTANCIAS

Los Arcos
.... 7,0 km
Sansol
.... 3,5 km
Ntra. Sra. Poyo
.... 8,0 km
Viana

N A V A R R A

El Busto

San

Aº

N. 111

Capilla
de San Blas

Cementerio

Odrón
A Acedo →

Río

LOS ARCOS

A Lodosa ←

Plaza

↓ A Estella

Sansol from Torres del Río

II. HISTORY, ART AND LEGENDS

The route out of Los Arcos leads through the Portal de Castilla and over the river Odrón, one of the rivers of 'deadly waters' which Aymeric Picaud describes in the *Pilgrims' Guide*. A short walk away from the river, opposite the cemetery, stands the Ermita de San Blas, built on the site of a former hospital for contagious patients. The cult of St Blase, the mythical early-Christian Armenian bishop who, amongst other miracles, cured the plague, entered Spain via the road to Santiago, probably brought by pilgrims from such cities as Paris or Trier, where there were relics of the saint.

Sansol, as its name suggests, came under the jurisdiction of the monastery of San Zoilo in Carrión de los Condes. The 18th-century baroque parish church is dedicated to St Zoilo, a Holy Martyr from Córdoba, whose relics are kept at the monastery, as are those of St Felix. This is possibly the site of a hospital mentioned by Aymeric Picaud, who states that *'between Los Arcos and the first hospital you come to, there flows a river which is deadly poisonous to all horses and men who drink from it.'*

However, these two are not the only noxious rivers according to Picaud. The river Linares which flows through Torres del Río is also described as *'deadly for all animals and people who drink thereof'*, while *'through a place called Cuevas, there flows a river which is also poisonous'*. Cuevas was one of eight villages incorporated into Viana by Sancho VII, and is now the area called Santa María de las Cuevas. The Arroyo de Perizuelas, which flows through it, must be the river Picaud was referring to. Taking into account these descriptions of the local rivers, it is hardly surprising that Picaud's general conclusion was that *'every river between Estella and Logroño is unhealthy for man and beast alike, and the fish are poisonous.'*

Torres del Río: the Church of the Holy Sepulchre

Torres del Río is the location of one of the architectural jewels of the Spanish stretch of the Camino de Santiago: the octagonal Romanesque *Church of the Holy Sepulchre,* which features a semicircular apse, a round tower and a lantern crowning the main cupola. (Lanterns such as this acted as beacons to guide pilgrims to their destination.) Unfortunately, the church's origins are undocumented, although these unusual Romanesque octagonal churches (such as those of Santa María at Eunate, of San Miguel at Almazán, province of Soria, or the church of Vera Cruz in Segovia) are usually linked to the Templars order, due to their similarity to the octagonal Church of the Holy Sepulchre in Jerusalem, which was under the protection of the Knights Templars for many years. Their exoticism, added to their obscure origins, has led them to be associated, perhaps wrongly, with the mysterious and unexplained sudden disappearance of the Templar Order. Some historians link the foundation of this church (12th century) with the order of the Holy Sepulchre or with the enormously powerful monastery of Irache, which reached its apogee in the 12th century. Inside, the most notable feature is the great cupola with

Central lantern in the Church of the Holy Sepulchre, Torres del Río

cross-ribbed vaults forming eight-sided stars, a type of vaulting characteristic of Moorish Spain and reminiscent of the Mosque at Córdoba. The rich iconography on the capitals includes some very interesting scenes, such as the curious Descent from the Cross. Also of note is a 13th-century Gothic crucifix in the apse chapel.

The Virgen del Poyo hermitage

While you are in Torres del Río, the Renaissance parish church of San Andrés also merits a visit.

The **Ermita de Santa María del Poyo** ('poyo' is the Spanish equivalent of the French word 'puy', and both are derived from the Latin *'podium'*) is a square building dating from the 16th century which houses a Gothic statue of its namesake, Legend has it that the hermitage was built on the spot where the statue appeared, as it refused to be moved.

After the ravine known as the 'Barranco Mataburros' (the 'Mulekiller'), you come to **Cornava,** which was an old Roman settlement and, like Cuevas, was one of the eight villages which formed **Viana** in 1219. Sancho VII 'the Strong' founded this defensive stronghold on the border with Castile, and granted it special status. In 1423, Charles III founded the Principality of Viana as an appanage for the heir to the throne of Navarre. On the third of March 1507, the infamous Cesare Borgia was killed in the battle of Mendavia, not far from Viana, and a magnificent mausoleum was built for him in the church of Santa María in Viana. This was violated at the end of the 17th century and his remains re-interred in a modest tomb outside the porch. A 19th-century white marble tombstone serves as his memorial.

Viana

The imposing walls and the old town's quadrangular ground plan (similar to Puente la Reina and Sangüesa) are a clear indication of Viana's past status as a heavily fortified frontier town. Viana was also a thriving market town, as well as an important halt on the route to Santiago. A pilgrims' hospital is recorded here as early as the 13th century, while towards the end of the 15th century, Künig von Vach credits Viana with four hospitals. Later on, in the 16th century, this was reduced to two, with the fusion of two of the hospitals into one entity, the 'Hospital Mayor de Nuestra Señora de Gracia'.

Viana: the walls

Viana is full of grand old mansions, some four storeys high, each bearing the family crest although, unfortunately, the state of preservation of some of them leaves a lot to be desired. Two municipal palaces, one in the Plaza del Coso and the other in the Plaza de los Fueros, are fine examples of civic architecture.

The Plaza de los Fueros, in the oldest and highest part of the town, is also the location of the *Church of Santa María,* a Gothic construction begun in the 13th century (shortly after Sancho VII founded Viana), completed in the 14th century and visibly altered between the 16th century and the 18th century. The church has three aisles, radiating chapels and a poligonal apse. The tower dates from the 16th century, as does the south portal with its exteriorised retable, which depicts scenes from the Redemption alongside classical scenes, such as the Labours of Hercules. 18th-century additions include the baroque ambulatory, the chapels of La Magdalena and

Emblazoned house, Viana

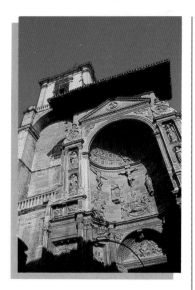

*Viana: the Church
of Santa María*

of San Juan del Ramo, the chapterhouse and the sacristy. The chapel of San Juan del Ramo is decorated with splendid frescoes, recently restored, by the classical Madrilenian painter Luis Paret (1746-1799), which depict the life of St. John the Baptist. The enormous 17th-century baroque retable dedicated entirely to the Virgin Mary is a particularly fine piece. The handsome organ dates from the 18th century. The splendid 14th-century Church of San Pedro, on the west side of the walls, is now in a lamentable state of repair.

*Viana: painting by Peret in the
Church of Santa María*

Viana. The Church of San Pedro

III. HISTORICAL PILGRIMS' ACCOUNTS

Aymeric Picaud: *'... between Los Arcos and the first hospital you come to, there flows a river which is deadly poisonous to all horses and men who drink from it. Through the place known as Torres ('Turres'), in Navarre, there flows a river which is deadly for all animals and people who drink thereof... Through a place called Cuevas ('Covas'), there flows a river which is also poisonous... Every river between Estella and Logroño is unhealthy for man and beast alike, and the fish are poisonous.'*

Künig von Vach: *'Viana ('Vianna') is four miles further on. There are two fountains at the entrance to the town, and there are four hospitals as you pass through.'*

Arnold von Harff: *'It is four leagues from Los Arcos to Viana ('Viennes'), a town situated on a small hill.'*

Laffi: *'We set off towards Viana ('Viannas')... Upon arriving, we were overjoyed to see such a beautiful place, with a fine cathedral which is better proportioned than any. It has a very handsome door with the most beautiful reliefs.'*

STAGE 8

VIANA • NAVARRETE

Logroño. the cathedral of Santa María la Redonda

VIANA • LOGROÑO •
NAVARRETE

PILGRIMS' REFUGES

Logroño: This magnificent, newly-built refuge ranks as one of the best to be found along the Pilgrims' Route. Located at no. 32 Calle Rúa Vieja (opposite *Santa María de Palacio*).
☎ (941) 26 02 34
Navarrete: The town council has just finished work on a splendid, comfortable refuge situated in a skilfully restored building at no. 2 Calle San Juan. ☎ (948) 44 00 05

ACCOMMODATION

Logroño:
HR** Los Bracos Sol.**
☎ (941) 22 66 08.
72 rooms. ♣♣♣
HR** Carlton Rioja.**
☎ (941) 24 21 00.
120 rooms. ♣♣♣
H** N. H. Herencia Rioja.**
☎ (941) 21 02 22.
88 rooms. ♣♣♣
HR* Ciudad de Logroño.**
☎ (941) 25 02 44.
95 rooms. ♣♣
H* Condes de Haro.**
☎ (941) 20 85 00.
44 rooms. ♣♣
H* Murrieta.** ☎ (941) 22 41 50.
113 rooms. ♣♣
H Soto Galo.** ☎ (941) 25 91 22.
44 rooms. ♣♣
HR* Isasa. ☎ (941) 25 65 99.
30 rooms. ♣♣
The following establishments offer **accommodation** at more reasonable prices:
La Numantina. Marqués de Vallejo. Niza. París. Rioja-Condestable. Gonzalo de Berceo. Mesón Pepa. Sebastián.

Navarrete:
Fonda La Carioca.
☎ (941) 44 00 06. ♣

CAMPSITES

Logroño:
La Playa. 1st Category.
☎ (941) 25 22 53

Navarrete:
Navarrete. 1st Category.
☎ (941) 44 01 69

RESTAURANTS

Logroño:
El Cachetero. Anzuelo de Oro. La Chata. Carabanchel. La Merced. San Remo. Mesón Asador Egües. Mesón Lorenzo. Zubillaga.
Navarrete:
La Clarisa. ☎ (941) 44 00 06
El Molino. ☎ (941) 44 05 64

PETROL STATIONS

On the N-111, at km 85.5; in the town of Logroño; on the N-232, at kms 416 and 413.

'Inde Grugnus.' (Aymeric Picaud: 'Pilgrims' Guide')

I. ROUTE

🚶🚶 Leave **Viana** on the west side of the town, and head steeply downhill towards the N-111, which you cross. You then take a dirt track that runs between the cemetery and the 'Marbu' biscuit factory. The path is wide and level and takes you through vineyards and olive groves on the way to the Ermita de la Trinidad de Cuevas, crossing a stream (the 'arroyo Perizuelas') en route. After the hermitage, the path bears right towards the N-111, catching up with it at the regional border between Navarre and La Rioja (at a petrol station), passing the 'Pantano de las Cañas' nature reserve on the left. The route joins the N-111 for a short distance, and then bears left off it along another dirt track. After crossing another road, this path takes you round the north face of the Cerro de Cantabria (about 3 kilometres) towards the outskirts of **Logroño.**
Heading down to the Mendavia road, you pass the cemetery on your right and cross the river Ebro over the famous 'Puente de Piedra' ('Bridge of Stone'), turning right subsequently and making your way down the Rúa Vieja, which runs parallel to the river behind the Church of Santa María del Palacio. Calle Barriocepo is the continuation of the Rúa Vieja, and the two roads meet at the spot where the 'Fuente de los Peregrinos' ('Pilgrims' Fountain') stands, opposite the Church of Santiago. You then go through the gateway known as the 'Puerta del Camino' and come out onto Calle de los Depósitos. Next, cross the Plaza del Marqués de Murrieta, go down the Avenida del Marqués de Murrieta and come out onto the Avenida de Burgos. At a petrol station, bear left off the avenue and make your way through an industrial estate. Next, you have to cross a ring road and go through an area of rubbish dumps, heading towards the 'Pantano de la Grajera' (artificial lake), skirting round the right hand edge. From here, proceed up towards the N-230 which runs alongside the path to the right. Continue along this road until it intersects with the N-120 (in the direction of Burgos), which leads downhill towards Navarrete, clearly visible up ahead. A kilometre outside **Navarrete,** bear right off the N-120 and follow a path through arable and pasture land: after crossing the A-68 Zaragoza-Bilbao motorway and passing the ruins of the old Hospital de San Juan de Arce this takes you directly into Navarrete.

🚲 The pedestrian route is mainly negotiable by bicycle. However, there are a couple of difficult parts: crossing the arroyo Perizuelas shortly before the Ermita de la Trinidad de Cuevas, and the stretch between Logroño and the N-230.

🚗 Milestones: N-111 km 80: Viana; N-120 km 10: Navarrete.

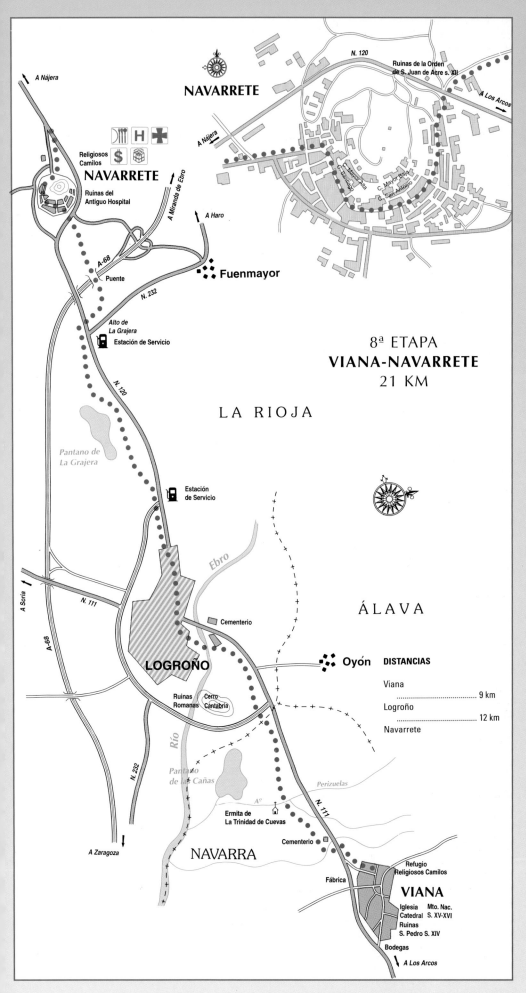

NAVARRETE

A Nájera

N. 120

Ruinas de la Orden
de S. Juan de Acre s. XII

A Los Arcos

A Nájera

C. Mayor Alta
C. Santiago
C. Mayor Baja
C. San Antonio

Religiosos
Camilos

NAVARRETE

Ruinas del
Antiguo Hospital

A Miranda de Ebro

A Haro

◆ **Fuenmayor**

A-68

Puente

N. 232

Alto de
La Grajera

Estación de Servicio

8ª ETAPA
VIANA-NAVARRETE
21 KM

N. 120

LA RIOJA

Pantano de
La Grajera

Estación
de Servicio

Ebro

ÁLAVA

Cementerio

A Soria

N. 111

A-68

LOGROÑO

◆ **Oyón**

DISTANCIAS

Ruinas
Romanas

Cerro
Cantabria

Viana
.... 9 km

Logroño
.... 12 km

Navarrete

Río

N. 232

Pantano
de las Cañas

Perizuelas

Aº

Ermita de
La Trinidad de Cuevas

N. 111

A Zaragoza

Cementerio

NAVARRA

Refugio
Religiosos Camilos

Fábrica

VIANA

Iglesia   Mto. Nac.
Catedral   S. XV-XVI
Ruinas
S. Pedro S. XIV

Bodegas

A Los Arcos

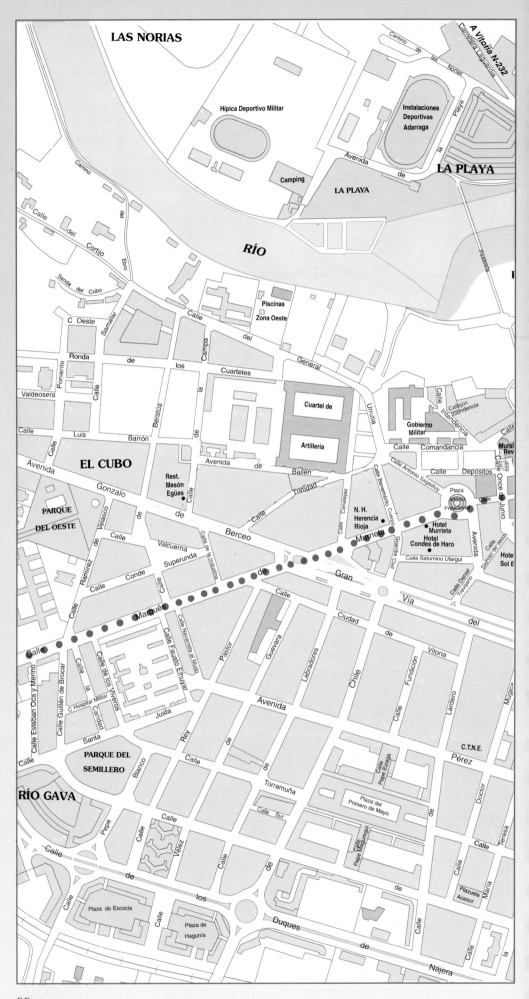

LAS NORIAS

Hípica Deportivo Militar

Instalaciones
Deportivas
Adarraga

LA PLAYA

Camping

LA PLAYA

A Vitoria N-232

Carretera Laguardia

Camino de las Norias

Avenida de la Playa

Pasarela

RÍO

Senda del Cubo

C Oeste

Ronda

Valdeosera

Calle

Poniente

Calle

Calle de los Cuarteles

Calle del Campa

Piscinas
Zona Oeste

Calle

de

General

Urrutia

Cuartel de

Artillería

Calle Intendencia

Callejón Intendencia

Gobierno
Militar

Calle

Mural
Rev

EL CUBO

Calle

Luis

Barrón

Samalar

Calle

Beratúa

Avenida

de

Gonzalo

Bailén

Comandancia

Calle

Depósitos

Calle Once de Junio

PARQUE
DEL OESTE

Velasco

Calle

de

Rest.
Mesón
Egües

Berceo

Calle

Calle

Trinidad

Calle

Calle Antonio Sagastuy

N. H.
Herencia
Rioja

Calle Barenfento Cuerpo

Plaza
Afénez
Provisional

Calle

Ramírez

Conde

Valcuerna

Superunda

Calle de la Industria

Marqués

de

Gran

Murrieta

Calle Canalejas

Guardia Civil

Hotel
Murrieta
Hotel
Condes de Haro

Avenida

Calle Saturnino Ulargui

Hote
Sol E

Calle

PARQUE
DEL OESTE

Calle

Via

del

Vitoria

Calle Daniel
Trevijano

Sierras de Jesús

Calle Esteban Oca y Merino

Calle Guillén de Brocar

Calle de la Caridad

C Hospital Militar

Calle de los Viveros

Calle Fausto Elhuyar

Calle Navarrete el Mudo

Pastor

Guevara

Ciudad

Chile

Fundición

Lardero

Múgica

RÍO GAVA

Justa

Santa

PARQUE DEL
SEMILLERO

Blanco

Rey

Calle

Avenida

de

Torremuña

Labradores

Calle Pepe Eizaga

Plaza del
Primero de Mayo

Pérez

C.T.N.E.

Doctor

de

Calle

Vélez

Calle

Calle

Sur

Calle Pepe Magunagui

Teresa

Calle

Pepe

de

los

Duques

Nájera

María

Calle

Plazuela
Acesur

Calle

Calle

de

Plaza de Escocia

Plaza de
Hagunía

88
Stage 7

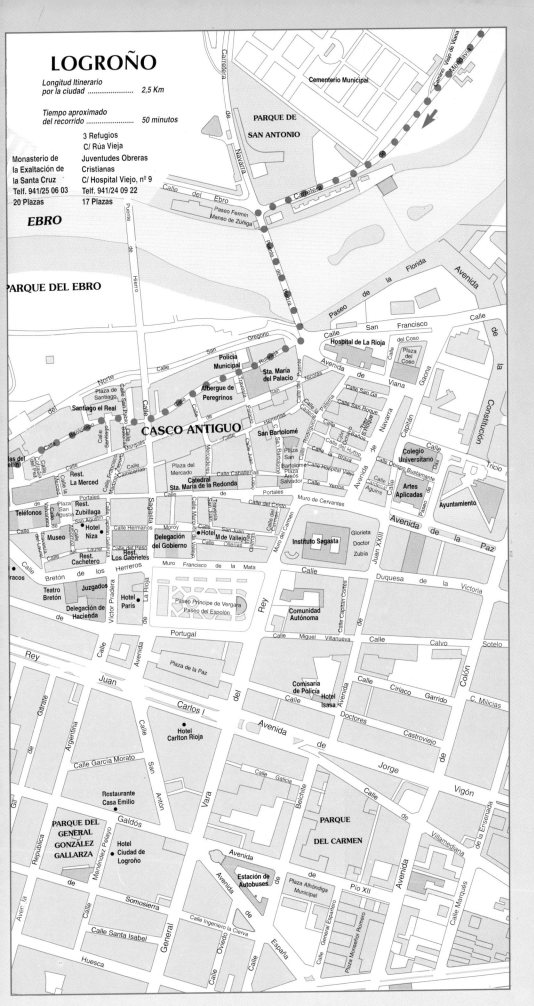

LOGROÑO

Longitud Itinerario
por la ciudad .... 2,5 Km

Tiempo aproximado
del recorrido .... 50 minutos

3 Refugios
C/ Rúa Vieja

Monasterio de
la Exaltación de
la Santa Cruz
Telf. 941/25 06 03
20 Plazas

Juventudes Obreras
Cristianas
C/ Hospital Viejo, nº 9
Telf. 941/24 09 22
17 Plazas

EBRO

PARQUE DEL EBRO

Cementerio Municipal

PARQUE DE SAN ANTONIO

CASCO ANTIGUO

89
Stage 7

Logroño: view of the city and the bridge over the Ebro

Logroño: Fuente de los Peregrinos

Logroño: Church of San Bartolomé

Logroño: looking towards the Cathedral

II. HISTORY, ART AND LEGENDS

The route out of **Viana** leads to the 17th-century baroque **Ermita de la Trinidad de Cuevas.** This was the site of the erstwhile village of Cuevas, one of the eight villages out of which Viana was formed in 1219, which Aymeric Picaud mentions in connection with its insalubrious river. As far back as the 13th century there are records of a church here belonging to the convent of the Trinitarians, an order which distinguished itself in caring for pilgrims.

As it enters the region of La Rioja, the pilgrims' way skirts around the hill which was the site of the ancient city of **Cantabria.** Current archaeological excavations are bringing to light new data regarding Cantabria, a pre-Roman settlement which was later Romanized and flourished until it was destroyed by the Visigothic king, Leovigild, at the end of the 6th century. Around 640, Braulio of Zaragoza refers to Leovigild's 'destruction of Cantabria' in his *Life of San Millán.*

The pilgrims' route enters **Logroño** via the great *Puente de Piedra* which crosses the mighty river Ebro. The present bridge dates from the end of the last century, and replaced the original medieval one, which was built on the orders of the great promotor of the Santiago pilgrimage, Alfonso VI. The bridge's strategic importance is demonstrated by the fact that it was repaired by St. Dominic of the Causeway and later by his assistant and disciple, St. John of Ortega. At one time it had twelve arches and three defensive towers. The origins of Logroño are obscure, but one theory is that it stands on the site of the ancient city of Vareia, which was near the river port of Tarraconense, destroyed by Leovigild in 574. When Sancho Garcés of Navarre and Ordoño II of León reconquered the area from the Moors in the 10th century, it was little more than an insignificant farming community. Logroño began to grow in importance after its destruction by El Cid in 1092, when Alfonso VI ordered the construction of the famous Puente de Piedra, with the intention of repopulating the area and creating a town strong enough to defend the strategic bridge over the Ebro. The town duly received a generous royal charter. The old city forms a long rectangle parallel to the river, with a double vertical axis formed by the parallel streets of the Rúa Vieja (the old pilgrims' route through Logroño) and the Rúa Mayor. Between the two streets stands the *Imperial Church of Santa María del Palacio,* built in the 12th century over a chapel belonging to the former royal palace, and donated by the 'Emperor' Alfonso VII to the Order of the Holy Sepulchre. Its most interesting features are the 14th-century ogival spire which rises directly from the lantern tower and the 16th-century high altarpiece by Arnald of Brussels. Continuing down the Rúa Vieja you come to the baroque *Fuente de los Peregrinos* (Pilgrims' Fountain) and the *Church of Santiago el Real.* According to tradition, this stands over an earlier church which was built by Ramiro I in the 9th century, after his legendary victory over the Moors at Clavijo. It is a single-aisled 10th-century Gothic construction, in which every piece of ornamentation is dedicated to St. James, starting with the baroque south portal which represents him in his two different guises: the 'Moor-slayer', an impressive 17th-century statue of the saint mounted on a spirited stallion and, above it, the gentle Pilgrim. The high altarpiece is presided over by a 15th-century statue of St. James and a 12th-century Romanesque statue of the Virgen de la Esperanza, the patroness of Logroño. At the end of the Calle Barriocepo (the continuation of the Rúa Vieja) the old gateway, known variously as the *Puerta del Camino*, 'Puerta de Carlos V' or 'Puerta del Revellín', still stands, through which pilgrims left the city walls.

Logroño cathedral

A short detour from the pilgrims' route takes you to the *Cathedral of Santa María de la Redonda*. This 15th-century Gothic construction was built around a small octagonal church, similar to those at Eunate and Torres del Río, which gives it its name: St. Mary of the Rotunda. Its famous twin towers were a later addition and date from the 18th century, as does the stone frontispiece of the west façade.

Nearby is the *Parish Church of San Bartolomé*, which dates from the 12th and 14th centuries and has three Romanesque apses and an elaborately carved Gothic portal.

The *Convent of San Francisco* was built beside the river. Local tradition linked it to St. Francis of Assisi, who stopped in Logroño on his way to Santiago de Compostela. During his stay he healed the son of a local nobleman who, in gratitude, built the convent. On his way back from Santiago, St. Francis was able to see the work in progress.

Logroño: Parish Church of Santa María de Palacio

The Provincial Hospital stands at the entry to the Puente de Piedra, on the site of the former *pilgrims' hospital of Roque Amador*. This curious name must be a Spanish corruption of the French name 'Rocamadour', the famous Marian shrine on the pilgrims' route from Le Puy (the 'Via Podensis') and the patron saint of the plague-stricken. Logroño had other hospitals apart from this one: the hospital of San Juan de Dios, the hospital of Santiago and, outside the city walls, the hospital of San Lázaro for lepers and contagious patients.

Just outside Navarrete stands the ruined **Hospital de San Juan de Acre,** founded by Doña María Ramírez *'on the road to Santiago, near Navarrete'.* The 13th-century portal has been kept as the entrance to the village cemetery.

Navarrete is a pleasant medieval town perched on a hill that was once crowned by a castle. It was the scene of numerous skirmishes between the Castilians and the Navarrese, and was resettled and granted special privileges by Alfonso VIII in 1195. At the top of the village stands the *Parish Church of the Assumption*, a magnificent triple-aisled 16th-century construction housing, amongst other treasures, a huge baroque high altarpiece depicting the Assumption. The village still retains its 16th-century layout, and has many fine old houses emblazoned with coats of arms, one of which has a small statue of St. James the Moorslayer in a niche.

Clavijo, 18 kilometres from Logroño, is the location of

Logroño: Church of Santiago el Real

Gate leading into Navarrete cemetery

one of Spain's best-loved and most symbolic ruined castles, the *Castle of Clavijo,* which stands perched on a forbidding rock. The fabled name of Clavijo is associated with the beginning of the Reconquest of Spain and the intervention of St. James the Apostle, who appeared for the first time as the Moorslayer at the legendary Battle of Clavijo (834), when Ramiro I of León defeated the army of Abdurrahman II. The story of St. James' appearance to the king in a vision, his participation in the battle astride a mighty white charger and the deliverance of the hundred virgins demanded as tribute by the Moors, are some of the most beautiful legends in Spanish history.

Navarrete: church of the Assumption

Castle of Clavijo

III. HISTORICAL PILGRIMS' ACCOUNTS

Aymeric Picaud: *'A mighty river called the Ebro flows through Logroño ('Grugnus'). Its waters are pure and full of fish.'*

Künig von Vach: *'After two miles you come to a city called 'Grüningen'. It is the first city in Spain. In Romance it is called Logroño ('Lagrona'). You will encounter a new currency: instead of crowns, you must get used to maravedís.'*

Arnold von Harff: *'It is a league from Viana to Logroño ('La grunea'), the city of the King of Spain. You cross a stone bridge. This is where the kingdom of Navarre ends... It is a league from Logroño to Navarrete ('Nauaret'), a town with a castle.'*

Laffi: *'...and we set off towards Logroño ('Grogno'), only one league away. It is the first city in the kingdom of Old Castile... We continued our journey towards Navarrete ('Navarreta'), two leagues away, where there is a castle shaped like a ship, situated on top of a hill, which is very strong and enclosed by mighty walls. And there is a beautiful cathedral which is large, well-maintained and with good offices.'*

STAGE 9

NAVARRETE • NÁJERA

San Millán depicted slaying Moors in the Monastery of Yuso

NAVARRETE • NÁJERA

PILGRIMS' REFUGES

Nájera: The regional government of La Rioja has set up a fully-equipped, 40-bed hostel in the buildings belonging to the Church of Santa María la Real.
☎ (948) 36 36 50

ACCOMMODATION

Nájera:
H** San Fernando.
Paseo San Julián, 1.
☎ (941) 36 37 00.
55 rooms. ♣♣
HS* Hispano .
☎ (941) 36 36 15.
13 rooms. ♣
San Andrés.
☎ (941) 36 90 30. 40 beds. ♣
El Moro.
☎ (941) 36 00 52.
30 beds. ♣

CAMPSITES

Nájera:
El Ruedo. 3rd Category.
☎ (941) 36 01 02

RESTAURANTS

Nájera:
Mesón Duque Forte.
Paseo San Julián, 15.
☎ (941) 36 35 20
El Mono.
Mayor, 43.
☎ (941) 36 30 28

PETROL STATIONS

On the N-120, at km 23; in the town of Nájera.

I. ROUTE

🚶 Take the N-120 in the direction of Nájera out of **Navarrete** (joining it at km 10.5). On the left you pass the cemetery, the entrance of which is the old portal from the ruined Hospital de San Juan de Acre, which bears a recently-placed memorial stone to the unfortunate Belgian pilgrim, Alice de Craemer. After about 5 km (at km 16) bear left off the road and join a red earth track which runs through vineyards. Shortly afterwards, cross over a road which leads to the village of Ventosa (visible to the left on a small hill). You then start a short and gentle uphill climb towards the Alto de San Antón, although the path only goes halfway up and runs along the hillside through scrub and bushes. At the top you will make out the ruins of the old monastery of San Antón. When you come to a white house by the edge of the path, make your way gently downhill, meeting up with a disused section of the old road and, shortly afterwards, with the N-120. Cross over the road and continue along a dirt track which runs parallel to the right of the road, through vineyards and almond trees. Between the path and the road you will see the small elevation known as the 'Poyo de Roldán' ('Roland's bench'), while a humble adobe hut used as a shelter by shepherds stands beside the path. Continue westwards, until you come to the secondary road which links the village of Huércanas (visible over to the right) and Alesón (which is off to the left). After crossing this road, you come to a concrete gravel pit which you can either cross over or go round to the right. A bit further on the path meets the (usually) dry riverbed of the river Yalde, which you can ford on foot. Next, cross a bridge over an irrigation channel which serves the market gardens and orchards on the outskirts of **Nájera,** through which you approach the town. Before entering Nájera, cross a ring road between industrial warehouses and a school.

🚲 The first 5 km of this stage are by road. The rest is on footpaths which are mainly transitable by bicycle. However, there are a few short stretches when cyclists will have to dismount, such as the point at which the path crosses the N-120 (between km 18 and km 19) and in parts of the Alto de San Antón stretch.

🚗 Milestones: N-120 km 10: Navarrete; km 16: turning to the footpath; km 16.5: turning to Ventosa; km 23: turning to San Millán de Cogolla and Valvanera, via Tricio; km 25: Nájera.

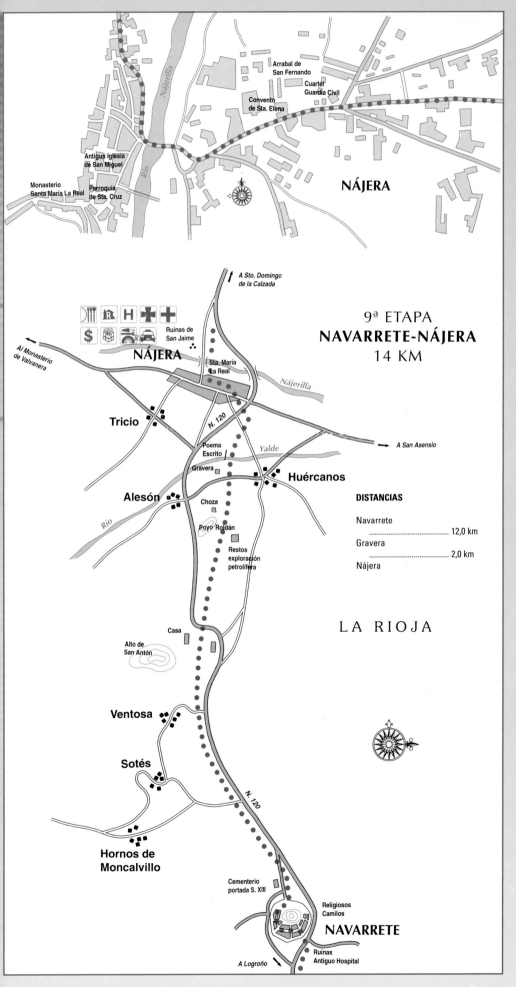

NÁJERA

Arrabal de
San Fernando

Cuartel
Guardia Civil

Convento
de Sta. Elena

Antigua Iglesia
de San Miguel

Monasterio
Santa María La Real

Parroquia
de Sta. Cruz

NÁJERA

Río Najerilla

A Sto. Domingo
de la Calzada

9ª ETAPA
NAVARRETE-NÁJERA
14 KM

Ruinas de
San Jaime

NÁJERA

Al Monasterio
de Valvanera

Sta. María
La Real

Najerilla

Tricio

N. 120

A San Asensio

Poema
Escrito

Yalde

Gravera

Huércanos

Alesón

Río

Choza

Poyo Roldán

Restos
exploración
petrolífera

DISTANCIAS

Navarrete
.... 12,0 km
Gravera
.... 2,0 km
Nájera

LA RIOJA

Casa

Alto de
San Antón

Ventosa

Sotés

N. 120

Hornos de
Moncalvillo

Cementerio
portada S. XIII

Religiosos
Camilos

NAVARRETE

A Logroño

Ruinas
Antiguo Hospital

Roland and Ferragut on the gate of Navarrete cemetery

Nájera

Nájera: Monastery of Santa María la Real

II. HISTORY, ART AND LEGENDS

The cemetery of Navarrete (completed in 1886) is the first place you come to at the beginning of this stage. The cemetery is entered through the attractive Romanesque splayed-arched portal which originally came from the pilgrims' hospital administered by the Order of San Juan de Acre, the ruins of which were off to your right just before you entered Navarrete. One of the ten capitals depicts the struggle between Ferragut and Roland, as seen at Estella and Villamayor de Monjardín, the legend of which is outlined below.

The ruined Monastery of San Antón is about 6 kilometres from Navarrete, and is situated at the top of the Alto de San Antón, a location clearly indicative of its role in assisting pilgrims. The Antonine order was one of the most ubiquitous on the pilgrims' route: we will come across them again in other places such as Castrojeriz. The isolated and wooded location made this an unsafe and risky stretch of the pilgrims' way, which would explain the presence of the Templars who are believed to have occupied part of the building.

The **Poyo de Roldán** is a small hill, and its name evokes the mythical victory of the hero, Roland, over the giant, Ferragut. According to one version of the legend, Roland went to Nájera to liberate the Christian knights that Ferragut, the Moorish giant who ruled Nájera, held prisoner in his castle. He climbed up the hill that bears his name, caught sight of the giant, picked up an enormous boulder and struck him on the head, killing him. Roland then entered the city and liberated all the prisoners. Another version has it that the hill is none other than the enormous boulder with which Roland killed the giant. It is interesting to note that in this local legend two contradictory traditions meet: that of the giant Errolán (inspired by Roland), the traditional enemy of the Basques who would hurl great rocks at them, and the cult of the hero Roland, as narrated in *The Pseudo-Turpin Chronicles*. According to this version, Ferragut takes several knights of Charlemagne's army prisoner, whereupon Roland begs the Emperor to let him fight the giant. After various clashes, the giant asks for a halt in the fighting to rest. On waking, Ferragut and Roland embark on a learned theological discussion and finally agree that the religion of the victor is the true religion. Naturally, Roland wins, this time by stabbing Ferragut in the navel, his only weak point, as he foolishly revealed before the duel. After this, Charlemagne's army enters Nájera and liberates the captive knights.

Nájera means 'place between the rocks' in Arabic, and this is revealing of both the origins and character of the city, which was reconquered in 923 by a joint Leonese and Navarrese army. In the 11th century, Sancho the Great made Nájera the capital of the kingdom of Navarre and the pilgrims' route was diverted here from the earlier and more difficult routes further north. Nájera was the first place where Christian money was minted during the Reconquest. In 1076 it was annexed to Castile and Alfonso VI, the other great promotor of the Santiago pilgrimage, increased its endowments and made it an important halt on the road to Santiago, repairing and building bridges, hostelries and hospitals. The bridge which spans the river Najerilla is attributed to St John of Ortega, who certainly repaired it in the 12th century. The present 19th century bridge was built over the original structure.

In 1052, Don García, the great king from Nájera, son of Sancho the Great, founded the monastery and Church of *Santa María la Real* and entrusted it to a religious community dedicated to St Isidore. He later added a pilgrims' hospital. There is a lovely legend regarding the founding of the monastery, which has it that Don García was out hunting one day, when his falcon disappeared into a cave in pursuit of a dove. When the king went in after them he discovered a statue of the Virgin Mary, lit by a lamp with a 'terrace' of Madonna lilies at her feet. This explains the title of the first Spanish Order of Chivalry, which was founded to commemorate this incident: the 'Orden de la Terraza'. All the elements of the legend —the statue of the Virgin Mary, the lamp and the Madonna lilies— can still be seen in the cave, which is now a part of the magnificent church.

The statue of Santa María la Real

In 1079, Alfonso VI, at the height of the 'Cluniac modernization' of his kingdoms, made the monastery a dependency of the Abbey of Cluny, in the face of general protest and the open defiance of the Bishop of Nájera, who moved his see to Calahorra.

Santa María la Real, now occupied by Franciscan monks, is the real jewel of Nájera, despite centuries of despoilment and disentailments. The narrow, triple-aisled church is 15th-century Gothic. Apart from the objects relating to the legend, the church houses magnificent Isabelline-Gothic choirstalls, a 14th-century Gothic statue of the Virgin Mary and a splendid Royal Pantheon containing the tombs of the Kings of Navarre. The incomparably elegant Knights' Cloister is another of the main attractions of the monastery complex: the arches are adorned with the most delicate Gothic plateresque tracery. Off the cloisters are the mausoleum of Don Diego López de Haro and the chapel of Queen Doña Mencía, both of which date from the 13th century.

Santa María la Real: the Pantheon of the Kings of Navarre

Santa María la Real: the cloisters

A road opposite the convent of Santa Elena leads from Nájera to the *Abadía de Valvanera,* a 15th-century Gothic sanctuary which houses a much-venerated 11th-century Romano-Byzantine statue of 'Nuestra Señora de Valvanera', patroness of La Rioja.

Further along the same road are the *monasteries of San Millán de Suso* and *San Millán de Yuso.* The monastery of San Millán de Suso (from the Latin 'sursum', 'above') is built high up on the hillside abutting the caves where the hermit, San Millán (473-574), and his disciples lived a life of retreat, and is composed of a mixture of Visigothic, Mozarabic and Romanesque elements. The original burial place of San Millán is marked by a splendid 11th-century recumbent statue of the saint, which is one of the oldest statues in Spain. The ancient cobbled atrium, the floor of which is lined with the tombs of the seven Infantes of Lara and their tutor, Don

Monastery of San Millán de Suso

Monastery of San Millán de Suso

Nuño Salido, is fancied to be the spot where Gonzalo de Berceo, a 13th-century Benedictine monk, wrote his poetry in the evolving vernacular of the day, rather than in Latin, thereby creating the earliest suriving literature by a known author in the Spanish language. His birthplace, Berceo, is close by.

Down below in the valley stands the grandiose monastery of San Millán de Yuso (from the Latin 'deorsum', 'below'), often called the 'Escorial of La Rioja'. Among its best-known treasures are the carved ivory reliquaries of San Millán and San Felices, his teacher. The famous *'Emilianese Glosses'*, the earliest known document in the Spanish language, used to be kept here. It is now kept as *manuscript number 60* at the Academia de la Historia in Madrid, and La Rioja is pressing for its return to the region.

Monastery of San Millán de Yuso

Monastery of San Millán de Yuso: the cloisters

III. HISTORICAL PILGRIMS' ACCOUNTS

Aymeric Picaud: *'Then* [comes] *the city of Nájera ('Nagera').*

Künig von Vach: *'...you can be glad to go from Navarrete ('Nazareto') to Nájera ('Nazera'). There you will be well-treated in God's name. The hostels have all you could possibly need, except the hospital of St. James, which is full of buffoons and the housekeeper plays all sorts of tricks on pilgrims...'*

Arnold von Harff: *'It is two leagues from Navarrete ('Nauaret') to Nájera ('Nazera'), a small town with a castle on a hill.'*

Laffi: *'Nájera ('Naxsera') is one of the most beautiful places in this region. It is situated on a plain and is traversed by a great river spanned by a fine bridge which unites the two parts of the town. There is an enormous hill of living rock, which overshadows the town to such an extent that neither the rain nor the sun reaches half of it (unless it be the morning sun). Here they are forever putting up buildings and churches, and there are three squares.'*

STAGE 10

NÁJERA • STO. DOMINGO DE LA CALZADA

Cathedral of Santo Domingo de la Calzada: the bell-tower

NÁJERA • AZOFRA • CAÑAS •
• CIRUEÑA •
SANTO DOMINGO DE LA CALZADA

Azofra: We owe this recently built parish refuge to the enthusiasm of Herbert Simon and his group from Cologne. Capacity of twenty. Equipped with beds and toilets.
☎ (941) 37 90 63 - 37 90 49

Santo Domingo de la Calzada: Situated in the *Casa de la Cofradía del Santo.* Calle Mayor, no.42. This is one of the best and most traditional refuges on the Pilgrims' Route and is lovingly cared for by the members of the said «Confraternity of the Saint».
☎ (941) 34 33 90 -34 26 09

ACCOMMODATION

Santo Domingo de la Calzada:
H**** P. Santo Domingo de la Calzada. Plaza del Santo, 3.
☎ (941) 34 03 00.
61 rooms. ♣♣♣
H*** El Corregidor.
Zumalacárregui, 14-16.
☎ (941) 34 21 28.
32 rooms. ♣♣
HS** Santa Teresita.
Pinar, 2 ☎ (941) 34 07 00.
79 rooms. ♣♣
HSR* Río. Etchegoyen, 2.
☎ (941) 34 00 85.
12 rooms. ♣

RESTAURANTS

Santo Domingo de la Calzada:
H*** El Corregidor.
Zumalacárregui, 14-16.
☎ (941) 34 21 28
Mesón El Peregrino.
Avda. de Calahorra, 22.
☎ (941) 34 02 02.
Specialities of La Rioja.
El Rincón de Emilio.
Plaza de Bonifacio Gil, 7.
☎ (941) 34 09 90.
Home cooking.
Los Arcos.
C/ Mayor, 68
☎ (941) 34 28 90

PETROL STATIONS

On the N-120 at km 33; and km 42'9.

'Inde Sanctus Dominicus.' (Aymeric Picaud: 'Pilgrims' Guide')

I. ROUTE

🚶🚶 Pick up the pilgrims' route behind the monastery of Santa María la Real, and make your way up a wide, steep road which comes out at a *pelota* court. A dirt track then leads uphill through pine trees and continues over uneven terrain, across irrigated farmland. Half a kilometre outside Azofra, which is visible up ahead, the track is succeeded by a small road.

Make your way through **Azofra** along the calle Mayor and leave the village at the 'Virgen de Valvanera' park on your left and the 'Fuente de los Romeros' (Pilgrims' Fountain) on your right. Cross the Alesanco, Cañas and San Millán de la Cogolla road and carry straight on past the last few houses of the village, heading northwestwards.

Soon you will come to the medieval boundary stone between the villages of Azofra and Alesanco, which is now a cross. Carry straight on for about a kilometre, until the path makes a right turn towards the nearby N-120, turns again 90° to the left and continues parallel to the road along a farm track, before crossing the secondary road which goes to San Millán de la Cogolla. From here there are two alternative routes:

a) Continue along the existing path which runs parallel to the N-120, with the disadvantage that the footpath gets lost to view a few times under crops. This path eventually comes out on the road which runs between Santo Domingo de la Calzada and San Millán de la Cogolla and Berceo. It has to be said that as this stretch is difficult to follow (even though it is the most authentic pilgrims' route) you may be advised to take the N-120 and enter **Santo Domingo de la Calzada** directly.

b) Follow a path to Cirueña, which gradually takes you further and further away from the N-120. Before long, the path climbs uphill towards the small plateau on which **Cirueña** is situated. You enter the village along a paved path, passing a thick holm oak grove, then follow the road out of Cirueña and, after a short distance, take a rough asphalted track off to the left. Carry straight on for about 6 km over very abrupt, hilly terrain towards **Santo Domingo de la Calzada,** which is visible on the horizon.

🚲 This stage is for the most part suitable for cyclists, with two difficult stretches: the steep climb out of Nájera and the ascent to Cirueña (should you choose alternative route (b).)

🚗 Milestones: N-120 km 25: Nájera; km 32: turning to Azofra, Cañas and San Millán de la Cogolla; km 43.7: turning to Cirueña and San Millán de la Cogolla; km 44: Santo Domingo de la Calzada.

10ª ETAPA
NÁJERA-
STO. DOMINGO DE LA CALZADA
20,7 KM

A Belorado

Río Oja

SANTO DOMINGO
DE LA CALZADA

Naves

A Berceo

Cirueña

Ciriñuela

Hervías

LA RIOJA

A San Millán
de la Cogolla

Cañas

Río Tuerto

Alesanco

Crucero

Parque Virgen
de Valvanera

Fuente de
Los Romeros

Azofra

Hospital
de S. Pedro

N. 120

Sta. María
la Real

Ruinas de
San Jaime

Al Monasterio
de Valvanera

Río

Río Nájerilla

NÁJERA

A San Asensio

A Navarrete

Río Oja

Ermita
del Santo

Convento
San Francisco

Parador
Nacional

Catedral
(Sepulcro Santo)

Refugio

Ermita de
San Lázaro

SANTO DOMINGO
DE LA CALZADA

DISTANCIAS

Nájera
.... 5,5 km
Azofra
.... 9,2 km
Cirueña
.... 6,0 km
Sto. Domingo de la Calzada

Monastery of Cañas: tomb of the founder

Santo Domingo de la Calzada cathedral: the chicken coop

A street in Santo Domingo de la Calzada

II. HISTORY, ART AND LEGENDS

Azofra, situtated on a low hill in the heart of the Cañas valley, is a typical wayside village, with houses flanking either side of the pilgrims' route. Apart from this, Azofra's jacobean past is also revealed in historical records and its artistic and architectural heritage. For instance, there are documents relating to the existence of a pilgrims' hospital, with a church and cemetery attached, dedicated to St. Peter. Furthermore, the Parish Church of Nuestra Señora de los Angeles houses a statue of St. James dressed as a pilgrim and of St. Martin of Tours, who is also closely linked to the Santiago pilgrimage. Further evidence of the village's longstanding jacobean tradition is the structure and location of the *'Fuente de los Romeros'* (Pilgrims' Fountain), which is so old that it is situated below current ground level.

Cañas is about 5 kilometres further on, and was the birthplace of St. Dominic of Silos (1000-1073), who was a monk and later prior at the neighbouring Monastery of San Millán, until King Don García of Nájera banished him from the kingdom. Dominic, who had already restored the priory in his hometown, sought refuge at the Castilian court and undertook the restoration of the decaying monastery of San Sebastián de Silos, converting it into the splendid monastery which became known as Santo Domingo de Silos. The *Monastery of Santa María de Cañas* is a Cistercian foundation of 1170, after the transfer of the Benedictine community of La Hayuela, having adopted St. Bernard's Rule. It is a magnificent church built in the severe Cistercian style of its time and houses a large 16th-century retable. The chapter house has been converted into a small but select museum, and amongst the treasures on display is the 13th-century Gothic tomb of Doña Urraca López de Haro, one of the finest sepulchral monuments in Spain. Cañas is another village where St. Francis of Assisi's visit on his way to Santiago is traditionally commemorated. Outside Azofra, at a spot known as 'la Picota', there is a narrow medieval boundary stone decorated with animal motifs which marks the boundary between the villages of Azofra and Alesanco.

The village of **Cirueña,** which has a church dedicated to St. Andrew, is where Count Fernán González was taken prisoner by the Navarrese. Halfway between **Ciriñuela** (which has a church dedicated to San Millán) and **Hervías** (whose church is dedicated to the Assumption) stood the Hospital of Santa María de Bellota (or Valleota), entrusted by Alfonso VIII to the Order of Calatrava.

There are few cities which have been as closely linked to the Camino de Santiago from the outset as **Santo Domingo de la Calzada.** St. Dominic was born in the nearby village of Viloria and studied at the Abadía de Valvanera and at the monastery of San Millán. Having been rejected by the monastery he became a hermit in the village which now bears his name, and devoted his life to helping pilgrims on their way to Santiago. In 1044 he built a pilgrims' bridge over the river Oja. He also built a pilgrims' hostel and hospital and, according to

Aymeric Picaud, he *'built the stretch of road between Nájera and Redecilla del Camino'*, part of which still survives. Alfonso VI took possession of La Rioja in 1076, and gave his unconditional support to St. Dominic. In 1109, St. Dominic died and was buried in the village, and around his tomb the 'Burgo de Santo Domingo' grew up, with a statute as an abbatial town.

The town is especially famous for the legend of the miracle of the roasted cock that crowed again, although other cities on the pilgrims' way have their own versions of the legend. Toulouse has the legend of *'le pendu dépendu'*, a miracle attributed to St. Amande or St. James. Barcelos, on the 'Caminho Português' has a legend known as *'o senhor do galo'*. Utrecht also has a version of the legend. The 'Liber miraculorum' (the second volume of the *Liber Sancti Iacobi*) places the miracle in Toulouse. Gonzalo de Berceo also recounts the miracle in his *'Cántigas de Santa María'*, as does Jacobus of Voragine in the *'Golden Legend'*. Be that as it may, the miracle of the roasted cock that crowed again belongs indiscutibly to Santo Domingo de la Calzada. Here's an outline of the story:

Santo Domingo de la Calzada cathedral: the Santo Domingo altar

In the 14th century, a man and his wife from Saintes, a part of the diocese of Cologne [this might explain why they are French pilgrims in some versions and German pilgrims in others —although Laffi goes so far as to state that they were Greek from Thessalonika] *were making the pilgrimage to Santiago de Compostela, accompanied by their son, Hugonell. They stopped for the night at an inn in Santo Domingo, where the innkeeper's daughter took a fancy to the young man, who virtuously resisted her advances. Thus spurned, she hid a silver goblet in Hugonell's baggage, and the following morning denounced him as a thief. The boy was arrested and hanged. As his parents were preparing to depart they heard their son's voice telling them that he was still alive, as St. Dominic was holding him up by the feet. They hastened to the house of the judge, who was just sitting down to dine on a pair of roast chickens, a cock and a hen, and told him the extraordinary tale. The judge retorted that the boy was no more alive than the cock and hen on his plate. At that, the birds jumped out of the plate, grew feathers again and began to flutter around and cackle and crow, thus demonstrating the hanged boy's innocence.*

Santo Domingo de la Calzada: portal of the cathedral

To commemorate this miracle, a late Gothic carved niche with a Renaissance grille decorates the west wall of the south transept, which is known as the *Gallinero* (or chicken coop) and which contains a pair of live white chickens, a cockerel and a hen. (A different pair is brought in every couple of weeks). The continuous presence of the birds only dates from the Holy Year of 1965: prior to this the birds could only be seen between 15th April and 13th October. Naturally, if a pilgrim hears the cock crow it means good luck.

Santo Domingo de la Calzada cathedral: the High Altar

St. Dominic's legacy are the monuments he built during his lifetime: the cathedral, the bridge and the pilgrims' hostel. The *Catedral del Salvador* is a Gothic construction built over St. Dominic's original Romanesque church and retains the typical ground plan of a Romanesque pilgrims' church: Latin cross shape, three aisles, ribbed vault and a

Santo Domingo de la Calzada: the bridge over the Oja

Choirstalls in Santo Domingo de la Calzada cathedral

The Bishop's House Santo Domingo de la Calzada

Santo Domingo de la Calzada: the town hall

Romanesque ambulatory behind the high altar. The graceful bell-tower, popularly known as 'la moza de la Rioja' ('the young lass of La Rioja') is a noteworthy 18th century Baroque addition. The most important features of the interior are the towering high altar retable by Damian Forment, St. Dominic's mausoleum with a Renaissance sepulchre and a Romanesque recumbent statue of the saint; various retables and numerous fine paintings; the choirstalls and the cloisters.

The Parador, which has been extended and restored recently, houses several fine pieces from the former *pilgrims' hospital.*

Pilgrims entered the ramparts (of which quite a few stretches survive) via the Puerta del Norte and made their way to the cathedral along the Calle de los Caballeros. The saint's grave at the edge of the road ('calzada') has contributed to the appreciable cracks in its surface.

On the way out of the city stands the 24-arched bridge over the river Oja, built by St. Dominic, which is spoiled by hideous modern cement parapets.

III. HISTORICAL PILGRIMS' ACCOUNTS

Aymeric Picaud: *'...in Spain you must visit the grave of St. Dominic ('Sanctus Dominicus'), who built the stretch of road in which he now rests, between the city of Nájera and Redecilla del Camino.'*

Künig von Vach: *'My advice is that you press on three miles to Santo Domingo ('Sant Dominicus') where food and drink await you at the hospital. Do not forget the chickens behind the altar... I know for a fact that it is true that they got up and flew away after being roasted, as I have seen the hole through which they flew away and the oven in which they were roasted.'*

Arnold von Harff: *'It is three leagues from Azofra ('Dofra') to Santo Domingo ('sent Dominicus'), a small and pleasant town. In the main church... lies St. Dominic himself, in his grand, lofty tomb... to the left of the high altar there is a cage built into the wall in which live a pair of white chickens, a cock and a hen.'*

Laffi: *'... next to the altar we saw the monument which narrates the miracle of the three pilgrims who were on their way to Santiago in Galicia, which is the story of the cock and the hen... We saw the cock and the hen inside an iron cage, to the left of the door... We asked the sacristan for feathers, and he obliged, and we have brought them back home out of devotion... St. Dominic of Silos ('San Domenico de Scillos'), after spending a few days with St. Dominic of the Causeway, returned to Silos...'*

STAGE 11

STO. DOMINGO DE LA CALZADA • BELORADO

St James the Moor-slayer in the Church of Santa María, Belorado

SANTO DOMINGO DE LA CALZADA •
GRAÑÓN • REDECILLA • CASTILDELGADO •
VILLAMAYOR DEL RÍO • VILORIA DE RIOJA •
BELORADO

'Inde Radicellas, inde Belfuratus.' (Aymeric Picaud: *'Pilgrims' Guide)'*

I. ROUTE

🚶 Leave **Santo Domingo de la Calzada** along the Calle Mayor (the actual pilgrims' way) which leads to the N-120 Burgos road. Cross the great bridge over the river Oja, which was originally built by St. Dominic himself, as was the stretch of road between here and Redecilla del Camino, now the N-120. Continue along the N-120 for about 5 kilometres, bearing off to the left at km 50 at the turning to Grañón, which is situated on a small hill.

As you enter **Grañón,** turn left and make a short detour to come out by a small fountain which stands beside the public scales and the *pelota* court. The calle Cuatro Cantones is opposite the fountain, and will take you right across the village, where you meet up with the path again. By a warehouse, the path makes a 90° turn to the left and heads steeply downhill away from the village, down towards the plain, where you turn right onto a farm track which runs across arable land. Continue along this track towards the N-120 which is over to your right. After about 300 metres, the path bends sharply to the left and continues parallel to the road as far as Redecilla, no more than 5 kilometres from Grañón.

You cross the regional border between La Rioja and Castilla y León (Old Castile) just outside **Redecilla,** the first village in the province of Burgos. Go through Redecilla along the main street, which runs to the right of the main road, and get back onto the road again upon leaving the village.

For the remaining 12 kilometres from Redecilla to Belorado the pilgrims' route unfortunately goes along the N-120, passing through **Castildelgado** (2 kilometres from Redecilla) and **Villamayor del Río** (5 kilometres from Castildelgado) on the way.

Shortly before km 58, after Castildelgado, a left-hand turning leads off the N-120 towards **Viloria de Rioja,** less than one kilometre away, which was the birthplace of St. Dominic of the Causeway. After visiting the village, return to the N-120 and continue along it until you reach **Belorado.**

🚲 This stage is suitable for cyclists throughout. The only slightly difficult stretches are the descent from the village of Grañón and the subsequent 5 kilometres to Redecilla, which are unpaved.

🚗 Milestones: N-120 km 45.5: Santo Domingo de la Calzada; km 50: turning to Grañón; km 55: Redecilla del Camino; km 56.8: Castildelgado; km 57.8: turning to Viloria de Rioja; km 61.5: Villamayor de Río; km 66: Belorado.

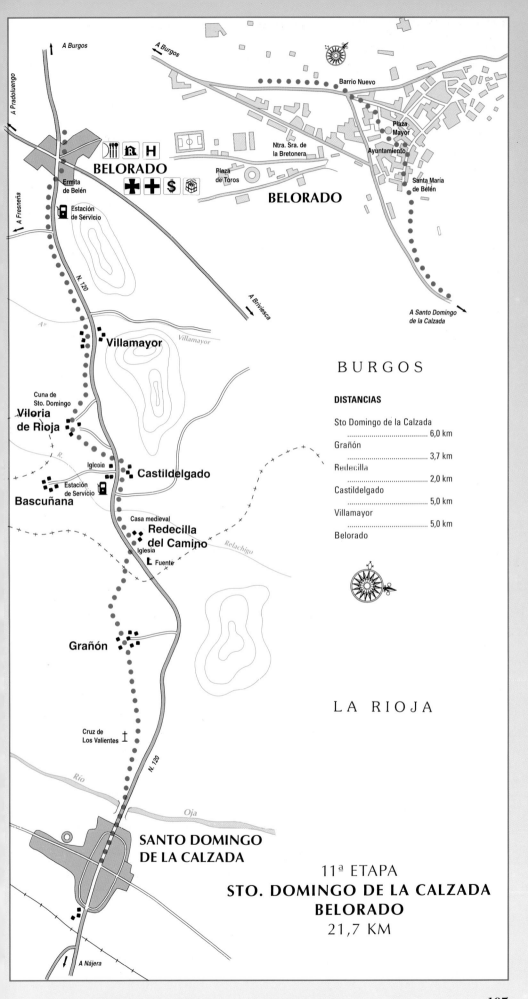

A Burgos
A Burgos

Barrio Nuevo

A Pradoluengo

Plaza
Mayor

Ntra. Sra. de
la Bretonera

Ayuntamiento

BELORADO

Ermita
de Belén

A Fresneña

Estación
de Servicio

Plaza
de Toros

Santa María
de Belén

BELORADO

A Briviesca

A Santo Domingo
de la Calzada

N 120

Aº

Villamayor

Villamayor

B U R G O S

Cuna de
Sto. Domingo

DISTANCIAS

**Viloria
de Rioja**

R.

Iglesia

Sto Domingo de la Calzada
.... 6,0 km
Grañón
.... 3,7 km
Redecilla
.... 2,0 km
Castildelgado
.... 5,0 km
Villamayor
.... 5,0 km
Belorado

Estación
de Servicio

Castildelgado

Bascuñana

Casa medieval

**Redecilla
del Camino**

Iglesia

Fuente

Relachigo

Grañón

L A   R I O J A

Cruz de
Los Valientes

N 120

Río

Oja

**SANTO DOMINGO
DE LA CALZADA**

11ª ETAPA
**STO. DOMINGO DE LA CALZADA
BELORADO**
21,7 KM

A Nájera

Grañón

Grañón. the Church of San Juan Bautista

A street in Redecilla del Camino

II. HISTORY, ART AND LEGENDS

On the left-hand side of the road, halfway between Santo Domingo de la Calzada and Grañón, you will see a sign for the *Cruz de los Valientes* (Cross of the Brave), which stands on the spot where a trial by ordeal was once held to settle a dispute over the ownership of some land, which both villages were claiming. The winner of the bizarre contest was one Martín García, the representative of Grañón, who asked his fellow villagers to say a Paternoster and an Ave Maria for him every Sunday in return for his feat.

Two factors have shaped the village of **Grañón:** its position on the frontier between the kingdoms of Castile and Navarre, and its strategic location on the stretch of the pilgrims' way built by St. Dominic of the Causeway. The village is built on a hill, the 'Cerro Mirabel', and grew up around the castle which records show was donated by the famous Castilian count, Fernán González, in the 10th century (although it is possible that the founding of the village goes back a century earlier, to King Alfonso III 'the Great' of León). As a frontier town, it was directly affected by the vicissitudes of Castile and Navarre. It had two monasteries, one dedicated to San Tomé and the other to St. Michael, which were both donated to San Millán de la Cogolla in 1063. In the 13th century the town became a dependency of Santo Domingo de la Calzada.

There was also a pilgrims' hospital in the village, almost certainly linked to one or other of the monasteries. Grañón still retains the grid layout typical of villages on the pilgrims' route.

The nucleus of the village was the Monastery of San Juan Bautista, over whose church the massive parish church of the same name was built in the 14th century. Its priceless high altarpiece, created between 1545 and 1556, was almost certainly the work of Natuera Borgoñón and Bernal Forment, and has recently been completely restored.

St. Dominic's roadbuilding activities took him as far as **Redecilla,** which is another typical wayside village in its layout. Its parish church is dedicated to the Virgen de la Calle (the Virgin of the Road), and a fine statue of her decorates the façade. Inside, one of the sculptural jewels of the pilgrims' way is to be found: a Romanesque *baptismal font* dating from the 12th century. The great bowl rests on a group of eight columns and is decorated with towers, windows and carved friezes, with what is possibly a snake curling around the base. A modern pilgrims' refuge stands on the site of the old Hospital de San Lázaro: a document in the Parish Archives records a curious incident concerning a 16th-century French pilgrim, by the name of Jean, who died there. His clothes were auctioned to pay for the burial, but no buyer came forward (for obvious reasons!) and so he was buried in the chancel of the church at the expense of the town council, which paid the 400 maravedis.

The Parish Church of San Pedro in **Castildelgado** is the final resting place of the village's most famous son, Don

Francisco Delgado, who was Bishop of Lugo and Jaén, Archbishop elect of Burgos and a Tridentine theologian. The village is named after him, having changed its name from Villaypún, although both names were interchangeable up until the 19th century. A pilgrims' hospital, founded by Alfonso VII, used to exist in the village. In **Viloria de Rioja,** the birthplace of St. Dominic of the Causeway, the ruins of the house where he was born still survived until very recently, but tragically have now been demolished. The Romanesque baptismal font in which he was christened still stands in the parish church.

Back on the main road, the pilgrims' route passes through **Villamayor del Río,** a small village next to a stream, before reaching **Belorado.** This historic town lies in the narrow valley of the river Tirón, in the shadow of a limestone outcrop which is crowned by the ruins of a castle that once defended the frontier of Castile. Lower down, there are anchorite cave dwellings hollowed out of the rock. One of them, for unexplained reasons, is linked to the name and memory of San Caprasio. This might be Caprasio, Bishop of Agen, mentioned by Aymeric Picaud, who hid trembling in a cave until his courage was restored by the example of the young maiden, Faith, who bravely accepted martyrdom. The basilica which was built over this Virgin Martyr's tomb at Conques (near Le Puy, in France) became one of the most famous places on the 'Via Podense'. An image of San Caprasio, brought from the caves, can be found in the Church of San Nicolás. Even the name of the town, Belorado, ('Belfuratus' in Picaud's *'Pilgrims' Guide'*) derives from these caves, which bore ('forare') into the rock face.

Redecilla del Camino: Romanesque baptismal font

Belorado: bridge over the river Tirón

King Alfonso I of Aragón, 'the Battler', resettled the town and granted it special privileges in 1116, converting it into a stronghold on the border with the kingdom of his stepson and rival, King Alfonso VII of León, 'the Emperor'. The old Hospital de Santa María de Belén was situated at the entry to the town and was dependent on the Bishop of Burgos. Today, only a chapel of the same name survives. Within the ramparts, of which several stretches still stand, are the Church of San Nicolás, the oldest in the town, and the Church of San Pedro, situated next to the Casa Consistorial in the Plaza Mayor. Outside the walls and on the other side of the 'arroyo Verdancho', is the *Parish Church of Santa María,* dating from the 16th century, which has a magnificent stone retable entirely dedicated to St. James. Both images of the Apostle appear: the Moor-slayer and the gentle pilgrim. The retable is completed by two reliefs showing scenes from the life of St. James. The high altar has a very fine statue of St. Mary.

Belorado: the Church of Santa María

Belorado refused to pay the annual tax to the church at Santiago de Compostela, the 'Voto de Santiago', imposed by Ramiro I after the victory at Clavijo. When the King tried to oblige them to pay it, the town alleged that it was not under the jurisdiction of the King of León. This gave rise to a lawsuit, settled in 1408, and the curious, rather longwinded document which resulted, signed by the King, is kept at the *Casa Consistorial.*

Retable in the Church of Santa María, Belorado

A stone statue in the school patio is visible from the road. It is dedicated to the illustrious Latinist, Raimundo de Miguel y Navas, who was born in Belorado, whose Latin dictionary was used by generations of Spaniards. On the way out of the town is the bridge built by St. John of Ortega, which still retains some of the original elements. The Ermita de San Lázaro is nearby, built on the site of a pilgrim' hospital of the same name, and houses a serene 14th-century Gothic Christ.

Viloria de Rioja

III. HISTORICAL PILGRIMS' ACCOUNTS

Aymeric Picaud: *'Then come... Redecilla ('Radicellas') and Belorado ('Belfuratus').'*

Künig von Vach: *'...after a fine bridge, you walk a mile to a town called Grañón ('Graneon'), and then another mile to a small town called Redecilla ('Redihile').'*

Arnold von Harff: *'... it is a league from Grañón ('Graneoin') to Redecilla del Camino ('Restilla de la Kamine'), a 'villa franca'.'*

Laffi: *'... we continued to Grañón ('Grignon'), two leagues away. It is a very small, poor place... in the morning we set off towards Redecilla ('Redicilia')... we continued on to Castildelgado ('Castel Guado')... a small place, but attractive and wealthy. We then started out towards Belorado ('Belferrato'), three leagues away.'*

STAGE 12

BELORADO • SAN JUAN DE ORTEGA

The Montes de Oca

BELORADO • TOSANTOS •
VILLAMBISTIA • ESPINOSA DEL CAMINO •
VILLAFRANCA • SAN JUAN DE ORTEGA

Villafranca Montes de Oca:
Until such a time when part of the magnificently restored *Hospital de San Antonio Abad* is fitted out as a refuge, as it rightly should be, for the time being pilgrims will be looked after at the local schools, which have 17 bunk-beds.

San Juan de Ortega:
This is one of the most traditional «hospital» complexes, one which exudes the true spirit and atmosphere of the Pilgrimage to Santiago. It is fervently and lovingly taken care of by the parish priest, himself one of the most outstanding characters to be encountered along the Pilgrims' Route. Large capacity and good facilities.
☎ (948) 56 04 38

RESTAURANTS
Villafranca Montes de Oca:
El Pájaro.

PETROL STATIONS
On the N-120, on entering and leaving Belorado.

'Inde Francauilla; inde nemus Oque.' (Aymeric Picaud: *'Pilgrims' Guide'*)

I. ROUTE

🚶🚶　Take the N-120 out of **Belorado** and cross the bridge over the river Tirón. Go past a petrol station and a Red Cross hut, bear left off the road on a level with the turning to San Miguel de Pedroso, and get onto an earth track. This path, obscured in some parts by vegetation, continues parallel to the N-120 for about 4 kilometres towards **Tosantos.** Opposite, on the other side of the village, the rupestrian Ermita de la Virgen de la Peña is visible.
The path continues to the village of **Villambistia,** just over 1.5 kilometres away. Make your way through the highest part of the village by the church and the cemetery, and come out along a poplar-lined lane. After just under 2 kilometres, you cross the N-120 and enter **Espinosa del Camino.** The pilgrims' route cuts through the middle of the village, crosses the stream known as the arroyo Palomar and then joins a wide farm track which climbs gently up to the top of a low hill, from which **Villafranca Montes de Oca** is visible. Next, head downhill towards the Ermita de San Felices, where you make a 90° turn towards Villafranca. Half a kilometre outside Villafranca you come out onto the N-120, which brings you into the village after crossing the river Oca. When you come to the Church of Santiago, bear right off the road between the church and the Hospital de San Antonio Abad (now a pilgrims' refuge). Upon leaving the village, the very steep climb, thickly-wooded with oaks, up into the Montes de Oca begins. After a kilometre, at the spring of Mojapán, the gradient becomes a little gentler, but the climb still continues uphill, through pine forests now, almost meeting up with the N-120 visible to the left (at the Monumento a los Caídos). The route then enters a forest track, which you leave at milestone MP-61 to make a short detour down to the Ermita de Valdefuentes and the Fuente del Carnero. Then return to the forest track which brings you, after about 6 kilometres, directly into **San Juan de Ortega.**

🚲　This stage is mainly suitable for cyclists, with the exception of the stretch between Villafranca Montes de Oca and the Ermita de Valdefuentes. Be warned, too, that the 6 kilometres between Valdefuentes and San Juan de Ortega are by no means easy.

🚗　Milestones: N-120 km 67: Belorado; km 71: Tosantos; km 72.8: Villambistia; km 78: Villafranca Montes de Oca; km 81.3: Alto de la Pedraja and Monumento a los Caídos; km 84.4: Ermita de Valdefuentes; km 93: turning to San Juan de Ortega.

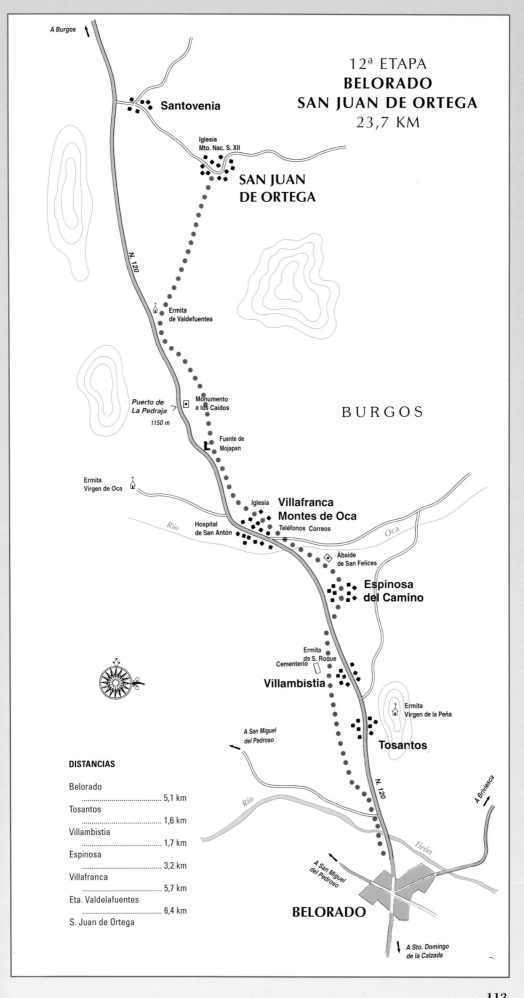

A Burgos

Santovenia

Iglesia
Mto. Nac. S. XII

**SAN JUAN
DE ORTEGA**

12ª ETAPA
**BELORADO
SAN JUAN DE ORTEGA**
23,7 KM

N. 120

Ermita
de Valdefuentes

Puerto de
La Pedraja
1150 m

Monumento
a los Caídos

BURGOS

Fuente de
Mojapan

Ermita
Virgen de Oca

Iglesia   **Villafranca
Montes de Oca**

Hospital
de San Antón   Teléfonos Correos

Río   Oca

Ábside
de San Felices

**Espinosa
del Camino**

Ermita
de S. Roque
Cementerio

Villambistia

Ermita
Virgen de la Peña

Tosantos

A San Miguel
del Pedroso

N. 120

A Briviesca

DISTANCIAS

Belorado
.... 5,1 km
Tosantos
.... 1,6 km
Villambistia
.... 1,7 km
Espinosa
.... 3,2 km
Villafranca
.... 5,7 km
Eta. Valdelafuentes
.... 6,4 km
S. Juan de Ortega

Río

Tirón

A San Miguel
del Pedroso

BELORADO

A Sto. Domingo
de la Calzada

Tosantos: Ermita de la Virgen de la Peña

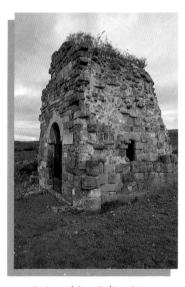

Parish church of Espinosa del Camino

II. HISTORY, ART AND LEGENDS

In **Tosantos,** to the right of the path and the main road, you will notice the rupestrian Ermita de Nuestra Señora de la Peña, which is dug out of the hillside. Inside, a 12th-century Romanesque statue of the Virgin is venerated.

The pilgrims' route next passes through **Villambistia,** where a stretch of the old road survives, and **Espinosa del Camino.** Here, in the parish church of the Assumption, there is a fine Romanesque sculpture of San Indalecio who, according to tradition, was one of the seven apostles who accompanied St. James in the evangelization of Hispania. He was made a Bishop, and converted the area of Auca (Villafranca Montes de Oca) to Christianity where, as we shall see, his memory is everywhere. His relics are worshipped with devotion at Jaca cathedral, in the Aragonese Pyrenees.

Half a kilometre outside Villafranca, on the right of the pilgrims' route, stands the **Ábside de San Felices** (San Felices' Apse), a small chapel built of hewn stone which is entered through a horseshoe arch. It is all that remains of a 10th-century Mozarabic monastery that was dedicated to San Millán's mentor, San Felices. Tradition has it that this is where the founder of Burgos, Count Diego Rodríguez, was buried. A memorial stone stands in remembrance.

Villafranca Montes de Oca is the ancient episcopal see of 'Auca' (Oca). Apart from the tradition of San Indalecio, the first recorded Bishop was one Asterio, whose signature appears in 589 at the Third Council of Toledo. Alfonso VI moved the episcopal see to the city of Burgos, an event recorded in a document of July 8th, 1075. The designation 'Villafranca' is a legacy of the Santiago pilgrimage, which gave rise to an important settlement of Franks, to repopulate Auca. It became an important landmark on the road to Santiago, and could boast a pilgrims' hospital of St. James as early as the 9th century (according to later sources), of which no traces survive except, perhaps, the name of the parish church. Large portions do, however, survive of the *Hospital de San Antonio Abad,* also known as 'Hospital de la Reina' in honour of its founder (1380), Queen Doña Juana Manuel, wife of Enrique II, including the main gate which is formed by a basket-handle arch, with the coat of arms of the Catholic Kings, Isabel and Ferdinand, carved above it, the chapel of San Antonio Abad, named after the former resident order, a few rooms and even some centuries-old surgical instruments. Its restoration as a pilgrims' hostel is superb.

The huge 18th-century *Church of Santiago* houses a pair of sculptures depicting St. James dressed as a pilgrim, one of which presides over the high altar. It also has a baptismal font made out of a real giant shell from the Philippines.

On the way out of the village, a road off to the left of the main road leads, after a few kilometres, to the Ermita de Nuestra Señora de Oca, a Romanesque sculpture of whom is enshrined there. Behind the shrine is the *Pozo de San Indalecio,* a stone water tank full of

Ruins of San Felices' Apse, Villafranca Montes de Oca

crystal-clear spring water, which commemorates the spot where San Indalecio was martyred.

The **Montes de Oca** was always one of the most feared stretches of the pilgrims' route due to their steepness, dense undergrowth and harsh climate but, above all, because they were infested with bloodthirsty bandits who would rob and murder passing pilgrims. The *Book of Miracles* in the *Codex Calixtinus* records 22 miracles, one of which it places in the sinister scenario of the Montes de Oca. The Montes de Oca were also, historically, the true frontier of Castile.

Several places used to exist where pilgrims could seek help in this difficult area, but all that remains is the portico of the church belonging to the monastery and hospital of **Valdefuentes,** now a chapel dedicated to St. James. Opposite this is the Fuente del Carnero.

Villafranca Montes de Oca: Church of Santiago

The sanctuary of **San Juan de Ortega,** situated in the heart of the Montes de Oca, and dedicated exclusively to helping pilgrims, is another of the landmarks of the pilgrims' way. It is named after its legendary founder, St. John of Ortega, who was born in 1080 in the nearby village of Quintanaortuño, on the banks of the river Ubierna. He was ordained on his return from a pilgrimage to Jerusalem, and became the principal helper of St. Dominic of the Causeway, building churches, hospitals, roads and bridges for pilgrims, many of which are still in use. He also offered material and spiritual help to pilgrims. After clearing a way through to the wild spot known as Ortega (from the Latin 'urtica' and the Spanish 'ortiga', nettle), he founded a community of Augustinian monks and built a chapel dedicated to St. Nicholas of Bari, whose miraculous intercession had saved him from drowning in a shipwreck on his way back from Jerusalem. He also built a pilgrims' hospital, of which no trace remains. In 1138, Pope Innocent II took the community under his protection and in 1142, Alfonso VII 'the Emperor' (to whom St. John was confessor and spiritual advisor) endowed him with all crown estates in the Montes de Oca. However, after St. John's death in 1163, the monastery gradually declined and became a shadow of what it had been during his lifetime. In 1431, the Bishop of Burgos, Pablo de Santa María, entrusted it to the Jeronymites, under whom it flourished again. Isabel la Católica herself visited the monastery in 1477, after seven years of unfruitful marriage, drawn by St. John's reputation as an intercessor in cases of infertility. The Queen was cured of her sterility and in her gratitude to St. John she had the *Chapel of San Nicolás de Bari* completely rebuilt in a more sumptuous style. St. John's splendid mausoleum is of a similar style and date, and comprises a recumbent statue of the saint under a baldachino, the work of Juan de Colonia and Gil de Siloe. St. John's magnificent 12th-century Romanesque tomb is intricately carved with scenes from his life. The beautiful Romanesque *monastery church* was begun by St. John of Ortega, and completed in Gothic style. Apart from the mausoleum, it features a fine central apse, a Romanesque capital depicting, once again, the clash between Roland and Ferragut and,

Villafranca Montes de Oca: the old hospital converted into a pilgrims' hostel

The Ermita de Valdefuentes

*San Juan de Ortega: the
monastery church*

St. John of Ortega's tomb

San Juan de Ortega mausoleum

above all, a marvellous capital showing the
Annunciation, the Visitation, Joseph's Dream and
Christ's Nativity. Each equinox (21st March and 22nd
September), at precisely 5pm solar time, a single shaft
of sunlight strikes this capital, illuminating it alone in
the surrounding gloom and creating the marvellous
illusion that the Holy Ghost is alighting on Mary's belly.
Miracle or artifice, it is clear that this is no ordinary
place.

III. HISTORICAL PILGRIMS' ACCOUNTS

Aymeric Picaud: *'After the land of the Navarrese,
on the other side of the Montes de Oca ('Nemus
Oque') in the direction of Burgos, Spanish territory
continues in Castilla y Campos ('Castella et
Campos').'*

Künig von Vach: *'It is three miles' walk to
Villafranca ('Vylfrancken'). Do not miss the
Hospital de la Reina... You must then climb up a
mountain: do not be in too much of a hurry.'*

Arnold von Harff: *'Villafranca ('Villa francka')... is
a town situated next to another, called Belorado
('Bilorato').'*

Laffi: *'... we continued our journey to Villafranca...
situated at the foot of a mountain... here pilgrims'
are treated with great charity, especially in the
hospital where the food is excellent... we
discovered a monastery where the parents of St.
John of Ortega are buried, and where St. John's
body rests in a marble tomb.'*

STAGE 13

SAN JUAN DE ORTEGA • BURGOS

Arch of Santa María, in Burgos

SAN JUAN DE ORTEGA • AGÉS •
ATAPUERCA • VILLAFRÍA •
BURGOS

PILGRIMS' REFUGES

Burgos: Until such a time when part of the superbly restored *Hospital del Rey* is fitted out as a refuge, as it rightly should be, for the time being pilgrims will be looked after at the *El Parral* Municipal Hostel, situated not far from the said *Hospital del Rey*.
☎ (947) 20 82 10 - 908 78 32 25

ACCOMMODATION

Villafría:
H La Aduana.
Ctra. Madrid-Irún km 245.
☎ (947) 48 42 52.
22 rooms. ♣
H Vitoria. Ctra. Madrid-Irún, km 245. ☎ (947) 48 36 00.
19 rooms. ♣
HR* Buenos Aires.
☎ (947) 48 37 70. 45 rooms. ♣
Meals available.
HSR Iruñako. ☎ 48 41 26.
31 rooms. ♣

Burgos:
♣♣♣
**Landa Palace. Almirante Bonifaz.
Husa Puerta de Burgos.
Condestable. Del Cid.
Ciudad de Burgos.**
♣♣
**Cordón. Corona de Castilla.
Fernán González. María Luisa.
Rice. Conde de Miranda. España.
Norte y Londres. Las Vegas. Villa
Jimena. Alarzón. Hilton. Lar.**
♣
**Manjón. Puerta Romeros. La
Tesorera. Ambos Mundos.
Carrales. Castellano. García.
Hidalgo. Joma. Niza. San Juan.
Temiño. Torres.**

CAMPSITES
Villafría:
Río Vena. 2nd Category.
☎ (947) 48 41 20

Burgos:
Fuentes Blancas. 1st Category.
☎ (947) 22 10 16

RESTAURANTS
Villafría:
**Aeropuerto. Jesús. Las Vegas.
Buenos Aires. Iruñako.**

Burgos:
Los Chapiteles. General
Santocildes, 2 ☎ (947) 20 59 98.
Castilian cuisine.
**Casa Ojeda. Fernán González.
Gaona. Mesón del Cid.
Papamoscas. Rincón de España.**

PETROL STATIONS
There are several at the entrance to Burgos.

'Inde urbs Burgas.' (Aymeric Picaud: 'Pilgrims' Guide')

I. ROUTE

🚶 A short distance from the monastery of **San Juan de Ortega** a road leads off to the left towards Santovenia and the N-120 to Burgos. There are three alternative routes from here:
a) Go along the above-mentioned road, passing through **Santovenia,** and come out onto the N-120 which takes you straight to Burgos, via **Zalduendo, Ibeas de Juarros** and **San Medel.**
b) Branch off to the right towards **Barrios de Colina,** passing through **Olmos de Atapuerca, Rubena** and **Villafría,** where you meet up with alternative route (c).
c) Cross over and carry straight on along a dirt track which goes up the hill. This route is described in detail below.
The path takes you across a high, level plateau, some 1 000 metres above sea-level, and runs through bushes and pine trees for about 3 km before reaching a clearing, from which the church of Santovenia is visible on a hill over to the left. A bit further on, you come to the Ermita de la Virgen del Rebollo, an outpost of **Agés,** from which a gentle slope leads down to the village. After just over 2 km, a narrow asphalted path leads into **Atapuerca.** On your way out of the village, bear left off the road and take a footpath which climbs the Sierra de Atapuerca. You soon reach a fork in the path: the right-hand fork bypasses the Sierra via Rubena, while the left-hand fork (the route you should follow) takes you up into the Sierra. At the top, the path runs for a short distance between barbed-wire fencing on the left and a quarry and telephone posts on the right. Make your way downhill along paths which, at times, become very faint, passing the villages of Villalval and Cardeñuela which you will see over to the left of the path. Outside the village of Orbaneja, cross a bridge over the A-1 motorway and then proceed along an asphalted track some 3 km to **Villafría,** crossing the Madrid-Irún railway line and another bridge on the way. From Villafría, the route runs along the Vitoria road, through an industrial estate, and enters **Burgos** via the **Gamonal** district. The most direct route to the cathedral is along calle de las Calzadas, calle de San Juan, calle Avellanos and calle de Fernán González.

🚴 Alternative routes (a) and (b) present absolutely no problem for cyclists. Route (c) is impracticable between Atapuerca and Orbaneja, and from Atapuerca cyclists should continue to Olmos de Atapuerca and then meet up with alternative route (b).

🚗 Milestones: N-120 km 94.5: Zalduendo; km 98: Ibeas de Juarros; km 111: Burgos.

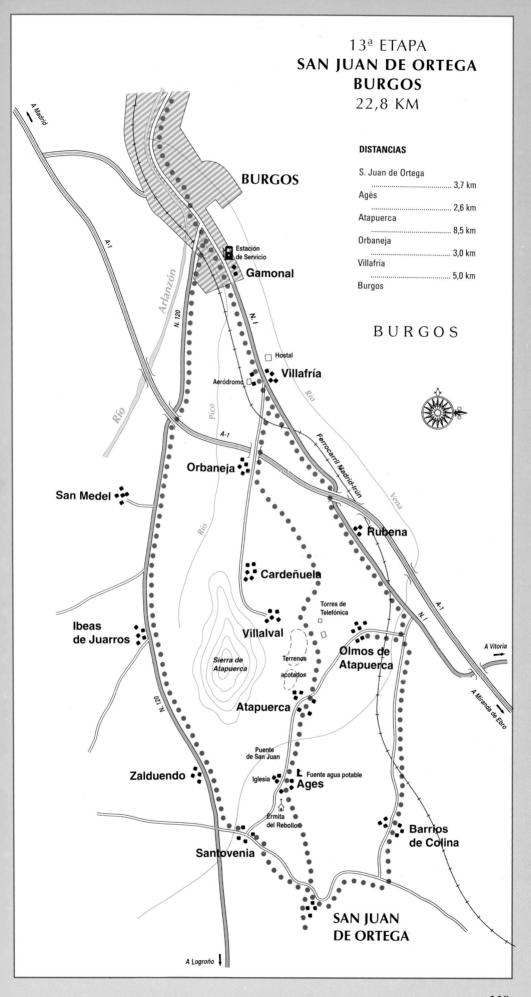

13ª ETAPA
SAN JUAN DE ORTEGA
BURGOS
22,8 KM

DISTANCIAS

S. Juan de Ortega
.... 3,7 km
Agés
.... 2,6 km
Atapuerca
.... 8,5 km
Orbaneja
.... 3,0 km
Villafría
.... 5,0 km
Burgos

B U R G O S

A Madrid

A-1

BURGOS

Arlanzón

N. 120

N. I

Río

Estación
de Servicio

Gamonal

Hostal

Villafría

Aeródromo

Pico

Río

A-1

Orbaneja

Ferrocarril Madrid-Irún

San Medel

Vena

Rubena

Cardeñuela

Torres de
Telefónica

Ibeas
de Juarros

N. I

A Vitoria

Sierra de
Atapuerca

Villalval

Terrenos
acotados

Ólmos de
Atapuerca

A Miranda de Ebro

Atapuerca

N. 120

Puente
de San Juan

Zalduendo

Iglesia

Fuente agua potable

Ages

Ermita
del Rebollo

Barrios
de Colina

Santovenia

SAN JUAN
DE ORTEGA

A Logroño

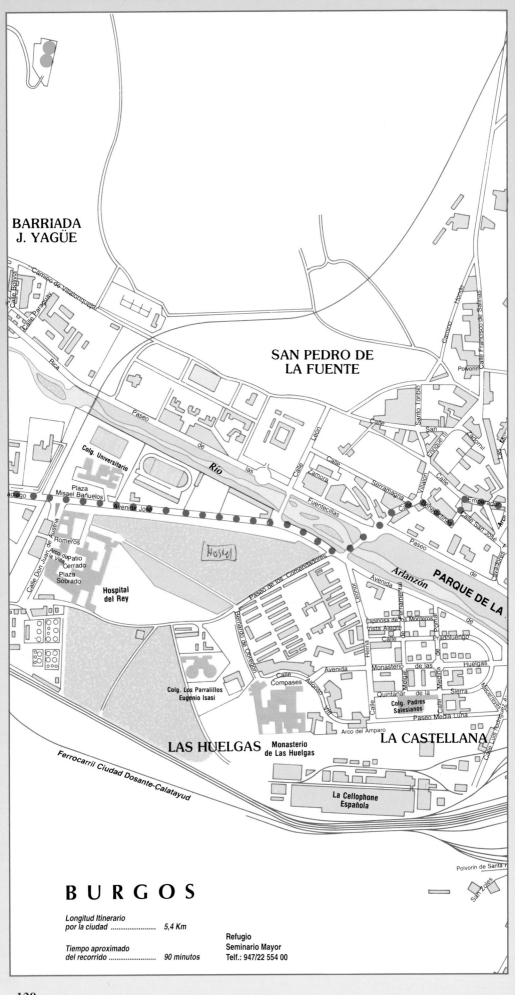

BARRIADA J. YAGÜE

SAN PEDRO DE LA FUENTE

Colg. Universitario

Plaza Misael Bañuelos

Avenida José

Río

Paseo

de

las

Hostel

Romeros

Arco de Patio Cerrado

Plaza Sobrado

Calle Don Juan de Austria

Hospital del Rey

Colg. Los Parralillos Eugenio Isasi

Paseo de los Comandadores

Bernardo de Obregón

Calle Compases

Calle Alonso VIII

Calle

Avenida

PARQUE DE LA

Arlanzón

Paseo

Avenida

Espinosa de los Monteros

Vista Alegre

Calle

Reina

Monasterio de las Huelgas

Quintanar de la Sierra

Colg. Padres Salesianos

Paseo Media Luna

Pradoluengo

Calle Medina

LA CASTELLANA

Arco del Amparo

LAS HUELGAS

Monasterio de Las Huelgas

Ferrocarril Ciudad Dosante-Calatayud

La Cellophone Española

Polvorín de Santa

San Isidro

B U R G O S

Longitud Itinerario
por la ciudad .... 5,4 Km

Tiempo aproximado
del recorrido .... 90 minutos

Refugio
Seminario Mayor
Telf.: 947/22 554 00

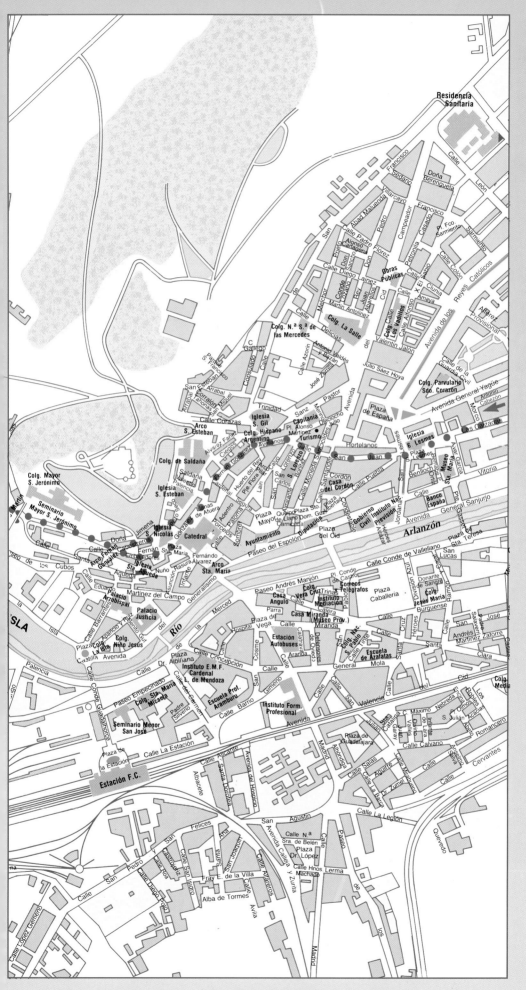

The bridge between Agés and Atapuerca

Gamonal: the Church of Santa María la Real y Antigua

Burgos cathedral

II. HISTORY, ART AND LEGENDS

A tombstone in the parish church of **Agés,** a small village at the foot of the Montes de Oca, is supposed to mark the original burial place of King Don García de Nájera (who was killed in the area), before his remains were transferred to the Monastery of Santa María la Real in Nájera. Standing to the left of the small road that links Agés and Atapuerca is a very pretty little one-arched bridge, built for pilgrims to cross the river Vena, which is a small work of genius by St. John of Ortega.

Just outside **Atapuerca** there is a stone known as 'el fin del rey' ('the end of the king') which, coupled with the tombstone at Agés, commemorates the Navarrese King Don García's dramatic death here in 1054 at the hands of his brother, King Fernando I of Castile and León, during their jousting contest over the areas of Briviesca and Montes de Oca. The village church is dedicated to St. Martin, one of the saints most closely linked to the Santiago pilgrimage and whose cult, as has already been seen, was imported by French pilgrims.

The Sierra de Atapuerca is honeycombed with caves. In 1992 some prehistoric human remains were found here which are so old that 'Atapuerca man' is possibly the earliest example of *homo sapiens* in Europe.

After passing **Orbaneja** and **Villafría,** you come to **Gamonal,** now a district of Burgos, which is the location of the splendid 13th-century Gothic church of **Santa María la Real y Antigua.** A Gothic stone cross, bearing a relief of St. James the pilgrim, stands in front of the church.

Burgos owes its very existence to the defensive towers (the 'burgos' referred to by the town's name) that rose up on the hill beneath which Count Diego Rodríguez Porcelos founded the town in the year 884. Once the frontier had been withdrawn, and owing to its strategic position as a crossroads of the routes leading from the sea and those of the Camino de Santiago, Burgos was to witness the beginning of intense commercial activity. This activity was to entail the emergence of a number of merchant districts that marked out the trail of the pilgrims' route to Santiago. The latter, skirting the hill on which the castle stood, wended its way along what today is *Calle de Fernán González*. The eventual fusion of the said districts gave rise to a centre of considerable economic importance, and it would not be long before Burgos also became a focus of political interest. The town was granted the status of 'Caput Castellae', the capital of the county and, subsequently, of the very kingdom of Castile. Furthermore, Burgos has been an episcopal see since 1075, as a result of the canonical transfer of the see that once belonged to Oca.

Pilgrims entered the city along what is now the Calle de las Calzadas ('Roads'), so called because in the Capiscol district the pilgrims' route from Bayonne met the 'Camino francés'. The 14th-century Gothic *Church of San Lesmes* (formerly the church of San Juan Evangelista) and the remains of the monastery and hospital of San Juan Evangelista stand outside the city walls. The monastery was founded for the Benedictines by Alfonso VI in about 1074 and placed under the charge of the French abbot Adelhelm, who was brought from the Abbey of La Chaise-

Dieu by the Burgundian Queen Doña Constanza, wife of Alfonso VI. Adelhelm, who dedicated his life to the welfare of pilgrims, became San Lesmes, the patron saint of Burgos. The importance of Burgos on the pilgrims' route to Santiago is demonstrated by the fact that, according to Künig von Vach, in the 15th century there were 32 hospitals in the city. Apart from the Hospital de San Juan Evangelista, Alfonso VI also founded the Hospital del Emperador. Later examples include the Hospital del Rey, the Hospital de San Lucas, the Hospital de San Lázaro and the Hospital de San Juan de Ortega. Furthermore, several religious communities, such as the Convent of San Agustín or the Monastery of Las Huelgas Reales, were equally devoted to the welfare of pilgrims.

After passing through the 13th-century Puerta de San Juan you come to the magnificent Gothic **Cathedral,** the first stones of which were laid in 1221 by Fernando III and which was consecrated in 1260. Although work on the cathedral lasted until the 16th century, it is stylistically surprisingly coherent. The grandiosity of its architecture and the richness of its interior decoration combine to make Burgos cathedral one of the most outstanding artistic monuments in Spain. From the famous Gothic towers to the tomb of El Cid in the crossing, everything is superlative, both from an artistic and historical point of view. Briefly, the main sights to see inside the Cathedral include the *Santo Cristo de Burgos,* the 15th-century *Capilla del Condestable* by Simón de Colonia, the *Escalera Dorada,* the *portals,* the *cupola* and the *rose window.* Of particular interest to pilgrims is the *Capilla de Santiago,* which is dominated by a 16th-century statue of St. James the Moor-slayer. Another figure of St. James graces the altar in the Capilla de Santa Tecla, and he is also to be found in a representation of the appearance of the Virgen del Pilar on one of the choirstalls, as well as on the Puerta de la Pellejería and in the Cathedral Museum, among other places.

Burgos has many other monuments which are well worth visiting. These include the 15th-century Gothic *church of San Nicolás,* the *Church of Santa Gadea* or *Santa Agueda* where, legend has it, El Cid forced King Alfonso VI to swear that he had played no part in the death of his brother, Sancho), the remains of the *Castle,* the 13th-century *Puerta de San Esteban,* the *Church of San Gil,* the *Casa del Cordón* and the *Gate and Arch of Santa María,* finished in 1553 by Francisco de Colonia. The *Cartuja de Miraflores* is outside the city and was built between 1454 and 1499 by Juan and Simón de Colonia (among others) and intended by Isabel la Católica as a pantheon for her parents, Juan II and Isabel of Portugal, whose splendid mausoleum was built by Gil de Siloé between 1489 and 1493. The superb high altar retable includes a magnificent image of St. James the pilgrim.

The **Hospital del Rey,** the most important pilgrims' hospital in the city, is on the way out of Burgos. It was built for the Cistercians by Alfonso VIII in 1195 and was under the auspices of the neighbouring monastery of Las Huelgas Reales. Despite its Romanesque origins, virtually all of what we see today dates from the 16th century. The plateresque *Puerta de Romeros* (Pilgrims' Gate) and the *Pórtico de la iglesia* (church door) are particularly fine: the latter is

The Church of San Nicolás, Burgos

The Cartuja de Miraflores, Burgos

Cartuja de Miraflores: the tomb of prince Alfonso

Chapel door at the Hospital del Rey, Burgos

The Convent of Las Huelgas Reales, Burgos

The Convent of las Huelgas Reales: the cloisters

The knighthood-bestowing statue of St. James, Las Huelgas Reales

decorated with exceptional woodcarvings depicting three generations of a family making the pilgrimage to Santiago, which is the work of Juan de Valmaseda and a very fine example of Spanish Renaissance art. After a most successful and elaborate restoration programme it was inaugurated as the University Law Faculty on 4th October, 1991. In the pilgrims' cemetery there is a shrine to San Amaro, another French saint who died in the service of pilgrims.

The **Monasterio de las Huelgas Reales** is a short walk away. It was founded by Alfonso VIII in 1187 for Cistercian nuns of royal or aristocratic lineage, under St. Bernard's rule, and the complex incorporates Romanesque and early Gothic elements as well as the transitional Gothic style of the Cistercians. The monastery church and the San Fernando Cloister are particularly fine. Several Castilian monarchs are buried here, including Alfonso VIII, the founder. Various kings were crowned here, Fernando III being the first, and knighthoods were bestowed by a seated statue of St. James with an articulated arm, which can still be seen today.

III. HISTORICAL PILGRIMS' ACCOUNTS

Aymeric Picaud: *'Then come... Atapuerca ('Altaporca') and the city of Burgos ('urbs Burgas')...'*

Künig von Vach: *'It is seven miles to Burgos ('Burgeß')... then you cross a fine bridge, and soon reach Burgos where there are 32 hospitals.'*

Arnold von Harff: *'Burgos ('Burgis') is a Spanish city under the sovereignty of the King of Castile. The city has a fine cathedral... Above the city the King has a fine castle on a hill, where there is a stream called 'Moneta' [this is perhaps an allusion to the Malatos bridge].'*

Laffi: *'Burgos is a really splendid, large city, and is the capital of Old Castile, where the King used to have his court. It is situated in a beautiful, wide plain, traversed by a delightful river which makes it pleasant and fertile. The cathedral is very ancient... it has a most splendid façade..; in short, it is a magnificent building...*
...at the edge of the city is the hospital, which is so huge that it seems a city in itself, and I do not believe there is another hospital which compares with it in the whole of Spain. It can accommodate two thousand people and great charity is shown to pilgrims and the food and the beds are excellent. There is a person here who accompanies a Franciscan friar..., who knows every language under the sun and who helps him run the hospital, which is called the Hospital del Rey ('Ospedale de Re').'

STAGE 14

BURGOS • CASTROJERIZ

Nuestra Señora del Manzano. Castrojeriz

BURGOS • VILLALBILLA •
TARDAJOS • RABÉ DE LAS CALZADAS •
HORNILLOS • HONTANAS •
CASTROJERIZ

PILGRIMS' REFUGES

At the villages of *Tardajos,* *Hornillos* and *Hontanas,* the traditional refuges made available thanks to the generosity of the local town councils are undergoing a series of welcome improvements.
Tardajos: ☎ (947) 45 11 89
Hontanas ☎ (947) 37 70 35

Castrojeriz: A well-equipped and well-run refuge with a large capacity. 32 bunk-beds.
☎ (947) 37 70 34 - 37 70 36

ACCOMMODATION

Villalbilla:
HSR* San Roque.
☎ (947) 29 12 29.
7 rooms. ♣♣

Castrojeriz:
HR** La Posada.
☎ (947) 94 76 10. ♣♣
HS** Mesón de Castrojeriz.
Cordón, 1.
☎ (947) 37 74 00.
7 rooms. ♣♣
Hostal El Mesón.
☎ (947) 37 74 00.
17 beds. ♣
Casa Antón.
☎ (947) 37 70 12.
15 beds. ♣

RESTAURANTS

Tardajos:
Fernando.

Castrojeriz:
Popular set meals available at:
Hostal el Mesón.
Casa Antonio.
Nisio.

CAMPSITES

Castrojeriz:
Camino de Santiago. 2nd Category. ☎ (947) 37 72 55

PETROL STATIONS

On the N-120: at Burgos; and at km 135; km 144. In Castrojeriz.

'Inde Alterdalia, inde Castrosorecia.' (Aymeric Picaud: *'Pilgrims' Guide')*

I. ROUTE

🚶 From the cathedral, make your way along calle Fernán González, calle del Emperador and calle Villalón (or alternatively via the river walk or other routes) to the 'Malatos' bridge over the river Arlanzón and thence to the N-620. On your left you pass the Monasterio de Las Huelgas Reales and, a bit further on, the Hospital del Rey. Shortly before the railway line, bear right off the road and take an asphalted track which runs through poplars and vegetable gardens alongside the Arlanzón, until you come to the Apeadero de la Alameda (a halt on the railway line), where you cross the rails. You then enter **Villalbilla,** and cross the railway line again on your way out of the village. Next, proceed about a kilometre along a dirt track which emerges onto the N-120 and immediately cross the Arlanzón over the Puente del Arzobispo and enter **Tardajos.**

In Tardajos, the pilgrims' route leaves the N-120, turning left into calle de Mediodía, which leads to the other side of the village. You then take an asphalted local road which crosses the little Urbel valley on the way to **Rabé de las Calzadas,** 2 kilometres away. Go through the village along the calle de Don Baldomero Pampliega, and make your way out again past the cemetery and the Ermita de Nuestra Señora del Monasterio on your left. The next 9 km take you along a rural road which slopes gently uphill through cornfields. On reaching the highest point of the plain, continue for a short distance, before beginning the sharp descent down the 'Cuesta Matamulos' (the 'Mulekiller Hill') towards the river Hormazuelas. Down in the valley, first cross the local road between Villanueva de Argaño and Estepar and then the river, before entering **Hornillos del Camino.** Pass through the village along the main street and keep going straight on along a farm track, towards Hontanas. Before long, you find yourself back on the high plain, where bare patches are interspersed with cultivated fields and pasture land. After about 6 hard, bleak kilometres you descend towards the valley of the arroyo Sambol (where there are ruins and a spring). From here, you regain the plateau and, shortly afterwards, cross the local road between Olmillos de Sasamón and Iglesias. Crossing a landscape characterized by great piles of stones known as 'majanos', cereals, pasture land and the odd patch of bushes, the path leads to Hontanas, which is hidden from view on the side of the plateau. On your way out of **Hontanas,** cross the little road that goes to Castrojeriz and continue parallel to it. Just before the ruins of the Monastery of San Antón, you turn onto the road which leads to **Castrojeriz,** about 9 km from Hontanas.

🚲 This stage is suitable for cyclists, although the 'Cuesta Matamulas' between Rabé and Hornillos might present some problems.

🚗 Milestones: N-120: km 120: Villalbilla; km 124: Tardajos; km 135: turning to Hornillos; km 144: from here, you are advised to leave the N-10 and continue along local roads to Hontanas and Castrojeriz.

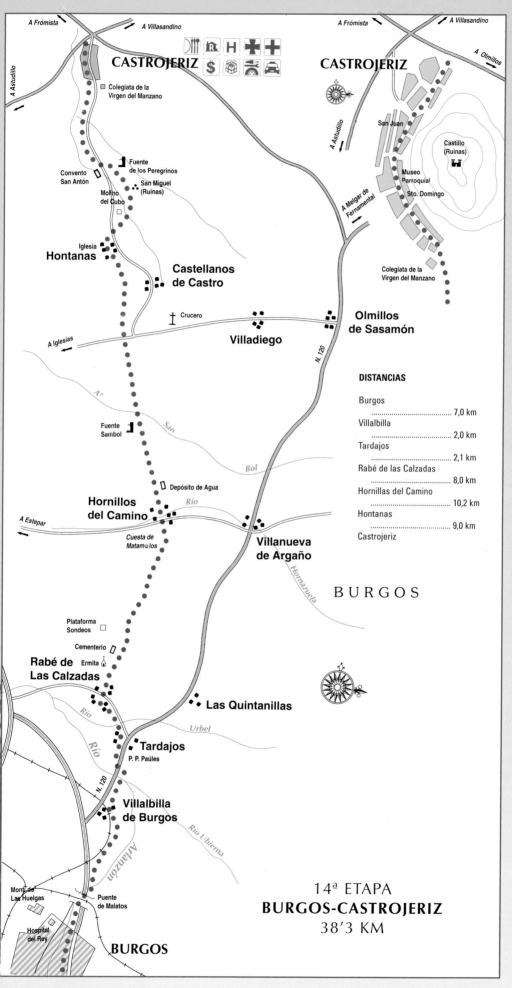

CASTROJERIZ

Colegiata de la
Virgen del Manzano

A Frómista   A Villasandino

A Astudillo

Convento
San Antón

Fuente
de los Peregrinos

San Miguel
(Ruinas)

Molino
del Cubo

Iglesia
Hontanas

**Castellanos
de Castro**

✝ Crucero

A Iglesias

Villadiego

Fuente
Sambol

Bol

Depósito de Agua

Río

**Hornillos
del Camino**

A Estepar

Cuesta de
Matamulos

Plataforma
Sondeos

Cementerio

**Rabé de
Las Calzadas**   Ermita

Las Quintanillas

Río

Urbel

Tardajos
P. P. Paúles

N. 120

Río

**Villalbilla
de Burgos**

Río Ubierna

Arlanzón

Mont. de
Las Huelgas   Puente
de Malatos

Hospital
del Rey

BURGOS

CASTROJERIZ

A Frómista   A Villasandino

A Olmillos

A Astudillo

San Juan

Castillo
(Ruinas)

Museo
Parroquial

Sto. Domingo

A Melgar de
Fernamental

Colegiata de la
Virgen del Manzano

**Olmillos
de Sasamón**

N. 120

DISTANCIAS

Burgos
.... 7,0 km
Villalbilla
.... 2,0 km
Tardajos
.... 2,1 km
Rabé de las Calzadas
.... 8,0 km
Hornillas del Camino
.... 10,2 km
Hontanas
.... 9,0 km
Castrojeriz

**Villanueva
de Argaño**

Hornazuela

BURGOS

14ª ETAPA
BURGOS-CASTROJERIZ
38'3 KM

*The pilgrims' route through
Hornillos del Camino*

*Ruins of the Monastery
of San Antón*

*St. James dressed as a pilgrim in
the Collegiate Church of Nuestra
Señora del Manzano*

II. HISTORY, ART, LEGENDS

The route out of Burgos across the 'Puente de Malatos' leads through the historic San Pedro district, the location of the Hospital del Emperador which was founded by Alfonso VI.

The parish church of **Villalbilla** is named after the Assumption. There are many churches of the Assumption along the pilgrims' way, although there is no particular link with the Santiago pilgrimage.

Just outside Tardajos, the **Puente del Arzobispo** leads across the river Arlanzón. Legend has it that this is where Alfonso VI had a serious fall from his horse whilst galloping in pursuit of enemy troops.

Tardajos is the old Roman town of *Augustobriga,* which was strategically located on the road which linked *Clunia* (Coruña del Conde, south of Burgos) and *Juliobriga* (near Reinosa, Cantabria). The parish church is dedicated to St. Mary, and the other village church, which is older, is dedicated to Mary Magdalene, a clear indication that this was once a place of hospitality to pilgrims. Furthermore, records show the existence of a pilgrims' hospital as early as the 12th century. The current Vincentian convent stands on the site of the former palace of the Archbishop of Burgos.

A popular refrain reflects how difficult it used to be to cross the swampy Urbel valley (which is now a pleasant two kilometre walk):

*'De Rabé a Tardajos,
no te faltarán trabajos;
de Tardajos a Rabé,
¡libera nos, Domine!'*

('From Rabé to Tardajos, you'll have your work cut out for you, from Tardajos to Rabé, spare us, Domine.')

Rabé de las Calzadas is named after the two roads ('Calzadas') which converged here: the Roman road between *Clunia* and *Juliobriga* and the *'Camino francés'*. The whole village has been very attractively restored. The village church is dedicated to St. Marina and retains a 13th-century portal.

Hornillos del Camino is one of the most unusual examples of a wayside village, consisting of a single street (the calle Real) which is the pilgrims' way itself. Alfonso VII donated the village to the Parisian monastery of St. Dionysius. Later, a Benedictine monastery under the auspices of the French monastery of Rocamadour was founded here and, until fairly recently, there was a figure of the Virgin of Rocamadour in the Gothic parish church of Santa María. Just outside the village are the ruins of the 'leprosarium' which was known as the Hospital de San Lázaro, in common with countless other hospitals for sick pilgrims along the pilgrims' way. Standing in the heart of the plain between Hornillos and Hontanas are the ruins of the former Convent of San Baudilio, which gives its name to the stream and the little valley in which it is situated: Samboal. The convent was a dependency of the Monastery of San Antón in Castrojeriz.

The hospitable village of **Hontanas** (from the Latin 'fontanas' meaning 'springs'), still retains a reminder of its Jacobean past: the 'Mesón de los franceses', which is the former pilgrims' hospital. The village church, dedicated to the Immaculate Conception, is a vast 14th-century construction.

Between Hontanas and Castrojeriz stand the impressive ruins of the 14th-century Monastery and Hospital of San Antón which, sadly, are very badly maintained. It belonged to the Antonine order, which has already been encountered in other places along the pilgrims' route, such as Villafranca Montes de Oca and the Alto de San Antón, near Nájera. The order was founded by a French noble named Guérin in St. Didier-de-la-Mothe (in the Dauphiné) in the year 1095, when the relics of the famous 3rd-century hermit, St. Anthony of Egypt, were transferred there from Constantinople. Before long, Pope Urban II authorised its statutes and the order spread throughout Europe and came to have as many as 369 hospitals. The order's main claim to fame was the ability to cure erysipelas or *'St. Anthony's fire'*, a contagious skin disease producing burning red blisters, which scourged Europe in the 10th and 11th centuries. Apart from his association with fire, St. Anthony was also patron saint of swineherds, which is interesting as the same disease affects pigs in the form of swine erysipelas, which the followers of St. Anthony also cured.

The Order's symbol was the τ *('tau'*, the 19th letter in the Greek alphabet), which appeared in blue on their black habits, and which they used in their healing ceremonies. Windows divided in sections reflecting the three strokes which make up the τ can still be seen in the ruins. Of the 14th-century buildings, a Gothic double arch (the Arco de San Antón) survives, under which the pilgrims' route still passes. To its left is the ogival church door, in the form of a splayed arch, adorned with six archivolts housing decaying statues. Opposite this is a wall with an alcove where the monks would leave provisions for pilgrims who arrived after the gates were locked.

The ground plan of **Castrojeriz** is reminiscent of that of the old quarter of Burgos, in that an extremely long main street runs along the south side of the hill, which is crowned by a castle. Few villages along the route have such an impressive number of monuments lining the pilgrims' way, even though some of them are partially ruined. Apart from its association with the Santiago pilgrimage, Castrojeriz was also important in the political life of the area. The 'Crónica Albeldense' refers to it as 'Castrum Sigerici', which takes its founding back as far as Visigothic times, if not further. During the 9th and 10th centuries, it was the scene of continuous fighting between Saracens and Christians, and in 1131 Alfonso VII finally won the town for Castile after routing the Aragonese garrison that defended it. On entering the town, you come to the former **Collegiate Church of Santa María del Manzano,** a superb building which was remodelled in the 18th century over the original 13th-century transitional Gothic structure. The 13th-century figure of Santa María del Manzano appears as 'Santa María d'Almaçan' in Alfonso X's 'Cántigas' (his

View of Castrojeriz and Santa María del Manzano

The ruined castle at Castrojeriz

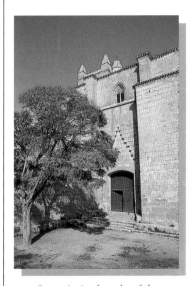

Castrojeriz: façade of the Church of San Juan

Castrojeriz: interior of the Church of San Juan

The Annunciation in the Church of San Juan, Castrojeriz

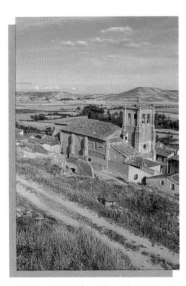

Castrojeriz: the Church of Santo Domingo

collection of 400 poems written in the Galician language). The great retable depicting the Annunciation is the work of the 18th-century artist, Rafael Mengs. The church also houses works by Carduccio and Bronzino, as well as a Gothic image of Nuestra Señora del Pópulo and a carving of St. James dressed as a pilgrim. In the Church of Santo Domingo there are six tapestries based on cartoons by Rubens, and a small museum displaying a variety of religious art from the 13th century onwards. The Church of San Juan is a magnificent Gothic construction with a spacious and elegant hall-church interior. The fine cloister is also worth a visit, although it is in a bad state of repair. In its heyday, Castrojeriz had other churches too, one of which was dedicated to St. James, and various monasteries, including one of the Franciscan order. Several hospitals lined the pilgrims' route as it passed through the village (there were four in Künig von Vach's day). The ruined castle is worth a visit, despite being somewhat difficult to reach, for the magnificent view of the surrounding countryside.

III. HISTORICAL PILGRIMS' ACCOUNTS

Aymeric Picaud: *'Then come... Tardajos ('Alterdalia'), Hornillos del Camino ('Furnellos') and Castrojeriz ('Castrosorecia').'*

Künig von Vach: *'Then you come to the Monastery of San Antón ('Sant Thonges kirch')... where they will give you as much bread as you need. Half a mile further on, you come to a castle called 'Fritz' (Castrojeriz); in German this signifies a long, sprawling town. There are four hospitals.'*

Arnold von Harff: *'It is two leagues from Burgos to the village of Tardajos ('Tardasius'), and a league from Tardajos to Rabé ('Rowe')... It is two leagues from Rabé to the village of Hornillos ('Hornilus'), and two leagues from Hornillos to the village of Hontanas ('Ala fontana'). It is two leagues from Hontanas to the 'villa franca' Castrojeriz ('Castresory'), a very long, sprawling town with a great castle on a hill. Pilgrims call it 'the long city'.'*

Laffi: *'...we came to the town of Hontanas ('Fontana'), which is hidden at the bottom of a little valley so you hardly see it... Wolves come in such numbers that if they see no fire they eat the livestock, night and day... we lingered a while and then set off towards Castrojeriz ('Castel Sorizz'), two leagues away. Our path was swarming with those cursed locusts, which not only eat the fruit and the grass, but also the vines and even the trees. It moves one to pity to see how people are dying of hunger, and the beasts too, as their pastures are devoured by these insects.'*

STAGE 15

CASTROJERIZ • FRÓMISTA

The triple-apsed east end of the Church of San Martín, Frómista

CASTROJERIZ • ITERO DE LA VEGA •
BOADILLA DEL CAMINO • FRÓMISTA

PILGRIMS' REFUGES

Itero del Castillo: Thanks to the efforts of Paolo G. Caucci von Saucken and his 'Confraternita di S. Jacopo di Compostella' from Perugia, the historical hermitage of San Nicolás has been restored and turned into a pilgrims' hostel.
☎ (947) 73 73 59

Itero de la Vega:
Recently refurbished refuge with capacity for about 15 guests.
☎ (979) 15 17 78

Boadilla: Old school buildings fitted out to sleep about 12 guests.

Frómista: Comfortable municipal hostel featuring good facilities and run by the parish priest.
☎ (979) 81 01 44

ACCOMMODATION
Frómista:
Hostería los Palmeros.
Plaza de San Telmo, 4.
☎ (979) 81 00 67.
Complete with restaurant
Hostal Camino de Santiago.
☎ (979) 81 00 53.
8 rooms. ♣
P. Marisa. ☎ (979) 81 00 23.
8 rooms. ♣

PETROL STATIONS
At Frómista.

'Inde Pons Fiterie; inde Frumesta.' (Aymeric Picaud: *'Pilgrims' Guide'*)

I. ROUTE

🚶 From **Castrojeriz** go down to the Castrillo de Cabezón road, and continue along it for a short distance after crossing the Villasillos road. Next, take a dirt track off to the left across the Odrilla valley, crossing the river over a small medieval bridge. You then continue straight on towards the foot of the small plateau which divides the Odrilla valley from the great basin of the Pisuerga river. The steep ascent up the 'cuesta de Mostelares' soon takes you to the top of the plateau, which you cross in a westerly direction, before starting a short, sharp descent which converges with a path known as the 'Collada del Camino Francés'. From here, you continue descending, very gradually, across an immense, cultivated plain, before reaching the 'Fuente del Piojo' (Fountain of the Louse) some 7 km away. A bit further on, the dirt track joins an asphalted path which, shortly afterwards. comes out onto the Castrillo de Cabezón road, which crosses the Pisuerga river —the border between the provinces of Burgos and Palencia— over the great Puente de Itero. On the Burgos side of the river, you pass the Ermita de San Nicolás on your left and the village of Itero del Castillo on your right. On the Palencia side, get onto a paved path which runs parallel to the river, which takes you to **Itero de la Vega.**
Leave Itero on an asphalted path which leads to the Melgar-Osorno road, which you cross, and then continue along a wide track across an open plain sown with cereals. Over to the left you will see Las Bodegas, before crossing the Pisuerga canal a bit further on. After some 2 km, the route rises gently uphill, running between some low hills on the right and the Alto del Paso Largo on the left. **Boadilla del Camino** is 3 km away, and you should head north through the village until you come to a fork in the road by a raised irrigation channel. Take the left fork, which soon meets the Canal de Castilla, and continue parallel along the left-hand bank of the canal as far as **Frómista,** which is 5 km at the most from Boadilla. Cross the canal by a lock and enter Frómista through a tunnel on the Astudillo road, which goes underneath the railway line.

🚲 The pedestrian route presents one major obstacle for cyclists, namely the 'cuesta de Mostelares' and the subsequent descent. Consequently, it is advisable to cover the Castrojeriz-Itero stretch (some 12 km) along the Castrillo de Cabezón road.

🚗 Milestones: Local road: Castrojeriz-Castrillo: 3 km; Castrillo-Itero: 9 km; Itero-Boadilla: 7 km; Boadilla-Frómista: 6 km.

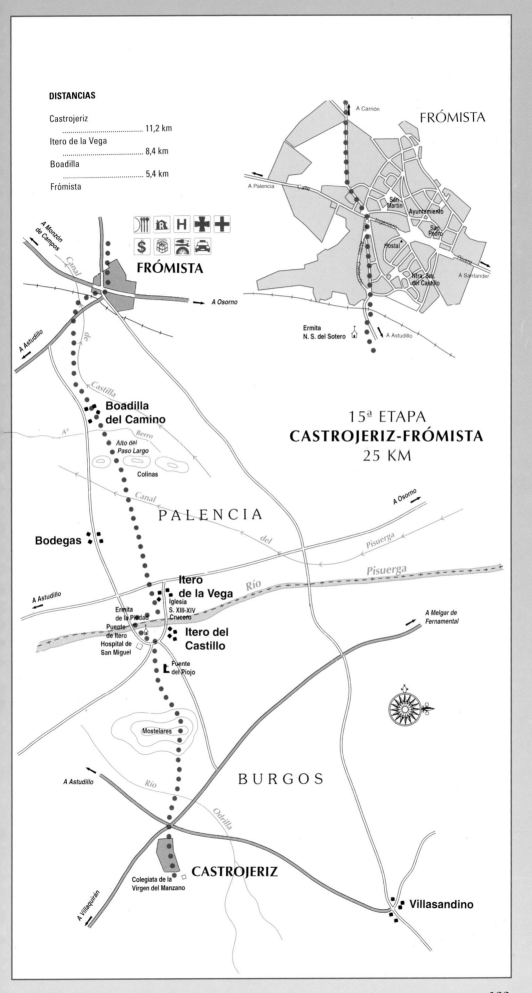

DISTANCIAS

Castrojeriz
.... 11,2 km
Itero de la Vega
.... 8,4 km
Boadilla
.... 5,4 km
Frómista

FRÓMISTA

A Carrión

A Palencia

San Martín

Ayuntamiento

San Pedro

Hostal

Ntra. Sra. del Castillo

A Santander

A Astudillo

Ermita N. S. del Sotero

A Monzón de Campos

Canal

FRÓMISTA

A Osorno

A Astudillo

Castilla

Boadilla del Camino

Aº Berro

Alto del Paso Largo

Colinas

Canal

PALENCIA

del

A Osorno

Pisuerga

Pisuerga

Bodegas

Itero de la Vega

Río

A Astudillo

Iglesia S. XIII-XIV Crucero

A Melgar de Fernamental

Ermita de la Piedad

Puente de Itero

Hospital de San Miguel

Itero del Castillo

Puente del Piojo

15ª ETAPA
CASTROJERIZ-FRÓMISTA
25 KM

Mostelares

BURGOS

A Astudillo

Río

Odrilla

CASTROJERIZ

Colegiata de la Virgen del Manzano

A Villaquirán

Villasandino

*The Puente de Itero
over the Pisuerga*

*Gothic village cross at Boadilla
del Camino*

*14th-century baptismal font in
the parish church at Boadilla
del Camino*

II. HISTORY, ART AND LEGENDS

Towards the end of the 15th century, Künig von Vach refers to three bridges on the stretch between Castrojeriz and Carrión de los Condes, and it is very probable that the first of these bridges is the one which crosses the little Odrilla river. It is so low that you can easily miss it, but it is a lovely Romanesque construction.

The second bridge in question, however, is very well-known: the **Puente de Itero** over the Pisuerga river, which was built on the orders of Alfonso VI, whose positive contribution to the pilgrims' way has been apparent since Nájera. It is a majestic eleven-arched Romanesque bridge, although it has been extensively restored. Just in front of the bridge, on the Burgos side of the river, are the ruins of the Ermita de San Nicolás, which is all that remains of the church of the former 12th-century pilgrims' hospital. The Confraternity of St. James of Perugia is lobbying hard to get it turned back into a pilgrims' refuge. To the left of the pilgrims' route is **Itero del Castillo,** a riverside stronghold which defended the border between the County of Castile and the Kingdom of León, and whose position as a frontier village is reflected in its name, which is a derivative of the Spanish word 'hito', meaning 'boundary stone'. The 17th-century pilgrim, Laffi, refers to this bridge as 'Ponte della Mulla', which might be a variant of the Basque word 'muga', signifying a boundary stone, or 'muria', which refers to a heap of stones, and by extension, a limit or boundary. This is also the point at which you enter the region known as **Tierra de Campos,** the ancient *'Campi Gothorum'* or *'Fields of the Goths'* which are mentioned in the *'Crónica Albeldense'*. This is one of the most unvarying and typical stretches of the pilgrims' way. Picaud refers to it as 'Castile and Campos', and sums it up in chapter VII of his 'Pilgrims' Guide' thus:

'It is a land full of treasures, of gold and silver, rich in wool and strong horses, and abounding in bread, wine, meat, fish, milk and honey. However, there are few trees...'

Itero de la Vega stands on the right-hand bank of the Pisuerga, and its name also denotes its position as a frontier village, while highlighting its agricultural background ('vega' means 'fertile valley'), in contrast to the other Itero with its fortified 'castillo'. To the left of the path, just outside the village, you pass the 13th-century Ermita de la Piedad, which has a lovely figure of St. James the pilgrim. The village church of San Pedro, which was built in the 16th century over an earlier one, still retains a 13th-century Gothic portal.

In **Boadilla del Camino** the *Parish Church of the Assumption* is worth a visit. This triple-aisled, 16th-century church houses some fine works of art, including a 16th-century high altarpiece, another retable with beautiful Renaissance panels and a splendid 14th-century Gothic baptismal font. Standing behind the church is a marvellous late Gothic *village cross* which dates from the 15th century and is profusely decorated with, among other ornamentation, the typical pilgrims' scallop shells. In Castile, this type of stone column was known as a 'rollo' and was a symbol of jurisdictional authority and the scene of both the trial and the execution.

On the way to Frómista, the pilgrims' route runs parallel to the **Canal de Castilla** for a few kilometres. This important feat of 18th-century engineering was the fruit of the enlightened policies of the Marqués de la Ensenada, and had a triple function: the transport of cereals, irrigation and grinding corn.

View of Frómista

Frómista is the final halt at the end of the sixth stage in Picaud's 'Pilgrims' Guide'. It was first a settlement of the Vacceos, a Celtic tribe, and later became a Roman town. The abundance of wheat and the similarity of its Latin name, 'Frumesta', with the Latin word 'frumentum' ('wheat'), has inspired the theory that its name is derived from this Latin noun. However, it is more likely that the name Frómista is derived from a Visigothic proper noun, a period during which the town enjoyed great importance. The town was completely destroyed after the Moorish invasion in the 8th century, and spent a century in 'no man's land'. It was resettled in the 10th century, and in 1066, Doña Mayor, Countess of Castile and wife of King Sancho III 'the Great' (perhaps the same lady who had the bridge at Puente la Reina built), founded a Benedictine monastery which later, in the 12th century, became a dependency of the Monastery of San Zoilo at Carrión de los Condes. The famous **Church of San Martín** is the only surviving part of the monastery complex and marks a climax in the development of the European Romanesque style along the pilgrims' route. Architecturally, it is closely related to its immediate predecessor, Jaca cathedral, as well as to the Basílica de San Isidoro at León and the cathedral at Santiago de Compostela itself. Its triple-apsed east end is attached to a three-aisled nave, and an octagonal dome on squinches rises out of the crossing, while the west façade is framed by a pair of circular stair turrets. The church's ornamentation is outstanding: the interior is decorated with carved capitals, while outside there is an amazing series of 315 beautiful carved corbels, each one different, running right around the eaves. Regrettably, the only surviving part of its original furnishings is a fine 13th-century transitional Gothic Christ. The church was massively over-restored at the end of the 19th century but now, a century later, the traces of this are wearing off.

The Church of San Martín at Frómista

Standing on a small hill outside Frómista, from where there is a good view of the town, is the *Ermita de Santiago,* or *del Otero* (knoll), in which a 12th-century Romanesque figure of the Virgen del Otero is enshrined. The Gothic *Church of San Pedro* houses a 16th-century figure of St. James the pilgrim, as well as several paintings which are attributed to Mengs or to Ribera. The *Church of Santa María del Castillo,* which is named after the fortifications on which it was built, boasts a lovely retable with panels attributed to the great Castilian painter, Fernando Gallego.

Frómista was once a major halt on the pilgrims' route (to the extent that it was known as 'Frómista del Camino'), and there are surviving records of two pilgrims' hospitals:

Interior of the Church of San Martín, Frómista

Frómista: capital inside the Church of San Martín

the Hospital de Santiago and the Hospital de Palmeros (now a restaurant). 'Palmeros' (Palmers) were pilgrims who went to Jerusalem, their symbol being a palm leaf, and the name later came to be applied to pilgrims in general. The place known today as the 'Huerto del Francés' or 'Huerto del Romero' is probably the site of the former pilgrims' cemetery. The village square is presided over by a statue of the Dominican friar, Pedro González Telmo, who was born in Frómista in 1190. He became San Telmo, or St. Elmo, the patron saint of sailors and of the Diocese of Tuy in Galicia, in whose cathedral he is buried, and the famous phenomenon 'St. Elmo's Fire' is named after him.

The Church of San Pedro at Frómista

Frómista: statue of St. Elmo

III. HISTORICAL PILGRIMS' ACCOUNTS

Aymeric Picaud: *'Tierra de Campos ('Campos')... is a land full of treasures, of gold and silver, rich in wool and strong horses, and abounding in bread, wine, meat, fish, milk and honey. However, there are few trees and it is full of evil, bad men.'*
'Then you come to Puente de Itero ('Pons Fiterie') and Frómista ('Frumesta').'

Künig von Vach: *'In a village two miles away there is a bridge... And another mile further on you come to a hospital built next to a bridge.'*

Arnold von Harff: *'It is two leagues from Castrojeriz to Puente de Itero ('Ponte fittir'). You cross a wide river over a stone bridge... It is a league from Boadilla ('Bobadilia') to the town of Frómista ('Fromeste'). All towns in Spain are surrounded by whitewashed walls and the inns are bad.'*

Laffi: *'... we crossed over a great bridge and climbed up a high mountain, and then reached a wide, open plain which was absolutely barren, in the middle of which we crossed a great bridge known as the 'Ponte della Mulla'. After crossing it... under a beating sun and plagued by cursed locusts we reached (with God's help) 'Formezza' (Frómista), a place which they call 'Formeste'... It is so large as to be almost a city, but it is suffering great privation as, due to the locusts, there has been no wheat, no wine, no fruit: nothing. In short, it is heartbreaking to see these places so devastated by these creatures. At night, the townsfolk come out into the streets armed with clubs and kill the locusts which gather under the walls during the day... covering the walls so thickly that they appear painted black. At night, they fall to the ground with cold and there they are killed, as otherwise it would be necessary to abandon the villages and even the cities. Here, in the Cathedral, we witnessed a beautiful miracle of the Holy Sacrament.'*

STAGE 16

FRÓMISTA • CARRIÓN

Christ in Majesty, the Church of Santiago at Carrión de los Condes

FRÓMISTA • POBLACIÓN DE CAMPOS •
REVENGA • VILLARMENTERO •
VILLOVIECO • VILLARMENTERO •
VILLALCÁZAR DE SIRGA •
CARRIÓN DE LOS CONDES

PILGRIMS' REFUGES

Población de Campos: Medium capacity refuge run by the town council.
☎ (979) 81 01 51 - 81 01 73

Villalcázar de Sirga:
Good municipal refuge at the *Casa del Peregrino.*
☎ (979) 88 80 13 - 88 80 41

Carrión de los Condes:
Here there is a good refuge that is very well run by the priest of the parish church of *Santa María del Camino.* It has a reasonable capacity and is well equipped. A comfortable, spacious refuge for pilgrims has also been set up in a building attached to the luxury *Hospedería de San Zoilo.*
☎ (979) 88 00 72

ACCOMMODATION
Carrión de los Condes:
HS* La Corte.
Santa María, 34. ☎ (979) 88 01 38
16 rooms. ♣
Hospedería de San Zoilo.
Monasterio de San Zoilo.
☎ (979) 88 00 50
Hotel Carmen.
☎ (979) 88 02 52.
6 rooms. ♣
Hotel Estefanía.
☎ (979) 88 01 60.
10 rooms. ♣
Hotel El Resbalón.
☎ (979) 88 04 33.
6 rooms. ♣

CAMPSITES
Carrión de los Condes:
El Edén. 2nd Category.
☎ (979) 88 01 85

RESTAURANTS
Carrión de los Condes:
Mesón Pisarosas. Piña Blasco, 27.
☎ (979) 88 00 58. Home cooking.
Open only during the winter.
Inés. Abel. El Edén. Mikus. El Resbalón.

Villalcázar de Sirga:
Mesón Villasirga.
Plaza Mayor, s/n.
☎ (979) 88 00 58. Home cooking and game specialities.

PETROL STATIONS
At Carrión.

'Inde Karrionus.' (Aymeric Picaud: 'Pilgrims' Guide')

I. ROUTE

🚶🚶 Upon leaving **Frómista,** the pilgrims' route enters the C-980, which forms a straight line between Frómista and Carrión de los Condes. Continue along here for about 3 km, until you come to Población de Campos which is off to the right. Before entering the village, make a small detour to the left to visit the Ermita de San Miguel, situated in a lush meadow in the shade of a poplar grove. From here, cross back over the C-980 and enter **Población de Campos,** and make your way through the centre of the village along the pilgrims' route, the aptly named 'Calle Francesa', passing the Ermita del Socorro on the left. On leaving the village there are two alternative routes to choose between:
a) The first possibility is to cross the river Ucieza and come out onto the C-980, which takes you first to **Revenga** and then to **Villarmentero.**
b) Alternatively, you can take a wide, paved path which runs along the right-hand bank of the river Ucieza, which takes you to **Villovieco.** On leaving the village, cross over to the left-hand bank of the river and continue alongside it for about a kilometre, after which you can enter **Villarmentero,** if you wish, and meet up with alternative route (a).
From Villarmentero, there is another choice of routes:
a) One alternative is to continue for about 7 km along the C-980, as far as **Villalcázar de Sirga.**
b) Otherwise, you should return to the river and continue alongside the left-hand bank along a willow and poplar-lined riverside path, typical of the Tierra de Campos area. Further downriver you come to the Ermita de la Virgen del Río, from where you bear left off the path onto the Arconada road, which brings you into **Villalcázar de Sirga.**
The most direct route to cover the 5 km from Villalcázar de Sirga (also known as Villasirga) to **Carrión de los Condes** is along the C-980, bearing left off it when you reach Carrión. The route through Carrión takes you past the Convent of the Order of St. Clare (Clarisas) and, once inside the walls, past the Church of Santa María and the Church of Santiago.

🚲 In common with most of the Castilian stages, the level ground allows cyclists to follow the pedestrian route with no difficulty.

🚗 Milestones: C-980: km 15.4: Población de Campos; km 11.3: Revenga de Campos, turning to Villovieco; km 10: Villarmentero de Campos; km 5.5: Villalcázar de Sirga; km 1: Carrión de los Condes.

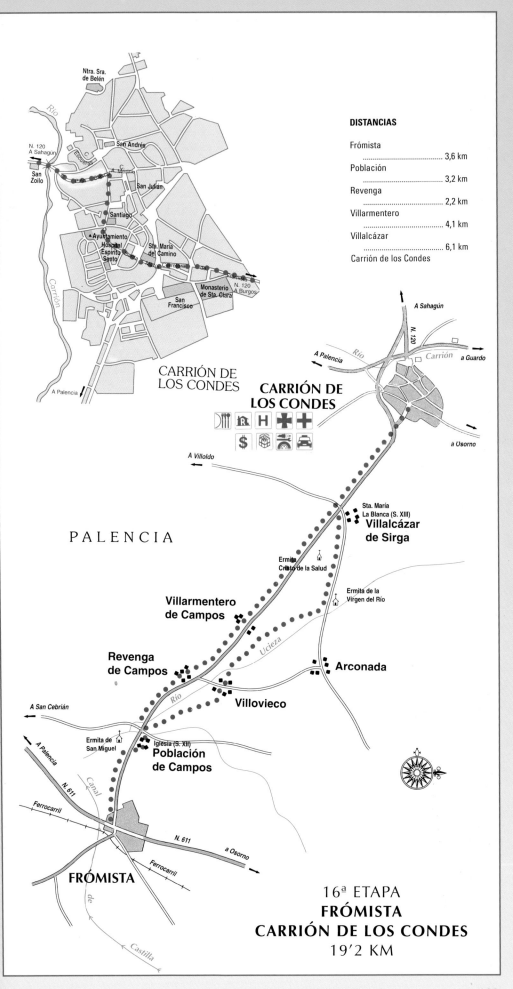

Ntra. Sra.
de Belén

Río

N. 120
A Sahagún

San Andrés

San Zoilo

A Merino

San Julián

Santiago

Ayuntamiento
Hospital
Espíritu
Santo

Sta. María
del Camino

Carretera

Monasterio
de Sta. Clara

N. 120
A Burgos

San
Francisco

Carrión

A Palencia

CARRIÓN DE
LOS CONDES

**CARRIÓN DE
LOS CONDES**

A Sahagún

N. 120

Río

A Palencia

Carrión

a Guardo

a Usorno

A Villoldo

PALENCIA

Sta. María
La Blanca (S. XIII)
**Villalcázar
de Sirga**

Ermita
Cristo de la Salud

Ermita de la
Vírgen del Río

**Villarmentero
de Campos**

Ucieza

**Revenga
de Campos**

Arconada

Río

A San Cebrián

Villovieco

Ermita de
San Miguel

Iglesia (S. XII)
**Población
de Campos**

A Palencia

N. 611

Canal

Ferrocarril

N. 611

a Osorno

Ferrocarril

FRÓMISTA

de

Castilla

**16ª ETAPA
FRÓMISTA
CARRIÓN DE LOS CONDES
19'2 KM**

Población de Campos: the Ermita de San Miguel

View of Villalcázar de Sirga

The Church of Santa María la Blanca at Villalcázar de Sirga

II. HISTORY, ART AND LEGENDS

Standing in the shade of a poplar grove just outside **Población de Campos** is the little Ermita de San Miguel, a 13th-century transitional Romanesque building. The parish church in Población de los Campos is dedicated to Mary Magdalene, who is strongly associated with the pilgrims' way and hospitality to pilgrims. There are records here of a former hospital of the Knights of St. John, but no traces remain of it. The 'Calle Francesa' (one of so many on the way to Santiago) is, of course, the pilgrims' way itself. The little Romanesque Ermita de la Virgen del Socorro, which you pass on the left, houses a Romanesque image of its namesake. Practically on a level with **Revenga de Campos** (whose baroque parish church is dedicated to St. Lawrence), those following the river path will come to the village of **Villovieco.** Its founder's name, Oveco, harks back to the resettlement of this area in the 10th and 11th centuries. The high altarpiece in the Parish Church of Santa María is decorated with several Jacobean motifs. Not far from here is a place called Arconada, where the Count of Carrión, Don Gómez, built a monastery and pilgrims' hospital in honour of Saints Facundo, Primitivo and Christopher. Near the ruins there are traces of what was possibly once the course of the 'Camino Francés'.

The village of **Villarmentero** is named after its resettler, who would have been one of several 'Armentarius' who appear in the local medieval records. Its parish church is dedicated to St. Martin of Tours, the cult of whom is strongly linked with the Santiago pilgrimage, as has already been seen. Its most outstanding features are the 16th-century Mudéjar *artesonado* ceiling and the plateresque high altarpiece.

A simple, archaic cross which stands a little way off the road, in the middle of the countryside, is almost certainly a relic of an earlier course of the pilgrims' way which got swallowed up in the local system of land redistribution.

There are few documented Templar institutions along the pilgrims' way, but one of them is to be found at **Villalcázar de Sirga** (commonly abbreviated to 'Villasirga'), with the clear vocation of protecting the pilgrims' route. All that remains of the magnificent Templar installations is the impressive 13th-century *Church of Santa María la Blanca.* This transitional Romanesque construction is built in the shape of a Latin cross, with a three-aisled, ribbed-vaulted nave and a double crossing, and has an enormously tall porch framing a richly carved portal. Inside, in the railed Capilla de Santiago, the famous seated stone image of the *Virgen Blanca* (White Virgin) is venerated, to whom the poet-king Alfonso X 'the Wise' attributes as many as twelve miracles in his collection of poems known as the 'Cántigas'. The Virgin is supposed to have cured several pilgrims on their way through Villasirga as they were returning uncured from Santiago de Compostela. The influence of the great Pedro Berruguete is evident in the polychrome reliefs and the

Interior of the Church of Santa María la Blanca, Villalcázar de Sirga

panels of the high altarpiece. Apart from the Virgen Blanca, the Capilla de Santiago also houses the beautiful Gothic tombs of the fifth son of Fernando III 'the Holy', the Infante Don Felipe (who was closely connected with the Templar order) and of his wife, Doña Leonor Ruiz de Castro. The carved reliefs showing different mourning and burial scenes, and the sumptuous attire of the couple, are especially evocative. The chapel is presided over by a retable depicting St. James and a 16th-century figure of him in pilgrim's dress.

The big solid house opposite the church emblazoned with the coat of arms of the Order of St. James, was called, until recently, the 'Casa de los Peregrinos'.

Carrión de los Condes is situated near the Celto-Roman settlement of 'Lacobriga', and was the most important town in the area known as 'inter Zeiam et Pisoracam flumen' ('between the rivers Cea and Pisuerga') and its most solid bastion during the Reconquest. With the apogee of Castile, Carrión became the object of the disputes between Castile and León. This was the seat of the Beni-Gómez, a noble Leonese family who are the Counts of Carrión that the pro-Castilian 12th-century epic poem 'El Cantar del Mio Cid' presents (with no real historical basis) as ridiculous anti-heroes, the unworthy sons-in-law of the great Castilian hero, El Cid. (The legend has it that they married the hero's daughters, took their riches and then beat, stripped and abandoned them on the way back to Carrión.) Fact or fiction, the fact of the matter is that the great Spanish medieval epic poem would be inconceivable without Carrión and its Counts. With a population of 10 000 Carrión de los Condes became, along with Sahagún, the great commercial and political centre of the 'Tierra de Campos'. In the 11th century, Count Gómez Díaz built a monastery over the relics of the Cordovan martyr, San Zoilo, which in the 12th century, came under the influence of Cluny via the Monastery of Sahagún on which it depended. After Sahagún, Carrión de los Condes was the most important pilgrims' centre in the area, and came to have at least seven recorded hospitals. Carrión is also famous for having been the birthplace of two illustrious figures in Spanish literature: Dom Sem Tob, author of a work called 'Consejos e documentos' around the year 1355, and the poet Don Iñigo López de Mendoza, the Marques of Santillana (1398-1458).

On entering Carrión you pass the 13th-century *Convent of Santa Clara* which is supposed to have given shelter to St. Francis of Assisi during his pilgrimage to Santiago. Amongst the magnificent exhibits in its well-endowed museum (which is well worth a visit) is a beautiful piece entitled 'Piedad' (Piety) by the brilliant 17th-century sculptor, Gregorio Fernández.

The 12th-century Romanesque church of Santa María del Camino stands beside the walls. Its south portal, flanked by two flying buttresses and framed by a porch, is carved with a variety of figures, unfortunately rather worn, which are thought to represent the miracle whereby Carrión was released from the shameful tribute of a hundred virgins imposed on Christian Spain from

Villalcázar de Sirga: statue of Santa María la Blanca

Church of Santa María la Blanca at Villalcázar de Sirga: the tomb of Don Felipe

The Church of Santa María del Camino at Carrión de los Condes

*Detail of the portal
of the Church of Santiago,
Carrión de los Condes*

*Portal of the Church of Santiago,
Carrión de los Condes*

*Carrión de los Condes:
the cloisters of the Monastery
of San Zoilo*

*Carrión de los Condes:
the tombs of the princes
in the Monastery of San Zoilo*

the times of King Mauregato. Inside the church a Romanesque figure of Santa María del Camino, the author of the miracle, is enshrined.

The Church of Santiago, which was recently somewhat controversially restored, was sacked and burned at the beginning of the 19th century by Napoleon's troops. The only surviving part is the impressive 12th-century west façade, with a frieze over the portal showing high relief figures of the Disciples flanked by symbols of the Evangelists, and dominated by a sublime Christ in Majesty. The archivolt is carved with 24 figures representing different trades, skills, games and battle scenes.

The above-mentioned Benedictine-Cluniac Monastery of San Zoilo stands outside the walls, across the medieval bridge on the opposite bank of the river Carrión. Its Renaissance cloister, designed by Juan de Badajoz in 1537, is one of the most elegant and richly-carved examples in Europe. In a side chapel are the tombs of the 'literary' Counts of Carrión.

Also in Carrión de los Condes are the churches of Nuestra Señora de Belén, of San Julián (protector of pilgrims) and of San Francisco, who is also linked to the Santiago pilgrimage.

III. HISTORICAL PILGRIMS' ACCOUNTS

Aymeric Picaud: *'Then comes Carrión ('Karrionus') which is a busy and industrious city rich in bread, wine and meat and all kinds of things.'*

Künig von Vach: *'A mile further on you come to a city called Carrión ('Garrion') with a fine bridge; there, in two convents, bread and wine are provided.'*

Arnold von Harff: *'It is a league from Frómista to Población ('Polacioin'), a 'villa franca' and another league from Población to Revenga ('Reuenga'), a large village. It is a league from Revenga to Villalcázar de Sirga ('Villa Schirga'), and two leagues from Villasirga to the city of Carrión ('Hokarioin').'*

Laffi: *'... we continued our journey to Carrión ('Carion'), a distance of four leagues. This is an ordinary, fairly prosperous town with several friaries, in particular, one of the Franciscan order. On our way out of Carrión we came to a large monastery where pilgrims are given a ration of bread and wine.'*

STAGE 17

CARRIÓN • SAHAGÚN

The Church of San Tirso, Sahagún

CARRIÓN •
CALZADILLA DE LA CUEZA • LEDIGOS •
TERRADILLOS DE LOS TEMPLARIOS •
MORATINOS •
SAN NICOLÁS DEL REAL CAMINO • SAHAGÚN

PILGRIMS' REFUGES

Calzadilla: Good refuge, recently refurbished.
Ledigos: Very basic facilities offered by the town council.
Terradillos: Parish-owned premises, no water.
Sahagún: A splendid, almost sumptuous refuge has been set up in the restored Church of La Trinidad. Featuring all the necessary facilities and having a capacity for 64 guests, this refuge constitutes a true reflection of the historical tradition and the present-day importance of Sahagún on the Pilgrims' Route to Santiago. ☎ (987) 78 00 01

ACCOMMODATION

Calzadilla de la Cueza:
Hotel Camino Real.
☎ (979) 88 31 87. 7 rooms. ♣.
Meals also available.

Sahagún:
HS** Alfonso VI. Antonio Nicolás, 6. ☎ (987) 78 11 44.
10 rooms. ♣
HS** La Codorniz. Arco, s/n.
☎ (987) 78 02 76. 26 rooms. ♣
HS* Hospedería MM.
Benedictinas. Dres. Bermejo y Calderón, 8.
☎ (987) 78 00 78.
24 rooms. ♣
HS* Pacho. Avenida Constitución, 86. ☎ (987) 78 07 75.
8 rooms. ♣
La Asturiana. Pza. de Lesmes Franco, 2. ☎ (987) 78 00 73.
10 beds. ♣. Meals also available.

San Pedro de Las Dueñas:
HS* Hospedería MM. Benedictinas.
☎ (987) 78 01 50. 15 rooms. ♣

CAMPSITES

Sahagún:
Pedro Ponce. 2nd Category.
☎ (987) 78 11 12

RESTAURANTS

Sahagún:
El Camino de Santiago.
Ctra. Palencia, km 1.
☎ (987) 78 01 77. Typical cuisine.
Luis. Plaza Mayor.
☎ (987) 78 10 85. Popular cuisine.
La Codorniz. Constitución, 93.
☎ (987) 78 02 76. Traditional cuisine.
Asador El Ruedo.

PETROL STATIONS

On the N-120: on the way out of Carrión; at km 214, in Cervatos de la Cueza; and at km 237, in Sahagún.

'Inde est Sanctus Facundus.' (Aymeric Picaud: 'Pilgrims' Guide')

I. ROUTE

[This is an extraordinarily long stage, which in practice can be divided in two parts. However, it is considered that the historical and artistic contents are best covered as one single stage.]

🚶🚶 Take the N-120 out of **Carrión** and cross the river, passing the Monastery of San Zoilo on the left. At the junction with the C-615 to Riaño, take an asphalted path, known as the 'Carretera del Indiano', which leads the 4 km to the ruins of the famous Abbey of Benevívere, which you pass. A bit further on, the asphalted path bends sharply, but the pilgrims' route carries straight on along a paved path (the old Roman road) to Calzadilla de la Cueza (approximately 13 km). One of the first landmarks along this paved path is the 'Fuente del Hospitalejo', which is on the right under some poplars. After about 4 km, cross the road that goes to Bustillo del Páramo and then cross, successively, three riverbeds (the 'Pozoamargo', the 'Rioseco' and the 'Valdemienzo') after which the church spire at **Calzadilla de la Cueza** comes into view. Take the N-120 out of Calzadilla as far as **Ledigos** (5 km), after which you bear left off it onto the local road to Población de Arroyo. Leave the road after about 200 metres and take a dirt track to **Terradillos de los Templarios.** Leave Terradillos on a path which runs parallel to the left of the N-120 as far as the Villada road, which you take for a short distance before getting onto another path that goes to San Nicolás del Real Camino, passing through **Moratinos** on the way. On the way out of **San Nicolás,** you cross the river Sequillo (no bridge) and, shortly afterwards, the provincial border between Palencia and León, where you return to the N-120 and continue along it for about 2 km. At km 235.1, there is a drinking fountain about 100 metres to the right of the road. Continuing along the N-120, just after the river Valderaduey, you turn right onto a path which takes you upriver to the Ermita de la Virgen del Puente, situated in a pretty grove of poplars, from where Sahagún is visible up ahead. A footpath takes you through a tunnel under the road and the railway line and leads into the San Martín district of **Sahagún.**

🚲 This stage is suitable on the whole for bicycles, with the exception of the 13-kilometre stretch between Benevívere and Calzadilla de la Cueza, which is very hard going on a bicycle due to the rough, loose stone surface.

🚗 Milestones: N-120 km 198: Carrión; km 217: Calzadilla de la Cueza; km 219: ruins of Santa María de las Tiendas; km 223: Ledigos; km 227: Terradillos de Templarios; km 229.5: Moratinos; km 231.5: San Nicolás del Real Camino; km 235.5: turning to the Ermita de la Virgen del Puente; km 237: Sahagún.

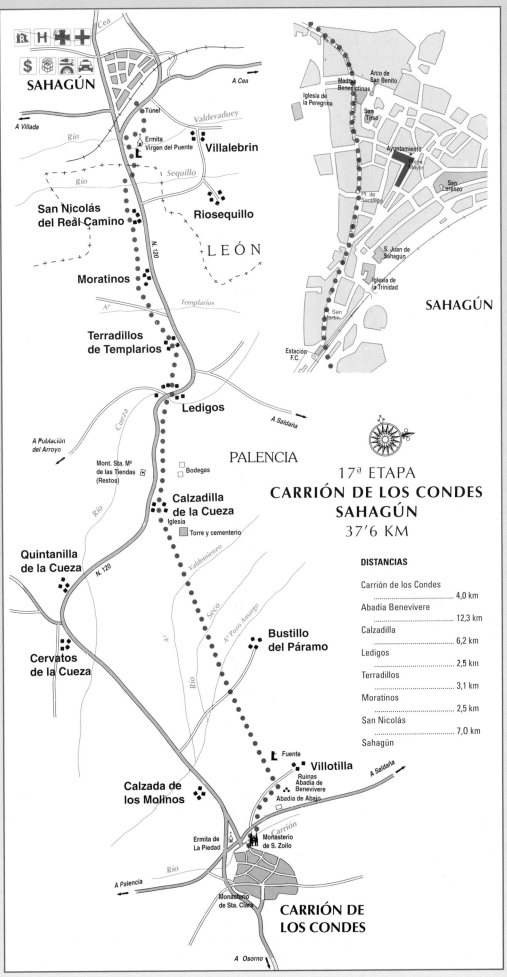

SAHAGÚN

A Cea →

A Villada →

Túnel

Valderaduey

Río

Ermita Virgen del Puente

Villalebrin

Sequillo

Río

San Nicolás del Real Camino

Riosequillo

LEÓN

Moratinos

N. 120

Aº

Templarios

Terradillos de Templarios

Ledigos

A Saldaña →

A Población del Arroyo →

Cueza

PALENCIA

Mont. Sta. Mª de las Tiendas (Restos)

□ Bodegas

Calzadilla de la Cueza

Iglesia

Torre y cementerio

Quintanilla de la Cueza

N. 120

Río

Valdemienzo

Seco

Aº

Cervatos de la Cueza

Aº

Río

Aº Pozo Amargo

Bustillo del Páramo

Fuente

Villotilla

Ruinas Abadía de Benevivere

Abadía de Abajo

A Saldaña →

Calzada de los Molinos

Carrión

Río

Ermita de La Piedad

Monasterio de S. Zoilo

A Palencia →

Monasterio de Sta. Clara

CARRIÓN DE LOS CONDES

A Osorno →

Arco de San Benito

Madres Benedictinas

Iglesia de la Peregrina

San Tirso

Ayuntamiento

Plaza Mayor

Pl. de Santiago

San Lorenzo

S. Juan de Sahagún

Iglesia de la Trinidad

SAHAGÚN

S. San Martín

Estación F.C.

17ª ETAPA

CARRIÓN DE LOS CONDES

SAHAGÚN

37'6 KM

DISTANCIAS

Carrión de los Condes
.... 4,0 km
Abadía Benevívere
.... 12,3 km
Calzadilla
.... 6,2 km
Ledigos
.... 2,5 km
Terradillos
.... 3,1 km
Moratinos
.... 2,5 km
San Nicolás
.... 7,0 km
Sahagún

Old road near Calzadilla de la Cueza

The Ermita de Nuestra Señora del Puente, near Sahagún

Convent of La Peregrina, Sahagún

II. HISTORY, ART AND LEGENDS

Only a few modest remains survive of the **Abbey of Santa María de Benevívere,** which was founded in 1065 and run by a community of Augustinian canons. Not surprisingly, given its location, it housed a pilgrims' hospital and the nearby 'Fuente del Hospitalejo' is a reminder of this. Between here and Calzadilla de la Cueza there is a good surviving stretch of the old Roman road (the *'via Traiana'* from Bordeaux to Astorga), which the pilgrims' way follows quite frequently. Not far away, in **Quintanilla de la Cueza,** the remains of a luxurious Roman villa have been found. Traces of a Roman settlement have also appeared in **Calzadilla de la Cueza,** and presumably the Roman villa mentioned above was linked to it. The village church of San Martín houses a lovely 16th-century retable which came from the former Monastery of Santa María de las Tiendas, a great abbey and pilgrims' hospital under the auspices of the Knights of the Order of St. James, which Laffi calls *'L'Ospitale del Gran Cavaliere'*. The scant remains of the monastery which can be seen to the left of the road make it hard to imagine its glorious past.

In the village church of **Ledigos,** which is dedicated to St. James the Apostle, there is a figure of the saint in pilgrims' dress. The name **Terradillos de los Templarios** suggests the presence of the Knights Templar in this humble backwater, although there are no records or surviving evidence to confirm this. The village church of San Pedro houses an interesting 13th-century crucifix.

Moratinos was resettled by the Mudéjars (Moors who remained in Christian Spain after the Reconquest), and is built around the pilgrims' way, which up until the 19th century was called 'Calle de la Francesa'. It has a simple church dedicated to St. Thomas.

The name of **San Nicolás del Real Camino** reveals the juxtaposition of the pilgrims' route with the 18th-century road (the 'Real Camino'). The presence of the Knights Templar is documented in this village. There was also a pilgrims' hospital which appears in French accounts as the *'Petit Cavalier'*, in contrast to Santa María de las Tiendas. The Templar's well-known devotion to the Virgin Mary perhaps explains the existence of a Romanesque figure of her in the humble parish church which, significantly, is dedicated to the multi-faceted medieval saint, Nicholas, the patron saint of travellers and pilgrims.

The Valderaduey is the most important river in the Tierra de Campos region, and derives from the old Iberian word 'Aratoi', meaning 'open country' or 'plain' which might, in turn, be remotely connected with the medieval name for the area, *'Campi Gothorum'*. The attractive *Ermita de la Virgen del Puente,* a characteristic local Mudéjar construction, is still a pilgrims' hospital and stands beside a small ruined Roman bridge which is waiting to be restored.

Sahagún stands on the banks of the river Cea, and is probably the continuation of the Roman 'Camala' of the *'Itinerarium Antonini'* (395. 2). This is where Saints Facundo and Primitivo were martyred (according to a later tradition, they were the sons of the Leonese centurion St. Marcel and his wife, St. Nonia). A monastery dedicated to these two saints was founded as early as the 9th century, and was rebuilt in 872, having been destroyed by the Moors, only to be destroyed again a year later. In 904 Alfonso III 'the Great' entrusted it to Abbot Valabonso, who gave refuge to monks fleeing from Córdoba. But it was to be Alfonso VI, a pupil and later a refugee at the monastery, who, from 1068, turned Sahagún into the Spanish equivalent of Cluny. He even had his court there from time to time, as is mentioned in the *Poema de Mio Cid* (line 2929), and his remains and those of his four wives now lie in the church of the Benedictine *Convent of Santa Cruz*. Line 1312 of the *'Poema de Mio Cid'* uses the name *'Sanfagund'*, which is a corruption of *'Sanctum Facundum'*, the name of the monastery and later of the town. This later became *'Safagún'* which finally evolved into the modern name of *'Sahagún'*. Alfonso VI instigated the reform of the Church and his kingdom from Sahagún, under the guidance of the great Benedictine monastery of Cluny in Burgundy, of which his wife, Constance, was a native. In 1080 the Cluniac priest, Bernard de Sédirac, was appointed Abbot of Sahagún and in 1085 became the first Archbishop of the reconquered Toledo. Sahagún also produced a whole series of ecclesiastical dignitaries, including Pedro, Archbishop of Osma. In 1085, the King founded the town of Sahagún, comprising the community which had grown up around the monastery, and granted it a special charter or 'fuero'. The fact that the inhabitants of this new town were from at least nine different countries, including Gascony, Brittany, Germany, England, Burgundy, Normandy, Toulouse, Provence and Lombardy, demonstrates the powerful attraction that Sahagún had for numerous pilgrims on their way to Santiago. Also in 1085, the 'Puente de Canto' was built, which leads into the famous *'Field of Charlemagne's Lances'* (discussed in the next stage). It is curious to note the obsession with Sahagún in later Carolingian literature, which makes Charlemagne the founder of the monastery and even the town. Aided by royal favours and endowments from Alfonso VI and his successors, Sahagún became the most powerful monastery on the pilgrims' route, with privileges and possessions stretching halfway across Spain. Its position and role on the pilgrims' route to Santiago was a key factor contributing to its greatness. The monastery had a very active *'scriptorium'* and produced priceless manuscripts, such as the *'Beato'* which is held at the Cathedral of Burgo de Osma, which dates from 1056 and was written by Brother Pedro and illuminated by Brother Martino. The pilgrims' hospital was famous for its 60 beds, vast wheatfields and the enormous *'vat of Sahagún'*. Sahagún's most illustrious sons were educated at the monastery, including the Augustinian St. John of Sahagún (1430-1479), the patron saint of Sahagún and Salamanca, the Franciscan friar Bernardino de Sahagún (1499-1590) who was the founder of modern ethnology and the Benedictine monk, Pedro Ponce de León (1514-1584), the pioneer in the education of the deaf and dumb. (All three are commemorated by modest statues in the town.) However, the Catholic kings favoured the monastery of San Benito at Valladolid, and Sahagún became a dependency of it, with a subsequent loss of privileges and importance. Even so, as late as the 18th century, it could still boast a flourishing university faculty. Then came the disentailments and devastating fire of the 19th century, which reduced Sahagún to barely a pale shadow of its former glorious self.

Of the former **Monastery of Santos Facundo y Primitivo** (sometimes erroneously called the monastery of San Benito),

Arco de San Benito, Sahagún

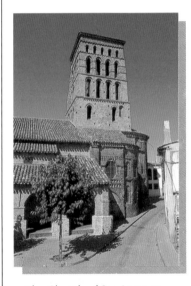

The Church of San Lorenzo, Sahagún

Tomb of Alfonso VI, Sahagún

The 'Virgen Peregrina', Sahagún

Monstrance by Enrique de Arfe,
Sahagún

Monastery of San Pedro
de las Dueñas, Sahagún

all that remain are an 19th-century tower and the 12th-century *Chapel of San Mancio*. Other sights worth seeing include the 12th-century Romanesque-Mudéjar *Church of San Tirso*, the 13th-century *Church of San Lorenzo*, with Gothic elements mixed with the Mudéjar style, the 13th-century *Convent of la Peregrina*, the *Chapel of San Juan de Sahagún*, which dates from the 16th century and above all, the magnificent *museum* at the Benedictine convent of Santa Cruz which has some outstanding pieces, including a monstrance by the gold and silversmith, *Enrique de Arfe* and a statue of the *'Virgen Peregrina'*. Don't miss it for the world.

III. HISTORICAL PILGRIMS' ACCOUNTS

Aymeric Picaud: *'You then come to prosperous Sahagún ('Sanctus Facundus'), the site of the field where (it is said), in olden times, the splendid lances which the victorious warriors thrust into the ground in the glory of God's Holy Name, sprouted leaves again.'*
'The Cea ('Ceya') [flows] through Sahagún...'
'You should visit the remains of the Holy Martyrs Facundo and Primitivo, whose church was built by Charlemagne.'
Künig von Vach: *'And a town called Sahagún ('Saguna'), which has a foul river and four hospitals.'*
Arnold von Harff: *'It is three leagues from Carrión to the village of Calzadilla ('Kaltzarilla'), then two leagues from Calzadilla to the village of Moratinos ('Moratinus') and two leagues from Moratinos to Sahagún ('Sagon'), a small town.'*
Laffi: *'... we reached Calzadilla ('Cascadegia'), four leagues away... Soon afterwards, we came to a very prosperous, large hospital which is called 'L'Ospitale del Gran Cavaliere' [Santa María de las Tiendas]. Here pilgrims are given a ration of bread, wine and cheese, of which there is an abundance in these parts as livestock is plentiful... Then we set off towards Sahagún ('San Fongon'). Upon arriving at this place, we saw the walls covered with so many locusts that it stirred our hearts to pity to see them. In the city, the women go out into the streets and round them up and kill them with sticks. We strolled around the town, curious to see it. The town has, among others, two particularly well-endowed and beautiful monasteries: the Monastery of San Benito and the Monastery of the Discalced Franciscans. We went to the Monastery of San Benito to see the refectory, which is so beautiful that I doubt it has its equal anywhere in the world. The ceiling is all of carved wood and is so splendid that no-one should miss it. The monks gave us dinner and treated us with great hospitality. After thanking them, we went to the Franciscan monastery to look for the Germans, who had gone to sell the monks pictures of the saints painted on parchment, and then we set off towards El Burgo Raneros ('Brunello')...'*

STAGE 18

SAHAGÚN • EL BURGO RANEROS

'The Field of Charlemagne's Lances', Sahagún

SAHAGÚN • CALZADA DEL COTO •
BERCIANOS DEL REAL CAMINO •
CALZADILLA DE LOS HERMANILLOS •
EL BURGO RANEROS

Section A: Calzada: Municipal refuge.

Bercianos: Municipal refuge.

El Burgo Raneros: The excellent «Domenico Laffi» municipal refuge, featuring 36 bunk-beds and magnificent facilities. It ranks as one of the most elegant and authentic refuges of the Pilgrims' Route. ☎ (987) 33 00 23

Section B: Calzadilla de los Hermanillos: The spacious and comfortable «Refugio de San Bartolomé».

ACCOMMODATION
El Burgo Raneros:
Fonda Lozano.
☎ (987) 33 00 60
Hostal El Peregrino
(both also have **restaurants**)
☎ (987) 33 00 69

'Iuxta quorum uillam sunt prat nemorosa...' (Aymeric Picaud: 'Pilgrims' Guide')

I. ROUTE

🚶 The way out of **Sahagún** leads over the 'Puente de Canto' which crosses the river Cea, whose deep valley forms the natural boundary of the Tierra de Campos region. On the right you pass the pretty poplar grove known as the *'Field of Charlemagne's Lances'*, a football ground and a campsite. Shortly afterwards, you enter a tunnel under the N-120, coming out onto the right-hand verge and continuing along it as far as **Calzada del Coto.** Here, there is a choice of two alternative routes:
a) Before entering **Calzada del Coto,** turn onto a splendid compacted earth track, flanked on either side by an uninterrupted line of plane trees, which runs parallel to the left of the Real Camino Francés. Built on the initiative of the regional government, this pleasant purpose-built path runs a full 32 km to Mansilla de las Mulas. It is for the exclusive use of pilgrims and has frequent benches and rest areas. Motor vehicles are strictly prohibited. After 6 km, you reach **Bercianos del Real Camino Francés** after passing some small lakes (which are dry during the hot months) and poplars on the right, and the Ermita de la Virgen de Perales on the left, just outside the village. Pass through Bercianos along the Calle Mayor, which emerges at the pond at the foot of the church hill, and immediately get back onto the tree-lined path which, after about 7 km, leads to **El Burgo Raneros.** This bleak, lonely stretch takes you across the small 'Arroyo del Olmo' valley, where there is a drinking fountain and a rest area, and past the village of Las Grañeras which is signposted off to the left.
b) Go into **Calzada del Coto** and follow the **'Calzada de los Peregrinos'** ('Pilgrims' Road') along the old Roman *'Via Traiana'*. After less than 2 km, cross the Palencia-La Coruña railway line and, shortly afterwards, enter the thick undergrowth of the Dehesa de Valdelocajos, after which you pass the farm of the same name. After a short while you cross a small valley, to the right of which is the rest area known as the *'Fuente del Peregrino'*, and after about 1 km, you reach **Calzadilla de los Hermanillos,** the only village you encounter between Calzada del Coto and Mansilla de las Mulas throughout alternative route (b). Leave Calzadilla on the old road, which was unfortunately asphalted twelve years ago, and continue until you reach the junction with the road to El Burgo Raneros. [The continuation to Mansilla de las Mulas is described in the following chapter (Stage 19: El Burgo Raneros-Mansilla) to make map-reading easier.]

🚲 Obviously, the easy tree-lined path which covers this stage of the route offers no problems to cyclists. A minor difficulty might be the state of the ground in alternative route (b).

🚗 Milestones: N-120 km 242.3: Calzada del Coto; km 256.5: Las Grañeras, El Burgo Raneros.

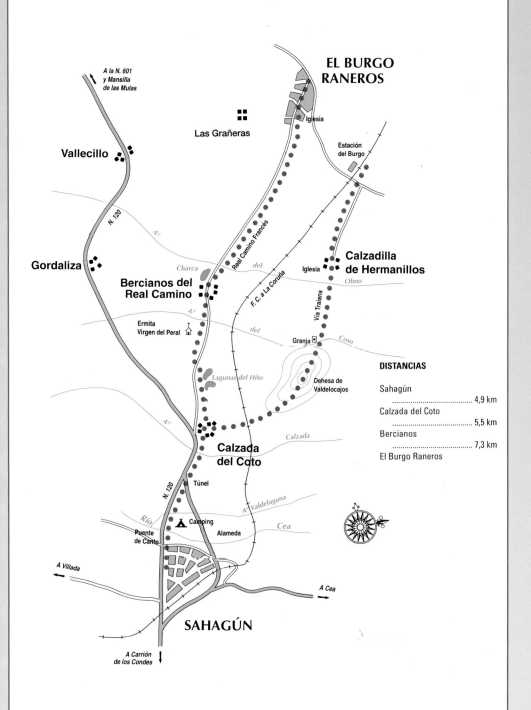

EL BURGO RANEROS

Las Grañeras

Iglesia

Estación
del Burgo

Vallecillo

A la N. 601
y Mansilla
de las Mulas

N. 120

A°

Charca

Real Camino Francés

del

**Calzadilla
de Hermanillos**

Iglesia

Olmo

Gordaliza

**Bercianos del
Real Camino**

F. C. a La Coruña

Vía Traiana

Ermita
Virgen del Peral

A°

del

Granja

Coso

Lagunas del Hito

Dehesa de
Valdelocajos

DISTANCIAS

Sahagún
.... 4,9 km

Calzada del Coto
.... 5,5 km

Bercianos
.... 7,3 km

El Burgo Raneros

A°

Calzada

**Calzada
del Coto**

Túnel

N. 120

A Valdelaguna

Río

Camping

Cea

Puente
de Canto

Alameda

A Villada

A Cea

SAHAGÚN

A Carrión
de los Condes

18ª ETAPA
**SAHAGÚN
EL BURGO RANEROS**
17,7 KM

*Bridge over the Cea
at Sahagún*

"Las Lanzas" poplar grove

*The Ermita de Nuestra Señora
de Perales*

II. HISTORY, ART AND LEGENDS

Sahagún is frequently described in medieval documents as being *'on a steep bank by the Cea'*, and the route out of the town does indeed take you down a pronounced slope. The solid *'Puente de Canto'* which crosses the river was built on the orders of Alfonso VI in 1085, and until 1992 was the only bridge in Sahagún.

The bridge emerges in a lush poplar grove which grows on the site of the *'Field of Charlemagne's Lances'*. The miraculous incident that happened here is recounted in *'The History of Charlemagne and Roland'*, written in the 12th century and erroneously attributed to the Archbishop of Reims, Turpin, which is the fourth book of the *'Liber Sancti Iacobi'* (commonly known as the *'Codex Calixtinus'*). Charlemagne was pursuing the Saracen caliph, Aigolando, during his expedition to drive the Infidel from the pilgrims' way and liberate the Apostle's tomb, when the following events occurred:

'...they came across him [Aigolando] *in the land known as Campos, beside the Cea, in some fields in a very fertile, flat place where, afterwards, upon Charlemagne's orders and with his help, the great and excellent Basilica of the Holy Martyrs Facundo and Primitivo was built... Some Christian soldiers were conscientiously preparing their weapons the night before the battle and thrust them upright into the ground, in front of the camp: that is to say, in the fields beside the river. When dawn broke the next day, those who were to receive the honour of martyrdom for their faith in God found their lances covered in bark and with leafy branches. More amazed than can be described, and attributing such a miracle to the divine power of the Lord, they cut them down to the ground and from the buried roots the great woods we see there today grew up, as many of the lances had ash shafts.'*

No fewer than 40 000 Christians were killed in the battle beside the Cea, among them Milon, Roland's father. Charlemagne's horse also perished.

This wonderful, legendary episode is depicted on one of the twelve embossed silver panels on the famous *'Karlschrein'*, the casket that holds the remains of the Emperor, in Aachen cathedral.

The neighbouring campsite is named after Pedro Ponce de León, the famous Benedictine monk who pioneered the education of the deaf and dumb.

Calzada del Coto appears with its present name in the earliest documents from the Monastery of Sahagún, which date from the 10th century. From the 9th century, the word 'calzata' was a clear reference, in Castile, to a road. In these early documents a 'Villa Zacharias' is mentioned frequently, which was associated with the district of Calzada. The village church is dedicated to St. Stephen.

From Calzada, the route divides into two branches. The first runs parallel to the **Real Camino Francés,** along the pleasant **tree-lined path** described in the previous section, which was inaugurated in 1991 and which makes for an easy, tranquil walk across the lonely Leonese plain as far as the lush banks of the river Esla. The East-West routes have always passed through this area and, as might be expected, it has a long and glorious tradition of road-building. Important vestiges remain of the old Roman road network, as shall be seen later. In the Middle Ages, written accounts of the Santiago pilgrimage confirm that the pilgrims' route (known as the 'Camino Francés') passed through here. Finally, in the 18th century, the enlightened, technocratic administration of Carlos III converted it into a 'Camino Real' or main road, which consequently became known as the **Real Camino Francés.**

Before reaching Bercianos you pass the **Ermita de la Virgen de Perales** (popularly known as 'La Perala'), who has a dedicated following in this region, having devoted herself to the Hospital del Cebreiro at the end of the 12th century. Bercianos del Real Camino Francés was resettled by natives of the El Bierzo region (west of León). The narrow silhouette of the parish church, the Iglesia del Salvador, stands out on top of a small hill. Inside, there is a Renaissance figure of John the Baptist and the 16th-17th century tomb of Doña Leonor de Quiñones, a local noblewoman.

Iglesia del Salvador at Bercianos

The 'Fuente del Romero' is located near the rest area in the Valle del Olmo, about 1.5 kilometres outside the village.

Eight hundred metres further up, you will see signs for **Las Grañeras** (the author's native village), which frequently appears in 10th-century documents from the Monastery of Sahagún as 'Graniera' or 'Granneras'. Some two kilometres further on, at the 'pago del Cimajo', the famous incident of the pilgrim being devoured by wolves must have taken place, as recounted by Domenico Laffi in his *Viaggio a San Giacomo:*

'... and we set off towards el Burgo Raneros ('Brunello'), four long leagues away, and after covering about three leagues across the plains we came upon a dead pilgrim, and two wolves appeared and began to devour the body. We scared them off and continued towards el Burgo, where we went in search of the priest so he could go and remove the corpse...'

Interior of the Iglesia del Salvador

The layout and name of **El Burgo Raneros** denote its connection with the pilgrimage. It must have been a 'burgo' of Sahagún and its single street used to be called the 'Camino Francés'. The earliest reference to it dates from 1126 and in 1386 the Abbess of Gradefes granted it a 'fuero'. The Cathedral Museum at León displays a lovely Romanesque figure of the Virgin Mary which used to be housed in the village church of San Pedro. In 1673, Laffi described its inhabitants' lifestyle and dedication to shepherding (see HISTORICAL PILGRIMS' ACCOUNTS), and it is curious to note his description of dwellings similar to the Celtic 'pallozas' to be found at Cebreiro, in Galicia. An illustrious figure from the village was Friar Pedro del Burgo (died 1467) who was Abbot of Sahagún for twenty years, as well as a sculptor

Monument marking the beginning of the special pilgrims' path. Las Grañeras

*The «Domenico Laffi» hostel.
El Burgo Raneros*

The tree-lined path

Typical landscape of this area

and architect: in 1457 he restored the Monastery of San Pedro de Cardeña, near Burgos. The recumbent statue from his tomb, the work of his disciples, is displayed in the Museum of the Benedictine convent of Santa Cruz in Sahagún.

The second branch of the route, which runs further north, follows the *Via Traiana,* and you will be sure to see some parts that look like the original paving stones. (It appears in an 18th-century cartography as the 'Calzada de los Peregrinos', the 'Pilgrims' Road'.) In the area known as the Dehesa de Valdelocajos two Roman milestones are still standing on the original site. The pretty, lilting name of **Calzadilla de los Hermanillos** is convincing proof of its pilgrimage-linked origins, being indicative of a detachment of Franciscan friars *('Hermanillos')* from the Monastery of Sahagún stationed at an intermediate point along the pilgrims' way *('calzadilla'),* dedicated to the welfare of pilgrims. At the high altar of the Parish Church of San Bartolomé there is a priceless 16th-century representation of the Calvary. In the neighbouring village of **Villamuñío,** the Parish Church of the Assumption has a lovely *artesonado* ceiling and a beautiful processional cross which is attributed to Juan de Arfe.

III. HISTORICAL PILGRIMS' ACCOUNTS

Aymeric Picaud: *'...then you come to Sahagún ('Sanctus Facundus')... which is the site of the field where (it is said), in olden times, the splendid lances which the victorious warriors thrust into the ground in the glory of God's Holy Name, sprouted leaves again.'*

Arnold von Harff: *'And then it is two leagues from Sahagún to Bercianos ('Bresianus'), a 'villa franca'. It is two leagues from Bercianos to the village of El Burgo Raneros ('Borgo riuero').'*

Laffi: *'... we set off towards El Burgo Raneros ('Brunello'), four long leagues away... and we found lodgings, but so poor that we had to sleep on the floor, as all the inhabitants of this village are shepherds and all the dwellings are straw-roofed huts.'*

STAGE 19

EL BURGO RANEROS • MANSILLA

The walls of Mansilla de las Mulas

EL BURGO RANEROS • RELIEGOS • MANSILLA DE LAS MULAS

PILGRIMS' REFUGES

Mansilla de las Mulas: The sheer enthusiasm of the local town council has given rise to what ranks as one of the most spacious and best-equipped hostels to be found on the Pilgrims' Route. It sleeps 46 and has all necessary facilities.
☎ (987) 31 09 41

ACCOMMODATION

Mansilla de las Mulas:
Hostal Las Delicias.
☎ (987) 31 00 94.
10 beds. ♣
Los Faroles.
☎ (987) 31 09 49.
35 beds. ♣

RESTAURANTS

Mansilla de las Mulas:
El Hórreo.
Carretera de Valladolid, 58.
☎ (987) 31 01 30. Quality meat and fish dishes.
Casa Marcelo. Los Faroles.
Olmo. Toño.
La Ruta de los Asturianos.

PETROL STATIONS

On the N-601, at km 9, in Mansilla de las Mulas.

'Inde est Manxilla.' (Aymeric Picaud: 'Pilgrims' Guide')

I. ROUTE

🚶 The **Real Camino Francés** option (continuation of *route (a)* from Stage 18): The village of **El Burgo Raneros** flanks the pilgrims' way, which is the street named Calle Real. On leaving the village, you pass a large pond (where the croaking of frogs can often be heard), close to which you get back onto the same tree-lined path as before and continue straight along it, parallel to the left-hand side of the León-Palencia railway line. For the next 10 km the path crosses a vast, monotonous plateau which extends as far as the eye can see to the first foothills of the Cordillera Cantábrica. This area is dotted with gullies: between El Burgo and Mansilla you will cross the Arroyo de Buen Solana, the Arroyo de Valdeasneros, the Arroyo de Utelga, the Arroyo Valdeviñas, the Arroyo del Valle Naval, the Arroyo de Valdearcos, the Arroyo de Santa María and the Arroyo Grande, some of which have shady rest areas. After passing the village of Villamarco (about 1 km off to the left) you cross the railway track, and from this point on the landscape becomes a little more interesting. You soon reach the little Arroyo de Santa María valley, where a pleasant and varied riverside wood grows and, shortly afterwards, enter **Reliegos,** following the Calle Mayor through the village. On leaving Reliegos, the descent begins down to Mansilla de las Mulas situated in the wide Esla valley. Exactly a 'legua de Castilla' (a Castilian league - 5.5 km) away, the tree-lined path comes to an end on the outskirts of Mansilla, after running 32 km from Calzada del Coto. Passing some rubbish dumps, you cross the Cistierna road and enter **Mansilla de las Mulas** through its archless south gate.

The **Calzada de los Peregrinos** or **'Via Traiana'** option (continuation of *route (b)* from Stage 18): Cross the road leading to El Burgo Raneros, and continue along the old Roman road parallel to the right-hand side of the railway track, within view of the other path (see above) which runs along the opposite side of the track. After 6 km, you come to the Apeadero de Villamarco (a halt on the railway line), after which you continue towards Reliegos, where a road leads off to the left into the village. You then descend towards Mansilla, a distance of about 5.5 km (a 'Castilian league'), crossing the Cistierna road and passing a modern housing development on the right, before turning left into Mansilla. The geographical characteristics (valleys, streams, landscape) are the same as those described above in route (a).

🚲 The **Real Camino Francés** option obviously offers no difficulty to cyclists. However, the surface throughout the **Calzada de los Peregrinos** or **Via Traiana** option is very rutted and eroded.

🚗 Milestones: N-120: km 256.5: turning to Las Grañeras and El Burgo Raneros; N-601 km 309: Mansilla de las Mulas.

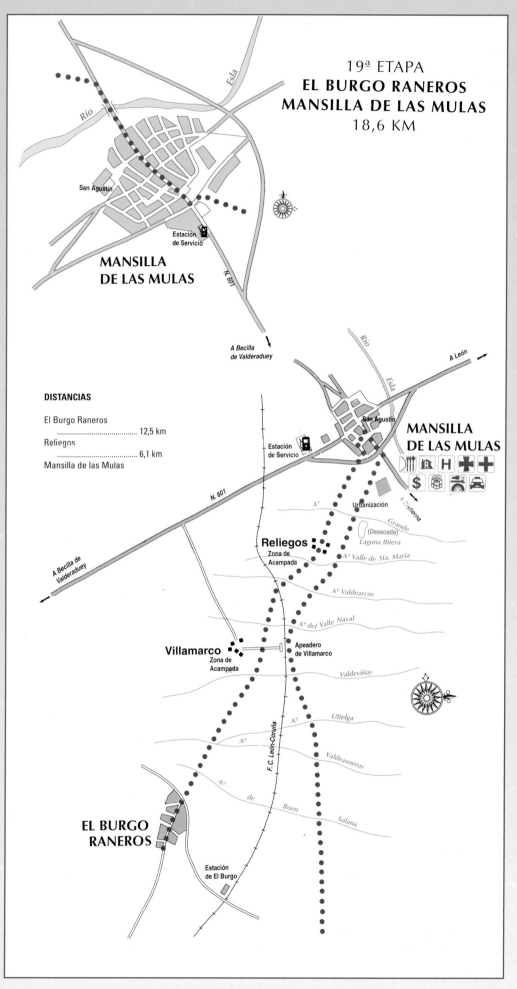

19ª ETAPA
**EL BURGO RANEROS
MANSILLA DE LAS MULAS**
18,6 KM

Río Esla

San Agustín

Estación
de Servicio

**MANSILLA
DE LAS MULAS**

N. 601

A Becilla
de Valderaduey

Río Esla

A León

DISTANCIAS

El Burgo Raneros
.... 12,5 km
Reliegos
.... 6,1 km
Mansilla de las Mulas

Estación
de Servicio

San Agustín

**MANSILLA
DE LAS MULAS**

A Cisterna

N. 601

Aº

Urbanización

Grande

(Desecada)
Laguna Ibiera

Reliegos
Zona de
Acampada

Aº Valle de Sta. María

Aº Valdearcos

A Becilla de
Valderaduey

Aº del Valle Naval

Villamarco
Zona de
Acampada

Apeadero
de Villamarco

Valdeviñas

Utielga

Aº

F. C. León-Coruña

Aº

Aº

Valdeasneros

Aº

de

Buen

Solana

**EL BURGO
RANEROS**

Estación
de El Burgo

II. HISTORY, ART AND LEGENDS

The first halt after El Burgo Raneros on the Real Camino Francés is the village of **Reliegos.** It is generally agreed that this is the *Palantia* of the *'Itinerarium Antonini'* and, this being the case, one of the main arteries of the Roman road network, the Via Traiana from **Burdigala** (Bordeaux) to **Asturica Augusta** (Astorga) would have passed through here, together with the Hispanic branch from **Tarraco** (Tarragona) to **Astorga.** The next *station* on the way to Astorga was **Interamnium,** which is possibly the present-day village of Ardón. The road from **Legio VII Gemina** (León) would also have converged here, after passing through Lancia. In its turn, the pilgrims' route to Santiago, the Real Camino Francés, passed through Reliegos, becoming the 'Calle Real' as it did so. The name of the parish church (which has no particular artistic merits) also testifies to the antiquity of the place, being dedicated to an early Pope, St. Cornelius, and to the Bishop of Carthage, St. Ciprian, both illustrious figures of the 3rd-century Christian church. A popular village refrain reflects its nature as a passing place:

'La legua de Castilla,
de Reliegos a Mansilla.'
('A Castilian league from Reliegos to Mansilla').

It is indeed a Castilian league (5.5 kilometres) to **Mansilla de las Mulas,** a historic town situated on the banks of the Esla, the mere sight of which offers a refreshing contrast to the starkness of the preceding stages of the journey. The two branches of the pilgrims' route from Calzada del Coto meet here. The first, the Real Camino Francés, enters the old quarter of Mansilla through the south gate, the *Puerta de Santiago,* which unfortunately has lost its arch. The second branch, the Calzada de los Peregrinos, enters through the east gate, the *Arco de la Concepción,* which is the only one to retain its great arched entrance intact.

Despite the efforts of certain authors —on philological grounds— to establish the origin of Mansilla as far back as the times of Ancient Rome, according to the archaeological research carried out here, the date of the town's birth is to be set no earlier than the first centuries of the Middle Ages. By a curious twist of popular etymology, it is traditionally interpreted as being composed of two very simple elements: *'Mano-en-silla'* or 'Hand on the saddle'. This explains the town's coat of arms, which emblazons the town hall and which consists of a hand on a saddle. The appellative *'de las Mulas'* (of the Mules), which perhaps also had some bearing on the choice of coat of arms, comes from the town's rich tradition of livestock fairs. Until fairly recently, Mansilla was the centre for buying and selling horses and cattle for farmers from as far afield as the mountains of León and the Tierra de Campos. The 'Plaza del Grano' ('Grain Square') recalls this farming and stockbreeding tradition.

Although the medieval history of Mansilla goes back as far as its 10th-century resettlement as *'Mansilla de illa*

The Puerta de Santiago, Mansilla de las Mulas

The walls, Mansilla de las Mulas

Portal of the Monastery of Gradefes

ponte', the town's earliest surviving documents date from as late as 1181, when King Fernando II of León granted it special status as a resettled village. He also granted it the Benavente 'fuero' and Mansilla was to be under the dominion of Benavente until 1594, the same year the castle was destroyed.

Architecturally, the town's main attraction are the extensive walls, of which the north stretch (parallel to the river Esla) is still almost intact. They are basically Romanesque, and were built during the resettlement at the end of the 12th century, using enormous stones from the river. Measuring some three metres thick, they are extremely solid and are of a similar type of construction to the walls of León. Of the four original gates, the Arco de la Concepción, on the east side, is the only one which is still intact.

There is little to suggest the former splendour of the town, except the Parish Church of Santa María which dates from the 18th century, and the Ermita de Nuestra Señora de Gracia, outside the city walls. Nearby, one can still see a type of wrestling contest peculiar to León, which consists of two opponents holding on to each other's leather belts and trying to push each other to the ground. Hardly anything remains of the former churches of San Martín, San Lorenzo and San Nicolás de Bari, or of the Convents of San Agustín or San Adrián. Records show that at one time the town could boast three pilgrims' hospitals, and the 1570 statutes of two of them (the Hospital de Sancti Spiritus and the Hospital de Santiago) still survive.

Mansilla is associated with one of the most colourful characters of Spanish Golden Age literature, the roguish Justina, from Francisco López de Ubeda's famous novel, *El Libro de Entretenimiento de la Pícara Justina,* published in 1605 in Medina del Campo. This unforgettable character opens an inn in Mansilla which is frequented by customers of all descriptions, including several pilgrims on their way to Santiago.

To the north, the Arco de San Agustín led out of the town dirctly to the solid stone bridge (mentioned in several pilgrims' accounts) built over the *'Astura'*, which was the name given to the river Esla by the Celtic tribe, the *Astures*.

There follows a description of four important monuments, which are close to Mansilla and connected in some way with it. Although they are not strictly speaking on the pilgrims' route, the following stretch between Mansilla and León passes close by them. Around km 311.5 on the N-601, a road leads off to Mansilla Mayor which brings you to the confluence of the rivers Porma and Esla. This is the site of the Cistercian monastery of **Santa María de Sandoval** which was built on lands given by Alfonso VII to his steward, Count Ponce de Minerva and Doña Estefanía, his wife, in 1142. Years later, the Counts built the monastery in circumstances described in a rather lovely legend, which has it that after many years of captivity in the land of the Infidel, the Count returned as a pilgrim to the Monastery of Carrizo where (unbeknown to him) his wife had built a pilgrims' hospital. As she approached to

Church of the Monastery of Gradefes

Monastery of Santa María de Sandoval

Portal of the Monastery of Sandoval

The Church of San Miguel de Escalada

San Miguel de Escalada: the portico

Celtic hillfort settlement on Cerro Lancia

undertake the ritual pilgrims' footwashing ceremony, she recognised her husband... Following Doña Estefanía's example, the Count had the Monastery of Sandoval built.

A hill some 200 metres to the right of the N-601 (at km 312.3) is the site of the former settlement of **Lancia,** the Asturians' largest stronghold and their last bastion until their defeat by the legate of Lusitania, P. Carisio, in the year 26 B.C., during the Cantabrian war. It appears in the old Roman *'Itineraria'* as an intermediate station between *Legio VII* (León) and *Palantia* (Reliegos). Somewhat further afield, two jewels of Leonese architecture are to be found. The first is the Mozarabic **Church of San Miguel de Escalada,** which was built by a community of monks from Córdoba at the beginning of the 10th century. The other is the **Convent of Santa María de Gradefes,** which was built as a Cistercian nunnery at the end of the 12th century. Both are well worth a visit.

III. HISTORICAL PILGRIMS' ACCOUNTS

Aymeric Picaud: *'Then comes Mansilla ('Manxilla')... The Esla ('Aisela') which flows through Mansilla.'*

Künig von Vach: *'It is then seven miles to a town called 'Mansile' (Mansilla), which you may enter freely and where you will find three good hospitals.'*

Arnold von Harff: *'It is two leagues from El Burgo Raneros to the village of Reliegos ('Religus'). It is three leagues from Reliegos to the town of Mansilla ('Mansila'). This is all in Spain. Then you cross a stone bridge over the river 'Isla' (the Esla).'*

Laffi: *'In the morning, upon rising, we set off towards Mansilla ('Mansila'), four leagues away...'*

STAGE 20

MANSILLA DE LAS MULAS • LEÓN

Jacobear: symbol on the Hostal de San Marcos, León

MANSILLA DE LAS MULAS •
VILLAMOROS DE MANSILLA •
PUENTE DE VILLARENTE • ARCAHUEJA •
VALDELAFUENTE • PUENTE CASTRO • LEÓN

León: In León the pilgrim is faced by the difficulties that are characteristic of all provincial capitals. As yet no true solution has been found.

ACCOMMODATION

Puente Villarente:
El Delfín Verde.
☎ (987) 31 20 65.
27 beds. ♣
La Montaña.
☎ (987) 31 21 61.
22 rooms. ♣

León:
♣ ♣ ♣
San Marcos. Alfonso V. Ciudad de León. Conde Luna. Riosol.
♣ ♣
Quindós. Don Suero. París. Londres.
♣
Reina. Orejas. Reino de León. Álvarez. Bayón. Covadonga. España. Europa. La Gárgola. Guzmán el Bueno. Oviedo. Quirós. San Martín.

RESTAURANTS

Puente Villarente:
Los Mesones. Ctra. Valladolid, s/n. ☎ (987) 31 22 15. In a former pilgrims' hospital.

León:
Medium-high price range:
Adonías Pozo. Casa Pozo. Sotomayor. Independencia. Formela. Bitácora. El Siglo.
Medium price range:
La Catedral. El Faisán Dorado. La Posada. Ruta Jacobea. Casa Teo. El Racimo de Oro. Rey Don Sancho. El Besugo. La Gitana. Gijón. San Martín. Bodega Regia. Las Calabazas. Don Quijote. El Llagar. El Palomo. Rancho Chico.
(All the above **restaurants** serve specialities of the León region and both traditional and modern cuisine.)

PETROL STATIONS
On the N-610: at km 316'1, in Puente de Villarente; at km 321'5, in Valdelafuente.
Within León itself (San Marcos, San Francisco and Padre Isla).

'Inde Legio.' (Aymeric Picaud: 'Pilgrims' Guide')

I. ROUTE

🚶 Leave **Mansilla de las Mulas** by way of the famous medieval bridge over the Esla, which leads to the N-601. After less than a kilometre, bear right off the main road on a level with the turning to Villafalé, and get onto a parallel dirt track a short distance from the road. (The turning to Mansilla Mayor and the Monastery of Sandoval is on the opposite side of the road, shortly after the turning to Villafalé.) After a kilometre, you pass along the base of a hill (recognisable by a cave on the hillside), at the top of which are the ruins of Lancia. A bit further on, in **Villamoros de Mansilla,** you cross over to the left-hand side of the N-601, go through the village and then cross back again to the right-hand side of the road and get onto another track similar to the one from Mansilla. After about 2 km, you cross the junction of the Gradefes and San Miguel de Escalada roads, before crossing the historic bridge over the river Porma. After the bridge, you pass what used to be a pilgrims' hospital on the left-hand side of the road, and continue along the N-601 through **Puente de Villarente.** A few kilometres further on (at km 316.5), bear right off the main road onto a small road that crosses the Canal del Porma, go past a fountain and a public washing place and climb a small hill to **Arcahueja,** leaving the village on another small road which leads to **Valdelafuente,** less than a kilometre away. From here, after passing a petrol station on the left, you return to the N-601 at about km 321, and follow the road to the Alto del Portillo, from where there is a lovely panoramic view of León. It is a continuous descent from here along the old road, past the Santa Isabel psychiatric clinic opposite a bus-stop, down to the **Puente Castro** district, where you cross the river Torío. You enter **León** via the typical old Santa Ana district, from where the following route leads to the cathedral: Calle de Barahona, Calle Puerta Moneda, Plaza del Mercado, Calle de la Rúa, Plaza de San Marcelo and Calle Ancha, which leads into the Plaza de Regla (or Plaza de la Catedral). From the Cathedral, the Calle del Cid leads to the Basílica de San Isidoro, a short walk away.

🚲 This stage presents no major problems for cyclists, although the cross-country stretch between km 317.5 and km 321 of the N-601 could be slightly tricky due to the inadequate signposting and the state of the ground.

🚗 Milestones: N-601 km 311: turning to San Miguel de Escalada (right) and Sandoval (left); km 312.3: Lancia; km 313: Villamoros de Mansilla; km 315: Puente de Villarente; km 319.5: Arcahueja; km 321: Valdelafuente; km 324: Puente Castro-León.

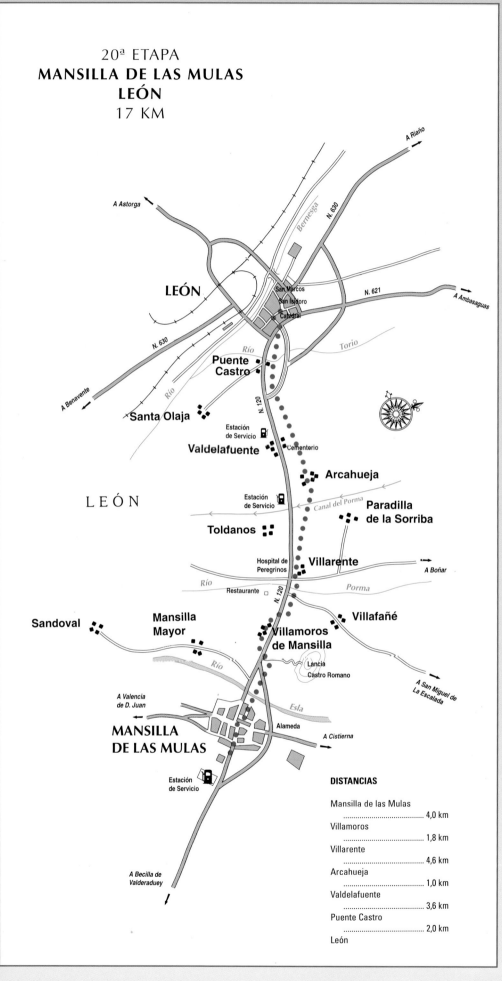

20ª ETAPA
MANSILLA DE LAS MULAS
LEÓN
17 KM

A Riaño

A Astorga

Bernesga

N. 630

LEÓN

San Marcos
San Isidoro
Catedral

N. 621

A Ambasaguas

N. 630

A Benavente

Río

Torio

Puente
Castro

Río

N. 120

Santa Olaja

Estación
de Servicio

Valdelafuente

Cementerio

Arcahueja

LEÓN

Estación
de Servicio

Canal del Porma

Paradilla
de la Sorriba

Toldanos

Hospital de
Peregrinos

Villarente

A Boñar

Río

Restaurante

N. 120

Porma

Sandoval

Mansilla
Mayor

Villafañé

Villamoros
de Mansilla

Lancia
Castro Romano

A San Miguel de
La Escalada

Río

A Valencia
de D. Juan

Esla

MANSILLA
DE LAS MULAS

Alameda

A Cistierna

Estación
de Servicio

A Becilla de
Valderaduey

DISTANCIAS

Mansilla de las Mulas
.... 4,0 km
Villamoros
.... 1,8 km
Villarente
.... 4,6 km
Arcahueja
.... 1,0 km
Valdelafuente
.... 3,6 km
Puente Castro
.... 2,0 km
León

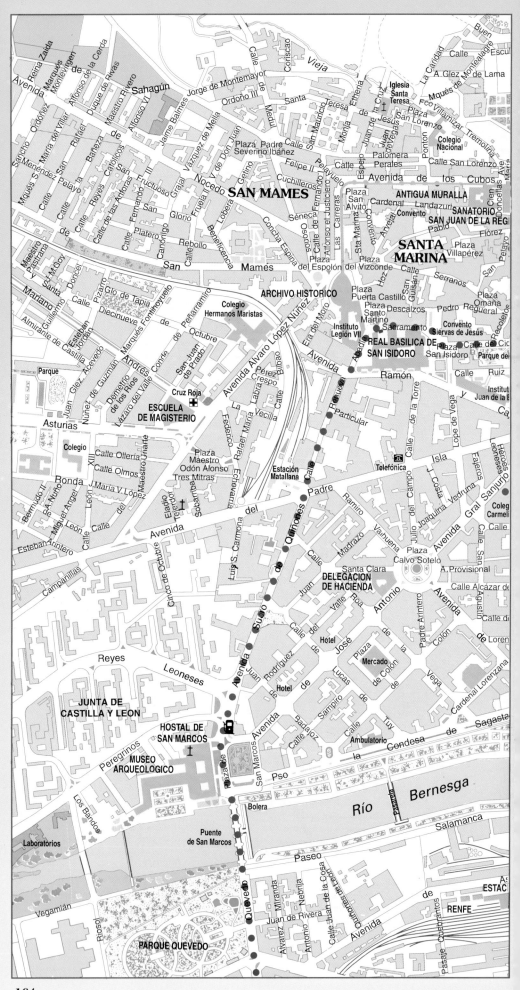

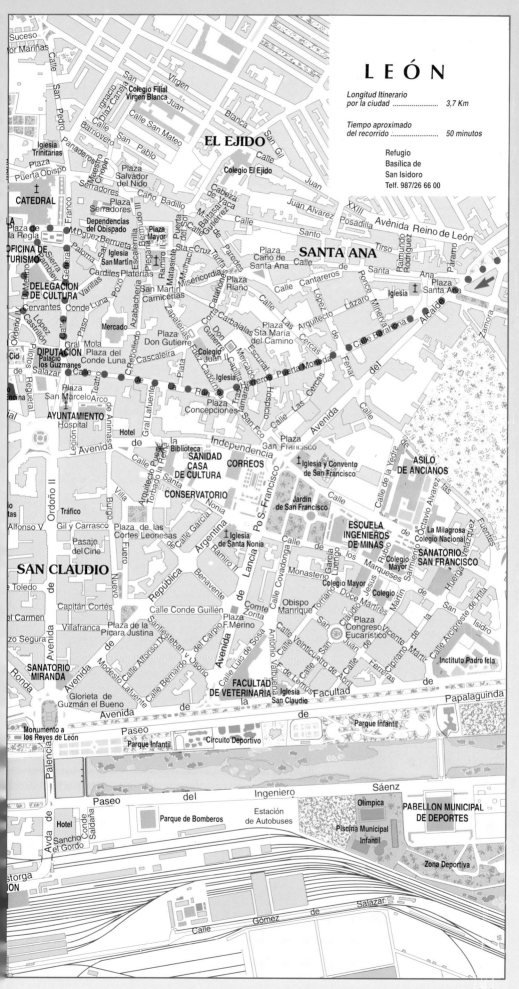

LEÓN

Longitud Itinerario
por la ciudad .... 3,7 Km

Tiempo aproximado
del recorrido .... 50 minutos

Refugio
Basílica de
San Isidoro
Telf. 987/26 66 00

The old hospital by the Puente de Villarente

The Puente de Villarente

II. HISTORY, ART AND LEGENDS

After **Villamoros de Mansilla** (which appears as *'Villamoros del Camino Francés'* in 17th and 18th-century documents) you come to the **Puente de Villarente,** which Aymeric Picaud describes as the *'an enormous bridge that crosses the Porma between Mansilla and León',* and which is also mentioned by Künig von Vach (see HISTORICAL PILGRIMS' ACCOUNTS). It is a twenty-arched construction of irregular shape, and has been restored and rebuilt over the centuries as a consequence of flooding. Recently, another clumsy attempt has been made at restoring this old monument. On your left, after crossing the bridge, you pass a former pilgrims' hospital, which was founded by the Archdeacon of Triacastela, an office held by a canon of the León chapter.

The village of **Arcahueja** used to be known as 'Santa María de Arcahueca', and **Toldanos** was a Mozarabic resettlement. León's equivalent of Santiago de Compostela's *'Monte del Gozo'* or *'Mount of Joy'* was the **Alto del Portillo,** from which the first glimpse was to be had of León described by Aymeric Picaud as *'the seat of the Royal Court'.* At the top, a modern cross substitutes the old one which marked the pilgrims' way and which now stands in the Plaza de San Marcos in the centre of León.

The name **Puente Castro** recalls the *'Castrum Iudeorum'* mentioned by Picaud, an important Jewish ghetto which grew up on the site of a Roman settlement, and which was destroyed in the 12th century. The bridge over the river Torío which gives the district its name dates from the 18th century.

León, like Rome, was originally a military garrison: in this case, the *'castra'* of the *'Legio VII Gemina'* which was formed out of Hispanic contingents by Galba, before he became Emperor in AD 69. Like Rome, too, it is *'quadrata':* the fence that defended the garrison was a rectangle measuring 550 by 380 metres, with a gate on each side. Little is known of the city after the Visigothic invasions, until it was conquered in the 8th century by the Moorish leader, Muza, during his campaign in the north of Spain and recuperated by Alfonso I in the same century. Ordoño I (850-866) and his successor Alfonso III 'the Great' rebuilt the city and resettled it with Mozarabic elements. In 914, Ordoño II made León the capital of the Kingdom of Asturias and León. It was devastated by the Moorish leader, Almanzor, in 988, and rebuilt again under Alfonso V. During the 10th and 11th centuries it was the most important capital city of Christian Spain, but with the definitive union of the kingdoms of Castile and León in the 13th century, it lost its capital city status.

Pilgrims entered the city via the suburb of *Santa Ana,* which had a church and neighbouring pilgrims' hospital administered originally by the Knights of the Holy Sepulchre and later by the Knights of St. John of Jerusalem. A lovely figure of St. James is still to be found in the church's neoclassical retable. The hospital for contagious patients, the Hospital de San Lázaro, was also outside the city walls.

The city grew in size with the building of new defensive walls in the 14th century, and from then on pilgrims entered the walled city either via the *Puerta de Santa Ana,* which led to the Arco del Rey in the original walls, or via the *Puerta Moneda,* which led directly to the Romanesque church of *Santa María del Mercado,* which once stood at the heart of the *'burgo*

Medieval Stone cross from the Alto del Portillo, now in front of the Hostal de San Marcos franco' located outside the former city walls. The church was originally known as *'Santa María del Camino'*, and still houses an image of the Virgen del Camino, the Patroness of León, a 15th-century Gothic Madonna which is referred to as 'Nuestra Señora del Mercado' to distinguish it from the image which is venerated in the Sanctuary of the Virgen del Camino outside the city. The Calle de la Rúa (formerly the 'Rúa de francos') leads to the 12th-century *Church of San Marcelo* (since restored) which is named after a centurion of the Seventh Legion who was martyred in the 3rd century. Inside, there are several sculptures by the great Gregorio Fernández.

The **Real Basílica de San Isidoro** is one of the great Romanesque treasures of the pilgrims' way, and is closely related to Jaca cathedral, the church of San Martín at Frómista and Santiago cathedral. It was consecrated on 21st December 1063 to receive the sacred relics of San Isidoro, Bishop of Seville, which had recently been brought from Seville on the initiative of Fernando I and his consort, Doña Sancha. Very soon, talk of the miracles attributed to San Isidoro attracted numerous pilgrims, to the extent that Aymeric Picaud, in Chapter VIII of his *'Pilgrims' Guide'*, classified the shrine as one of the four *'saints' bodies which pilgrims should visit'* on the Spanish stretch of the road to Santiago, together with those of Santo Domingo de la Calzada, Saints Facundo and Primitivo in Sahagún and St. James himself in Santiago. The complex consists of a church in the shape of a Latin cross, with three aisles and three apses, crowned with a square belfry, the *Torre del Gallo*. The two doors on the south side, the *Puerta del Cordero* and the *Puerta del Perdón,* are decorated with rich statuary which bears the hallmark of Master Esteban, who sculpted the carvings on the Puerta de Platerías at Santiago cathedral. Fernando I and Doña Sancha had a Royal Pantheon built in the crypt, and 23 monarchs are buried there. Around 1160, the ceiling was decorated with remarkable frescoes, which have earned it the nickname of *'the Sistine Chapels of Spanish Romanesque art'*. The Basilica also houses one of the richest collections of medieval sacred objects in Europe, including such incomparable pieces as an illuminated Bible dating from 960, the casket containing the remains of San Isidoro, a chalice belonging to Doña Urraca (daughter of Fernando I) and the Peñalba cross.

León cathedral is the masterpiece of the Gothic style in Spain, and is pure French in inspiration. Work on it commenced at the beginning of the 12th century, on a site that had previously been occupied by the Roman baths, followed by the palace of Ordoño II and the Romanesque cathedral. The ground-plan consists of a Latin cross shape, with a three-aisled nave, a pentagonal apse with a single ambulatory and five radiating chapels. The interior is a miracle of luminosity due to the glazed triforium consisting of over 100 windows. Indeed, the stained glass is the most characteristic and beautiful feature of this soaring cathedral, dubbed 'the Jewel of León' for good reason. Among the fine Gothic statuary decorating the exterior, there is an image of St. James dressed as a pilgrim to the right of the central door.

The pilgrims' route through León ends at the **Monastery and Hostal of San Marcos.** It origins go back to 1151, when Doña Sancha donated lands near the bridge over the river Bernesga for a church and hospital for the needy. In 1523, the Valladolid chapter of the Order of St. James of the Sword, with the backing

San Isidoro el Real:
the Pantheon

Page of the San Isidoro Bible

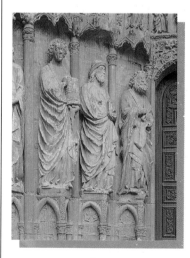

Statue of St James
on the portal of the cathedral

León cathedral

The Santa María la Blanca portal, León cathedral

Stained glass windows, León cathedral

The Hostal de San Marcos, León

of Ferdinand the Catholic, ordered the construction of the present-day structure, as their institution's headquarters. The complex consists of a simple two-storeyed pilgrims' hospital (recently restored), and a sumptuous plateresque monastery, the work of Juan de Orozco and others. The exterior decoration, which includes a representation of St. James the Moor-slayer over the entrance, as well as crosses, scallop shells and so on, clearly reveals the monastery's association with the Order of St. James. It was by far the most frequented pilgrims' hospital in León, which in its heyday had 17 hospitals, among them those of Santo Sepulcro, San Lázaro, San Marcelo, Santa María del Camino, San Isidoro, San Antonio, San Andrés, Capellanes and the Confraternity of St. James.

III. HISTORICAL PILGRIMS' ACCOUNTS

Aymeric Picaud: *'An enormous bridge crosses the Porma between Mansilla and León... Then you come to León ('Legio'), seat of the Royal court, full of all manner of good things... Next, you should visit the venerable remains of San Isidoro, Bishop, Confessor and Doctor, who instituted a pious rule for his priests, and who enlightened Spaniards with his doctrines and honoured the entire Holy Church with his glorious works.'*

Künig von Vach: *'Then you come to two bridges, one after another. León ('Leon') is two miles further on and is by no means a small city. You will find numerous hospitals there.'*

Arnold von Harff: *'It is three leagues from Mansilla to León ('Lioin'). This is one of the four most important cities in Spain, although it is not completely enclosed by walls. There is a splendid cathedral dedicated to Nuestra Señora de Regla ('de regula'). It is a bishopric.'*

Laffi: *'... we set off towards León ('Lione'), three leagues away, and arrived there around noon. Once inside the city, we went immediately to the Bishop to have our dimissory letters signed... and we visited the cathedral, which is very old and beautiful, although less so than Burgos cathedral... In truth, there are some ancient buildings here, as this was the capital of the Kingdom of León and the residence of the Kings themselves. There are quite a number of friaries and convents. The city is ringed by walls and stands in a plain. A great river flows through the west side of the city, and on its bank there is a very large, well-endowed hospital facing the river, which is called the Hostal de San Marcos and which has a beautiful church, and there are some monks who give a ration of food to pilgrims... And in the morning we went to Mass at San Isidoro... and they gave us alms for three months... We strolled around the city again, which is really beautiful, rich and spacious. There is a very big market which is full of all manner of merchandise.'*

STAGE 21

LEÓN • VILLADANGOS

The Virgen del Camino, in the Sanctuary of the same name

LEÓN • TROBAJO DEL CAMINO •
LA VIRGEN DEL CAMINO •
VALVERDE DE LA VIRGEN •
SAN MIGUEL DEL CAMINO •
VILLADANGOS DEL PÁRAMO

PILGRIMS' REFUGES

Villadangos:
This is another of the luxury refuges to be found along the Pilgrims' Route, in this case as it passes through León province. It has a large capacity and features excellent bathroom facilities, hot water, bunk-beds, a kitchen, etc.
☎ (987) 39 00 03

ACCOMMODATION

Trobajo del Camino:
HS* El Abuelo. Los Mesones, 6-8.
☎ (987) 80 10 44.
26 rooms. ♣
HSR* Bella. Santiago Apóstol, 8.
☎ (987) 80 28 10.
12 rooms. ♣

La Virgen del Camino:
HSR** Soto. Ctra. León-Astorga, km 5. ☎ (987) 80 29 25.
29 rooms. ♣
HS* Central. Ctra. León-Astorga, km 7. ☎ (987) 30 20 41.
15 rooms. ♣
HSR* Julio César.
Cervantes, 5. ☎ (987) 30 01 29.
8 rooms. ♣

Villadangos del Páramo:
HR** Avenida III. Ctra. León-Astorga, km 17. ☎ (987) 39 03 11.
20 rooms. ♣♣
HS** Alto Páramo.
Ctra. León-Astorga, km 18.
☎ (987) 39 04 25.
15 rooms. ♣
HS** Avenida II. Ctra. León-Astorga, km 17. ☎ (987) 39 01 51.
10 rooms. ♣
HS** Montico. Ctra. León-Astorga, km 17. ☎ (987) 39 00 01.
26 rooms. ♣

RESTAURANTS

Trobajo del Camino:
El Abuelo.

La Virgen del Camino:
Las Redes. Ctra. León-Astorga, s/n.
☎ (987) 30 01 64. Shellfish.

San Miguel del Camino:
La Casa de las Chuletas.

Villadangos del Páramo:
Sol de León.
La Pradera.

PETROL STATIONS
On the N-120 at km 308'7; and km 322'2.

'Bernesgua, que iuxta eandem urbem defluit'
(Aymeric Picaud; 'Pilgrims' Guide')

I. ROUTE

🚶 The route out of **León** from the Basílica de San Isidoro is along Calle de Renueva and Calle Suero de Quiñones, and across the bridge over the river Bernesga next to the Hostal de San Marcos (which you pass on the right). You then continue along the N-120 for a kilometre or so before crossing the railway line, where you bear left off the main road, which curves round to the right. Almost immediately, you cross back onto the N-120 and make your way through **Trobajo del Camino** along a road which runs parallel to the main road and which eventually leads back onto it. After a short distance, bear left off the main road again, thus avoiding an enormous curve as the road climbs up towards the Sanctuary of the Virgen del Camino. Before the road straightens out, cross over to the right-hand side and take a path which leads up to the top of a hill which is crowned by a ruined stone cross. From this point, the route passes through a very unattractive area of rubbish dumps, scrap heaps and warehouses, until it reaches the Sanctuary of the **Virgen del Camino** (about 3 km from the centre of Trobajo). After visiting the sanctuary, return to the N-120 and bear left off it almost immediately onto a path which runs alongside the local cemetery and then continues for a long stretch parallel to the main road on its way across the overwhelmingly arid plain. You then descend towards the Arroyo Fruévano valley where you return to the N-120, shortly before the intersection with the A-66 motorway to Oviedo. Proceed along the main road for 2 km to **Valverde de la Virgen,** where the Arroyo de la Oncina (after which the valley is named) meets its affluent, the Arroyo de Raposeras. A kilometre further on, bear right off the N-120 into **San Miguel del Camino,** and make your way through the village along a parallel road. On leaving the village, return to the N-120, cross over to the other side, and continue parallel to it (off the road) for about 8 km, until you reach **Villadangos del Páramo.** On the way, the path gets lost to view several times and approaches the main road on various occasions, before crossing the Arroyo Valdecelada, opposite the 'Camino de Santiago' housing development on the other side of the main road.

🚲 Between León and the Sanctuary of the Virgen del Camino, cyclists are advised to follow the N-120. Although it is by no means an easy ride (not to mention hazardous) it is more straightforward than the pedestrian route described above. Between Virgen del Camino and Villadangos, the path and the road have very little to choose between them.

🚗 Milestones: N-120 km 305: Trobajo del Camino; km 310.7: Sanctuary of the Virgen del Camino; km 314: Valverde de la Virgen; km 315: San Miguel del Camino; km 321.4: 'Camino de Santiago' housing development; km 323: Villadangos del Páramo.

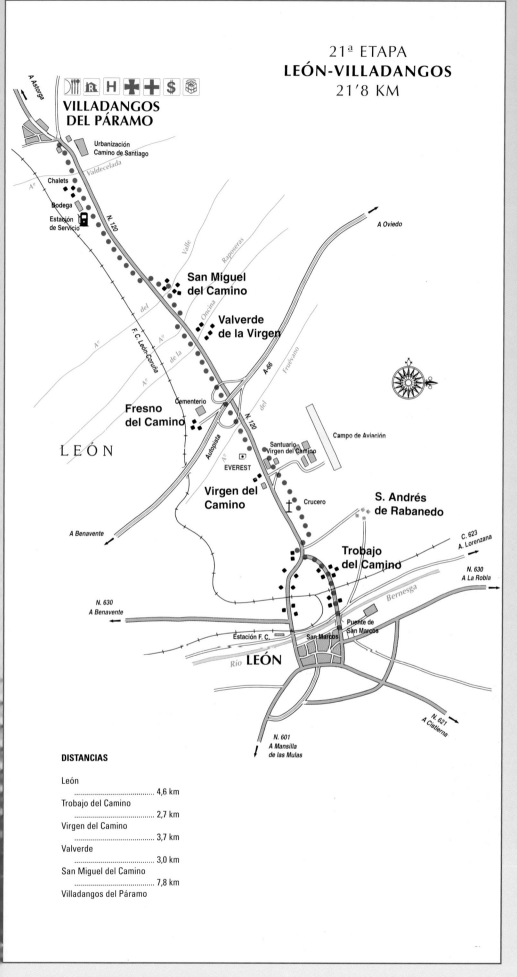

21ª ETAPA
LEÓN-VILLADANGOS
21'8 KM

VILLADANGOS
DEL PÁRAMO

Urbanización
Camino de Santiago

Valdecelada

Chalets

Bodega

Estación
de Servicio

N 120

A Astorga

A Oviedo

San Miguel
del Camino

Valverde
de la Virgen

A-66

Raposeras

Valle

del

Oncina

de la

Fruévano

F. C. León-Coruña

Cementerio

Fresno
del Camino

LEÓN

N. 120

del

Campo de Aviación

Santuario
Virgen del Camino

Autopista

EVEREST

Virgen del
Camino

Crucero

S. Andrés
de Rabanedo

A Benavente

C. 623
A. Lorenzana

Trobajo
del Camino

N. 630
A La Robla

N. 630
A Benavente

Bernesga

Estación F. C.

San Marcos

Puente de
San Marcos

Río LEÓN

N. 621
A Cisterna

N. 601
A Mansilla
de las Mulas

DISTANCIAS

León
.... 4,6 km
Trobajo del Camino
.... 2,7 km
Virgen del Camino
.... 3,7 km
Valverde
.... 3,0 km
San Miguel del Camino
.... 7,8 km
Villadangos del Páramo

Puente of San Marcos, León

The Apostolate on the Sanctuary of the Virgen del Camino

The Sanctuary of the Virgen del Camino

II. HISTORY, ART AND LEGENDS

The route out of León takes you across the Puente de San Marcos next to the Hostal de San Marcos, which has carried pilgrims across the river Bernesga since the 16th century when it was built as a replacement to the earlier bridge.

At this point, pilgrims who intended visiting the holy relics in the 'Cámara Santa' at Oviedo cathedral would part company with those going straight to Santiago. Before crossing the Bernesga, they would follow a route similar to the present N-630, parallel to the river, which took them up through La Robla and thence to the Collegiate church of Santa María de Arbas, a place of refuge on the difficult trek though the Pajares pass (the Asturian equivalent of the mountain routes through Roncesvalles, the Montes de Oca, 'Monte Irago' or El Cebreiro). Once over the mountains, they would continue via Pola de Lena and Mieres del Camino to the long-awaited shrine at Oviedo, which sometimes vied in importance with Santiago itself.

Trobajo del Camino, now a suburb of León, has a parish church dedicated to St. John the Baptist, as well as a small 18th-century chapel dedicated to St. James, which was once run by a Confraternity of St. James. The statue of St. James the Moor-slayer in the parish church is taken from the chapel. A ruined stone cross similar to the one at the Alto del Portillo stands just outside the village on a small hill, from where there is also an exceptional panoramic view of León.

Next you come to **La Virgen del Camino** (practically a continuation of Trobajo), a village which grew up around the Sanctuary dedicated to the Patroness of León. The present building dates from 1961, and is the work of the Dominican monk and architect, Fray Francisco Coello de Portugal. The massive modernist sculpture of the Apostolate which runs around the façade is the most well-known feature of the new sanctuary. The thirteen bronze statues (the 12 Apostles and the Virgin), each measuring 6 metres and weighing 700 kilos, are the work of the Catalan sculptor José María Subirachs, and are one of the most representative compositions of Spanish modernist religious sculpture. The stylised silhouettes are a clever replica of the Gothic style of León cathedral. Of the earlier 17th-century church, the baroque retable dating from 1730 has been retained and it is presided over by the famous 15th-century figure of the *Virgen del Camino* which stands on an opulent silver portable platform dating from 1715. The Madonna at the church of Santa María de Mercado on the pilgrims' route through León used to be known as the Virgen del Camino. However, from the beginning of the 16th century the cult of the new Virgen del Camino spread like wildfire, and the name was reserved exclusively for the image venerated in the sanctuary outside the city, while the former bearer was renamed 'la Virgen del Mercado'. Municipal records of León dating from 1514 mention the mysterious event which is supposed to have taken place at this deserted spot a few years earlier, when the Virgin appeared to a

The Virgen del Camino (unadorned)

shepherd, Alvar Simón, and ordered him to build her a shrine. From that moment on, the cult of the Virgen del Camino spread throughout the Kingdom of León. Among the numerous votive offerings which are kept in the sanctuary, the most curious are the strongbox and chains with which the merchant Alonso de Ribera was held prisoner by the Moors. He was liberated through the intercession of the Virgen del Camino, who miraculously spirited him back home inside the strongbox, still shackled with the chains.

Valverde de la Virgen

The pilgrims' route continues across the stark Leonese plain, whose one saving grace are the oases of vegetation (mainly poplars) growing on the banks of the rivers and streams which flow across it from the Cordillera Cantábrica. In Spanish, the plain is known as the *'páramo',* a term already used by the pre-Roman inhabitants of this northern plateau. The Romans substituted this word with the Latin 'campus', which is where the name *'Tierra de Campos'* comes from. However, the word 'páramo' has survived, not only as a generic term for a wide barren plain, but also as the name of this large area of the province of León, which extends from the Tierra de Campos to the Maragatería, and which shares many of the geographical characterisitics of the former.

San Miguel del Camino

The little village of **Valverde de la Virgen** (until fairly recently known as 'Valverde del Camino') is situated in the valley formed by the Arroyo de la Oncina and the Arroyo de Raposeras. Despite its insignificance, it is mentioned by name (one of the commonest place names in Spain) in 10th-century documents. Its modest parish church is dedicated to Santa Engracia, a centuries-old cult which is only found in Hispanic countries.

Situated in another of the pleasant little valleys that break the monotony of the plain is **San Miguel del Camino,** another small village flanking the pilgrims' way. Its links with the pilgrimage have been very strong throughout the centuries and there was a pilgrims' hospital in the village at least as early as the 12th century. A lovely 15th-century image of St. James once graced the village church, but it is now in León.

The hostel at Villadangos del Páramo

Villadangos del Páramo is also situated in a valley and is iconographically one of the most Jacobean villages along the pilgrims' route. According to some writers, Villadangos was *'Vallata',* an Asturian town on the *'Via Traiana'* which appears in the old *'Itineraria'.* After this, it disappears from history. It re-emerged during the high Middle Ages as one of the resettled villages in the wake of the first phase of the Reconquest, and in the earliest medieval documents it appears as *'Viadangos'.* In the year 1111, it was the scene of a bloody battle between troops loyal to Queen Doña Urraca and her son Alfonso VII 'the Emperor' and the army of the Aragonese king, Alfonso I 'the Battler', Doña Urraca's ex-husband. Perhaps the memory of this important battle accounts for the fact that all the representations of St. James, the village's patron saint, tend to emphasise his warlike aspect, rather than his gentler side as pilgrim or Apostle. Indeed, in the Parish Church of Santiago one of the most

Villadangos: portal of the Church of Santiago

The High Altar at the Church of Santiago, Villadangos

famous depictions of him in his Moor-slayer guise is to be found presiding over the high altar, sword in hand and attired in period military dress, topped with an 18th-century tricorn hat. Another image of St. James, in this case dressed as a pilgrim, can be seen beside it, while in the bottom section of the retable there are two reliefs illustrating scenes from the life of the Apostle: the appearance of the Virgen del Pilar and the battle at Clavijo. An image of St. Claude, another of the sons of St. Marcel (an ancient local cult) completes the retable. The church doors are carved with two charming painted folk art reliefs depicting the mythical victory of King Ramiro I of León over Abdurrahman II at Clavijo through the intervention of St. James. The reliefs are accompanied by some inscriptions which are extremely difficult to decipher, due to having been thoughtlessly repainted over the years.

St. James the Moor-slayer, Villadangos

The plain, near Villadangos

III. HISTORICAL PILGRIMS' ACCOUNTS

Aymeric Picaud: *'The Bernesga ('Bernesgua'), in the same city* [León], *but on the other side, that is to say, in the direction of Astorga.'*

Künig von Vach: *'And there* [on the way out of León] *the pilgrims' way divides into three branches, one of which goes to San Salvador* [Oviedo cathedral] *('Sant Salvator'), for which you must leave the city by the North Gate. But if you wish to go to Astorga, you must cross three bridges and then climb a mountain...'*

Arnold von Harff: *'It is two leagues from León to San Miguel del Camino ('sent Michaele'), a small village, and two leagues from San Miguel to the village of Villadangos ('Villa dangus').'*

Laffi: *'We left the city* [León], *passing the Hospital where the monks serve the pilgrims' ration... and, after crossing the great bridge I mentioned before, we made our way up to the top of a hill, where they are building a lovely church dedicated to a miraculous image which they call Santa María del Camino ('Beata Vergine del Camino'). We then reached San Miguel del Camino ('San Michele'), two leagues away, a very small village of straw-roofed huts...'*

STAGE 22

VILLADANGOS • ASTORGA

The cathedral and Bishop's Palace, Astorga

VILLADANGOS • SAN MARTÍN DEL CAMINO •
PUENTE DE ÓRBIGO • HOSPITAL DE ÓRBIGO •
VILLARES DE ÓRBIGO •
SANTIBÁÑEZ DE VALDEIGLESIAS •
SAN JUSTO DE LA VEGA • ASTORGA

PILGRIMS' REFUGES

Hospital de Órbigo: Within the beautifully restored building referred to as *Casa de la Vega* lies yet another magnificent municipal hostel. Situated on the banks of the River Órbigo, it has 36 beds. Casa parroquial: ☎ (987) 38 84 44
Casa de la Vega ☎ (987) 38 82 50
Astorga: Comfortable municipal hostel with a capacity for 36 people. It is run by the Astorga «Friends of the Pilgrims' Route to Santiago Association» and is located amidst beautiful surroundings at no.26, *Calle Matías Rodríguez.*
☎ (987) 61 62 20

ACCOMMODATION

Hospital de Órbigo:
HR Paso Honroso.** Ctra, Nal. 120, km 335. ☎ (987) 36 10 10. 12 rooms. ♣ ♣
HS Don Suero de Quiñones.** Álvarez Vega, 1. ☎ (987) 38 82 38. 11 rooms. ♣ ♣
HS El Kanguro Australiano.** Ctra. León-Astorga, km 31. ☎ (987) 38 90 31. 14 rooms. ♣
San Justo de la Vega:
HSR* Ideal. Real, 26. ☎ (987) 61 66 81. 22 rooms. ♣
Astorga:
HR* Gaudí.** Eduardo de Castro, 6. ☎ (987) 61 56 54. ♣ ♣
M* Pradorrey.** Ctra. Madrid-La Coruña, km 330. ☎ (987) 61 57 29. ♣ ♣
HSR Gallego.** Avda. Ponferrada, 78. ☎ (987) 61 54 50. ♣ ♣
HSR La Peseta.** Pza. de San Bartolomé, 3. ☎ (987) 61 72 75. ♣
San Narciso. Santana. Casa Sacerdotal. Coruña. Delfín.

CAMPSITES

Hospital de Órbigo:
Don Suero de Quiñones. 2nd Category. ☎ (987) 38 84 48

RESTAURANTS

Hospital de Órbigo:
Avenida. Fueros de León, 31. ☎ (987) 38 82 11.
Mesón Piscifactoría. La Vega, s/n ☎ (987) 33 81 14. ♣
Coto Cero. Flamingo. Parrillada. La Pista.
Astorga:
Regional cuisine within the medium price range: **Bardal, Gaudí** and **La Peseta.** More economical: **El Maragato, Las Murallas, Peñicas, La Paloma, París, Plaza, Río, Teleno, Ruta leonesa, Serrano...**

PETROL STATIONS

On the N-120 at km 335; On the N-VI at km 325; in Astorga.

'Inde est Orbega, inde est urbs Osturga.'
(Aymeric Picaud: 'Pilgrims' Guide')

I. ROUTE

🚶 The road through **Villadangos** comes out at a magnificent poplar grove and, after crossing a stream, you should make your way along a path which runs parallel to the right of the N-120 to **San Martín del Camino,** about 4.5 km away. On leaving the village, return to the path, which runs close to the main road as it makes its way across irrigated arable land which now covers the previously arid plain. After 6.5 km, having crossed one of the many irrigation channels which are a feature of this stretch of the route, you turn right towards **Puente de Orbigo,** cross over the great bridge and enter **Hospital de Orbigo** along the Calle Mayor, passing the remains of the old hospital on the left and the Church of San Juan on the right. At the end of a street named 'Camino de Santiago', the road forks towards the N-120 on the left and to **Villares de Orbigo,** 2 km away, along a farm track. From Villares de Orbigo, an asphalted track leads to **Santibáñez de Valdeiglesias** (some 2.5 kilometres away), from where you take a path which, after about a kilometre, starts to climb up Monte de la Colomba, through holm oaks. At an excavation on the left the path forks, and you should take the left-hand fork, which leads to a bare valley. Bear right at the next fork onto a paved path which runs through holm oaks and scrub and which emerges onto a wide track. Almost immediately, you bear right off this track onto a forest path which climbs up through the undergrowth. From the top, you descend to a pleasant little valley, cross the Arroyo Grillo, climb up again to a plateau and continue in the direction of the peak of El Teleno and the city of Astorga which are visible in the distance, passing a large field and a sheep-fold on the right. Upon reaching another intersection, take the central fork to the Cross of Santo Toribio, from where you go down the Camino de la Cañada to **San Justo de la Vega.** (Had you taken the straighter right-hand path at the intersection [the *Camino de la Piedra Fincada*], you would have entered San Justo along the Calle del Hospital.) Leave the village by way of the Calle de los Vientos and go up to the N-120 via a bridge over the river Tuerto. Shortly afterwards, bear right off the main road onto a parallel path which, after 3 km, brings you into **Astorga** via the Calle Puertasol, after crossing the railway line and a Roman bridge.

🚲 Cyclists are advised to stick to the N-120 throughout this stage, as almost all the unsurfaced stretches present some degree of difficulty.

🚗 Milestones: N-120 km 327.1: San Martín del Camino; km 334.6: Puente de Orbigo; km 335: Hospital de Orbigo; km 345: turning to San Justo de la Vega; km 350: Astorga.

ASTORGA

A La Coruña

S. Pedro

N. VI

A Madrid

Catedral
Sta. Marta

Muralla Romana

A León

S. Francisco

C. Iglesia

ASTORGA

Plaza
de Toros

N. VI

A Rabanal

A La Bañeza   N. VI

Puente
Romano

Río   Tuerto

**San Justo
de la Vega**

N. 120

Crucero
de S. Toribio

**San Román
de la Vega**

Grillo

Sierra de
La Paloma

Aº

22ª ETAPA
VILLADANGOS-ASTORGA
26 KM

Santibáñez

Canal

**Estebánez
de la Calzada**

**Villares
de Órbigo**

**Benavides
de Órbigo**

LEÓN

A Viloria

Hotel   **Hospital
de Órbigo**

Ayuntamiento

Río   Órbigo

Pte. Romano

**Puente
de Órbigo**

**Sta. Marina
del Rey**

A Carrizo

A Sta. María
del Páramo

**San Martín
del Camino**

Huerga

**Celadilla
del Páramo**

A Bustillo

de la   Páramo

N. 120

Riego

Lavadero

Canal   del

Aº

**VILLADANGOS
DEL PÁRAMO**

Urbanización
Cª de Santiago

A León

Aº

DISTANCIAS

Villadangos del Páramo
.... 3,0 km
San Martín
.... 7,0 km
Puente Órbigo
.... 2,0 km
Villares
.... 2,0 km
Santibáñez
.... 8,0 km
San Justo
.... 4,0 km
Astorga

The Puente de Órbigo or 'Passo honroso'

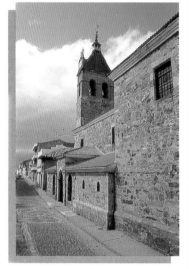

Hospital de Órbigo: the parish church and the main street

Bust of Santiago Alfeo

The 'Pero Mato'

II. HISTORY, ART AND LEGENDS

The village church at **San Martín del Camino** is dedicated to the Bishop of Tours, St. Martin, the patron saint of pilgrims. It has a modern altar at which, curiously, statues of other protectors of pilgrims, such as St. Michael, San Roque and San Antonio Abad, are grouped together. Records show that there was a hospital for indigent pilgrims here in the 17th century.

The village of **Puente de Orbigo,** on the left bank of the Orbigo, has a parish church dedicated to St. Blase, which suggests the past existence of a hospital for sick pilgrims. The bridge over the Orbigo is one of the most famous along the pilgrims' route, both for its architectural qualities and its history. It has been the scene of a number of violent confrontations, including the battle between the Swabians and the Visigoths in 452, the clash between the Moors and the army of Alfonso III 'the Great' (c. 900) and the famous incident that took place in the Holy Year of 1434 which gave the bridge its nickname, 'el Passo Honroso', when a Leonese knight, Don Suero de Quiñones, persuaded nine other knights to join him in challenging any adventurers who dared cross the bridge between July 10th and 9th August to joust with them. Don Suero declared himself imprisoned by his love for a certain lady, and calling on St. James as his witness, vowed to break 300 lances as a ransom to escape from his 'prison'. Over 30 days, the Leonese and his knights vanquished French, Italian, German, Portuguese and Spanish contenders. When the contest was over, they all went to Compostela, where Suero de Quiñones offered the Apostle a golden bracelet of his lady's in thanksgiving. This bracelet has been associated with the collar which adorns the bust of Santiago Alfeo in the reliquary chapel at Santiago cathedral, which bears the following inscription:

'Si a vous ne playst avoyr mesura,
certes ie di que ie suy sans ventura.'

After crossing the bridge, you enter **Hospital de Orbigo.** Both the name of the town and the dedication of its church to St. John are indicative of the presence of the Hospitallers, who ran a pilgrims' hospital here.

The parish church of **Villares de Orbigo** is dedicated to St. James, who presides over the high altar as the Moor-slayer. The church of the Trinity at **Santibáñez de Valdeiglesias** houses a couple of fine figures of San Roque the pilgrim and St. James the Moor-slayer.

Shortly before entering **San Justo de la Vega,** you come to a granite cross situated on a hilltop which is dedicated to St. Toribio, a 5th-century bishop of Astorga, and marks the spot where he is supposed to have shaken the dust from his sandals after being forced to leave his diocese. A clear remnant of the pilgrimage is the fact that, until 1965, there was a figure of San Roque in the village church of San Justo and San Pastor. Also, villagers can still remember a time when there was a *'Casa de los Pobres'* (House of the Poor) on the Calle Hospital, which would certainly have been the successor of the former pilgrims' hospital.

Astorga ('Asturica Augusta') was an important Asturian enclave, and gained prominence in Roman times as the seat of the 'Conventus Iuridicus'. Its position at the junction between two of the most important Roman roads - the **Via Traiana** from Bordeaux *(Burdigala)* and the Via de la Plata from Mérida *(Emerita Augusta)* - profoundly influenced its development, and explains the entrepreneurial, commercial and itinerant nature of the Maragatos, the local ethnic group whose capital was Astorga. Legend has it that Astorga was an episcopal see founded by St. James himself. Historical records show the existence of a bishop by the 3rd century, and at the end of the 4th century it was one of the places most affected by Priscillian's heresy. As a Swabian city it was destroyed by the Visigoths after the battle of Orbigo, and under Visigothic rule in the 7th century it became an important centre of the monastic movement, the main focus of which was the El Bierzo region, and whose most important names were Santo Toribio, San Fructuoso and San Valerio. Astorga came to have 21 pilgrims' hospitals, the largest number after Burgos, which clearly reveals its importance on the pilgrims' route.

The walls of Astorga

Pilgrims entered the *walls* through the Puerta del Sol, which still retains some Roman elements. The Arrabal de San Andrés was the location of the Hospital de San Esteban, the Hospital de San Feliz and the Hospital de las Cinco Llagas (an amalgamation of five earlier hospitals) which still existed until fairly recently. The route continued along the Calle de San Francisco, which was the old commercial street occupied by Jewish and Frankish merchants. This is the location of the Church of San Francisco (thought to be evidence of St. Francis' sojourn in the city) and the Church of San Bartolomé, which dates from the 11th century. The city's hallmark is the pair of clockwork figurines in full Maragato traditional dress (known as the *Maragatos*), which strike the hours on the clock on the beautiful Town Hall façade. The **cathedral,** consisting of a triple-aisled nave with side chapels and three polygonal apses, was started in 1471 in the Gothic style. Among its most outstanding features are the Renaissance *high altar* (the masterpiece of the Andalusian artist Gaspar Becerra), a Romanesque figure of the *Virgen de la Majestad* and Gregorio Fernández's 'Inmaculada'. On the outside, apart from the two great towers (the first thing pilgrims see in the distance on the approach to Astorga), the most noteworthy features are the low reliefs above the main door and the figure of *Pero Mato,* the Maragato who took part in the Battle of Clavijo, which crowns one of the apse pinnacles. The *Diocesan Museum* houses some valuable pieces. The former Hospital de San Juan, founded in the 12th century, is next to the cathedral. Between the baroque Church of Santa María and the Gothic chapel of San Esteban is the *Celda de las Emparedadas,* the cell in which loose-living women were locked up, to whom pilgrims would traditionally give part of their food. Standing opposite the cathedral is Antonio Gaudí's neo-Gothic **Bishop's Palace,** built between 1889 and 1913. Inside is the *Museum of the Ways,* dedicated to all the roads that lead to Astorga, with a special section on the pilgrims' way which includes several valuable figures

The façade of Astorga town hall

Astorga cathedral

Interior of Astorga cathedral

*The High Altar,
Astorga cathedral*

*The Bishop's Palace and
Museum of the Ways*

*The Jacobean Room in the
Museum of the Ways*

of St. James dressed as a pilgrim. There are also some noteworthy reminders of Astorga's Roman past, including stone tablets and sculptures.

Other remnants of Astorga's Roman past are the famous *Ergástula* (the slave prison), the triple-arched *Roman bridge* which present-day pilgrims still cross on their way into Astorga and mosaics and other objects unearthed in recent excavations.

Pilgrims made their way out of Astorga via the Puerta del Obispo, the location of the Chapel of the Confraternity of Santiago de los Pelliteros, and then through the Arrabal de Rectivía, outside the city gates, and thence towards either Monte Irago or the Puerto de Manzanal.

Don't leave Astorga without sampling its delicious mantecadas (butter buns), one of the most famous delicacies in Spanish pastrymaking.

III. HISTORICAL PILGRIMS' ACCOUNTS

Aymeric Picaud: *'Then comes Orbigo ('Orbega') and the city of Astorga ('Osturga')...'*

Künig von Vach: *'... you come to a great stone cross, and then you must turn to the left and thus will you reach Astorga ('Storgeß').'*

Arnold von Harff: *'It is two leagues from Villadangos to the village of Puente de Orbigo ('Ponte de Orfigo'), which is situated on both sides of the river Orbigo next to a stone bridge. It is three leagues from Puente de Orbigo to Astorga ('Storgis'), a Spanish walled city. At the southern tip of the city there is a castle ringed by beautiful towers.'*

Laffi: *'... and we continued towards Puente de Orbigo ('Ponte dell'aqua'), four leagues away, where we spent the night, although in great discomfort as we were obliged to sleep on the floor, as the inhabitants are so poor that they we had to give them alms, in addition to payment for the shelter of their hovels. The next morning we left Hospital de Orbigo and, passing through two small villages, reached Astorga ('Storga'), which is part of the domain of the Marquis of Astorga. It is quite a fine city, situated on a hillside... and ringed by tall, strong walls built of heavy stone... There are three gates: one towards the East... which is so small that one can only go through it in single file, and I think it is mainly used as an exit more than anything else; and another towards the North... through which one enters upon arriving at the city..., and another towards the West... On the right is the Cathedral which is old and beautiful and finished with precious marbles with statues and reliefs, and very well kept up by the Canons... On the right of the Cathedral is the Bishop's Palace and to the left the Hospital, where they are very charitable to pilgrims.'*

STAGE 23

ASTORGA • RABANAL

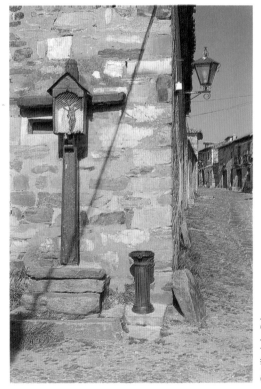

Castrillo de los Polvazares

ASTORGA • VALDEVIEJAS •
MURIAS DE RECHIVALDO •
SANTA CATALINA DE SOMOZA • EL GANSO •
RABANAL DEL CAMINO

Murias de Rechivaldo: Simple municipal hostel that proves very useful during the so-called «high season» of the pilgrimage. It has 12 beds.

Santa Catalina de Somoza: Simple 12-bed municipal hostel that is useful in the months when pilgrim traffic is at its peak.

Rabanal del Camino: The Confraternity of Saint James in England has reconstructed the old parish house at Rabanal and has fitted it out as a pilgrims' refuge. Run as it is by the members of the Confraternity themselves, the «Gaucelmo» Refuge is one of the best-liked and most original of those to be found along the Pilgrims' Route.
☎ (987) 63 94 92 - 63 94 68

ACCOMMODATION
Castrillo de los Polvazares:
Hostería Cuca la Vaina.
☎ (987) 69 10 78. ♣♣
Also has restaurant.

RESTAURANTS
Castrillo de los Polvazares:
Mesón El Arriero.
☎ (987) 61 60 21
Mesón Maruja Botas.
Mesón La Magdalena.
☎ (987) 61 85 39

Murias de Rechivaldo:
Mesón El Rancho.
☎ (987) 61 92 70

'Inde Raphanellus.' (Aymeric Picaud: 'Pilgrims' Guide')

I. ROUTE

🚶 Leave **Astorga** by way of the N-VI, looking out for a turning on the left onto the provincial road LE-142 to Santa Colomba de Somoza, Rabanal and Foncebadón. After just over a kilometre, you pass the village of **Valdeviejas** on the right and the Ermita del Ecce Homo on the left. Approximately two km further on, you come to **Murias de Rechivaldo,** after crossing the poplar-lined river Jerga. The LE-142 continues to Castrillo de los Polvazares, just over a kilometre away, but the pilgrims' route bears left off it and continues for 2.5 km (during which you will spot the remains of the cobblestones of the old road underfoot), before crossing it again at the point where a smaller road leads off it to Santa Catalina de Somoza, El Ganso, etc. This narrow and very basic asphalted road covers the first stage of the gradual ascent up to the Foncebadón pass, the historic *'Monte Irago'.* After 2 km, you reach **Santa Catalina de Somoza,** pass through it along the Calle Real and come back out onto the road, which then climbs gently uphill to the village of **El Ganso,** 4.5 km away. The road goes through the middle of El Ganso, passing the Church of Santiago on the right at the end of the village. Just under 5 km further on, you cross the Puente de Pañoto over the Arroyo de las Reguerinas, passing the turning to Rabanal Viejo and the Roman mine of *'La Fucarona'* on the right, 2.3 km and 1 km respectively from the Puente del Pañoto. However, the pilgrims' route continues along the same road as before, which takes you through a pinewood and past the *'Pilgrim's Oak',* a magnificent old tree which grows on the left-hand side of the road. A few hundred metres further on, you pass the Ermita del Santo Cristo and come out onto the LE-142 at the entrance to **Rabanal del Camino.** A paved street off to the right of the road leads up to the parish church of the Assumption and the *Refugio Gaucelmo.*

🚴 Throughout this stage, cyclists can follow the pedestrian route with no difficulty.

🚗 Milestones: LE-142 km 1.7: Valdeviejas; km 4: Murias de Rechivaldo; km 5.1: Castrillo de los Polvazares; km 6.4: turning to Santa Catalina de Somoza and El Ganso. On this minor road: km 2: Santa Catalina de Somoza; km 6: El Ganso; km 11: turning to Rabanal Viejo and La Fucarona; km 13: junction with the LE-142 at Rabanal del Camino.

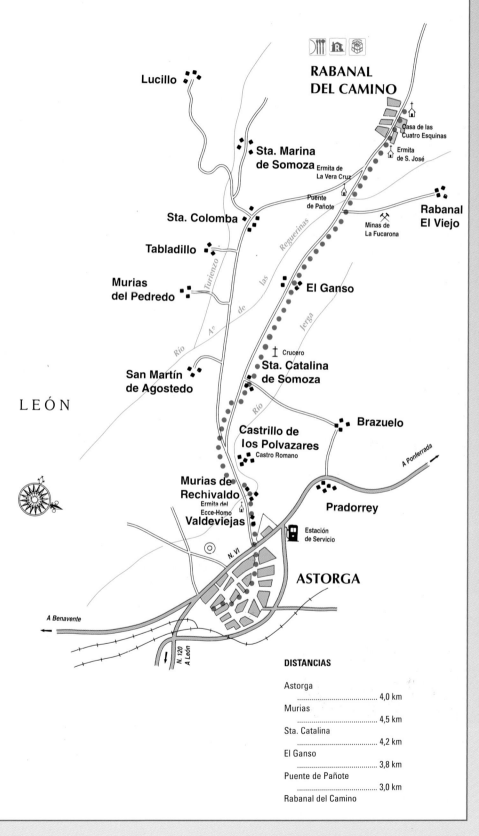

23ª ETAPA
ASTORGA
RABANAL DEL CAMINO
19'5 KM

Lucillo

RABANAL DEL CAMINO

Casa de las Cuatro Esquinas

Ermita de S. José

Sta. Marina de Somoza

Ermita de La Vera Cruz

Puente de Pañote

Rabanal El Viejo

Minas de La Fucarona

Sta. Colomba

Tabladillo

Murias del Pedredo

El Ganso

Turienzo

Reguerinas

de las

A°

Río

Jerga

† Crucero

Sta. Catalina de Somoza

San Martín de Agostedo

LEÓN

Río

Brazuelo

Castrillo de los Polvazares

Castro Romano

Murias de Rechivaldo

Ermita del Ecce-Homo

Valdeviejas

Pradorrey

Estación de Servicio

N. VI

ASTORGA

A Ponferrada

A Benavente

N. 120 A León

DISTANCIAS

Astorga

.... 4,0 km

Murias

.... 4,5 km

Sta. Catalina

.... 4,2 km

El Ganso

.... 3,8 km

Puente de Pañote

.... 3,0 km

Rabanal del Camino

Castrillo de los Polvazares

Stone cross at Valdespino de Somoza

Pilgrims on the mountainsides at La Somoza

La Maragatería: typical scene

II. HISTORY, ART AND LEGENDS

On leaving Astorga, pilgrims may choose between two alternative routes: either to carry on westwards through Rabanal, or to head northwestwards across the Puerto de Manzanal, thereby avoiding the climb up *'Monte Irago'*, a route chosen by many pilgrims, including Hermann Künig von Vach. This latter route follows the N-VI on its way to Ponferrada via Bembibre. Montealegre, shortly after the Puerto de Manzanal, was the location of a pilgrims' hospital administered by the Hospitallers of St. John, and the 12th-century Church of San Juan is a reminder of their presence at this important pass on the pilgrims' route.

Valdeviejas, only one kilometre from Astorga, has a parish church dedicated to San Verísimo who once gave his name to the whole village, which used to be called 'Villa Sancti Verissimi'. Records dating from 1481 show the existence of a pilgrims' hospital which was originally named after its founder, Sancha Pérez, and subsquently after the Confraternity of the Martyrs who administered it. The Calle de los Mártires which runs between Astorga and Valdeviejas is named after the Confraternity.

Standing on a small plain outside Valdeviejas is the Ermita del Ecce Homo, a medieval chapel which was restored in the 18th and 19th centuries.

Murias de Rechivaldo is the first typical Maragato village you come to. It was, like many others in the region, a village of muleteers, the age-old occupation of the Maragatos. The village church, dedicated to San Esteban, dates from the 18th century and its most Jacobean features are a relief of the Virgen del Pilar set in a niche over the door and a statue of San Roque Peregrino.

Castrillo de los Polvazares is just off the pilgrims' route, on the LE-142. It is the most typical Maragato village and was immortalised by the writer, Concha Espina, in her novel *The Maragato Sphinx,* a portrait of the village and its centuries-old customs, which can be applied to other villages in the region. The village is very well-preserved (especially its cobbled streets) and has recently become a tourist attraction. It is also famous for its 'Cocido maragato', a type of stew. The remains of an ancient hill fort ('castro') are to be found on a hill known as 'La Mesa', not far from Castrillo.

The next village is **Santa Catalina de Somoza,** situated in the Somoza (from the Latin *'sub montia'*) region at the foot of *'Monte Irago'*. The village has always been famous for its hospitality to pilgrims, to the extent that in some pilgrims' accounts (see Arnold von Harff's account at the end of this chapter) it is simply called *'Hospital'*. The pilgrims' hospital was dedicated to the Virgen de las Candelas. The Parish Church of Santa María houses a relic of St. Blase, the village's patron saint and one of the saints most frequently associated with pilgrims' welfare and health along the route. In common with many other villages along the pilgrims' way, the Calle Mayor is the pilgrims' route through the village.

In **El Ganso,** you will see straw-roofed houses for the first time. This type of roofing goes back to prehistoric times, and remained in use for centuries: Domenico Laffi, writing in 1673, encountered straw-roofed houses at Villadangos in the Leonese plain (Stage 21) and at El Burgo Raneros in the Tierra de Campos region (Stage 18). This type of roofing is thought to be indicative of these regions' Celtic extraction, although it only survives now in this area of the Bierzo and in some particularly backward, conservative areas of Galicia. Records show the existence of a pilgrims' hospital and a monastery in El Ganso, both under the auspices of Premonstratensian nuns dependent on the Monastery of Cluny. The parish church is dedicated to St. James, the village's patron saint, and has a fine 16th-century figure of him in pilgrims' dress.

El Ganso

Along the road which leads to Rabanal Viejo are the remains of a Roman gold mine, the **Mina de la Fucarona,** situated in an area of similar geological characteristics to the famous 'Médulas' of Ponferrada. **Rabanal del Camino** is the final halt of the ninth stage of Aymeric Picaud's itinerary. He calls it 'Captivus', which seems to suggest the existence of another place called Rabanal (which would be Rabanal Viejo). At one time it was an important stop on the pilgrims' way, being the last milestone before the final stage of the climb up 'Monte Irago', and had several churches and pilgrims' hospitals, some of which still stand as tangible evidence of the village's important Jacobean past.

The Calle Real: the pilgrims' route through Rabanal del Camino

Standing on the left-hand side of the road as you approach the village is the Ermita del Santo Cristo de la Vera Cruz. At the beginning of the Calle Mayor (the pilgrims' route through Rabanal) is the 18th-century Ermita de San José, where an image of St. James is enshrined alongside 18th-century images of St. Joseph and St. Barbara. Further along the street is the former Hospital de San Gregorio and the *Casa de las Cuatro Esquinas* (The House of the Four Corners), which is famous for having lodged Philip II during his stay in Rabanal. Finally, at the top of the village you come to the *Parish Church of Santa María,* one of the few Romanesque specimens to be found in this area, although so retouched that its Romanesque origins are scarcely recognisable. Its era and name both point to the presence of the Templars in Rabanal at the beginning of the 12th century, although concrete evidence of this is scant. The Order's base in Rabanal would possibly have been a dependency or outpost of Ponferrada, with the function of ensuring safe passage for pilgrims on this difficult, lonely stretch up 'Monte Irago' (or 'Mount Rabanal' as it was sometimes called). It is probable that the Knights Templars offered all kinds of help and assistance to pilgrims, apart from protection.

The Parish Church of Santa María at Rabanal del Camino

The Ermita del Santo Cristo, Rabanal del Camino

Capilla de San José, Rabanal del Camino

The 'Refugio Gaucelmo', Rabanal del Camino

The early 13th-century French work, the *'Anseïs de Cartage'*, which is set mainly on the Spanish stretch of the road to Santiago, places one of its episodes in Rabanal *('Mont de Ravanel')*. There, the Breton knight, Anseïs, faithful servant of Charlemagne and King of Spain and Carthage through his grace, marries the Saracen princess, Gaudisse. The work displays a good knowledge of Spanish geography, as in the scene in which Anseïs contemplates the sweeping view from Rabanal as far as Astorga *('Estorges')*.

III. HISTORICAL PILGRIMS' ACCOUNTS

Aymeric Picaud: *'Then comes Rabanal del Camino ('Raphanellus'), also called 'Captivus'.*

Künig von Vach: *'But if you wish to follow my instructions, go right and you will avoid all the mountains, which are over to the left. My advice is that you avoid Rabanal ('Rabanel') at all costs.'*

Arnold von Harff: *'It is two leagues from Astorga to the village of Santa Catalina ('Hospitale'). It is a league from Santa Catalina to El Ganso, and two leagues from El Ganso to the village of Rabanal del Camino ('Rauaneel ala kamine'). This is where Spain ends and it becomes known as the land of Galicia ('Galicien'), subject also to the King of Castile. In this village, you climb up the mountain of Rabanal. Also in this land of Galicia or Spain, the women generally wear silver or gold ear-rings.'*

Laffi: *'We left that place and set off in the direction of Rabanal ('Ravanal'), five leagues away, but we passed through two or three villages before arriving. Rabanal, which they call 'Rabanalcillo' ('Ravanacilla') is situated halfway up a mountain and is quite a fertile sort of place. We spent the night there and the next morning completed our ascent of the mountain, and it was the day of St. John the Baptist...'*

STAGE 24

RABANAL • PONFERRADA

The 'Cruz de Ferro'

RABANAL • FONCEBADÓN •
MANJARÍN • EL ACEBO • RIEGO DE AMBRÓS •
MOLINASECA • CAMPO • PONFERRADA

Manjarín: Basic mountain refuge.

El Acebo: Simple local premises.

Molinaseca: Comfortable refuge recently set up in the magnificent newly-restored Hermitage of San Roque. ☎ (987) 45 30 85

Ponferrada: There are plans for a large refuge on a site next to the *Cementerio del Carmen.* At present, members of the parish of La Encina make a great effort to receive pilgrims in a brotherly manner. ☎ (987) 41 19 78

ACCOMMODATION
Ponferrada:
HR**** Del Temple. Avda. Portugal, 2. ☎ (987) 41 00 58. 114 rooms. ♣♣♣
HR*** Bérgidum. Avda. de la Plata, 4. ☎ (987) 40 15 12. 71 rooms. ♣♣
HR** Conde Silva. Avda. de Astorga, 2. ☎ (987) 41 04 07. 60 rooms. ♣♣
H** Madrid. Avda. de la Puebla, 44. ☎ (987) 41 15 50. 55 rooms. ♣
HSR** Marán. Antolín López Peláez, 29. ☎ (987) 41 18 00. 24 rooms. ♣
HSR** Monteclaro. ♣
HSR* Conde de Lemos. ♣
HSR* García. ♣.
HSR* La Madrileña. ♣
HSR* Roma. ♣
HSR* San Miguel. ♣
HSR* Santa Cruz. ♣
HSR* Tres Portiñas II. ♣

RESTAURANTS
Molinaseca:
Mesón Real. Ctra. Ponferrada-Astorga, km 6. ☎ (987) 41 18 66
Casa Ramón.
Mesón del Peregrino.

Ponferrada:
Azul-Montearenas. Ctra. Madrid-La Coruña, km 380. ☎ (987) 41 70 12
Los Almendros. (Lombillos). ☎ (987) 42 49 80
Ballesteros. Fueros de León, 12. ☎ (987) 41 11 60
Bahía. Embajadores. El Gamo. Mesón El Comendador. Mesón El Pescador. La Perla. Moniemar. Ríos Bajos. América.

PETROL STATIONS
On the N-120 at km 335; On the N-VI at km 325; in Astorga.

'Inde portus Montis Yraci, inde Siccamolina, inde Ponsferratus.' (Aymeric Picaud: 'Pilgrims' Guide')

I. ROUTE

🚶 Leave **Rabanal** on a path off to the right of the LE-142, which returns to the road (at km 23.4) after just over a kilometre. Continue along the LE-142 as it climbs up towards *'Monte Irago'* through oak treees and clumps of broom and heather. Bear left off the road at km 27.5 to go through the ruined village of **Foncebadón,** and carry on uphill out of the village past some ruins and a drinking fountain on the right. From here, the path traces a wide curve around the edge of a hillock, which the road crosses on the right. With the **Cruz del Ferro** visible up ahead, return to the LE-142 which takes you up to the cross and the Ermita de Santiago. A tortuous 2.5 km further on, the road reaches the ruins of **Manjarín,** and at km 36, a magnificent view over the west face of *'Monte Irago'* awaits you. The pilgrims' route bears right off the road at km 37.5, and returns to it for a short stretch 1 km further on, before bearing off it again (to the left) at km 39. From here, you descend through open countryside to **El Acebo** (km 40.2), pass through the village and then continue along the LE-142 as far as km 42.6, where you take a path into **Riego de Ambrós.** Turn right in the village square and make your way down to the lovely valley of the Arroyo Prado Mangas, and briefly follow its course before returning to the LE-142 at km 11. A bit further on, bear right off the road down towards the valley of the Río de la Pretadura, and then make your way through poplars and rockroses up to a promontory on the right-hand side, which you skirt around. You then head back down to the LE-142 and join it at km 7, shortly before **Molinaseca,** which you enter via a bridge over the river Meruelo. Go straight down the Calle Real and get back onto the LE-142 and continue along it as far as km 4.2, where you take a path off to the right through the undergrowth. After a short while, you return to the road at km 3.5 and cross over to take a stony path which leads down to **Campo.** On leaving the village, the route passes through a rubbish dump near the banks of the river Boeza. The Puente de Escaril takes you across the Arroyo Moriscal and into the Puente de Boeza district, from where you enter the centre of **Ponferrada** via the Puente Mascarón over the Boeza. The route to the Basílica de la Encina is along Calle Hospital, Calle Salinas, Plaza del Temple and Calle del Comendador.

🚴 Cyclists are advised to follow the LE-142 from Rabanal to km 3.5, where they should take the stony path to Campo and then follow the pedestrian route.

🚗 Milestones: LE-142: km 27.5: Foncebadón; km 29.8: Cruz de Ferro; km 32: Manjarín; km 40.2: El Acebo; km 43: Riego de Ambrós; (counting backwards from here to Ponferrada): km 6.8: Molinaseca; km 2.4: turning to Campo; km 0: Ponferrada.

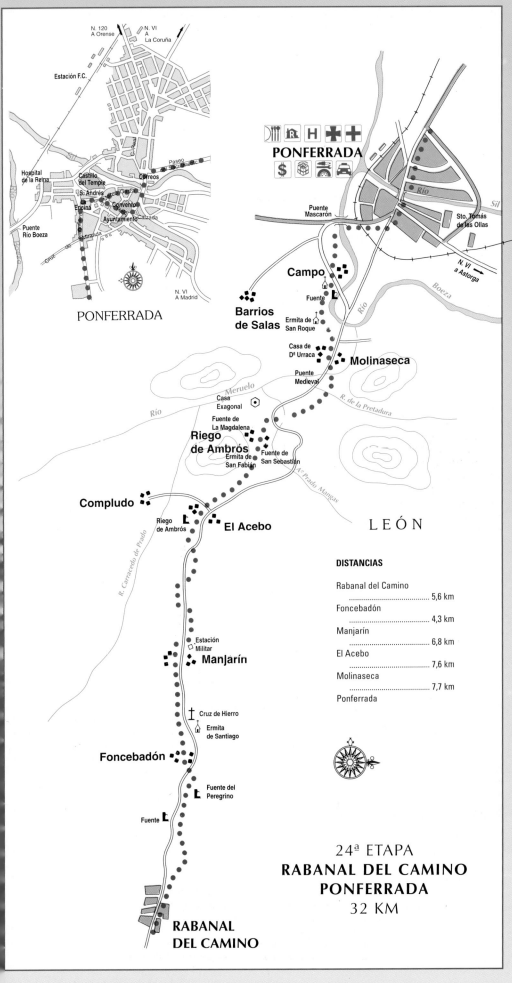

The Cruz de Ferro

Close to the top of *'Monte Irago'* is the desolate ruined village of **Foncebadón,** once an important halt on the road to Santiago, which appears in records as early as the 10th century. The hermit Gaucelmo (who died in about 1123) built a hospital and hostelry here for pilgrims crossing the punishing Foncebadón pass. The document dates from 1103 by which Alfonso VI, on the petition of Gaucelmo himself, granted special immunity to the Foncebadón hostelry and the Church of San Salvador de Irago. Medieval records show that the village could also boast a hospital dedicated to St. John and a church of Santa María Magdalena dependent on the hospital. Later, a community of hermits was established here, becoming a dependency of the Astorga chapter, which created the rank of Abbot of Foncebadón. Although the village is totally ruined, it is easy to see that the pilgrims' route passed right through the middle.

The pass is crowned by the **Cruz de Ferro** (1 504 metres above sea-level), one of the simplest, yet most ancient and symbolic monuments along the pilgrims' route. Aymeric Picaud's dreaded *'Mons Yragus'*, which Künig von Vach warns us so vehemently against *('my advice is that you avoid Rabanal at all costs')*, was crossed by a cautious Laffi on Midsummer's Day. Today, a simple iron cross attached to a five metre-long wooden stake and stuck in a heap of stones marks the spot. Whenever pilgrims add a stone to the pile they become part of an ancient tradition which pre-dates even the Romans, who called these stone heaps (which also served as boundary markers) *'mounts of Mercury'*, after the god of travellers. It was Gaucelmo, the protector of pilgrims in this perilous area, who Christianised this ancient monument (whose original significance is lost in the mists of time) by sticking a cross in it.

*The ruined village
of Foncebadón*

The village of **Manjarín** is now totally abandoned and ruined, but there was a pilgrims' hospital here in the 16th century.

According to an unwritten tradition, the villagers of **El Acebo** were freed from taxes if they marked the pilgrims' route with 800 stakes. The Parish Church of San Miguel houses a polychrome stone sculpture which is supposed to be St. James, although the absence of the traditional distinguishing features has led many to conclude that it could be the Saviour or St. John the Evangelist, the namesake of the former church. The statue is very beautiful and wears a tunic decorated with fleur-de-lys, one of the symbols of St. James according to the *'Codex Calixtinus'*. On the way out of the village there is a simple monument to the memory of Heinrich Krause, a German pilgrim who was killed here while cycling to Compostela. A 5-kilometre detour takes you steeply downhill to **Compludo,** a place where San Fructuoso founded his first monastery dedicated to San Justo and San Pastor. In this secluded, virtually inaccessible and idyllic spot there is a famous medieval *forge* operated by water by means of an ingenious, centuries-old procedure.

El Acebo

The parish church of **Riego de Ambrós** is dedicated to Mary Magdalene, who is strongly identified with the pilgrimage and particularly with pilgrims' welfare.

On entering **Molinaseca** you pass the Capilla de la Virgen de las Angustias, a handsome 18th-century baroque chapel built against the hillside. Molinaseca is considered by some to have been the station known as '*Interamnio Flavio*' on the Roman Road from Braga to Astorga. Whether this is so or not, its Romanesque bridge over the river Meruelo is a good indication of its importance as a passing place. On the other side of the bridge you come to the Calle Real, which is the pilgrims' route through the village (it was called the Calle de los Peregrinos until recently) and which was the location of the pilgrims' hospital. The village has many historic mansions emblazoned with coats of arms and its outstanding monument is the magnificent neoclassical Church of San Nicolás, which houses a figure of San Roque Peregrino, who shares the role of protector of pilgrims with St. James.

On the right of the pilgrims' route through **Campo** there is a rustic medieval fountain in the form of a subterranean cistern, which brings to mind the much more artistic and elegant '*Fuente de los Moros*' at Villamayor de Monjardín. The solid 18th-century parish church is dedicated to St. Blase, which suggests the existence of a pilgrims' hospital in the past.

Figure of St. James, El Acebo

Ponferrada (Aymeric Picaud's '*Pons ferratus*') first came to prominence in the 11th century as a result of the iron bridge over the Sil which was built on the orders of Osmundo, Bishop of Astorga, and which made the town an obligatory passing place for pilgrims bound for Santiago. Previously, it had been nothing more than a minor Asturian, and then Roman, settlement, despite its location on an important road. It was destroyed by the Visigothic leader Teodorico in the 5th century, and again by troops of the Caliphate of Córdoba in the 9th century, before being rebuilt by Alfonso III 'the Great'. In the 12th century, the Knights Templar established one of their most important Spanish bases in Ponferrada and built the magnificent castle which still stands today.

Outside Compludo

Pilgrims crossed the river Boeza either via the 'Paso de la Barca' (to the right of Campo on the present LE-142), whose name recalls the time before the bridge was built and the river was crossed by boat, or via the medieval *Puente Mascarón*. From there, they made their way along the Calle Hospital, the location of the *Hospital de la Reina*, which was built on the orders of Isabel la Católica in 1498. A bit further on is the *Church of San Andrés*, which houses the Gothic *Cristo de las Maravillas*, which is traditionally attributed to the Templars. The impressive **Templar Castle**, one of the oldest and finest examples of Spanish military architecture, stands next to the church on a prominent site overlooking the river Sil and is an eloquent testimony to the extent of the controversial Order's presence in this region. The nearby **Basílica de Nuestra Señora de la Encina,** dedicated to the patroness of the Bierzo, was built between 1573 and 1660, and houses an early 16th-century image of its namesake. According to legend, the Virgin was discovered by the Templars in a holm-oak tree (or 'encina') which they were cutting down to build their castle.

Ponferrada has other fine monuments, including the *Convento de los Concepcionistas* and the *Town Hall*, reached through the *Arco del Reloj* which is crowned by a

The forge at Compludo

Stone cross, Molinaseca

Ponferrada: the Templar Castle

The Torre de La Encina

Apse of the Church of Santo Tomás de las Ollas

clock tower, the famous *Torre del Reloj*. There are several places worth visiting in the vicinity of Ponferrada, including the Mozarabic *Church of Santiago de Peñalba,* one of the treasures of the pre-Romanesque period in Spain and the *Church of Santo Tomás de las Ollas,* which also has Mozarabic elements. Also of interest are the *Church of Santa María de Vizbayo* and the impressive ruined *Abbey of San Pedro de Montes,* which was founded by San Fructuoso in the 7th century, restored by San Genadio in 895 and artistically active until the Disentailment.

III. HISTORICAL PILGRIMS' ACCOUNTS

Aymeric Picaud: *'Then you come to the Monte Irago pass ('portus montis Yraci'), Molinaseca ('Siccamolina') and Ponferrada ('Pons ferratus').'*

Künig von Vach: *'By this route* [via the Puerto de Manzanal] *you soon reach Ponferrada ('Bonforat'). First, you should ask the way to Santa Marina de Torre ('Sancte Maurin'). You leave Astorga three miles over to the left; then you come to one village after another and good people and a safe road. People give bread and wine generously. In Ponferrada there is a fine castle.'*

Arnold von Harff: *'It is four leagues from Rabanal to El Acebo ('Villa nova'), a village situated in the Rabanal pass. It is one league from El Acebo to the village of Riego de Ambrós ('Reodambro'), and one league from Riego de Ambrós to Molinaseca ('Molina zeka'). It is one league frrom Molinaseca to Ponferrada ('Munferar'), a town with powerful fortifications and plentiful wine.'*

Laffi: *'We started our descent down the west face* [of 'Monte Irago'] *and then reached 'Sette Molini', which they call 'Molina Secca', six long leagues away. This is the first village you come to after crossing the great mountains, and it is situated in a lovely valley traversed by a river which flows from the East and which never runs dry. It is more abundant in fruit and grass than in grain... From here we set off towards Ponferrada, a fine, prosperous sort of place. It has a beautiful large main square and many convents and fine buildings. We spent the night here and the next morning strolled around the streets a little. We came upon a church where a requiem mass was being celebrated, so we went inside to watch. The closest relatives of the deceased remained seated in a special pew while the mass was sung. When it was over, they went to the church door and gave alms to all as they left the church, after which they returned home accompanied by the entire village. They were dressed in black in a long gown which resembled a friar's habit, with a double train which dragged along the ground, and an enormous hat covering their eyes...'*

STAGE 25

PONFERRADA • VILLAFRANCA

The Puerta del Perdón, Church of Santiago at Villafranca

PONFERRADA • COMPOSTILLA •
COLUMBRIANOS • FUENTES NUEVAS •
CAMPONARAYA • CACABELOS • PIEROS •
VILLAFRANCA DEL BIERZO

PILGRIMS' REFUGES

Cacabelos: The town council provides accommodation at the Pabellón de Deportes or Sports Hall. ☎ (987) 54 60 11

Villafranca del Bierzo:
The refuge in Villafranca is owned by J. Arias Jato. It is one of the most welcoming and friendly places the pilgrim will visit. A splendid new refuge has been erected by the town council opposite the Church of Santiago.
☎ (987) 54 02 91

ACCOMMODATION
Cacabelos:
HR** Santa María.
☎ 54 95 88. ♣♣
Miralrío. ☎ (987) 54 60 20.
10 rooms. ♣
El Molino. ☎ (987) 54 68 29.
4 rooms. ♣
Mesón Humeral. ☎ (87) 54 92 43.
30 beds. ♣

Villafranca del Bierzo:
H*** P. De Villafranca del Bierzo.
Avda. Calvo Sotelo, s/n.
☎ (987) 54 01 75.
40 rooms. ♣♣♣
HS** Casa Méndez. Espíritu Santo.
☎ (987) 54 24 08.
12 rooms. ♣
HR* San Francisco. Pza. Generalísimo, 6.
☎ (987) 54 04 65. 20 rooms. ♣♣
HSR* La Charola. Dr. Aren, 19.
☎ (987) 54 02 20. 6 rooms. ♣
HSR* Comercio. Puente Nuevo, 2.
☎ (987) 54 00 08.
14 rooms. ♣
HS*El Cruce. ♣
HSR* Ponterrey.

RESTAURANTS
Cacabelos:
Gato. Avda. de Galicia, 7.
☎ (987) 54 70 71
La Moncloa. Cimadevilla, 99.
☎ (987) 54 61 01
El Castro. Mary Crys.
Mesón Apóstol.

Villafranca del Bierzo:
La Charola.
Ctra. Madrid-La Coruña, km 406. ☎ (987) 54 00 95.
Abundant home cooking.
Capricho. Ctra. Madrid-La Coruña, km 6.
☎ (987) 54 25 06
Casa Méndez. Pza. Concepción, 1. ☎ (987) 54 24 08.
Panchi. El Padrino. Venecia.

PETROL STATIONS
On the N-VI at km 401, Cacabelos;
and at km 409, Villafranca.

'Inde Carcauellus, inde Villafranca.'
(Aymeric Picaud: 'Pilgrims' Guide')

I. ROUTE

🚶🚶 The pilgrims' route leads down calle Mateo Garza to the bridge over the river Sil, crosses it and continues along the Carretera de Madrid. A few metres further on, the Paseo Huertas del Sacramento leads off to the right along the river until it crosses the railway track and passes the slag heap of the electrical power plant of **Compostilla** on the left. You then cross the Bajo Bierzo canal and carry on into Compostilla, passing the parish church on the left. On reaching **Columbrianos** which, like Compostilla, is a suburb of Ponferrada, you emerge onto the Villablino road (C-631), only to bear left off it a few metres further down along calle de las Eras, also known as the *Camino Real.* After going through a tunnel underneath the railway track, you soon come out onto the road to Vega de Espinareda and, a couple of kilometres later, past houses and vegetable patches, reach Fuentes Nuevas. After following the *Calle Real* through the village, you continue on through fertile farmland to **Camponaraya,** just over a kilometre away. In Camponaraya, follow the road (the old N-VI) to the outskirts of the village, where you take a path on the left opposite a wine-growing cooperative. After following the path through vineyards, you reach a low, flat hilltop, after which the path drops down into the pretty Arroyo Magaz valley, crosses the river and runs through a leafy riverside wood until it crosses the road. On the far side, you continue down a farm track through vineyards and then up a small hill, before dropping into Cimadevila, from where you enter **Cacabelos** along the *Calle de los Peregrinos.* The N-VI leads out of Cacabelos and across a bridge over the river Cúa, passing the beautiful *Chapel of Nuestra Señora de las Angustias* on the right. 2 km later you come to Pieros (km 403.5), passing the hilltop ruins of *'Castrum Bergidum'.* At km 406.8, bear right off the road along a path which, after crossing the Arroyo de los Valtuilles stream, narrows through dense vegetation before leading out onto a wider track known as the *Camino de la Virgen,* coming from Valtuille de Arriba. Less than 2 km from there, you reach the Iglesia de Santiago at the entrance to **Villafranca del Bierzo.**

🚲 This stage is straightforward until Camponaraya. Between Camponaraya and Cacabelos the rough terrain of the pilgrims' route may cause some difficulties, and the same applies to the final stretch between the last exit off the N-VI (at km 406.8) and Villafranca del Bierzo.

🚗 Milestones: The old N-VI km 385: Ponferrada; km 395: Camponaraya; km 401: Cacabelos; km 403: Pieros and 'Castrum Bergidum'; km 406.8: turning onto the path; km 409: Villafranca del Bierzo.

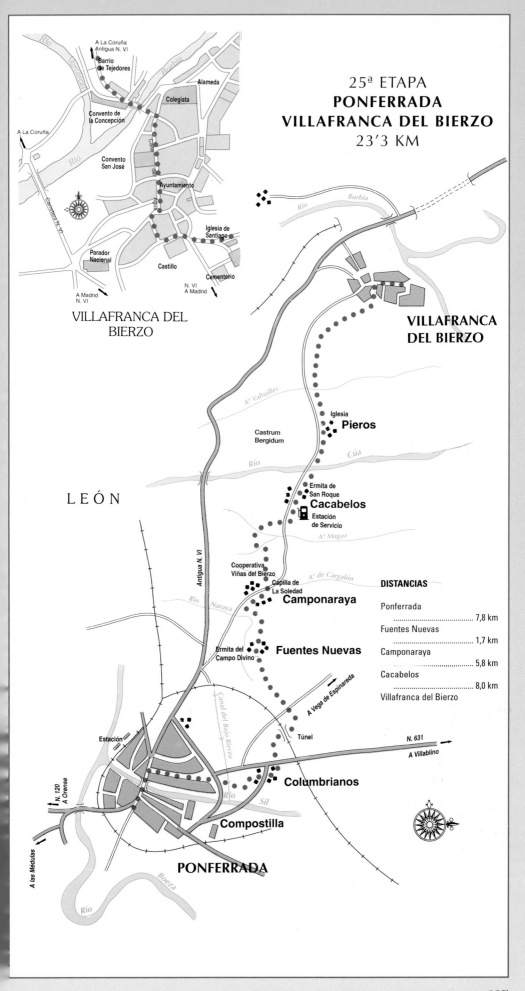

VILLAFRANCA DEL BIERZO

A La Coruña
Antigua N. VI

Barrio
de Tejedores

Alameda

Colegiata

Convento de
la Concepción

A La Coruña

Convento
San José

Ayuntamiento

Iglesia de
Santiago

Parador
Nacional

Castillo

Cementerio

A Madrid
N. VI

N. VI
A Madrid

Calle del AGUA

Carretera N. VI

Río Vardenza

Río Burbia

25ª ETAPA
**PONFERRADA
VILLAFRANCA DEL BIERZO**
23'3 KM

Río Burbia

**VILLAFRANCA
DEL BIERZO**

Aº Valtuilles

Iglesia
Pieros

Castrum
Bergidum

Río Cúa

L E Ó N

Ermita de
San Roque

Cacabelos

Estación
de Servicio

Aº Magaz

Cooperativa
Viñas del Bierzo

Aº de Cargalón

Capilla de
La Soledad

Camponaraya

Río Naraya

Ermita del
Campo Divino

Fuentes Nuevas

A Vega de Espinareda

Antigua N. VI

Túnel

N. 631

A Villablino

DISTANCIAS

Ponferrada

.... 7,8 km

Fuentes Nuevas

.... 1,7 km

Camponaraya

.... 5,8 km

Cacabelos

.... 8,0 km

Villafranca del Bierzo

Estación

Canal del Bajo Bierzo

N. 120
A Orense

Columbrianos

Río Sil

Compostilla

PONFERRADA

A las Médulas

Río Boeza

Río

Las Médulas

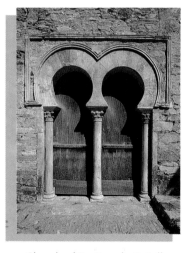

Carracedo Monastery. Mirador de la Reina vantage point.

View of Cacabelos

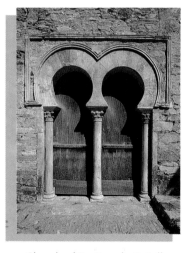

Church of Santigo de Peñalba

II. HISTORY, ART AND LEGENDS

Compostilla, a more ancient settlement than Ponferrada, is today the industrial heart of the town. The modern *Church of Nuestra Señora del Refugio* was built on the site of the hermitage of the same name, of which very ancient records survive. Its name indicates that this was once the site of a pilgrims' hospital or hostelry.

Columbrianos still conserves the remains of ancient pre-Roman forts. Apart from the Parish Church of San Esteban, there are two hermitages dedicated to St. John and St. Blase respectively, names suggestive of the existence of an institution dedicated to pilgrims' welfare at one time, and in fact not far from there is the site of an old pilgrims' hospital.

Continuing on down the path known to this day as the *Camino Real,* you come to **Fuentes Nuevas,** where the Parish Church of Santa María and the Ermita del Campo del Divino Cristo are worth a visit.

There are records of two pilgrims' hospitals in the attractive, large village of **Camponaraya,** which stands beside the river Naraya. The parish church is dedicated to San Ildefonso, the Holy Bishop of Toledo. Both he and one of his works, the treatise *'De uirginitate Sanctae Mariae',* are mentioned in connection with the first foreign pilgrim on record, Bishop Godescalco, who made a copy of the work in the Monastery of Albelda to take back with him to his see at Le Puy.

After it was destroyed by an earthquake, **Cacabelos** was rebuilt in 1108 by Bishop Diego Gelmírez of Compostela, to whose bishopric it belonged. It was then that the *Church of Santa María de la Plaza* was built, the apse of which still survives, incorporated into the rest of the building which is clearly of later construction (16th-century). At the entrance to the church there is a beautiful statue of the Virgin, carved in stone, which dates back to the 13th century. Cacabelos not only enjoyed a privileged position on the pilgrims' route and fertile land, but was also much-favoured by the Kings of Castile and León themselves, and particularly by the bishopric of Compostela. Its inhabitants were under direct royal jurisdiction and, after the creation of the Castro de la Ventosa in 1209, King Alfonso IX granted them additional privileges.

The layout of Cacabelos is typical of a village on the pilgrims' way. One long road, the present-day *'Calle de los Peregrinos',* forms a backbone from east to west, with houses lining it on either side. At the very beginning of the street you come to the *Plaza de San Lázaro,* formerly located on the outskirts of the village where there was a hermitage and a hospital of the same name. A chapel stands there to this day, dedicated to San Roque who appears dressed as a pilgrim. On the way out of the village, on the far side of the river Cúa, the 18th-century *Sanctuario de la Quinta Angustia* stands on the site of a hermitage which was once attached to a pilgrims' hospital. The altarpiece inside portrays Baby Jesus playing cards with St. Anthony of Padua and is a curiosity well worth seeing! Apart from this, the **Archaeological Museum** deserves a visit for its large display of exhibits from the rich pre-Roman and Roman past of the region. Less than two kilometres outside Cacabelos is the hill known as the *'Cerro de la Ventosa'*, enclave of the famous *'Castrum Bergidum'*, the capital of the Asturians, which eventually lent its name to the whole region now known as *'El Bierzo'*.

Not far from Cacabelos are the sadly neglected remains (despite recent restoration) of the **Monastery of San Salvador de Carracedo,** founded at the end of the 10th century and later converted into the extremely important Cistercian **Abbey of Santa María la Real.**

At the foot of *'Castrum Bergidum'* lies the village of Pieros, where the Parish Church of San Martín de Tours conserves a dedicatory inscription stating that it was consecrated by the Bishop of Astorga, Osmundo, who also ordered the construction of the *'Pons ferratus'* over the river Sil at Ponferrada.

Villafranca del Bierzo is another town which grew up and flourished as a result of its position on the road to Santiago. During the reign of Alfonso VI, a settlement for 'francos' was founded on the banks of the river Burbia at its confluence with the river Valcarce, close to *'Bergidum Flauium'*, the historical heart of the Bierzo. In addition to this, a community of Cluniac monks settled there, brought to Spain by the king and subsequently placed at strategic points along the pilgrims' route including Villafranca, a vantage point at the mouth of the Valcarce valley and an obligatory halt on the way to Cebreiro.

Villafranca del Bierzo: the Church of Santiago

Before entering the town, pilgrims arriving along the Camino de la Virgen passed the single-aisled Romanesque *Church of Santiago,* famous for its richly-carved north portal, the *'Puerta del Perdón'*, which gave onto the pilgrims' way. The Spanish Pope, Calixto III (1455-1458), granted a concession to pilgrims unable to continue their journey, allowing them to stop at this church and receive the absolution and plenary indulgence they would have received on reaching the Apostle's tomb in Compostela. The *Hosptial de Santiago* was nearby, and is mentioned in various historical documents. Opposite stands the solid 16th-century *Castle of the Marquesses of Villafranca,* who exerted a great influence on the history and artistic heritage of the town. It is now owned by the Alvarez de Toledo family and is the favourite haunt of the composer, Christopher Halffter. The pilgrims' route through Villafranca is along the Calle del Agua, which is lined with historical monuments. On the right, the *Church of San Francisco,* in common with other similarly-named churches along the way, commemorates the passing of St. Francis of Assisi on his way to Compostela. On the other side of the street stands the *Convento de la Anunciada,* built in the 17th century as a Franciscan convent on the former site of the Hospital de San Roque, possibly because it was traditionally believed that St. Francis had lodged there. At the end of the street is the *Collegiate Church of Santa María de Cruñego,* designed by Gil de Hontañón and built on the site of the first foundation of Cluniac monks, *'Santa María de Cluniaco'*. It was raised to the status of a Collegiate church in 1529, and its Chapter continued until 1862, boasting some very distinguished members. The grandeur of its three-aisled nave and domed crossing are matched by the magnificent Berruguetian altarpiece and other noteworthy features. The hospital, run by French monks to

Castle of the Marquesses of Villafranca del Bierzo

The Collegiate church at Villafranca del Bierzo

*The Church of San Nicolás,
Villafranca del Bierzo*

*The Calle del Agua, Villafranca
del Bierzo*

*The Church of San Miguel
at Corullón*

care for their fellow-countrymen, must have stood nearby. The magnificent *Church of San Nicolás* (a recurring name on the pilgrims' route) is well worth a visit. Its façade, an imitation of the 'Gesú' at Rome, denotes its status as a Jesuit College founded by the Marques of Villafranca at the beginning of the 17th century. Inside, the *Cristo de la Esperanza*, the patron saint of Villafranca, is venerated. Six kilometres south of Villafranca, in Corullón, are the Romanesque churches of San Miguel and San Esteban and a 14th-century castle. You can also visit the nearby Church of San Fiz de Visonia, also Romanesque, which was founded by San Fructuoso and run by the Hospitallers. (It is also known as the Church of San Juan.)

III. HISTORICAL PILGRIMS' ACCOUNTS

Aymeric Picaud: *'Then comes Cacabelos ('Carcauellus'), followed by Villafranca ('Villa Franca') at the mouth of the river Valcarce ('Vallis Carceris')... The river Burbia ('Burbia'), which flows under Villafranca bridge; the Valcarce ('Carcera'), which runs through the valley of the same name ('Vallis Carceris').'*

Künig von Vach: *'You must cover three more miles before reaching Cacabelos ('Kakafelos') and five more before Villafranca ('Willefrancken'). When you get there, drink the wine sparingly as it burns like a candle and can scorch your very soul.'*

Arnold von Harff: *'It is two leagues from Ponferrada to the village of Camponaraya ('Campo de narea'). It is one league from Camponaraya to Cacabelos ('Karkabelle'), a large village. Here you enter the domain of the Count of Benavente. It is two leagues from Cacabelos to Villafranca ('Villa Francka'), a town situated in a valley strewn with vineyards, which belongs to the Count of Benavente.'*

Laffi: *'We set off towards Cacabelos ('Cacavellos'), which stands in the middle of a plain and, after crossing beautiful fruit-filled fields, we reached Villafranca ('Villa Franca'). It is a most beautiful place set in a valley between four very high mountains, at the confluence of two great rivers. It is the last village in the Kingdom of León, although it could well be called a town, since it is large and prosperous. There are many friaries and nunneries, a large square and many fine buildings. There is also a large hospital for pilgrims. In the morning we visited the Jesuit Fathers to hear Mass, and they gave us alms and breakfast. In this great town, and I say great because there are towns less great and less noble than this, people are quite charitable to pilgrims, especially those wearing a 'ferraiolo', known here as a cape.'*

STAGE 26

VILLAFRANCA • EL CEBREIRO

The Church of Santa María, Cebreiro

PEREJE • TRABADELO • PORTELA •
AMBASMESTAS • AMBASCASAS •
VEGA DE VALCARCE •
RUITELÁN • HERRERÍAS • LA FABA •
LAGUNA DE CASTILLA • EL CEBREIRO

PILGRIMS' REFUGES

Vega de Valcarce: Simple municipal refuge.

El Cebreiro:
Next to the ancestral *'pallozas'*, the Xunta or Regional Government of Galicia has constructed a superb refuge that sleeps 80. It is equipped with a stable for horses.
☎ (982) 36 71 25

ACCOMMODATION

Trabadelo:
HS** Nova Ruta. Ctra. Madrid-La Coruña, km 420.
☎ (987) 56 64 31.
14 rooms. ♣

Vega de Valcarce:
HS** Valcarce.
Madrid-la Coruña, km 418.
☎ (987) 56 13 09. 40 rooms. ♣♣
P. Fernández. ☎ (987) 54 30 27.
10 rooms. ♣

Pedrafita do Cebreiro:
HS** Rebollal.
Ctra. Nal. VI.
☎ (982) 36 71 15.
18 rooms. ♣
HSR** San Giraldo de Aurillac. Next to the Sanctuary of El Cebreiro. ☎ (982)36 71 25.
6 rooms. ♣

PETROL STATIONS

On the N-VI km 415, in Trabadelo;
and at km 433, in Pedrafita.

'Inde portus montis Ferbruarii.' (Aymeric Picaud: 'Pilgrims' Guide')

I. ROUTE

🚶 The pilgrims' route folows the Calle del Agua through **Villafranca del Bierzo,** which leads to the bridge over the Burbia. From here to Trabadelo (about 10 km from Villafranca) there are two alternative routes:
a) One option is to follow the N-VI as it zigzags through the narrow Valcarce valley. This is the authentic pilgrims' route, but the walk along the edge of the road is unpleasant and downright dangerous due to the heavy traffic.
b) The second alternative is to follow a new route via the *Cerro del Real,* which is more demanding, but goes through unspoiled countryside. This is the route which is outlined below.
From the *Barrio de Tejedores* you start a steep, 3-kilometre ascent, between heather and broom to the right and pines, chestnuts and oaks to the left. As you climb, you get a magnificent view over the Valcarce valley and Villafranca, with the peak of El Teleno in the background. On reaching the top of the Cerro del Real, make your way along the ridge, from where you will see **Pereje** in the valley far below, which you gradually leave behind. To the right is the little Arroyo Real valley, with Pradela at the bottom. When you reach a stone wall, the path forks: take the left-hand path which leads through woods of Spanish chestnuts, the path getting lost to view from time to time. Soon you reach an asphalted path which winds downhill to **Trabadelo,** where it meets up with alternative route (a). From Trabadelo to **Portela** follow the old N-VI which is now used for local traffic, crossing the new road at km 419.2 to enter **Ambasmestas.** The old road then passes through **Ambascasas, Vega de Valcarce** (2 km from Ambasmestas), **Ruitelán** (1.5 km from Vega de Valcarce) and **Herrerías** (2 km from Ruitelán), which has a district known as **Hospital Inglés.** A small road leads uphill out of Herrerías and, after 1 km, you bear left off it onto a path which leads down to the river Valcarce. Cross the river at a small stone bridge and then begin an arduous 2-kilometre uphill climb to **La Faba,** along a path that is initially paved with huge flagstones. From La Faba, the path continues climbing for 2 long kilometres between immense banks of heather to **Laguna de Castilla,** the last village in the province of León. About 1 km further on you reach a stone marking the boundary between Castile and Galicia and indicating the distance to Santiago de Compostela: 152 km. After a climb of one more kilometre you reach the mountain-top village of **Cebreiro.**

🚲 Between Villafranca and Ambasmestas, cyclists should follow the old N-VI. From Ambasmestas, either continue along the old N-VI to Pedrafita and Cebreiro or take an idyllic, but arduous, cross-country road through Herrerías, La Faba and Laguna de Castilla to Cebreiro.

🚗 Milestones: N-VI km 406: Villafranca; km 410.8: Pereje; km 415: Trabadelo; km 418: Portela; km 419.2: Ambasmestas; km 421: Vega de Valcarce; km 433: Pedrafita del Cebreiro.

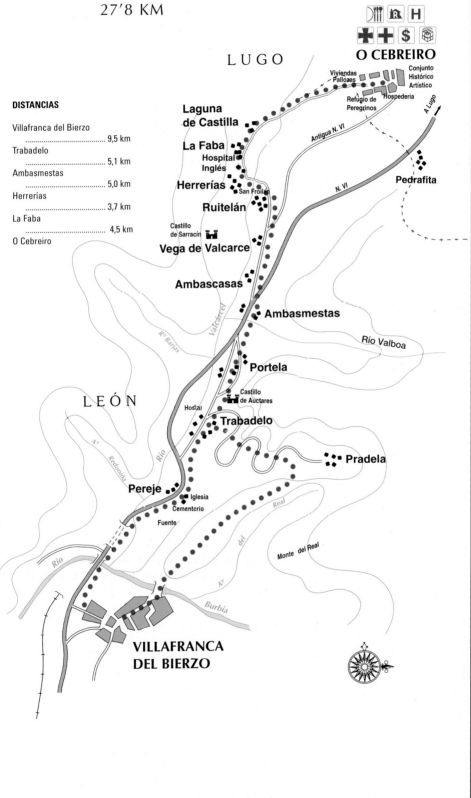

26ª ETAPA
VILLAFRANCA DEL BIERZO
O CEBREIRO
27'8 KM

DISTANCIAS

Villafranca del Bierzo
.... 9,5 km
Trabadelo
.... 5,1 km
Ambasmestas
.... 5,0 km
Herrerías
.... 3,7 km
La Faba
.... 4,5 km
O Cebreiro

LUGO

O CEBREIRO

Viviendas Pallozas
Conjunto Histórico Artístico
Refugio de Peregrinos
Hospedería

Laguna de Castilla

La Faba
Hospital Inglés

Herrerías
San Froilán

Antigua N. VI

N. VI

A Lugo

Pedrafita

Ruitelán

Castillo de Sarracín

Vega de Valcarce

Ambascasas

Ambasmestas

Río Valboa

Valcárcel

Rº Balras

Portela

Castillo de Auctares

LEÓN

Hostal

Trabadelo

Pradela

Aº Redoniña

Río

Pereje
Iglesia
Cementerio
Fuente

Real

del

Monte del Real

Aº

Burbia

Río

VILLAFRANCA
DEL BIERZO

Villafranca del Bierzo:
the Barrio de Tejedores

Pereje: the Calle Mayor

II. HISTORY, ART AND LEGENDS

The narrow Valcarce valley is characterised by the abundance of 'castros' or fortresses which guarded, or menaced, the pilgrims' way, including the *Castro de la Redoniña* outside Villafranca, the *Castillo de Auctares,* the *Castro de Veiga* and the *Castro Sarracín* in Vega de Valcarce. The local medieval lords used to send their bailiffs to exact a toll from any kind of passer-by, pilgrims included, and would not hesitate to resort to violence in the face of non-compliance. A document, dated 1072, has survived by which King Alfonso VI suppressed the right to charge tolls to pilgrims, and which mentions some of the abuses perpetrated against pilgrims by the Lord of Auctares.

The first milestone of this stage, for those following the course of the river down in the valley, is **Pereje,** a village which still retains part of its medieval layout. It was once the object of a celebrated lawsuit between the Cluniac community of Santa María de Cruñego at Villafranca and the monks of Aurillac responsible for Cebreiro, in which none other than Alfonso IX of León, Queen Doña Urraca and Pope Urban II became involved. The dispute arose because the Abbot of Cebreiro had built a church and pilgrims' hospital at Pereje, which entered under the religious jurisdiction of the Cluniacs of Villafranca.

It seems probable that **Trabadelo** could also boast a pilgrims' hospital at one time, situated near the *Chapel of San Lázaro.* In the ancient parish church, dedicated to St. Nicholas (who is closely linked to the pilgrimage) a medieval seated statue of the Virgin Mary is venerated. The neighbouring hill known as the Cerro de Aldares is the probable site of the above-mentioned castle of Auctares, infamous for its malevolent toll-collectors. In the *'Itinerarium Antonini'* of the 4th century A.D., a station called 'Uttaris' is mentioned on the road which linked *Asturica Augusta* (Astorga) and *Lucus Augusti* (Lugo), which can almost certainly be identified with Auctares.

The next village in the narrow Valcarce valley, **Portela,** derives its name from the Galician word for a narrow pass. Nearby, situated at the point where the river Balboa meets the river Valcarce, is **Ambasmestas,** a name which refers to a place where two currents of water merge. Remnants of the old Roman road still survive here and, until not so long ago, a triple-arched bridge built of slabs of slate, similar to the bridge at Astorga.

The prosperous town of **Vega de Valcarce** stands between the former Castro de Veiga (of which no trace remains) and the Castro Sarracín, the *'Castro Sarracenicum'* mentioned by Aymeric Picaud in his *'Pilgrims' Guide'* and founded in the 9th century by Sarraceno, Count of Astorga and the Bierzo. Vega de Valcarce is the head of the Valcarce valley and enjoys a privileged position. The local devotion to Mary Magdalene, the patroness of sinners and penitents and a recurring name along the pilgrims' way, testifies to the town's links with the pilgrimage.

Close by is the little village of **Ruitelán,** where there is a church dedicated to St. John the Baptist and a chapel dedicated to St. Stephen. There is also a place on the hillside which is supposed to have been the retreat of the

The river Valcarce

hermit *San Froilán* of Lugo (833-905), who later became Bishop of León.

Herrerías must be the place Laffi describes as *'Salvaterra'* (see Historical Pilgrims' Accounts), and possibly Picaud's *'Villaus'*. (Archaeological and documentary evidence support these suppositions.) The iron industry in the area goes back to at least the 17th century, and the great building which served as an iron foundry until early this century can still be seen. By the river, an eyecatching modern fountain has replaced the old *'Fuente de Quiñones'*, which a local tradition linked to Don Suero de Quiñones, the redoubtable jouster of the *'Passo honroso'* (the Puente de Orbigo). Just before leaving Herrerías, you come to the district known as **Hospital Inglés,** which was mentioned in a Papal Bull issued by Pope Alexander III in 1178. The previous year, King Henry II of England contacted King Fernando II of León expressing a wish to make the pilgrimage to Santiago from his possessions in Aquitaine. Perhaps the hospital for English pilgrims was connected in some way to Henry II's proposed pilgrimage. Traces still remain of the hospital church and the pilgrims' cemetery.

La Faba, whose village church is dedicated to St. Andrew, is the last parish belonging to the Diocese of Astorga. Slightly further up, the province of León comes to an end at **Laguna de Castilla.**

Cebreiro is another of the emblematic places on the pilgrims' way and is situated at an altitude of 1.293 metres, a short distance from the Roman road which passed through the Puerto de Pedrafita. Since the remotest origins of the pilgrimage, its pilgrims' hospital was one of the most important hostelries along the pilgrims' way. Historical records show that in 1072, Alfonso VI entrusted the monastery to French monks from the Abbey of St. Giraldo d'Aurillac. It later passed into the hands of the Benedictines, who administered it until the Disentailment. The simple, ancient *Church of Santa María la Real* is one of the landmarks of Cebreiro and is a pre-Romanesque construction of a kind typical of the area, with a three-aisled interior and a rectangular apse. Inside, the lovely 12th-century Romanesque statue (restored in 1971) of the patroness of the area, Santa María la Real, is venerated. On her saint's day (8th September), up to 30,000 pilgrims visit her shrine from throughout the area. The priceless 12th-century chalice and paten on display commemorate the famous *'Miracle of Cebreiro'* which probably occurred at the beginning of the 14th century, when a peasant from the neighbouring village of Barxamaior struggled up through a terrible snowstorm to receive communion at Cebreiro. The officiating monk, whose faith was much less solid than the peasant's, secretly despised him for bothering to come. Suddenly, the sacramental bread and wine turned literally into the flesh and blood of Christ inside the paten and chalice. The anonymous protagonists of the miracle are buried in the Capilla del Milagro. In 1486 the Catholic kings donated the golden reliquary which is displayed alongside the chalice and paten in a glass-fronted safe. Cebreiro is also famous for its *'pallozas'*, the straw-roofed dwellings that we have recorded previously in several parts of León and which are the continuation of a prehistoric

The museum at Cebreiro

'Pallozas' at Cebreiro

The statue of Santa María la Real at Cebreiro

View of Cebreiro

One of the 'pallozas' at Cebreiro

The 'Chalice of the Miracle'

View of the surrounding countryside from Cebreiro

tradition. Two of them now house an ethnography museum.

Don Elias Valiña Sampedro, the parish priest for many years, is buried in the church. He was a pioneer in the recuperation of the Jacobean tradition and the pilgrims' way, and in 1966 he restored the old monastery buildings and opened the magnificent, comfortable hostel. His bust presides over the patio.

III. HISTORICAL PILGRIMS' ACCOUNTS

Aymeric Picaud: *'Then come Castro Sarracín ('Castrum Sarracenicum') and 'Villaus' [Herrerías?]; followed by the Cebreiro pass ('Portus montis Februarii') and the hospital at the summit.'*

Künig von Vach: *'[after Villafranca] you must cross a bridge and when you reach a second, let me make this clear, do not go up to La Faba ('Allefaber') but pass it on the left-hand side and cross over the bridge which is on the right... After four miles, you reach the city of Lugo ('Lucas').'*

Arnold von Harff: *'It is four leagues from Villafranca to Vega de Valcarce ('Weichga'), a small village with a fortress belonging to the Count of Benavente. You then climb up a high mountain known as 'Male Faba' [Cebreiro]. It is two leagues from Vega de Valcarce to La Faba ('Alla faba'), a village situated on the hillside, and one league from La Faba to Santa María del Cebreiro ('Marie de Sebreo'), a small hamlet at the top of Mount 'Malefaber'.'*

Laffi: *'We set off across a great bridge on the west side and followed the course of the river until we reached Herrerías ('Salvatierra'), two leagues away, a village situated beside the river. Here they extract iron ore from the mountainside and then take it down to the village where there is a furnace for smelting. There is a great water-driven iron tilt hammer and enormous tongs and bellows. The village is only small, and almost all the dwellings are of straw, and it is the first place you come to in the Kingdom of Galicia. On the top of a mountain there is a castle which guards the mouth of the river by which you enter Galicia, as this is the place where the border is. Here you leave the river and start to ascend a great mountain, which is called Mount Cebreiro ('Cerviero')... the next morning... we reached La Faba ('Malafava'), halfway up the mountain... Then we continued up to the summit, where there is a Benedictine monastery, who give pilgrims a ration of bread and wine and other tokens of charity, and there is even a pilgrims' hospital. Here there is a great and holy relic of a host which turned into the true flesh of Our Lord Jesus Christ and a glass flask which contains the wine which became the true blood of Our Lord, and the miracle occurred as follows...'*

STAGE 27

EL CEBREIRO • (SAMOS) SARRIA

The Monastery of Samos

CEBREIRO • LIÑARES • HOSPITAL DA CONDESA •
PADORNELO • ALTO DE POIO • FONFRÍA •
BIDUEDO • FILLOVAL • AS PASANTES • RAMIL •
TRIACASTELA • SAMOS • BALSA • SAN XIL •
MONTÁN • FONTEARCUDA • FURELA • BREA •
PINTÍN • CALVOR • AGUIADA • SAN MAMEDE •
SAN PEDRO DO CAMIÑO • VIGO • SARRIA

PILGRIMS' REFUGES

Hospital da Condesa: A restored building with 18 beds.
☎ (982) 16 13 36
Triacastela: Here there is a large tourist complex that has been restored with good taste. It includes a hostel with a capacity of 80. ☎ (982) 58 80 87
Calvor: Comfortable municipal hostel sleeping 22, all necessary facilities. ☎ (982) 16 77 69
Sarria: In the Calle Mayor an old stately home is being fitted out by the Regional Government of Galicia to serve as a refuge. It has a capacity for 40 people.
☎ (982) 53 08 50
Samos: Solemn refuge under the protection of the historical, emblematic and welcoming Monastery of the Benedictine Friars. ☎ (982) 54 60 46

ACCOMMODATION

Triacastela:
Fernández. ☎ (982) 54 70 48.
8 beds. ♣
Villasante. ☎ (982) 54 70 16.
12 beds. ♣

Samos:
HR* A Veiga. Ctra. Sarria-Pedrafita. ☎ (982) 54 60 52.
15 rooms. ♣

Sarria:
H*** Alfonso IX. Rúa do Peregrino, 29. ☎ (982) 53 00 05.
60 rooms. ♣♣♣
H** Villa de Sarria. Benigno Quiroga, 49.☎ (982) 53 19 38.
23 rooms. ♣♣

RESTAURANTS

Sarria:
A Ponte Ribera. Rúa do Peregrino, 29. ☎ (9 82) 53 00 05. In the Hotel Alfonso IX.

PETROL STATIONS

At km 12, Samos; and km 1, Sarria.

(*) Important note: To celebrate the 'Holy Year of Compostela, 1993', the **Xunta de Galicia** (the regional Galician government) has inaugurated an easy alternative route along a purpose-built compacted earth track from Cebreiro to Santiago de Compostela. This follows the similar exemplary initiative taken by the regional government of Castile and León in 1991, between Sahagún and Mansilla de las Mulas. It avoids the danger and inconvenience of the long stretches along the main road, although some of the magic of the old 'corredoiras' (cart-tracks) is lost. For those who prefer to keep to the old road, and in order to leave written evidence of it, we have chosen to describe the old, zig-zagging route.

'Inde Linar de Rege, inde Triacastella.'
(Aymeric Picaud: 'Pilgrims' Guide')

I. ROUTE (*)

🚶 From **Cebreiro** the road goes down the side of Monte Pozo de Aréa to **Liñares** (3 km away), where you bear left off the road into the village and then cross it again on the outskirts of the village, before climbing up to the Alto de San Roque. Shortly afterwards, you return to the road until you reach **Hospital da Condesa,** where you turn right off the road and then return to it about 100 metres later. After 2 km you bear right off the road and, after passing through **Padornelo,** begin the short, steep ascent to the **Alto de Poio.** From there you follow the road to the outskirts of **Fonfría,** where you take another path off to the right which descends parallel to the road as far as the entrance to **Biduedo,** where you cross over and continue along the left-hand side of the road until **Filloval.** After Filloval, you cross back over the zig-zagging road and drop down another 2 km to the entrance of **As Pasantes,** where you cross the road one last time. The descent then continues down a shady *'corredoira'* (cart-track) to **Ramil** and, 1 km further on, to **Triacastela.** From the *Plaza do Concello,* the pilgrims' way follows two alternative routes to Sarria:
a) The first alternative is to head left on the same road as before for about 10 km, until you reach the Monastery of **Samos.** Sarria is 12 km further on, along the same road.
b) The second option is to take the route via San Xil, which is described below.
Turn right off the *Plaza do Concello* and follow the little river Valdoscuro along an old path shaded by birches, oaks, chestnuts and poplars, to **Balsa.** From there, you continue uphill and come out onto an asphalted track by a large, modern pilgrims' fountain, shortly before reaching the hamlet of **San Xil,** which you pass on the left. Further on up the path, you continue the ascent to the Alto de Riocabo, where you turn off to the right onto a *'corredoira'* which comes out onto another asphalted track, right at the entrance to the scattered hamlet of **Montán.** You then carry on to **Fontearcuda** and **Furela,** on the other side of the road. After that, the road takes you through **Brea** and **Pintín,** past the Church of San Esteban at **Calvor,** and through **Aguiada, San Mamede, San Pedro do Camiño** and **Vigo,** now part of **Sarria.** Once in the town, you cross the bridge over the river Ouribio and follow the Rúa do Peregrino, the Escalinata Mayor and the Rúa Mayor to the Mercedarian Monastery of La Magdalena.

🚲 Between Cebreiro and Triacastela, cyclists have no option but to follow the road. After Triacastela, alternative route a) follows the road, while on alternative route b), the stretches along the *'corredoiras'* present insuperable difficulties.

🚗 Milestone: km 35: Cebreiro; km 32: Liñares; km 30: Hospital da Condesa; km 26.3: Alto do Poio; km 23.1: Fonfría; km 15.7: Filloval; km 10: Triacastela; (kilometre numbering system changes) km 12: Samos; km 1: Sarria.

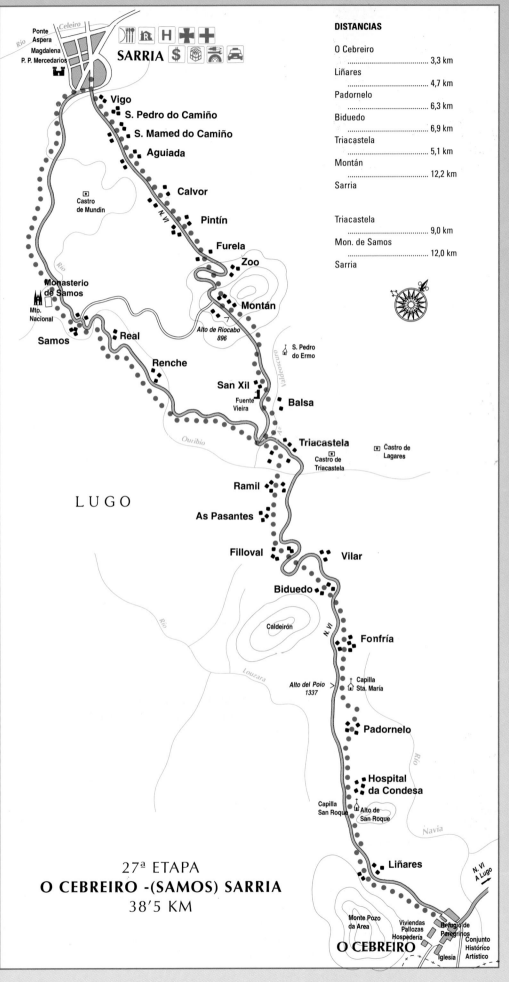

SARRIA

Ponte
Aspera
Magdalena
P. P. Mercedarios

Vigo
S. Pedro do Camiño
S. Mamed do Camiño
Aguiada
Calvor
Pintín
Furela
Zoo
Montán
Alto de Riocabo 896
S. Pedro do Ermo
Monasterio de Samos
Mto. Nacional
Samos
Real
Renche
San Xil
Fuente Vieira
Balsa
Triacastela
Castro de Triacastela
Castro de Lagares
Ramil
As Pasantes
Filloval
Vilar
Biduedo
Caldeirón
Fonfría
Alto del Poio 1337
Capilla Sta. María
Padornelo
Hospital da Condesa
Capilla San Roque
Alto de San Roque
Liñares
Monte Pozo da Area
Viviendas Pallozas Hospedería
Refugio de Peregrinos
Conjunto Histórico Artístico
Iglesia

O CEBREIRO

Castro de Mundín

L U G O

N. VI A Lugo

DISTANCIAS

O Cebreiro
.... 3,3 km
Liñares
.... 4,7 km
Padornelo
.... 6,3 km
Biduedo
.... 6,9 km
Triacastela
.... 5,1 km
Montán
.... 12,2 km
Sarria

Triacastela
.... 9,0 km
Mon. de Samos
.... 12,0 km
Sarria

27ª ETAPA
O CEBREIRO -(SAMOS) SARRIA
38'5 KM

Hospital da Condesa

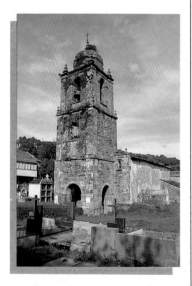

View of the parishes of Vilar and Vilavella from Triacastela

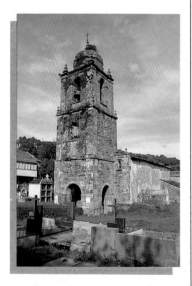

Triacastela: the tower of the Parish Church of Santiago

II. HISTORY, ART AND LEGENDS

Liñares, the small village downhill from Cebreiro, is referred to in Aymeric Picaud's *Pilgrims' Guide* as *'Linar de Rege'*. The name comes from the flax plantations which the Crown established at Cebreiro to supply its cloth requirements. The very ancient Parish Church of San Esteban is built along the same lines as the Church of Santa María at Cebreiro.

After Liñares, thre is an uphill climb to the **Alto de San Roque,** where there was once a chapel dedicated to San Roque, the leper saint of Montpellier who made the pilgrimage to Rome in the 14th century. The origins of the village of **Hospital da Condesa** are linked to an old hospital which, according to some sources, was founded as early as the 9th century by Doña Egilo, the wife of Count Gatón, famous for bringing settlers to the Bierzo region. If this is the case, this would make it one of the oldest hospitals along the pilgrims' way. The village church, like that of Liñares, is designed along the same lines as the church at Cebreiro. In **Padornelo,** the dedication of the village church to St. John is the only remaining vestige of the presence of the Knights of the Order of St. John of Malta in the area. The village cemetery now occupies the site of the old Church of La Magdalena, which was attached to the pilgrims' hospital. The Church of Santa María, another commission of the Order of St. John of Malta, was built in a strategic position at the **Alto de Poio.** At **Fonfría,** pilgrims encountered the fourth hospital since Cebreiro in under 15 kilometres, and a fifth awaited them at **Biduedo,** at the priory of the Order of St. John.

After the small hamlets of **Filloval, As Pasantes** and **Ramil,** you reach **Triacastela** (a name that means *'three castles'*, none of which survive), which was founded in the 9th century by Count Gatón of El Bierzo. The 18th-century Church of Santiago, which stands beside the pilgrims' way, is a reconstruction of an earlier Romanesque church, of which part of the masonry remains and houses a figure of St. James, the patron saint of the town. The stonemasonry tradition of Triacastela (see HISTORICAL PILGRIMS' ACCOUNTS) continues to this day, and there are quarries producing raw materials for cement manufacture in the vicinity. As this was the end of Aymeric Picaud's 11th stage (Villafranca-Triacastela) it was only natural that there should have been several pilgrims' hospitals in the town. In the out-buildings of one of them, said to have been a prison for riotous pilgrims, you can still read the 'graffiti' left by the prisoners. In the *Plaza do Concello,* where the pilgrims' route forks, there is a monument to pilgrims built to commemorate the 'Holy Year of Compostela, 1965'.

The road to **San Gil** takes you through the village and on through other typical villages such as **Montán,** which is mentioned in ancient accounts of the pilgrimage, where there is a Romanesque church dedicated to St. Mary. You then come to **Furela, Pintín** and **Calvor,** whose Church of San Esteban conserves architectural elements dating back to Visigothic times. The next villages are **Aguiada,** where there was probably once a hospital for pilgrims and **Vigo**

de Sarria, once the ancient country seat *('uicus')* of a nobleman from Sarria.

The other branch of the pilgrims' route leads to the great **Monastery of Samos,** one of the most ancient monasteries in Spain, which was originally founded by the Apostle of Galicia, San Martín Dumiense, in the 6th century. A 7th-century Visigothic gravestone confirms its great age. The monastery's links with the pilgrimage to Santiago and with hospitality to pilgrims are evident from its position on the road to Santiago, coupled with the fact that it belongs to the Benedictine order, which prescribes hospitality in Chapter 53 of the *'Regula Benedicti'.* Despite this, Samos was never comparable to the other Benedictine monasteries at Sahagún, Nájera, Leyre, Carrión or Villafranca, whose principal mission was to offer aid to pilgrims. Of the few medieval remains still to be found, mention should be made of the small Mozarabic Chapel of the Saviour (or 'Chapel of the Cypress') dating from the late 9th and early 10th centuries, which might have been a place where pilgrims were lodged. The main part of the impressive monastery complex dates almost exclusively from the 16th and 17th centuries and the predominant styles are therefore Renaissance and baroque. The façade of the fine neoclassical church displays the figures of St. Benedict and the patron saints of the Abbey, the Antiochian martyr couple, Saints Julian and Basilisa. Between the church and the monastery is *'Feijoo's cloister',* dating from the 17th century, which is presided over by a statue of Feijoo, the famous Benedictine reformer. Beside it stands the elegant 16th-century *'Cloister of the Nereids',* together with the 17th-century refectory and the magnificent library which was badly destroyed in a terrible fire on 24th August, 1951. The Monastery of Samos is a symbol of culture and learning throughout Galicia, and the figure of the eminent and learned Benedictine monk, Father Benito Jerónimo Feijoo (1676-1774), who joined the order in Samos in 1688 and was to become so closely linked with the monastery, makes Samos a cultural symbol for the rest of Spain too.

The noble town of **Sarria** first appeared in records as far back as the 6th century, although there was a pre-Roman settlement there. Originally repopulated after its reconquest by Bishop Odoario of Lugo (circa 750), its existence was given an important boost by Alfonso IX of León, who died in the town in 1230. During the Golden Age of Spanish art and literature, Sarria contributed some eminent names, such as the writer and theologian Fray Luis de Granada, and the sculptor Gregorio Fernández, part of whose work can be admired in several places along the pilgrims' way.

The old part of the town stands on the side of a hill which is crowned by the castle. The pilgrims' route through the town led them up the Calle Mayor, and the first place they would have stopped at is the Church of Santa Marina. The present church is modern, but it stands on the site of the old Romanesque church of the same name which was built in the 12th century. A little further on, the *Parish Church of El Salvador* stands in fairly good repair, and is representative of the Galician Romanesque style, with a single rectangular nave and semi-circular apse. Close by is

The Monastery of Samos

Monastery of Samos: the Cloister of the Nereids

Monastery of Samos: Feijoo's Cloister

View of Samos

Sarria: the Calle Mayor and the Church of Santa Marina

Sarria: the Monastery of La Magdalena

Sarria: Church of El Salvador

the old building said to have been the *Hospital de San Antonio*.

Sarria castle is situated in the highest part of the town. Only one section of its masonry survives: the rest was destroyed during the *'Irmandiños wars'* in the 15th century. These 'wars' were violent rebellions of the local people against the feudal nobility, which virtually escalated into civil war, similar to the *'Cabochan'* uprising in France or the *'Lollard'* uprising in England at about the same time.

The *Monastery of La Magdalena* is located in the same area of the town, and is said to have been founded as a hospital in the early 13th century by the Knights of St. John of Jerusalem. It is now run by Mercedarian monks. Among the most noteworthy features of the monastery, which was renowned for its hospitality, are the plateresque façade of the church and some surviving Gothic elements in the cloister.

III. HISTORICAL PILGRIMS' ACCOUNTS

Aymeric Picaud: *'Once in Galicia, you come to Liñares ('Linar de Rege') and Triacastela ('Triacastella') on the hillside itself, a place where pilgrims pick up a stone and carry it to Castañeda to provide limestone for the work on the basilica of the Apostle.'*

Arnold von Harff: *'It is one league from Cebreiro to Hospital da Condesa ('Hospital de gundis'). It is one league from Hospital da Condesa to the village of Fonfría ('Mumfrea') and to Biduedo ('Bordeos'), a small village on the side of Mount Cebreiro. It is two leagues from Biduedo to Triacastela ('Trecastelle')... It is two leagues from Triacastela to the village of 'sent Michaele de la Costa' [San Miguel de Monseiro?]. From there to the village of Aguiada ('Agiata') it is one league. From Aguiada to Sarria ('Zarea'), a 'villa franca' with a fortress, it is one league.'*

Laffi: *'Having seen this holy relic, we continued through those mountains, passing some shepherds' villages, and then started a long descent down to a plain where we came to a fairly large town with fine buildings, which is known as Triacastela ('Tre Castelli') and is six leagues from Cebreiro. After this town, you come to a very beautiful plain, full of fruits of all kinds and houses and vegetable gardens. You then cross a river where there are lots of mills and climb up a little way to Sarria ('Saria'), two leagues on. It is a very beautiful, prosperous place, with handsome buildings; there is a monastery where the friars are clothed in white and give pilgrims their ration. Overlooking it is a fine, solid castle, ringed by high walls...'*

STAGE 28

SARRIA • PORTOMARÍN

The Church of San Nicolás, Portomarín

SARRIA • VILEI • BARBADELO • RENTE •
MERCADO DA SERRA • XISTO • DOMIZ •
LEIMAN • PERUSCALLO • CORTIÑAS •
LAVANDEIRA • BREA • FERREIROS • MIRALLOS •
PENA • COUTO • ROZAS • MOIMENTOS •
MERCADOIRO • MOUTRAS • PARROCHA •
VILACHÁ • PORTOMARÍN

PILGRIMS' REFUGES

Barbadelo: Comfortable, recently restored hostel with 22 beds.
☎ (982) 53 04 12

Ferreiros: Functional, recently fitted out hostel with 22 beds.
☎ (982) 54 12 40 - 15 74 96

Portomarín: Traditional, long-standing hostel belonging to one of the most active town councils of the whole Pilgrims' Route. 102 beds. In addition it has camping facilities and the local livestock market is used as stables.
☎ (982) 54 50 70 - 54 51 43

ACCOMMODATION

Portomarín:
H*** Pousada de Portomarín.
Avda. de Sarria, s/n.
☎ (982) 54 52 00.
34 rooms. ♣ ♣ ♣
HSR** Mesón de Rodríguez.
Fraga Iribarne e Portomarín.
☎ (982) 54 50 54.
4 rooms. ♣
Bodegas Pérez.
☎ (982) 54 50 40. ♣

RESTAURANTS

Portomarín:
Casa Ferreiro.
Rúa del Peregrino, s/n.
☎ (982) 54 50 17
Bodegas Pérez.
Aviación Española, s/n.
☎ (982) 54 50 40

CAMPSITES

La Casona de Alvarado.
Sta. Mariña, s/n.
☎ (982) 50 00 83

PETROL STATIONS

In Portomarín.

(*) See WARNING
on STAGE 27

'Inde Barbadellus, Inde Pons Minee.' (Aymeric Picaud: 'Pilgrims' Guide')

I. ROUTE (*)

🚶 Set off from the monastery of La Magdalena in **Sarria** and make your way steeply downhill to the C-546 (Monforte-Lugo road), passing the muncipal cemetery on the right. Turn right onto the road and continue along it for a short distance, before bearing left off it and crossing the river Celeiro via the *'Ponte Aspera'*. Continue parallel to the river until you cross the railway line (not far from the site of the erstwhile village of **Sancti Michaelis,** which is indicated by a stone marker) and follow the line for about 100 metres. You then cross a stream, turn right and head uphill in the shade of an oak grove towards the village of **Vilei.** Here you take an asphalted track leading to the Church of Santiago de **Barbadelo,** from where you make your way through a varied landscape of oaks, fields and scattered farmhouses to the villages of **Rente** and **Mercado de Serra.** You then cross the C-535 (Sarria-Portomarín road) and proceed along an asphalted track for about 2.5 km through **Xisto, Domiz, Leiman** and **Peruscallo,** passing clumps of chestnuts and oaks (the typical Galician variety, *Quercus robur*) and fields enclosed by the typical slate walls or *'chantos',* one of the most characteristic features of areas where the Celtic cultural inheritance is most strongly-rooted. Next, follow local roads for 1.5 km, passing through the villages of **Cortiñas, Lavandeira** and **Brea,** through countryside which is more rugged and less fertile than before. About half a kilometre from the foot of Monte Morgade is the tiny village of the same name, after which you cross the Arroyo Ferreiros and start a gentle uphill climb towards the village of **Ferreiros.** An oak-lined *'corredoira'* (cart-track) then leads up towards an asphalted track which you cross and then make your way down to the villages of **Mirallos** and **Pena,** after which an asphalted track leads to **Couto** and **Rozas.** You then climb up the Pena do Cervo before descending towards **Moimentos, Mercadoiro** and the fertile valley of the river Bocelo, the location of **Moutras.** Continue for just over a kilometre as far as **Parrocha** and follow an asphalted track out of the village and, after 600 metres, a path into Vilachá, from where the modern village of **Portomarín,** situated overlooking the right-hand bank of the river Miño, comes into view. Cross into Portomarín via the great bridge over the Miño, which also carries the traffic coming on the C-135 from Sarria.

🚴 The pedestrian route has a large number of difficult stretches for cyclists: almost all the *'corredoiras'* have an uneven and slippery surface. However, in the dry season it would be worth the effort to follow this itinerary in spite of the difficulties, to enjoy a route of true ethnological originality.

🚗 Milestones: C-535 km 32: Sarria; km 14: Paradela; (change in the kilometre numbering system) km 23.5: Portomarín.

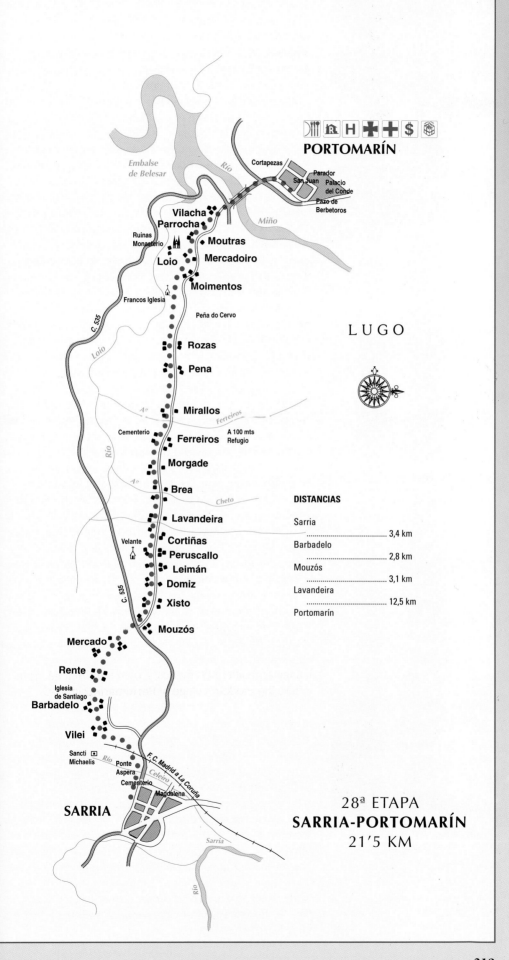

PORTOMARÍN

Cortapezas

Parador
Palacio
del Conde
San Juan
Pazo de
Berbetoros

Embalse
de Belesar

Río

Miño

Vilacha
Parrocha

Ruinas
Monasterio

Moutras

Loio

Mercadoiro

Moimentos

Francos Iglesia

Peña do Cervo

C. 535

Loio

LUGO

Rozas

Pena

Río

Aº

Mirallos

Ferreiros

Cementerio

Ferreiros

A 100 mts
Refugio

Morgade

Aº

Brea

Cheto

Lavandeira

Velante

Cortiñas

Peruscallo

Leimán

C. 535

Domiz

Xisto

Mouzós

Mercado

Rente

Iglesia
de Santiago
Barbadelo

Vilei

Sancti
Michaelis

Río

Ponte
Aspera

F.C. Madrid a La Coruña

Celeiro

Cementerio

Magdalena

SARRIA

Sarria

DISTANCIAS

Sarria

.... 3,4 km

Barbadelo

.... 2,8 km

Mouzós

.... 3,1 km

Lavandeira

.... 12,5 km

Portomarín

28ª ETAPA
SARRIA-PORTOMARÍN
21'5 KM

Stone cross at Sarria

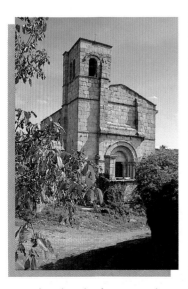

Puente del Aspera

II. HISTORY, ART AND LEGENDS

The route out of Sarria from the monastery of La Magdalena takes you down through the **San Lázaro district,** which is named after a chapel dedicated to the patron saint of the sick and plague-ridden. As has already been seen on numerous occasions, a chapel dedicated to this saint on the outskirts of a town means that at one time there was a hospital there for pilgrims with contagious diseases.

After leaving Sarria via the *Ponte Aspera,* a small Romanesque bridge over the river Celeiro, you come to the site where archaeologists place the ancient settlement of **Sancti Michaelis,** the only place in this area mentioned by Aymeric Picaud in his *Pilgrims' Guide,* who makes no reference whatsoever to Sarria. After passing the scattered hamlet of **Vilei,** the pilgrims' way leads to the **Church of Santiago de Barbadelo,** a notable example of Galician Romanesque architecture, with a single-aisled nave and a square tower divided into three sections. The main portal is worthy of special attention: four columns crowned with capitals support two archivolts adorned with human and animal motifs, while the tympanum is presided over by a crude human figure with outstretched arms. Interesting carvings depicting plants and geometrical motifs abound. The church used to be attached to a monastery of which no trace remains, although records of it still exist dating from as early as the 9th century. Furthermore, the district in which the church is located is known as 'Mosteiro', which is a clear derivative of the word 'monasterium'. Records speak of a 'mixed' monastery of both monks and nuns under the auspices of Samos, and it is safe to say that its principal activities would have been those related to hospitality to pilgrims. The *Liber Sancti Iacobi* mentions Barbadelo in two passages. One of them (Book I, chapter 17) constitutes one of the most revealing texts regarding the roguery and villainous practices prevalent on the pilgrims' way during the Middle Ages. From this passage, it can be deduced that Barbadelo was, at that time, a place which attracted numerous pilgrims:

'Others [referring to innkeepers] *go to Barbadelo or to Triacastela in search of* [pilgrims] *and after approaching them, greeting them and talking about a thousand other things, they say: 'My brothers who travel to Santiago, I am a prosperous citizen of that city, and have come here not to seek lodgers, but to speak with a brother of mine who lives in this place. If you wish to enjoy first-class hospitality in Santiago, stay at my house; tell my wife and my relatives to take care of you in the name of the love they bear me. I will give you a sign to show them.'... When the pilgrims arrive at the house and take up lodging there, and once they have eaten the first meal, the innkeeper's wife sells them a wax candle worth four coins, for eight or ten. In this way, innkeepers swindle pilgrims going to Santiago.'*

The Church of Santiago de Barbadelo

After this interesting halt on the pilgrims' way, the route penetrates deep into a landscape which has changed little over the centuries. A succession of tiny villages, each similar to the other, alternate with fields and dark clumps of oaks. After Barbadelo you pass through **Rente** and **Xisto,** the latter being the Galician word for slate, the main building material in rural Galicia. There then follows a series of simple and typical villages: **Domiz, Leimán, Peruscallo** (close to which is the Romanesque Church of Santa María de Velante), **Cortiñas, Lavandeira, Casal** and **Brea.**

The pilgrims' route now leaves the municipal district of Sarria and enters **Paradela,** which has a 12th-century Romanesque church dedicated to St. Michael. Within the Paradela district lies the humble village of **Ferreiros,** where blacksmiths used to offer all manner of invaluable services to pilgrims such as those recalled by Künig von Vach, including 'nailing studs in boots', shoeing horses, and so on. The next village is **Mirallos** (the location of the Romanesque Church of Santa María de Ferreiros) followed by **Pena, Couto, Moimentos, Mercadoiro, Moutras, Parrocha** and **Vilachá,** a lovely string of lyrical Galician place-names. The **Monastery of Santa María de Loyo,** the birthplace of the Order of Santiago, lay to the south of Vilachá. This is where, towards the end of the 12th century, the first statutes of this great Spanish Order of Chivalry were drawn up. Today, only a few scant ruins remain of the once grandiose monastery complex.

After crossing the river Miño you enter **Portomarín.** In 1956 work began on the Belesar reservoir and the old village and the remains of the old medieval bridge were submerged under water. In 1962, the new Portomarín was inaugurated at its new position higher up the bank. Portomarín (Aymeric Picaud's *'Pons Minee'*) was historically important as a crossing-point over the Miño, and its origins can be traced back as far as Roman times. In 993 it appears in documents with the name *'Villa Portumarini'.* The antagonism between Doña Urraca and her husband, Alfonso I 'the Battler', obliged the Queen to destroy the bridge, which was rebuilt around 1120 by Pedro *Peregrino* (see HISTORICAL PILGRIMS' ACCOUNTS). Pedro Peregrino, whose background is clear from his surname, also built the headquarters of the Order of St. John and a hospital (in 1126). The importance of Portomarín is demonstrated by the fact that three great military religious orders had headquarters there: the Knights of Santiago and the Templars were installed on the left-hand bank of the Miño, while the Order of St. John of Jerusalem had one of its most important bailiwicks in the San Nicolás district to the right of the river. The *Church of San Pedro* stood at the heart of the San Pedro district, on the left-hand bank of the river and downstream from the bridge, and two pilgrims' hospitals were attached to it, one of which was dedicated to contagious patients. Only the Romanesque portal survives, with an inscription from 1182, which was taken to the new Portomarín, together with the 17th-century Pazo de Berbetoros. Next to the medieval bridge was the

Remains of the Monastery of Loyo

Remains of the old Portomarín submerged by the reservoir

The bridge leading into the new Portomarín

Portomarín: San Pedro

Steps up to the Chapel of the Virgen de las Nieves, Portomarín

Portal of the Church of San Nicolás, Portomarín

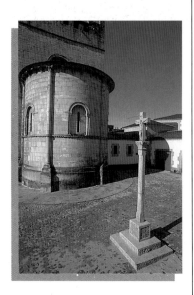

Apse of the Church of San Nicolás, Portomarín

Church of Santa María de las Nieves, which was granted to Pedro Peregrino by Doña Urraca and Alfonso VII, and it was there that he built a pilgrims' hospital known as *'Domus Dei'*. Its memory survives today in the *Chapel of the Virgen de las Nieves*, mounted on one of the arches of the old medieval bridge which was saved for posterity and erected at the mouth of the new bridge. In the San Nicolás district to the right of the river (the most important district in old Portomarín) was the impressive fortified *Church of San Nicolás*, sometimes referred to as the 'Church of San Juan' due to having been the headquarters of the Order of St. John of Jerusalem. The church was reconstructed stone by stone on the new site, and is an unusual example of Romanesque architecture consisting of a wide single-aisled nave and a single rounded apse. It has three portals, a lovely rose window on the western side and is fortified with battlements and four towers.

III. HISTORICAL PILGRIMS' ACCOUNTS

Aymeric Picaud: *'Then come 'Sancti Michaelis', Barbadelo ('Barbadellus') and Portomarín ('Pons Minee')... The Miño ('Minea'), which flows through Portomarín ('Pontem Minea')... These are the names of some of the builders who rebuilt the pilgrims' way to Santiago: Andrés, Rotgerio, Alvito, Fortus, Arnaldo, Esteban and Pedro, who rebuilt the bridge over the river Miño which was destroyed by Queen Doña Urraca.'*

Arnold von Harff: *'It is four leagues from Sarria to Portomarín ('Ponte marine'), a town on the banks of a great river called 'Mino' [the Miño], which is spanned by a stone bridge.'*

Laffi: *'We set off towards Portomarín ('Porto Marino'), three leagues away. It is a charming place and is traversed by a great river abundant in fish, particularly eels and delicious trout, off which we dined splendidly. On the other side of the river there are numerous vineyards and orchards. The land on either side of the river is linked by a lovely large bridge, which gives this area its name, and it is called 'Ponte del Min' [cf. 'Pons Minee'].'*

STAGE 29

PORTOMARÍN • PALAS DE REI

Portal of the church at Vilar de Donas

PORTOMARÍN • TOXIBO • GONZAR •
CASTROMAIOR • HOSPITAL DA CRUZ •
VENTAS DE NARÓN • PREBISA • LAMEIROS •
LIGONDE • EREIXE • PORTOS • LESTEDO •
VALOS • MAMURRIA • BREA • PALAS DE REI

Gonzar: Recently refurbished, functional refuge with 20 beds.
☎ (982) 15 78 40

Ventas de Narón: Recently refurbished 22-bed refuge.
☎ (982) 54 52 32

Ligonde: Recently refurbished 20-bed hostel.
☎ (982) 15 34 83

Palas de Rei: Recently restored, urban stately home that has been fitted out in great comfort to serve as a hostel with 50 beds. Located opposite the Town Hall. The local livestock market is used as stables.
☎ (982) 37 41 14 -37 41 26

ACCOMMODATION
Palas de Rei:
P Ponterroxán.
Roxán, s/n.
☎ (982) 38 01 32. 33 beds. ♣
Curro.
☎ (982) 38 00 44. 10 beds. ♣
Guntina.
☎ (982) 38 00 80. 20 beds. ♣

PETROL STATIONS
On the N-547 at km 35: Palas de Rei.

(*) See WARNING
on STAGE 27

'Inde Palacium Regis.' (Aymeric Picaud: 'Pilgrims' Guide')

I. ROUTE (*)

🚶🚶 From the refuge, make your way down the steep, porticoed main street of **Portomarín** to the C-135, and turn off it almost immediately to cross a narrow footbridge over an arm of the Belesar reservoir. You then begin a gentle climb round the north side of Monte San Antonio, with the river Torres on your right. After approximately 2 km, you come back out onto the C-135 at the San Mamed turning, the tiny hamlet of Cortapezas standing on the right and a pottery on the left. After 2 km, you reach **Toxibo** and 3 km further on, **Gonzar,** after which you bear left off the road down a dirt track leading to the little village of **Castromaior.** You then continue through softly undulating countryside so typical of this region, studded with small oak trees, pines and gorse. You soon come out onto the road and follow it up a gentle slope for about 1 km until coming to another left turn towards **Hospital da Cruz,** where you cross the N-540 and take an asphalted track for the next 10 km. After the first 1.5 km you reach **Ventas de Narón,** after which the path slopes gently up the Sierra de Ligonde and drops down into **Prebisa, Lameiros** and **Ligonde.** You continue downhill before crossing the river Ligonde, and then climb up to **Eirexe** and carry on up to the Monterroso road, where you begin your descent to **Portos.** On your way out of the village, there is a turning off to the right to the famous Romanesque church at Vilar de Donas, situated about 3 km away on the far side of the N-547. After 1 km you come to **Lestedo,** passing the cemetery and the Church of Santiago on your left, after which a short uphill climb brings you to **Valos.** Finally, 1 km further on (after passing the small hamlet of **Mamurria**), the path comes out onto the N-547 at Brea. From there, it is about 3 km down a path running parallel to the left of the main road, to Palas de Rei. You pass the municipal sportsground on the left as you enter the town.

🚲 The route outlined above is suitable for cyclists, with the exception of the climb up Monte San Antonio at the beginning of the stage.

🚗 Milestones: C-135, km 56: Portomarín; km 67: Hospital da Cruz, and junction with the N-540. N-547: km 29: turning to Vilar de Donas; km 32: the path comes out onto the road at Brea; km 34: Palas de Rei.

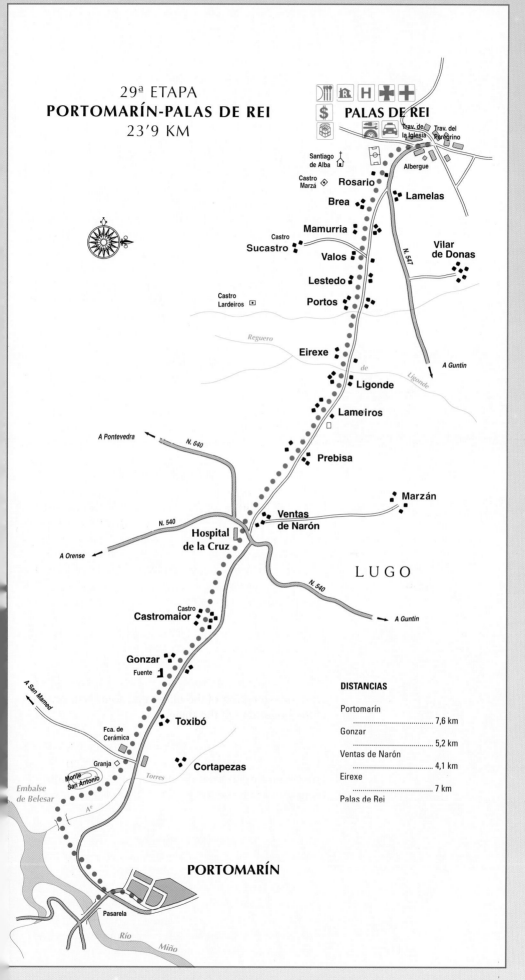

29ª ETAPA
PORTOMARÍN-PALAS DE REI
23'9 KM

PALAS DE REI

Trav. de la Iglesia · Trav. del Peregrino

Santiago de Alba
Albergue
Castro Marzá
Rosario
Lamelas
Brea
Mamurria
Castro **Sucastro**
Valos
Vilar de Donas
Lestedo
Castro Lardeiros
Portos

Reguero

Eirexe
de
Ligonde
A Guntin
Ligonde
Lameiros

A Pontevedra
N. 640
Prebisa

Marzán
N. 540
Ventas de Narón
Hospital de la Cruz
A Orense

LUGO

N. 540
A Guntin

Castro
Castromaior

Gonzar
Fuente

A San Mamed

Toxibó

Fca. de Cerámica

Granja
Cortapezas
Monte San Antonio
Torres
Aº
Embalse de Belesar

DISTANCIAS

Portomarín
.... 7,6 km
Gonzar
.... 5,2 km
Ventas de Narón
.... 4,1 km
Eirexe
.... 7 km
Palas de Rei

PORTOMARÍN

Pasarela
Río Miño

River Miño

Country lane near Ereixe

The portal of the church at Vilar de Donas

II. HISTORY, ART AND LEGENDS

As soon as you leave Portomarín, the road starts to climb up *Monte de San Antonio,* a name which, despite the lack of records and archaeological remains, suggests the existence of an Antonine monastery-hospital such as those that were found at frequent intervals along the pilgrims' way.

You then descend to **Toxibó** and **Gonzar,** where the parish church is dedicated to St. Mary.

In **Castromaior,** in addition to the small Romanesque Church of Santa María, there are the ruins of the 'castro' which lends the village its name, the first of several which stand to the left and right along this stretch of the route: Castro Lardeiros, Castro Simone (between Eirexe and Lestedo), Castro de Valos (south-east of Castromaior) and Castro de Marzá (to the south of Palas de Rei).

Hospital da Cruz owes its name to an old pilgrims' hospital, of which nothing remains, although it is known to have still existed as late as the 18th century. It had an adjacent chapel dedicated to St. Stephen but this, too, has disappeared without trace.

Although the toponym **'Ventas de Narón'** is relatively recent, it does reflect a certain connection with transport and road travel. Moreover, the chapel of La Magdalena on the outskirts of the village may be an indication of the more recent existence of a pilgrims' hospital. 'Narón' brings to mind *'Naharon',* the place where, not long after the discovery of the tomb of St. James in Compostela, the Christians routed the troops sent by the Emir of Córdoba to Galicia. The fact that Ventas de Narón is equidistant from both Portomarín and Palas de Rei, has led to suggestions that it might be the place referred to as *'Sala Regine'* that Aymeric Picaud's *Pilgrims' Guide* situates halfway between these two towns.

After **Prebisa** and **Lameiros** (where there is a chapel dedicated to St. Lazarus), the pilgrims' route reaches **Ligonde,** formerly an important halt on the road to Compostela. Its Church of Santiago, though almost entirely neoclassical, conserves the portal of its Romanesque predecessor. Both the church and the hospital must have belonged to the Order of St. James, and the hospital's little pilgrims' cemetery can be seen to this day.

After passing through **Eirexe** and **Portos,** a small detour takes you to **Vilar de Donas,** the site of the most outstanding small Romanesque church of the twenty or more specimens to be found in the Palas de Rei area. The first reference to the *Church of El Salvador* dates from 1184, when it was taken over by the *Knights of the Order of St. James.* From then on, it became the Order's official burial place in Galicia. The church nevertheless appears to have had its origins two centuries earlier, when Don Arias de Monterroso and his wife founded a nunnery there (this explains the use of *'Donas',* Galician for *'Dueñas'*). The church is classified as a national monument, and has a Latin cross ground plan, a single-aisled nave and a semicircular apse flanked by two absidioles. Its beautiful portal, in the form of a semicircular splayed arch, is particularly impressive, with richly-carved archivolts and capitals. Three stone statues adorn a protective porch: St. Michael the Archangel in the centre, flanked by St. Bartholomew and the Virgin and Child. Inside, many important artistic treasures are conserved. Lining the walls are the tombs of several knights of the Order of St. Jame and there is a magnificent Gothic baldachin dating from the 15th century, crowned by a structure reminiscent of the nearby fortress of Pambre. At the main altar, a stone retable portrays scenes of the Descent from the Cross and the Miracle of the Eucharist, an allegorical or possibly testimonial representation of the extraordinary event which occurred at Cebreiro. A priest raises up the Eucharistic bread to a kneeling worshipper; on the altar is the figure of Christ with the symbols of the Passion. Finally, the 15th-century Gothic frescoes in the main chapel are almost unique examples of their kind in Spain. They portray the Annunciation and include two figures which, according to some, are the *'donas'* who founded the convent, popularly known as Bela and Elvira. However, recent studies may have demonstrated that the figures in fact represent a 15th-century lady and gentleman, possibly King Juan II and Queen María of Aragón.

Back on route, after passing through **Lestedo** (whose church is dedicated to St. James), **Valos, Brea** and **Alto do Rosario,** the pilgrims' way reaches **Palas de Rei,** the end of a stage in Aymeric Picaud's *Pilgrims' Guide.* Once more, the *Liber Sancti Iacobi* (Book I, chapter 17) refers to the region, but this time in a totally different tone:

'Innkeepers' servants along the Road to Santiago who, taking pleasure in seduction for illicit gain, are inspired by the Devil himself to get into pilgrims' beds at night, are fully reprehensible. Harlots who go out to meet pilgrims in wild parts between Portomarín and Palas de Rei for this purpose should not only be excommunicated, but also stripped of everything and exposed to public ridicule, after having their noses cut off.'

Aymeric Picaud's *Pilgrim's Guide* refers to the town as *'Palacium Regis'* ('Royal Palace'), and it would be a logical assumption that its history dates back to far distant times, particularly in view of the number of Celtic forts to be found in the district and the fact that it is situated close to the Roman road between *Lucus Augusti and Asturica Augusta* (Lugo and Astorga). However, there are no documentary records of the existance of Palas de Rei until the 9th century, when the *'Caelicolae'* of Alfonso III mentions the local Church of San Tirso. The claim that it had been an episcopal see in the 5th century remains unfounded, and the suggestion that the Visigothic king, Witiza, held his court there is nothing but another unconvincing attempt to explain the meaning of the name of this town, a question still to be resolved. Despite the town's importance on the pilgrims'

Vilar de Donas: tombs of the Knights of Santiago

Vilar de Donas: frescoes

A typical Galician 'horreo'

Rustic bridge

The portal of the Church of San Tirso, Palas de Rei

Pilgrim's monument, Palas de Rei

route, the only vestiges of its Jacobean past are the Romanesque portal of the Parish Church of San Tirso, and the façade of one of the houses, another medieval building, which is decorated with scallop shells and was probably a pilgrims' hospital.

In contrast with the lack of historical monuments in Palas de Rei itself, the artistic wealth of the surrounding area is quite considerable. In addition to the twenty-odd Romanesque churches already mentioned (out of a total of 43 parishes), some as important as Vilar de Donas, there are the castles of Pambre and Felpós, the 'literary' 'Pazo de Ulloa', to name but a few examples.

STAGE 30

PALAS DE REI • ARZÚA

The Castle of Pambre

PALAS DE REI • SAN JULIÁN DO CAMIÑO •
PALLOTA • OUTEIRO DA PONTE •
PONTECAMPAÑA • CASANOVA • CAMPANILLA •
COTO • CORNIXA • LEBOREIRO • DISICABO •
FURELOS • MELLID • CARBALLAL • RAIDO •
A PEROXA • BOENTE • CASTAÑEDA • PEDRIDO •
RÍO • RIBADISO DE BAIXO • RIBADISO DE RIBA •
RIBADISO DA CARRETERA • ARZÚA

PILGRIMS' REFUGES
Mato-Casanova:
Recently fitted out refuge, with 20 beds. ☎ (982) 17 34 83

Mellid: Beautifully built, magnificent refuge that offers all necessary facilities. 130 beds and stables facilities.
☎ (981) 50 72 75 - 50 62 66

Ribadiso: The old pilgrims' hospital (the last one to operate on the Pilgrims' Route) has been restored in an exquisite and very successful manner, along with an extensive area surrounding it. It has 62 beds, in addition to a camping area. ☎ (981) 50 08 70

Arzúa: The old School of Music has been successfully converted to serve as a hostel offering 50 beds.
☎ (981) 50 04 55

ACCOMMODATION
Melide (Mellid):
HS* Estilo II.
Progreso, 6. ☎ (981) 50 51 53.
5 rooms. ♣
Bar Sony.
☎ (981) 50 54 73. ♣
Bar Xaneiro.
☎ (981) 50 50 15. ♣
Bar Alongos.
☎ (981) 50 51 02. ♣
Bar Estilo. ☎ (981) 50 51 53. ♣

Arzúa:
H** Suiza.
Lugar de Río Vello - Arzúa.
☎ (981) 50 08 62. 9 rooms. ♣♣
Casa Frade.
☎ (981) 50 00 19. ♣
Bar Carballeira.
☎ (981) 50 00 94. ♣
Casa Teodora.
☎ (981) 50 00 83

PETROL STATIONS
On the N-547 at km 35, in Palas de Rei; and at km 64, in Arzúa.

(*) See WARNING
on STAGE 27

'Inde Campus Leuurarius, inde Castaniola.' (Aymeric Picaud: 'Pilgrims' Guide')

I. ROUTE (*)

🚶🚶 Take the N-547 out of **Palas de Rei,** and bear left off it on a long bend at km 36. You then descend along a paved 'corredoira' to **San Xulián do Camiño** (about 3 km from Palas). From there, an asphalted track takes you to **Pallota,** where you turn right onto a track which descends through dense vegetation to **Outeiro da Ponte.** After crossing the river Pambre and passing **Pontecampaña,** you climb gently up through pines and oaks to the top of a low hill, passing **Casanova** on the way up. You then drop down towards the river Villar valley, and make your way across a wide stretch of meadowland before crossing the river. 1 km further on you come to the village of **Campanilla,** where you rejoin the N-547, which crosses the border between the provinces of Lugo and La Coruña between the villages of **Coto** and **Cornixa.** After this brief spell on the main road, you take a finely-paved, cypress-lined road leading to **Leboreiro.** This is followed by **Disicabo,** where you cross the river Seco over the Magdalena bridge and get onto a compacted earth track, flanked by poplars, which leads into **Furelos,** passing through a shady copse on the way. On leaving the village, you return to the same track as before and, about 1 km further on, enter **Mellid** through the San Pedro district. Once in the town, you turn left off the N-547 towards the Santa María district and, after crossing the river Lázaro and passing through **Carballal,** you take an asphalted path through a leafy oak and eucliptus wood to **Raido.** You then come out onto the N-547 and turn off it again almost immediately down a dirt track on the left, which leads through pines and ferns, crosses the Valverde stream and drops down through **A Peroxa** to Boente. On the outskirts of the village, you go through a tunnel under the N-547 (which curves round to the right on a wide bend), and make your way downhill and across the river Boente, after which you climb back uphill and get onto an abandoned branch of the N-547 which takes you to **Castañeda.** From here, the pilgrims' way heads off to the left, passing through **Pedrido,** and drops down into **Río.** You then cross the Arroyo Ribeiral and climb up towards a small hill covered with eucaliptus. At the top of the hill, you will see the road cutting across the pilgrims' route down in a deep gorge which is only negotiable down some incredibly steep and perilously flimsy wooden steps. Once you reach the other side, the path drops quickly down to the river Iso, after which you pass through **Ribadiso de Baixo** and **Ribadiso de Riba,** go through a tunnel under the N-547 and come straight out into **Ribadiso da Carretera.** On leaving the village, take the N-547, which soon leads into **Arzúa.**

🚲 Some stretches of the route between Boente and Arzúa (about 8 km) are very rough, even when the surface is in good condition, and it is therefore advisable to follow the N-547 for this part of the journey.

🚗 Milestones: N-547: km 35: Palas de Rei; km 49: Melide; km 54: Boente; km 59: Castañeda; km 62: Ribadiso; km 64: Arzúa.

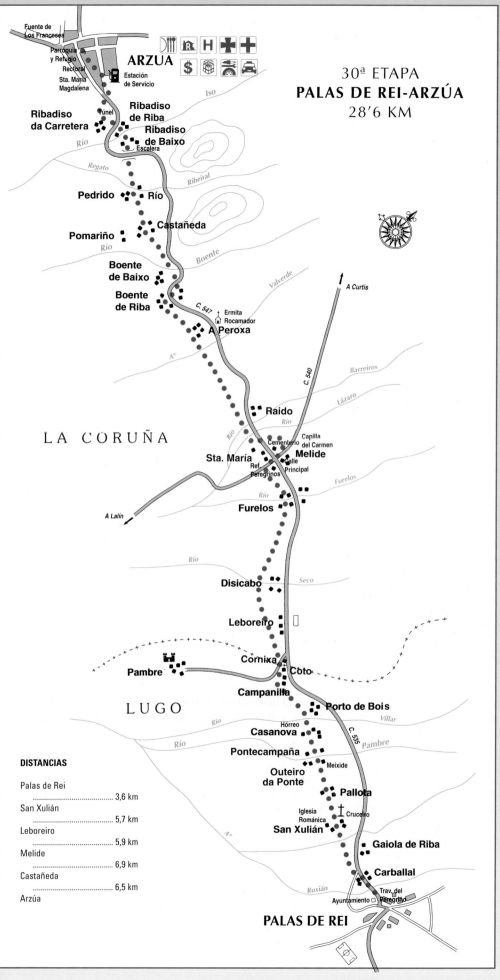

Fuente de
Los Franceses

Parroquia
y Refugio

Rectoral
Sta. María
Magdalena

ARZUA

Estación
de Servicio

Túnel

Ribadiso
de Riba

Ribadiso
da Carretera

Ribadiso
de Baixo

Escalera

Iso

Río

Regato

Ribeiral

Pedrido   **Río**

Pomariño

Río

Castañeda

Boente
de Baixo

Boente

Boente
de Riba

C. 547

Ermita
Rocamador

A Peroxa

Valverde

A Curtis

C. 540

Barreiros

Lázaro

A°

LA CORUÑA

Raido

Río

Río

Capilla
del Carmen

Cementerio

Melide

Sta. María

Ref.
Peregrinos

Calle
Principal

Furelos

Río

Furelos

A Lalín

Río

Disicabo

Seco

Leboreiro

Cornixa

Pambre

Coto

Campanilla

LUGO

Río

Porto de Bois

Villar

Hórreo

Casanova

Río

Pontecampaña

C. 535

Pambre

Meixide

Outeiro
da Ponte

Pallota

Iglesia
Románica

Cruceiro

A°

San Xulián

Gaiola de Riba

Carballal

Ruxián

Trav. del
Peregrino

Ayuntamiento

PALAS DE REI

30ª ETAPA
PALAS DE REI-ARZÚA
28'6 KM

DISTANCIAS

Palas de Rei
.... 3,6 km
San Xulián
.... 5,7 km
Leboreiro
.... 5,9 km
Melide
.... 6,9 km
Castañeda
.... 6,5 km
Arzúa

Apse of the Church of San Julián do Camiño

The 'Pazo de Ulloa'

The pilgrims' route through Leboreiro: the stone bridge

Medieval bridge at Furelos

II. HISTORY, ART AND LEGENDS

On leaving Palas de Rei, you enter an area whose toponymy is dominated by an ancient devotion to St. Julian, one example of which is the river called *'Ruxián'* (which means 'River Julian'). St. Julian's historical links with the pilgrimage are vague and questionable, being based on the legend recorded by Jacobus de Voragine in his famous work *'Legenda Aurea'*: Julian, a noble soldier, accidentally kills his parents. To expurgate his sins he founds a hospital, which he runs with his wife, Adela, until visited by an angel who tells him that he has been granted divine pardon. The small 12th-century Romanesque Parish Church of **San Julián (Xulián) do Camiño** also testifies to the centuries-old devotion to this saint.

To the south of the route is the *Palace of Villamayor de Ulloa,* the inspiration for Emilia Pardo Bazán's *'Los Pazos de Ulloa'*, and the *Castle of Pambre,* a magnificent example of medieval military architecture. Built in the 14th century, it was one of the few fortresses to withstand the attacks of the *'Irmandiños'* in the 15th century. The rectangular castle wall is flanked by four towers, and in the centre stands the solidly-built keep.

The area around **Porto de Bois** ('the Pass of the Oxen') was the scene of a fierce battle between Henry of Trastamara and the Duke of Lemos, a follower of the legitimate monarch, Pedro I 'the Cruel'. Luck was on the side of Henry of Trastamara, who inflicted a crippling defeat on the Duke, while his army was falling back towards Santiago.

Coto is the last village in the province of Lugo, after which you enter La Coruña province via **Cornixa** and **Leboreiro,** following the ancient medieval road which has been greatly restored. Leboreiro was an important halt on the pilgrims' way in the Middle Ages, as is demonstrated by Aymeric Picaud's *Pilgrims' Guide,* in which it is referred to as *'Campus Leuurarius'* ('the hare field'). Nestling among the village houses is the transitional Romanesque Parish Church of Santa María, which has a single-aisled nave and a circular apse. On the tympanum of the portal there is a beautiful carved figure of the Virgin. Opposite the church is a building which was once a pilgrims' hospital, founded by the Ulloa family, whose coat of arms is still to be seen on the façade, and which is known to have existed as far back as the 12th century.

In the next village of **Disicabo,** the pilgrims' way crosses the little medieval Magdalena bridge and comes out onto an open piece of ground bearing the same name which, as we have seen on many occasions, is a name closely associated with hospitality to pilgrims. It may be called this after some ancient hospital, possibly the one at Leboreiro.

You enter **Furelos** across the magnificent *'ponte velha'*, a medieval bridge with four arches which spans the river after which the village is named. At the heart of the village, which still retains its medieval air, stands the Parish Church of San Juan, beside which was a pilgrims' hospital which appears in documents dating back to the 12th century.

In **Melide** (Mellid), pilgrims who had left the route after León to visit the relics in the Cathedral of San Salvador at Oviedo rejoined the *'Camino Francés'*, having journeyed via Salas, Grandas de Salime or Ribadeo, and finally through the city of Lugo. Situated in an area that is particularly rich in pre-Roman remains, it is impossible to ascertain the precise date of origin of this busy market town. The pilgrims' route enters Mellid through the San Pedro district. Only the portal survives of the Romanesque church of San Pedro after which the district was named, which has since been taken to the *Campo de San Roque.* At one time a pilgrims' hospital would have depended on the church. Further down the calle Principal, and slightly set back from it, is the place where the *Monastery and Hospital of Sancti Spiritus* was built in the 14th century, over the site of an earlier hospital, and situated at the point where pilgrims from Oviedo entered the town. The former monastery church is now the parish church, and houses some interesting 15th-century frescoes depicting St. James the Moor-slayer.

Continuing down the calle Principal you come to the baroque Capilla del Carmen, formerly the site of a castle belonging to the bishopric of Compostela. On the outskirts of Melide, past the cemetery, you come to the *Santa María de Melide* district, which grew up around the Romanesque church of the same name. The church has a single-aisled, barrel-vaulted nave and a semicircular apse, which is decorated with a series of interesting frescoes of a slightly later date than the church itself.

A little further on, you come to the place where the hospital and church of San Lázaro once stood overlooking the river Lázaro. Sadly, they have now disappeared without a trace.

North of the route, very near **A Peroxa,** is the *Chapel of San Vicente de Vitiriz,* also known as the *Chapel of Rocamadour,* a French cult which entered Spain via the pilgrims' way.

Boente must have been an important halt on the Galician stretch of the pilgrims' way at one time, as it is mentioned in Picaud's *Pilgrims' Guide* and has a parish church dedicated to St. James. The church houses, amongst other treasures, an attractive figure of St. James, not dressed as a pilgrim as he is usually seen, but seated like the statues in Santiago cathedral. There must have been a pilgrims' hospital here at one time, although nothing remains of it.

Castañeda is famous for the mention Aymeric Picaud made of it (see HISTORICAL PILGRIMS' ACCOUNTS) as the site of the furnaces where the lime was prepared for use during the construction of Santiago cathedral. On their way through Triacastela (an area full of quarries, as we have seen), pilgrims would pick up a stone and carry it to the furnaces at Castañeda. The parish church at Castañeda is dedicated to St. Mary.

In **Ribadiso,** just after crossing the river Iso over a charming medieval bridge, you come to the old

Frescoes in the Church of Santa María de Melide

Mellid: the town hall

Mellid: the parish church

The bridge at Ribadiso

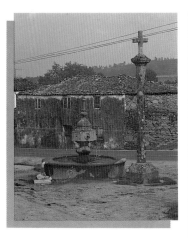

Boente: Fuente de la Saleta and stone cross

Arzúa: the parish church and the main square

High altar in the church at Arzúa

Hospital de San Antón de Ponte de Ribadiso, another Antonine foundation dating from the 15th century, which has recently been restored and converted into a magnificent pilgrims' hostel.

Arzúa is the place referred to as *'Villanoua'* in the *Pilgrims' Guide,* as is confirmed by two later French guides which mention *'Arcerouze, dit Villeneufe'* and *'Arsetouse, dicte Villeneuve'.* Following the pilgrims' route along the Calle Coma do Lugar and the Calle de la Rua through the old part of the town, the first place of interest is the former *Convent of La Magdalena,* a 14th-century Augustinian foundation which once had a refuge for poor pilgrims, but which is now in a deplorable state of ruin.

Close by is the modern Parish Church of Santiago, where there are two statues of St. James, one dressed as a pilgrim at the high altar, and the other as the Moor-slayer.

In As Barrosas, on the outskirts of Arzúa, there is a chapel dedicated to St. Lazarus, which probably harks back to an old hospital. To the north of the route are the Church of Santa María de Arzúa and the Capilla del Salvador.

III. HISTORICAL PILGRIMS' ACCOUNTS

Aymeric Picaud: *'Then come Leboreiro ('Campus Leuurarius'), Santiago de Boente ('Sanctus iacobus de Boento'), Castañeda ('Castaniolla') and Arzúa ('Villanoua').'*

'... in Galicia you come to Triacastela, on the hillside, a place where pilgrims pick up a stone and carry it to Castañeda to obtain lime for the work on the basilica of the Apostle.'

Arnold von Harff: *'It is one league from Palas de Rei to San Xulián do Camiño ('sent Johan a la kamine'), a small village where you cross a stone bridge. It is one league from San Xulián to the village of Furelos ('Foriole'), and one league from Furelos to 'Villa rumpeta' [Mellid?], a 'villa franca'. It is two leagues from 'Villa rumpeta' to the small village of Boente [sic], and one league from Boente to the small village of Castañeda ('Castineer'). It is one league from Castañeda to Ribadiso ('Riuidis'), a small town, and one league from Ribadiso to the village of Arzúa ('Ursowe').'*

Laffi: *'... we continued out journey towards Mellid ('Melid'), a distance of six leagues [from Ligonde]. We strolled around the town, which is a charming place —though not very large— and which has a beautiful monastery run by discalced friars and some fine houses.'*

STAGE 31

ARZÚA • SANTIAGO DE COMPOSTELA

The figure of St James on the Pórtico de la Gloria, Santiago cathedral

ARZÚA • AS BARROSAS • RAÍDO • CORTOBE •
PEREIRIÑA • CALZADA • CALLE • FERREIROS •
BOAVISTA • SALCEDA • BREA • SANTA IRENE •
RÚA • BURGO • ARCA • AMENAL • CIMADEVILA •
SAN PAIO • LABACOLLA • VILAMAIOR •
SAN MARCOS • SANTIAGO

PILGRIMS' REFUGES

Santa Irene: Old refurbished stately home with 36 beds and stable facilities. ☎ (981) 51 10 00

Arca-O Pino: Newly-built, magnificent and sophisticated refuge featuring all necessary amenities. It has 80 beds and stable facilities. ☎ (981) 51 11 10

Monte do Gozo - Santiago de Compostela: Giant hospital complex, featuring 800 free beds and all kinds of facilities. Situated within a residential area, there is also a campsite, an auditorium and the European Pilgrimage Centre (Centro Europeo de Peregrinación). ☎ (981) 58 48 17

ACCOMMODATION

O Pino: O'Pino 24. ♣
Santiago de Compostela:
♣ ♣ ♣
H***** Reyes Católicos. ♣
H***** Araguaney. ♣
HR*** Compostela. ♣
H**** Peregrino
HR**** Los Tilos. ♣
♣ ♣
H*** Castro. ♣
HR*** Gelmírez. ♣
H*** Santiago Apóstol. ♣
H** Congreso. ♣
HR** Rey Fernando. ♣
H** Santa Lucía. ♣
HR** Universal. ♣
HR* B'Nor. ♣
HS*** Hogar San Francisco. ♣
HSR*** Windsor. ♣
HSR** Alameda. ♣
♣
Garcas. Balboa. Cantábrico. Fornos. Galicia. Mapoula. Maycar. México S.A. Mi Águila. Miño. La Paz. El Rápido. San Lázaro. San Paio. La Senra. Suriña. Suso. Vilas. Virgen de la Roca. A Concha de Santiago...

CAMPSITES

Santiago de Compostela.
1st Category. ☎ (981) 88 80 02
As Cancelas. 2nd Category.
☎ (981) 58 02 66
Las Sirenas. 2nd Category.
☎ (981) 88 25 05

RESTAURANTS

Santiago de Compostela:
Anexo Vilas. Alameda. El Asesino. Camilo. Carretas. Don Gaiferos. Fornos. A Charca. Las Huertas. La Tacita de Oro.

PETROL STATIONS

On the N-547 at km 85, in Arca; On the N-544 at km 713.5, Labacolla. In Santiago.

(*) See WARNING on STAGE 27

'Inde Compostella apostolica urbs.' (Aymeric Picaud: *'Pilgrims' Guide'*)

I. ROUTE (*)

🚶 Follow the Rúa do Carmen out of **Arzúa,** and make your way down through vegetable patches and fields to the oak grove of **As Barrosas,** which you pass on the left. You then come out onto the N-547 and go down it for a short distance, before bearing left onto a dirt track which climbs up to **Raído,** on the other side of the river of the same name. You then return to the N-547, continue along it for about 400 metres and bear right off it onto a farm track which goes through the hamlets of **Cortobe, Pereiriña, Calzada, Calle, Ferreiros** and **Boavista,** after which you get onto a dirt track which takes you the 1.5 km to **Salceda,** on the edge of the N-547. A road leads out of the village and onto the main road, which you follow for a short distance, before bearing left off it once again onto a track which leads through a pine and eucaliptus wood, passing Xen and Ras, to **Brea,** where it crosses the N-547 and then returns to it half a kilometre later. Continue along the main road for 1 km, and on reaching the **Empalme de Santa Irene,** you turn off once again to the right onto a road which crosses back over the main road after about 700 metres and enters the village of **Santa Irene,** before returning to the main road past the hostel. You leave the N-547 for another short spell and then cross back over it by a sawmill and go down to **Rúa** and then on to **Burgo.** After 1 km you cross back over the main road by a petrol station and head towards **Arca.** The pilgrims' route skirts round the edge of this village and continues for 3 km to **Amenal,** where you cross the main road once again and go down a street which soon turns into a leafy, overgrown path which leads to **Cimadevila,** where you get onto a forest path which starts climbing uphill, passing Santiago airport (Labacolla) on the left. 2 km further on you turn onto the N-544 and go down towards the turning to **San Paio** on the right. On leaving the village, you cross another road 1 km further on and enter **Labacolla.** From here, make your way down to the river Labacolla, passing the hamlet of **Vilamaior** and the headquarters of **TV Galega** (the Galician TV station) and **TVE** (Spanish TV) on the way. Soon you come to the hamlet of **San Marcos,** near the summit of the *Monte del Gozo,* from where **Santiago de Compostela** comes into view. From the Capilla de San Marcos you descend towards the N-544, passing the enormous Monte del Gozo hostel complex on the left. The N-544 leads into the San Lázaro district of Santiago, passing the church on the left. The pilgrims' route then enters the Polígono de Fontiñas and continues through the Concheiros district and along the Rúa de San Pedro, to the Porta do Camiño. After passing through the gate, you go down the Rúa das Casas Reais and the Rúa das Animas to the Plaza de Cervantes, and then follow the calle de la Azabachería (passing underneath the Arco del Obispo) which brings you into the Plaza del Obradoiro itself.

🚲 Cyclists should have no difficulty following the pedestrian route.

🚗 Milestones: N-547 km 77.1: Salceda; km 82: Santa Irene; km 87: Arca; km 88.2: Amenal; N-544: km 714: Labacolla.

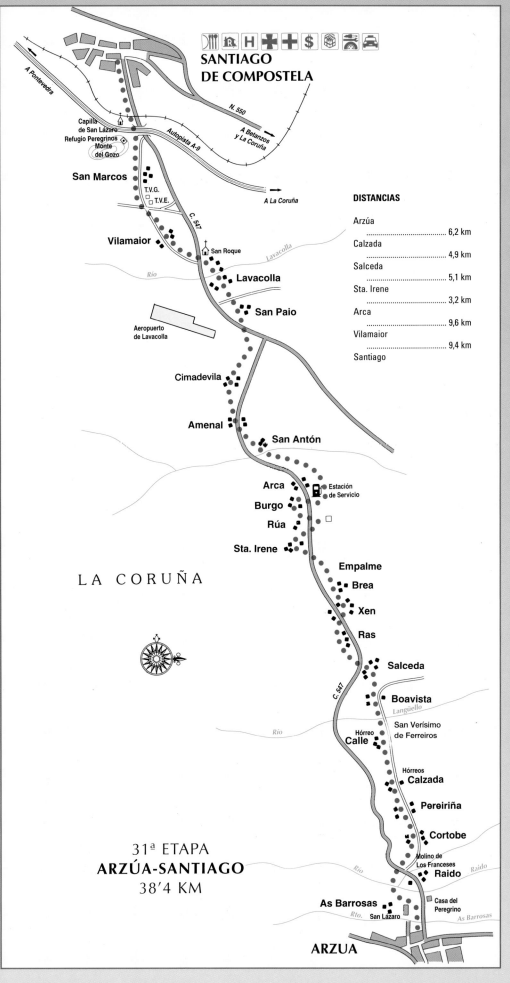

SANTIAGO DE COMPOSTELA

A Pontevedra

N. 550

A Betanzos y La Coruña

Capilla de San Lázaro

Refugio Peregrinos

Monte del Gozo

Autopista A-9

A La Coruña

San Marcos

T.V.G.

T.V.E.

C. 547

Vilamaior

San Roque

Lavacolla

Lavacolla

Río

San Paio

Aeropuerto de Lavacolla

Cimadevila

Amenal

San Antón

Arca

Estación de Servicio

Burgo

Rúa

Sta. Irene

LA CORUÑA

Empalme

Brea

Xen

Ras

Salceda

Boavista

C. 547

Langüello

Río

San Verísimo de Ferreiros

Hórreo

Calle

Hórreos

Calzada

Pereiriña

Cortobe

Molino de Los Franceses

Río

Raido

Raido

As Barrosas

Casa del Peregrino

Rto.

San Lázaro

As Barrosas

31ª ETAPA
ARZÚA-SANTIAGO
38'4 KM

ARZUA

DISTANCIAS

Arzúa	
....	6,2 km
Calzada	
....	4,9 km
Salceda	
....	5,1 km
Sta. Irene	
....	3,2 km
Arca	
....	9,6 km
Vilamaior	
....	9,4 km
Santiago	

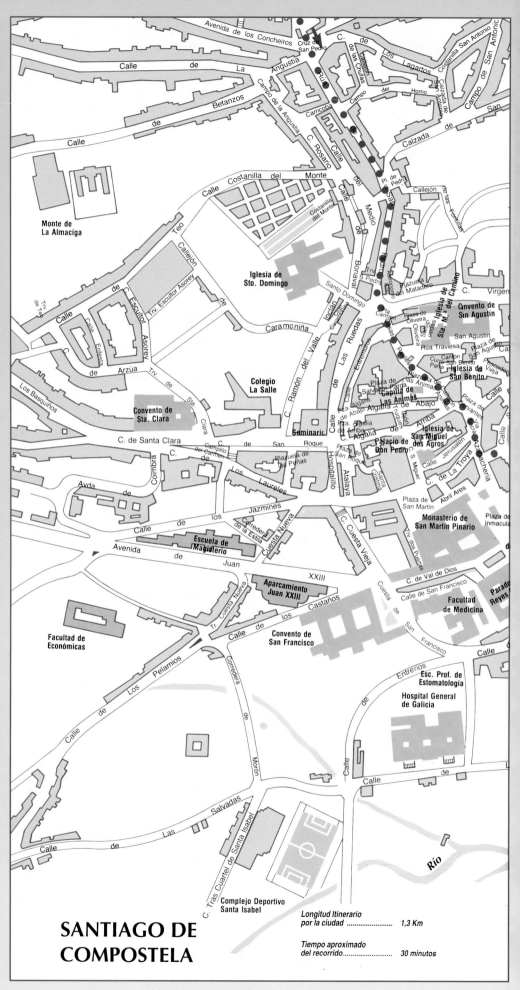

SANTIAGO DE COMPOSTELA

Longitud Itinerario
por la ciudad .... 1,3 Km

Tiempo aproximado
del recorrido.......................... 30 minutos

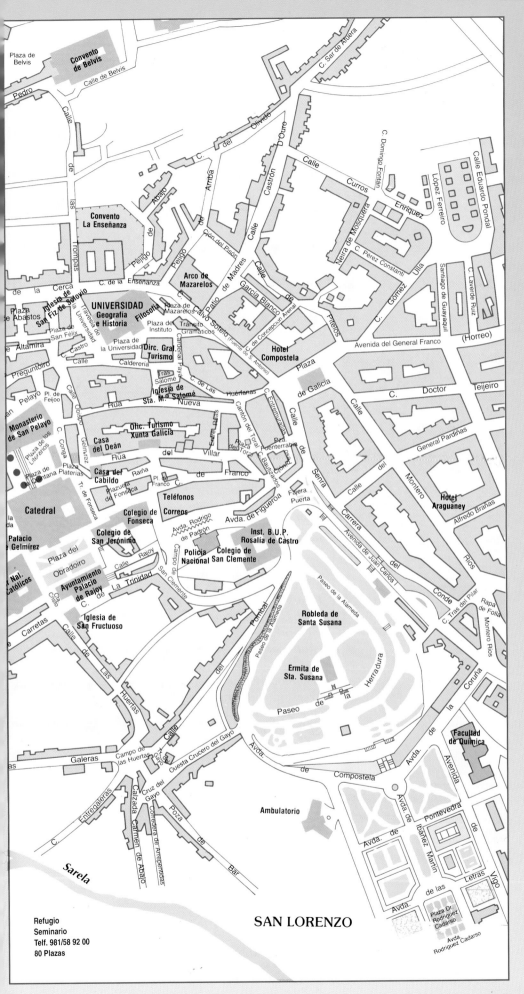

SAN LORENZO

Refugio
Seminario
Telf. 981/58 92 00
80 Plazas

*A wood near
O Pino*

*View of Santiago
de Compostela*

*The old altar of St. James in the
Monastery of San Paio
de Antealtares*

II. HISTORY, ART AND LEGENDS

The first stretch of this last stage of the journey is dotted with small hamlets hidden amongst the eucalyptus trees, all a short distance from one another. It is striking that as many as four different place-names on this stretch alone are references to the pilgrims' way: **'Brea'** (a frequently-recurring name, which is derived from the Latin word 'uereda'), **'Calzada', 'Rúa'** and **'Calle',** all words which are recognisably connected with roads.

After Calle, you come to the village of **Ferreiros,** which is mentioned in almost all the old pilgrims' guides from Aymeric Picaud onwards. Its Parish Church of San Verísimo is extremely ancient, but has been recently restored.

In **Santa Irene,** you should visit the small 18th-century chapel dedicated to the Portuguese martyr, Santa Irene, a rather uncommon devotion.

After passing **Arca do Pino** and **Amenal,** the pilgrims' way continues towards Labacolla, passing through **San Paio** on the way, a small village with a medieval air which is protected from the encroaching modernity of the airport and the main road by thick undergrowth. The name of the village is a contracted version of the Galician rendering of *San Pelayo,* who was born near Tuy and martyred in Córdoba in 925, and whose cult extends throughout Galicia.

The parish church of Sabugueira, in **Labacolla,** is also dedicated to San Pelayo. Labacolla, now famous for its airport, is named after the river Labacolla, or *'Lauamentula',* as it was called in Picaud's time, who has this to say in his *'Pilgrims' Guide':*

'And there is a river called 'Lauamentula', because in a leafy spot along its course, two miles from Santiago, French pilgrims on their way to Santiago take off their clothes and, for love of the Apostle, wash not only their private parts ('mentulas'), but the dirt from their entire bodies.'

Having performed these ablutions (which were a ritual over and above mere hygienic necessity) in order to cleanse and purify themselves before visiting the Apostle's shrine, pilgrims would hurry to reach the summit of the **Monte del Gozo** (*'Mount of Joy'*), so called because it was from there that they caught their first glimpse of the Holy City of **Compostela.** (You might sometimes see it written *'Monxoi',* which many writers claim is the Galician rendering, although the term does not seem to be used by local residents, even the most elderly amongst them.) The Monte del Gozo must have witnessed many a scene of uncontainable emotion throughout the centuries, some of which are brought to life in the old pilgrims' tales (see HISTORICAL PILGRIMS' ACCOUNTS). Today, this once idyllic and moving spot has been ruined by the unavoidable construction of a gigantic hostel complex which sprawls downhill from the **Capilla de San Marcos.** The pilgrims' route then passes the *Parish Church of*

San Lázaro, the only surviving part of a leprosarium founded in the mid-12th century. The route through Santiago is packed with reminders of the pilgrimage. First, you go up through the *'Barrio de los Concheiros'* ('Concheiros' —from 'concha', meaning 'shell'— is the nickname habitually given to pilgrims in Galician). Then you come to the Rúa de San Pedro, which was the location of the ancient *Monastery of San Pedro de Foras,* so called as it stood outside the city walls, as opposed to the *Monastery of San Pedro de Antealtares* (later renamed 'San Paio'), which was situated inside the walls. The Church of San Pedro is one of the ten churches in the city of Santiago mentioned by Aymeric Picaud in the *Pilgrims' Guide,* who wrote that *'it is situated on the Camino Francés'.* Pilgrims then crossed the city walls through what is now known as the *'Puerta del Camino',* which is referred to as the *'Porta Francigena'* by Aymeric Picaud, and which is the principal and most-transited of the city gates. Once inside the walls, the pilgrims' route continued along the present-day Rúa das Casa Reais and the Rúa das Animas, across the Plaza de Cervantes and up the calle de la Azabachería. Taking Aymeric Picaud as our source, this modern route would appear to be the equivalent of the medieval *'Via Francigena',* which led *'pilgrims of French nationality'* all the way to the cathedral. This street was packed with *'money-changers, innkeepers and merchants of all descriptions',* and came out into the great market square then known as **Paraíso,** situated in front of the north façade of the cathedral, where (as Aymeric Picaud describes):

'They sell scallop shells to pilgrims... as well as wineskins, shoes, deerskin knapsacks, bags, straps, belts and all sorts of medicinal herbs and other spices, and many other products besides.'

Today, the square is known as the *Plaza de la Azabachería* (the street leading up to it being the calle de la Azabachería), after the workshops of craftsmen specialising in jet jewellery ('azabache') which used to be found here.

You now find yourself right outside **Santiago cathedral,** the reliquary of the precious body of the Apostle St. James, the eagerly awaited goal of our long pilgrimage. Before beginning a quick summary of the most important parts of the cathedral, we must make it clear that this is not intended as a comprehensive guide. We suggest that pilgrims obtain one of the many excellent guidebooks available, which will help them on their tour of the cathedral and of the many other superb monuments in Santiago which are worth visiting, such as the *Monastery of San Martín Pinario,* the *Palacio de Gelmírez,* the *Monastery of San Paio de Antealtares,* the *Monastery of San Francisco,* the *Colegio de Fonseca,* the former *Monastery of Santo Domingo de Bonaval* (with its Pantheon of illustrious Galicians), the *Collegiate Church of Santa María del Sar* and the *Church of Santa María Salomé.*

Human remains in the crypt at Santiago cathedral

Plaza de la Azabachería

The Monastery of San Martín Pinario

Pilgrims in the Plaza del Obradoiro

The Palacio de Rajoy in
the Plaza del Obradoiro

The cathedral from the Plaza
del Obradoiro

Hostal de los Reyes
Católicos

Puerta de las Platerías

Standing in the **Plaza de la Azabachería,** you face the north façade of the cathedral. The old 12th-century Romanesque facade was pulled down in 1757 and substituted by the existing neoclassical, overly-academic façade, which was built under the supervision of the famous Ventura Rodríguez. Some of the components and statues salvaged from the Romanesque façade, described in minute detail by Picaud in the *Pilgrims' Guide,* are recognisable in the Museum or grafted onto other parts of the cathedral. Walking from here round the cathedral, through the Arco del Obispo below the *Palacio de Gelmírez,* you come to the grandiose **Plaza del Obradoiro,** which is lined with some of the greatest monuments in Santiago de Compostela. As you face the cathedral, on your left stands the *Hostal de los Reyes Católicos,* the splendid pilgrims' hospital founded in 1492 after the reconquest of Granada, and one of the most important and elegant examples of the Spanish plateresque style (it was a functioning hospital until 1954). To your right stands the *Colegio de San Jerónimo,* founded by Archbishop Fonseca (1507-1523), the late 15th-century façade of which was salvaged from the former Hospital de la Azabachería. It is now the seat of the *Rectorate* of Santiago University. Behind you is the impressive neoclassical façade of the *Palacio de Rajoy,* built by the illustrious Archbishop Bartolomé Rajoy y Losada (1751-1772) following plans by the French architect, Charles Lemaur. It is now the *Town Hall* and a part of the *Xunta de Galicia* (the autonomous regional government of Galicia) is also housed there. Finally, facing you is the spectacular, world-famous Obradoiro façade, the universal symbol of the city of Santiago. Completed in 1750 by the Galician architect, Fernando de Casas y Novoa, and crowned by soaring twin towers, it shields the old Romanesque exterior and the beautiful Pórtico de la Gloria. The double-ramp staircase leading up to it is an earlier feature, and was commissioned in 1606 by Archbishop Maximiliano de Austria, a native of the province of Jaén, who entrusted the work to Master Ginés Martínez Aranda, a member of a family of stonemasons from Castillo de Locubín, also in Jaén province.

The history of Santiago cathedral goes back many centuries. Between 830 and 840, King Alfonso II 'the Chaste' commissioned a modest church to be built over the recently-discovered tomb of the Apostle, and in 899, Alfonso III 'the Great' had a grander basilica built over the original construction. Around the year 1000, Bishop San Pedro de Mezonzo ordered the construction of a new church, after Alfonso III's basilica was razed to the ground by the Moorish hordes of Almanzor in mid-August 997. Finally, in about 1075 work began on the present building, promoted by Bishop Diego Peláez, which was consecrated on April 3rd, 1211 by Archbishop Pedro de Muñiz (who is buried in the cathedral). The cathedral is a synthesis of the techniques and styles to be found in the other great Romanesque temples along the pilgrims' way: Toulouse cathedral, the very early cathedral at Jaca, the Church of San Martín at Frómista, the Church of Santiago at Carrión de los Condes (with its superb carved frieze) and San Isidoro at León. Prominent artists and architects worked on the building, including Bernardo, Esteban and the great Master Mateo, and the touch of some of them is often thought to be apparent in some of these other great Romanesque monuments. The cathedral is a Latin cross shape measuring 98 metres long and 67 metres wide at the crossing, with a three-aisled, barrel-vaulted nave divided by semicircular arches. A gallery runs around the whole building. Above the crossing there is a 32-metre high central cupola. The ambulatory links the aisles behind the High Altar, a characteristic feature of pilgrims' churches of which this cathedral must be the supreme example. Although Aymeric Picaud was writing as early as 1130, he gives the measurements of the cathedral and lists the nine chapels it had then. The modern pilgrim will share Picaud's aesthetic appreciation of the interior:

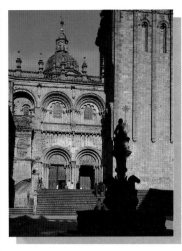

Plaza de las Platerías

'In this church there is no fault; it is admirably constructed, large, spacious, light, with harmonious diemensions, well proportioned as to length, width and height; it is more splendid than words can express... Anyone who walks around the upper parts and who started off unhappy would leave happy and contented after having contemplated the perfect beauty of this church.'

Picaud gives a detailed description of the north façade (Azabachería) and it is a shame that it is no longer of any practical benefit, since it was pulled down in the 18th century. However, his *Pilgrims' Guide* is an excellent companion for viewing the south façade and the **Puerta de Las Platerías,** which is described with great verve, especially the scene representing the Woman Taken in Adultery. One of the most beautiful and well-known carvings is the figure of King David playing the harp. The left doorpost of the right-hand door bears an inscription dated 1103, which is a good indication of the date of the façade as a whole. Moving to the east side of the cathedral, you come to the solemn, restrained Plaza de la Quintana, onto which the Puerta Santa or *'Puerta del Perdón'* opens. Dating from 1611, it is adorned with 24 magnificent sculptures by Master Mateo, taken from the original Romanesque choir. The **Puerta Santa** remains closed and is only opened during Holy Years (when the 25th July —St James' day— falls on a Sunday). Somewhat tucked back between the Puerta de las Platerías and the Puerta Santa is the Pórtico Real, the work of the architect Peña de Toro from Salamanca, and probably the earliest example of the baroque style in Santiago de Compostela. Work on the **Torre del Reloj** started in 1316, and was completed in 1680 by Domingo de Andrade who turned it into the elegant, well-proportioned baroque tower we see today. But the architectural jewel of the cathedral is

King David on the Puerta de las Platerías

Carved figures on the Puerta Santa

The Torre del Reloj

The Pórtico de la Gloria

Pórtico de la Gloria: the Apostles

unquestionably the **Pórtico de la Gloria.** It is worth reading the Latin inscription on the lintels:

'ANNO AB INCARNACIONE DOMINI MCLXXXVIII, ERA ICCCXXVI, DIE KL. APRILIS, SVPER LIMINARIA PRINCIPALIVM PORTALIVM ECCLESIE BEATI IACOBI SVNT COLLOCATA PER MAGISTRVM MATHEVM, QUI A FVNDAMENTIS IPSORVM PORTALIVM GESSIT MAGISTERIVM.'

This states that the lintels were placed on April 1st, 1188 (1226 according to an old system of counting the years beginning 38 years before the start of the Christian era), and that *Master Mateo* directed the work from the outset. Biblical scenes are faithfully represented in this work of pure poetry, which is considered to be the masterpiece of Spanish Romanesque art. Mounted on the archivolts and tympanums, more than 200 sculpted figures can be seen in lively, realistic poses, distributed amongst the three arches of the doorway which each lead into one of the aisles. One of the most well-known features is the central column which is carved with the *Tree of Jesse* (Christ's family tree), above which sits St. James, serenely smiling, and welcoming each exhausted pilgrim. The depth of the finger marks worn into the hard marble of the Tree of Jesse by pilgrims ritually placing their right hand upon it in thanksgiving for their safe arrival, gives an idea of the countless millions of pilgrims who have passed this way throughout the centuries.

You now make your way down the nave towards the High Altar, beneath which is the crypt housing the relics of St. James. Excavations were carried out in 1878, 1946 and 1959, during which an area of 750m^2 under the nave was explored which, under special circumstances, can be visited. The excavations brought to light some interesting data. The Apostle's tomb, discovered between 820 and 830, was a small stone mausoleum situated in a necropolis that had been in use from the 1st century B.C. until the end of the 6th century A.D., which leads to the conclusion that the story regarding St. James being buried in Santiago has an archaeological and historical basis, far removed from the tales of miracles and mystical visions traditionally associated with it.

Facing the High Altar, you have before you the rather overpowering baroque alcove surrounding the throne seating an imposing stone statue of St James dressed as a pilgrim: the famous Romanesque statue, gilded and sparkling with precious stones, which pilgrims traditionally embrace. Above it, a vigorous image of St James the Moor-slayer crowns the ensemble. A thick rope hangs above our heads, from which the famous gigantic silver censer known as the 'botafumeiro' is swung on special occasions. The fragrant smoke from the burning incense served a double purpose: it fulfilled a ritual and also purified the air which must have been rather heavy from the mass of pilgrims packed into the cathedral. Eight men, called in

Galician the *'tiraboleiros'* (from the Latin word *'turibulum'* meaning 'censer') swing it from side to side of the crossing, tracing a semicircle which at its highest point (nearly touching the roof) measures 50 metres across.

To your right are the *sacristy* and the *cloisters* (16th-century) by Juan Gil de Hontañón. In rooms off the cloisters are the archives containing the ancient manuscript of the *'Liber Sancti Iacobi'*, commonly known as the **'Codex Calixtinus'**. As a result of a recent laudable initiative of the Archbishop and the Cathedral Chapter, a splendid facsimile edition has been produced of this incomparable jewel of Jacobean literature.

The **Treasury and Reliquary Chapel** also merit a visit. Among the innumerable priceless exhibits, look out for the *reliquary bust* of St. James the Less, round whose neck hangs the bracelet brought in offering to the Apostle by the famous knight, Suero de Quiñones, after his victorious jousting contests on the *'passo honroso'*. The reliquary chapel houses the tombs of Raymond of Burgundy (who died in 1107 and was the husband of Doña Urraca and the brother of Pope Calixtus II), Doña Berenguela (the wife of Alfonso VII 'the Emperor', who died in 1149), Fernando II of León (died 1188) and Alfonso IX of León (died 1230). On display in the vestibule is the engraved tombstone of **Bishop Theodomir** (died 847), the discoverer of St. James' tomb, which was unearthed during the excavations in 1959. It bears the following inscription:

'IN HOC TVMULO REQVIESCIT
FAMVLVS DEI THEODEMIRUS
HIRIENSIS SEDIS EPISCOPVS QVI OBIIT
XIII KALENDAS NOVEMBRES ERA DCCCLXXXVA.'

After this, you descend to the crypt where the relics of St James and his two disciples, Theodore and Athanasius, are enshrined in a silver coffer worked in 1886 by the local silversmiths, Rey and Martínez. The relics were placed here after the excavations of 1878, directed by the eminent local Canon, A. López Ferreiro.

Our task is over and we leave you here, devout pilgrim, at the feet of the Apostle, after having accompanied you on your long, arduous journey of nearly 1000 kilometres. Perhaps you still have the energy to visit the earliest traces of the arrival of St. James' body in Spain at **Padrón,** the ancient Iria Flavia, or the mystical, far-westerly point known to the ancients as **'Finis Terrae'**. Both places are within easy reach if you feel inclined to visit them.

We take our leave with one request: when you go up to embrace the statue of St. James with your private prayers, please grant us the favour that the families of departing French pilgrims would beg of their loved ones:

'Priez pour nous à Compostelle.'

View down the central aisle of the cathedral

Bishop Theodomir's engraved tombstone

The statue of St James on the altar

The coffer containing the relics of St James

Page of the 'Codex Calixtinus'

Retable in the reliquary chapel

III. HISTORICAL PILGRIMS' ACCOUNTS

Aymeric Picaud: '...Compostela ('Compostella'), the sublime city of the Apostle, which enjoys all delights; the city in whose custody are the mortal remains of St. James, for which reason it is considered the most blessed and exalted city in Spain.'

'... and there is a river, called Labacolla ('Lauamentula')... two miles from Santiago... the river Sar ('Sar'), which flows between the Mount of Joy and the City of Santiago, is considered pure. The Sarela ('Sarela'), which flows towards the west on the other side of the city, is also considered pure.'

Künig von Vach: 'Then, nine miles [from the destroyed city], you come to Santiago ('Sant Iacob'), believe me: the city they call Compostela ('Compostell'). From a mountain top, at the foot of a cross stuck in a mound of stones, pilgrims marvel at how beautiful the city is. May the pure Virgin Mary and her beloved Son help us devotedly reach St. James so that, in the life to come, we may find our reward and receive the celestial crown that God has granted St James and all the Saints in the Heavenly Court. Amen.'

Arnold von Harff: 'It is one league from Arzúa to the hamlet of Ferreiros ('Villa fereire'). It is two leagues from Ferreiros to 'Trykasa' [present-day Rúa?], a hamlet. It is three leagues from 'Trykasa' to Compostela ('Compostella'). Compostela is a small, beautiful and charming city, situated in Galicia and subject to the Crown of Castile. Inside the city there is a fine, large church. Over the High Altar there is an image of St James with a silver crown above it. [German] pilgrims reach it from behind the altar and place the crown on their heads, for which reason people laugh at us Germans. Furthermore, it is claimed that the body of St. James the Apostle lies beneath the High Altar. Others refute this, saying it really rests in Toulouse in the Languedoc, as I have already written. Offering generous gifts, I persistently tried to get them to show me the holy remains. They replied that whoever did not believe firmly that the holy body of the Apostle St. James lay in the Altar, but doubted it, and so wished to see the body, would at once go mad like a rabid dog. This gave me a clear enough picture and we continued towards the sacristy, where they showed us the head of St. James the Less and many other relics. In the cathedral forecourt you will find innumerable scallop shells, large and small, for sale, which you can purchase and hang from your cape to show that you have been there...'

Laffi: *'In the morning we walked towards a town called 'Ferreros' [Ferreiros], two leagues away, and then we reached Amenal ('al Menar') after a journey of three leagues... We continued until we came to a spring, where we washed well and changed our clothes, as we knew we were close to Santiago. We then climbed uphill for half a league before reaching the summit of a hill which is called the Monte del Gozo ('Monte del Gaudio'), from where we were rewarded with the longed-for sight of the city of Santiago ('San Giacomo'), some half a league away. On seeing it, we fell to our knees and began to weep for joy and to sing the 'Te Deum', but we could not recite more than two or three lines, being unable to speak for the tears that streamed out of our eyes with such force that our hearts trembled, and our continuous sobs interrupted our singing. At last, our tears ceased and we resumed singing the 'Te Deum' and thus singing, continued our descent until we came to the city outskirts, which are large and beautiful, and full of buildings in construction. After passing through the outskirts, we reached the city gates.'*

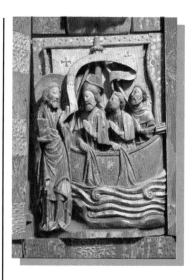

Detail of the retable

The 'Botafumeiro'

St James the Moor-slayer

BIBLIOGRAPHY

Below is a basic bibliography, for purely practical purposes, divided into two sections:

1.— Specialist reference works:

BEDIER, J., *Les légendes épiques. Recherches sur la formation des Chansons de Geste,* Paris, 1912, 4 vols.; 1929 (repr. 1966).

CONANT, K. J., *The early architectural history of the Cathedral of Santiago de Compostela,* Cambridge, 1926.

DAVID, P., *Études sur le Livre de Saint-Jacques, atribué au pape Calixte II,* in 'Bulletin des Études portugaises', t. X, 1945, pp. 1-41; t. XI, 1947, pp. 113-185; t. XII, 1948, pp. 70-223; t. XIII, 1949, pp. 52-104.

DÍAZ Y DÍAZ, M. C., *El códice calixtino de la Catedral de Santiago,* Santiago de Compostela, 1988.

ESCALONA, R., *Historia del Real Monasterio de Sahagún,* Madrid, MDCCLXXXII.

FOULCHE-DELBOSC, R., *Bibliographie des voyages en Espagne et en Portugal,* reimpr., Madrid, 1991.

GANZ-BLÄTTLER, U., *Andacht und Abenteuer. Berichte europäischer Jerusalem —und Santiago— Pilger (1320-1520),* Tübingen, 1990.

GUERRA CAMPOS, J., *Bibliografía (1950-1969). Veinte años de Estudios Jacobeos,* in 'Compostellanum', 16, 1971, pp. 575-736.

HERBERS, K. *(Bibliografía en Lengua alemana sobre el culto de Santiago desde 1980-86),* in 'Compostellanum', 1986, t. XXXI, 3-4, pp. 475-479.

—*Der Jakobuskult des 12. Jahrhunderts und der 'Liber Santi Jacobi'. Studien über das Verhältnis zwischen Religion und Gesellschaft im hohen Mittelalter,* in 'Historische Forschungen', 7, Wiesbaden, 1984.

—(Editor), *Deutsche Jakobspilger und ihre Berichte,* Tübingen, 1986.

—*Historia Compostelana,* 'Corpus Christianorum. Continuatio Medievalis', LXX, Ed. E. Falqué Rey, Turnholt, 1988. In 'España Sagrada', H. Flórez, Madrid, 1765, t. XX.

HUIDOBRO, L., *Las Peregrinaciones Jacobeas,* Madrid, 1951, 3 vols.

LÓPEZ ALSINA, F., *La Ciudad de Santiago de Compostela en la Alta Edad Media,* Santiago de Compostela, 1988.

LÓPEZ ALSINA, F.; MORENO ÁLVAREZ, J., *Los Tumbos de Compostela,* Madrid, 1985

LÓPEZ FERREIRO, A., *Historia de la Santa A. M. Iglesia de Santiago de Compostela,* Santiago, I: 1898; II: 1899; III: 1900; IV: 1902; V-XI: 1902-1911.

MENACA, M. de, *Histoire de Saint Jacques et de ses miracles au Moyen Age (VIIIème-XIIème siècles)*, Nantes, 1987.

MORALES, A. de, *Relación del viage de Ambrosio de Morales, chronista de S. M. el Rey D. Phelipe II a los Reynos de León, Galicia y Principado de Asturias. El año de MDLXXII*, edited by P. E. Flórez, Madrid, 1765, repr. Madrid, 1985.

PLÖTZ, R. *Der Apostel Jacobus in Spanien bis zum 9 Jahrhundert (Spanische Foschungen der Görresgesellschaft, 1. Reihe, 'Gesammelte Aufsätze zur Kulturgeschichte Spaniens', 30*, Münster, 1982, pp. 19-145.

VÁZQUEZ DE PARGA, L.; LACARRA, J. M.; URIA RIU, J., *Las peregrinaciones a Santiago de Compostela*, Madrid, 1948-1949, 3 vols.

WHITEHILL, W. M., *Liber Sancti Jacobi. Codex Calixtinus: I. Texto, Transcripción de W. M. Whitehill; II. Música, por Dom Germán Prado, OBS; III. Estudio e Índices*, Santiago de Compostela, 1944.

2.— Other reference works:

ARRIBAS BRIONES, P., *El Camino de Santiago en Castilla y León*, Burgos, 1982.

BARRET, P.; GURGAND, J. N., *La aventura del Camino de Santiago*, Madrid, 1982.

BONET CORREA, A., *Santiago de Compostela. El camino de los peregrinos*, Barcelona-Madrid, Orbis, 1985.

BOTTINEAU, Y., *El Camino de Santiago*, Barcelona, 1965.

BRAVO ECHEVARRÍA, P., *Cancionero de los peregrinos de Santiago*, Madrid, 1967, reimpr. 1971.

BRAVO LOZANO, M., *Guía del peregrino medieval. ('Codex Calixtinus')*. Introd., trad. y notas por, Sahagún, 1993, 12 ed.

CAUCCI VON SAUCKEN, P., *Guida del pellegrino di Santiago. Libro quinto del Codex Calixtinus, secolo XII*. Milan, 1989.

CHOCHEYRAS, J., *Ensayo histórico sobre Santiago en Compostela*, Barcelona, 1989.

DOMKE, H., *Spaniens Norden. Der Weg nach Santiago*, Munich, 1973.

FERNÁNDEZ SÁNCHEZ, J. M.; FREIRE BARREIRO, F., *Santiago, Jerusalén, Roma. Diario de una peregrinación a éstos y otros Santos Lugares…*, Santiago 1880-1882, 3 vols.

FITA, F.; VINSON, J., *Le Codex de St-Jacques, Livre IV*, París, 1882. 'Revue de linguistique et de littératures comparées', 15, 1882, pp. 1-20, 225-268 y 268-270.

GOICOECHEA ARRONDO, E., *Rutas Jacobeas. Historia-Arte-Caminos*, Estella, 1971.

—*El Camino de Santiago*, León, 1988.

GRUBER, R., *Tagebuch eines Pilgers nach Santiago de Compostela, en 'Año Santo Compostelano'*, Linz, 1976.

HERBERS, K., *Der Jakobsweg. Mit einem mittelalterlichen Pilgerführer unterwegs nach Santiago de Compostela,* Tübingen, 1990.

KING, G. G., *The Way of Saint James,* New York, 1920, 3 vols.

KÜNIG VON VACH, H. [Haebler, K.], *Das Wallfarhrtsbuch des Hermannus Künig von Vach und die Pielgerreisen der Deutschen nach Santiago de Compostela,* Strassburg, 1899.

LA COSTE-MESSELIERE, R. de (ed.), *Pèlerins et chemins de St. Jacques en France et en Europe du Xe siècle à nos jours,* Paris, 1965.

LAFFI, D., *Viaggio in Ponente a San Giacomo di Galizia e Finisterrae...,* Bologna, 1681. Nueva edición a cura di Anna Sulai Capponi, Perugia.

LAMBERT, E. *Le Pèlerinage de Compostelle,* Paris-Toulouse, 1957-58.

MANIER, G. [Bonnault d'Hoüet, Barón de], *Pèlerinage d'un paysan Picard à Saint Jacques de Compostelle au commencement du XVIIIe siècle,* Mondidier, 1890.

MARTÍNEZ SOPENA, P., *El Camino de Santiago en Castilla y León,* Salamanca, 1990.

MORALEJO, A.; TORRES, C.; FEO, J., *Liber Sancti Iacobi. Codex Calixtinus,* Traducción castellana, Santiago, 1951.

MUENZER, J., *Viaje por España y Portugal,* Madrid, 1991.

PASSINI, J., *El Camino de Santiago [Descripción topográfica],* Madrid, 1987.

PÉREZ DE URBEL, Fray J., *Santiago de Compostela en la Historia,* Madrid, 1977.

PORTELA SANDOVAL, F. J., *El Camino de Santiago,* Madrid, 1971, 3 vols.

ROMERO DE LECEA, C.; GUERRA CAMPOS, J.; FILGUEIRA VALVERDE, J., *Libro de la Peregrinación del Códice Calixtino, Edición facsimilar del l. V del 'Codex Calixtinus',* Madrid, 1971.

RUIZ DE LA PEÑA SOLAR, J. I.; SUÁREZ BELTRÁN, S.; SANZ FUENTES, M. J.; GARCÍA GARCÍA, E.; FERNÁNDEZ GONZÁLEZ, E., *Las peregrinaciones a San Salvador de Oviedo en la Edad Media,* Oviedo, MCMXC.

TATE, B.-M., *The Pilgrim Route to Santiago,* Oxford, 1987.

VALIÑA SAMPEDRO, E., *El Camino de Santiago. Guía del Peregrino,* León, 1985.

— *El Camino de Santiago. Estudio histórico-jurídico,* Madrid, 1971. Lugo, 1990.

VIELLIARD, J., *Le Guide du Pèlerin de Saint-Jacques de Compostelle,* Macon, 1938, Paris, 1981, deuxième tirage 1984.

VILLANUEVA, C. y otros, *El Pórtico de la Gloria. Música, arte y pensamiento,* Santiago de Compostela, 1988.

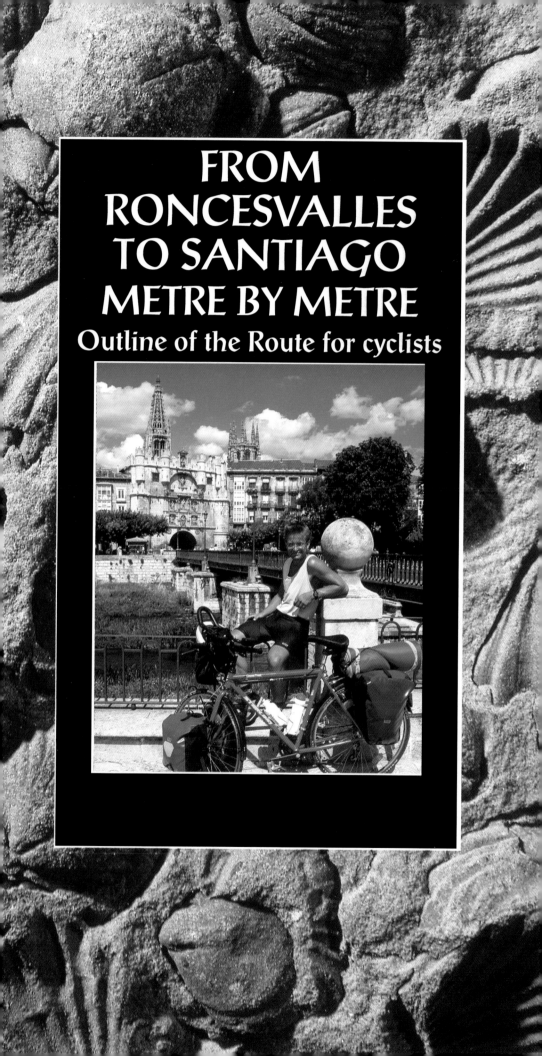

FROM RONCESVALLES TO SANTIAGO METRE BY METRE

Outline of the Route for cyclists

Members of the Expedition:

Emiliano Para	Measurer
Jorge Touriño	Measurer
Simón Iglesias	Measurer
Carlos Barreiro	Measurer
José M. Mangas	Measurer
Goyo García	Doctor-Photographer
Cuco da Torre	Mechanic
Miguel Fuentes	Organization
José Antonio Pérez	Organization
Juan Carlos Pérez	Organization
Lino García	Support
Isaac Rodríguez	Support
Manuel Fandiño	Supplies
Manuel Rodríguez	Driver
Joaquín Varela	Driver
David Fuentes	Equipment

RONCESVALLES - PAMPLONA

ROUTE	PART	STAGE	TOTAL	HGT.	REMARKS
RONCESVALLES (arco Rsda.)	0		0	960	Tree-lined path; visible roots.
RÍO URROBI	3.183	3.183	3.183	885	Path gates.
ESPINAL (Crossroads)	3.340	6.523	6.523	870	Steep climb, last part on foot up
CLIMB TO ALTO MEZQUÍRIZ	1.203	7.726	7.726	935	a conifer-lined path with steps.
ALTO MEZQUÍRIZ (Road)	680	8.407	8.407	925	Good earth track.
BAJADA ALTO MEZQUÍRIZ (Road)	1.201	9.608	9.608	810	
RIVER	1.073	10.681	10.681	765	Steep descent with dangerous torrent
VISCARRET	544	11.225	11.225	780	courses; some road sections.
LINZOÁIN (Pelota court)	2.329	13.554	13.554	740	Very stony, steeply-rising path.
HIGH AREA	1.471	15.025	15.025	845	
ROLAND'S STEPS	1.257	16.282	16.282	825	Very uneven paths with loose stones.
HILL	1.024	17.306	17.306	845	
ERRO HILL (Road)	768	18.073	18.073	815	Very dangerous descent from Erro Hill, with
ZUBIRI (Puente de la Rabia)	3.486	21.559	21.559	526	loose stones and many torrent courses.
ILARRAZ ROAD	942	22.501	22.501	545	
CROSSING	1.710	24.211	24.211	575	Various types of road, asphalted sections
ESQUÍROZ (Fountain)	31	24.241	24.241	570	and areas of sown land.
ESQUÍROZ (Crossroads)	1.741	25.982	25.982	540	
LARRASOAÑA	940	26.922	26.922	555	Tree-lined path along River Arga to
ZURIÁIN	3.735	30.657	30.657	510	Zabaldica; the next section, following the
IROZ	2.073	32.730	32.730	510	hillside is a dangerous one and is not
ARRE ROAD	3.412	36.141	36.141	495	to be recommended.
PAMPLONA (La Taconera Park)	6.269	42.411	42.411	449	Asphalted road to Pamplona.

RONCESVALLES - PAMPLONA 42.411 m.

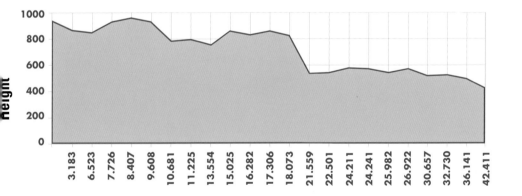

Metres

PAMPLONA- VILLATUERTA

ROUTE	PART	STAGE	TOTAL	HGT.	REMARKS
PAMPLONA (La Taconera Park)			42.411	449	Asphalted road all the way.
CIZUR MENOR	4.212	4.212	46.623	457	On crossing the railway line, an earth track
ZARIQUIEGUI	6.131	10.344	52.755	607	leads steeply up to Alto del Perdón.
ALTO DEL PERDÓN (Hut)	2.360	12.704	55.115	780	Difficult last section.
UTERGA (Church)	3.489	16.193	58.604	515	Descent with many loose stones.
MURUZÁBAL	2.582	18.775	61.186	478	Road.
CAÑADA REAL (Start)	204	18.978	61.389	460	Good paths.
OBANOS	1.546	20.524	62.935	415	Path through farmlands to Pte. la Reina.
PUENTE LA REINA (Pilgrim)	1.792	22.317	64.728	347	Good paths.
RUINS (Top of the hill)	4.052	26.369	68.780	410	Good path, last section rises sharply.
CROSS (Hilltop)	721	27.089	69.500	470	
CIRAUQUI (Baptismal font)	3.419	30.508	72.919	505	
ROMAN ROAD (Cossroads)	579	31.087	73.498	455	Section of badly preserved Roman road.
RIVER SALADO (Crossroads)	4.146	35.234	77.644	415	Path descends to the N-III tunnel.
LORCA (Church)	765	35.999	78.409	480	
HIGH AREA (Road)	1.633	37.632	80.042	500	Road to Villatuerta.
VILLATUERTA (Sports centre)	2.783	40.415	82.825	440	

PAMPLONA - VILLATUERTA 40.415 m.

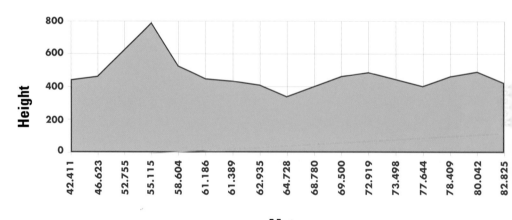

VILLATUERTA - NÁJERA

ROUTE	PART	STAGE	TOTAL	HGT.	REMARKS
VILLATUERTA (Sports centre)			82.825	440	On crossing the river Iranzu, we climb sharply
FOUNTAIN	1.614	1.614	84.439	450	up to the village; we cross streets and descend
ESTELLA (Suspension bridge)	363	1.976	84.802	465	to the fountain. Last section down steps.
ESTELLA (Petrol station)	2.889	4.865	87.690	483	Paths and streets in good condition.
IRACHE (Crossroads)	4.602	9.467	92.292	570	Steeply rising broad earth track.
AZQUETA	1.805	11.272	94.097	560	Path through holm oak groves.
MEDIEVAL FOUNTAIN (of the Moors)	1.434	12.706	95.531	640	Very steep climbs; difficult sections.
VILLAMAYOR DE MONJARDÍN (Church)	361	13.066	95.892	645	
LOS ARCOS	12.289	25.356	108.181	444	Good earth tracks.
SANSOL	6.997	32.352	115.178	504	
TORRES DEL RÍO	733	33.085	115.910	470	Sharply rising earth trak.
BORGOTA CROSSROADS	3.713	36.798	119.623	575	Very hard climb along paths.
VIANA (Church)	7.020	43.818	126.643	472	
LOGROÑO (Stone bridge)	9.007	52.825	135.650	384	Asphalted sections and good paths.
LOGROÑO (La Grajera)	5.762	58.587	141.413	464	Dangerous crossing: dual carriageway.
HILL AREA	3.614	62.201	145.026	535	
HILL (Beyond Navarrete cemetery)	6.204	68.405	151.230	575	Road sections and good paths.
HILL (Road)	3.001	71.405	154.230	615	
SAN ANTÓN HILL	1.849	73.254	156.079	670	
NÁJERA (River bridge)	7.689	80.943	163.769	485	

VILLATUERTA - NÁJERA 80.943 m.

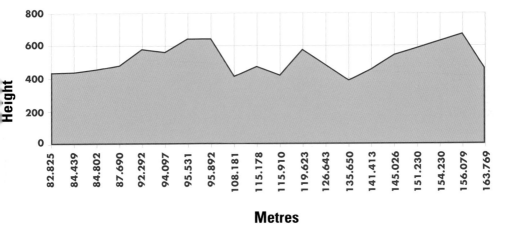

NÁJERA - BURGOS

ROUTE	PART	STAGE	TOTAL	HGT.	REMARKS
NÁJERA (River bridge)			163.769	485	
NÁJERA (High area)	1.472	1.472	165.241	555	Hard climb; good path through pinewood.
AZOFRA	4.596	6.068	169.837	550	Earth tracks.
ROLLO (Stone cross)	1.550	7.618	171.387	570	
HILL	5.946	13.564	177.333	695	Very hard climb on good path.
CIRUEÑA	1.837	15.401	179.169	735	
STO. DOMINGO DE LA CALZADA	5.957	21.357	185.126	639	Rapid descent on good earth track.
GRAÑÓN	6.358	27.715	191.483	712	Asphalted road and track.
HILL	2.131	29.846	193.615	725	Climb up good path.
REDECILLA DEL CAMINO	1.675	31.521	195.289	725	Alternating roads and
VILORIA DE LA RIOJA	3.696	35.216	198.985	785	earth tracks.
BELORADO (Sta. María Church)	8.192	43.408	207.177	770	Descent along road.
VILLAMBISTIA	6.728	50.136	213.905	850	
ESPINOSA DEL CAMINO	1.704	51.840	215.608	895	Excellent earth tracks.
HILL (Hut)	1.502	53.341	217.110	945	
VILLAFRANCA MONTES DE OCA	1.751	55.092	218.861	948	Last section along roads.
MOJAPÁN FOUNTAIN	546	55.638	219.406	990	Extremely hard climb over stony ground,
HILLTOP	3.052	58.690	222.458	1.135	through oak woods.
PEROJA STREAM	614	59.303	223.072	1.095	Good path.
HILL	79	59.382	223.151	1.115	Very steep slopes, some sections on foot only
CRUCES (Carnero Fountain)	1.512	60.894	224.663	1.135	
SAN JUAN DE ORTEGA	6.416	67.310	231.079	1.000	Mountain path through pinewood.
AGÉS (Fountain)	3.708	71.018	234.786	970	
ATAPUERCA	2.621	73.639	237.407	950	Good asphalted tracks.
HILL (cross)	2.076	75.715	239.484	1.060	Steep climb with loose stones and badly
VILLAVAL	2.852	78.567	242.335	940	signposted last section.
CARDEÑUELA	1.795	80.362	244.130	920	Good condition tracks lead
BURGOS (Fernán González Arch)	13.261	93.623	257.391	860	to the streets of Burgos.

NÁJERA - BURGOS 93.623 m.

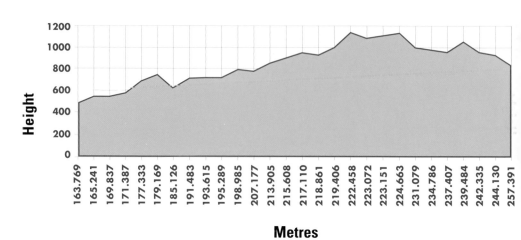

BURGOS - CARRIÓN

ROUTE	PART	STAGE	TOTAL	HGT.	REMARKS
BURGOS (Fernán González Arch)			257.391	860	
TARDAJOS	10.002	10.002	267.393	827	Road.
RABÉ DE LAS CALZADAS	2.103	12.105	269.496	835	Earth tracks in good condition.
ALTO DEL PÁRAMO	4.287	16.392	273.783	925	
HORNILLOS DEL CAMINO	3.863	20.254	277.646	825	Sharp descent down earth tracks.
PIEDRAS (formerly Fuente Sambol)	3.695	23.950	281.341	920	
CROSSROADS (Olmillos Church)	3.238	27.188	284.579	900	«Tierra de Campos» plains.
HONTANAS	3.331	30.519	287.910	930	
SAN ANTÓN CONVENT	5.641	36.160	293.551	775	Elm-lined roads.
CASTROJERIZ (Sto. Domingo Church)	2.433	38.594	295.985	808	
CROSS (Beyond River Odrilla)	3.601	42.194	299.585	790	Earth tracks.
TOP OF MOSTELARES HILL	1.260	43.454	300.845	900	Difficult climb, stony sections.
EL PIOJO FOUNTAIN	4.127	47.581	304.972	795	Earth paths.
ITERO DE LA VEGA	3.378	50.958	308.350	786	Track leading to the river
HILL	4.151	55.109	312.501	840	followed by a stony path.
BOADILLA DEL CAMINO	4.381	59.491	316.882	795	Wide paths suitable for cars.
FRÓMISTA	5.455	64.946	322.337	780	Very good path along the
POBLACIÓN DE CAMPOS	3.629	68.575	325.966	790	«Canal de Castilla».
REVENGA DE CAMPOS	3.277	71.852	329.243	800	Road.
CARRIÓN DE LOS CONDES	12.321	84.174	341.565	830	

BURGOS - CARRIÓN 84.174 m.

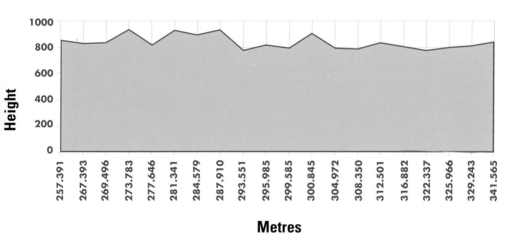

CARRIÓN - EL BURGO RANEROS

ROUTE	PART	STAGE	TOTAL	HGT.	REMARKS
CARRIÓN DE LOS CONDES			341.565	830	
BUSTILLO CROSSROADS	9.374	9.374	350.939	855	Very stony, narrow path.
CALZADILLA DE LA CUEZA	7.000	16.374	357.939	860	
CROSS (Rest area)	4.542	20.917	362.481	900	Climbing road section.
TERRADILLOS DE LOS TEMPLARIOS	4.360	25.276	366.841	880	
MORATINOS	3.140	28.416	369.981	855	Earth paths and tracks.
SAN NICOLÁS DEL REAL CAMINO	2.565	30.982	372.546	840	
SEQUILLO RIVER	238	31.220	372.785	835	We take the road to Calzada del Coto
SAHAGÚN (Trinity Church)	6.822	38.043	379.607	829	and then continue along the «Motorway
BERCIANOS DEL CAMINO	10.433	48.476	390.041	855	of the French Route» featuring newly
EL BURGO RANEROS	7.309	55.785	397.350	878	planted trees and very good signposting.

CARRIÓN - EL BURGO RANEROS 55.785 m.

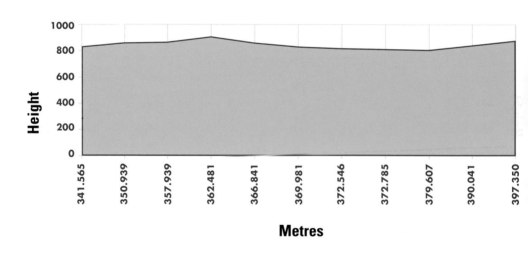

EL BURGO RANEROS - LEÓN

ROUTE	PART	STAGE	TOTAL	HGT.	REMARKS
EL BURGO RANEROS			397.350	878	The «Motorway» leads us
RELIEGOS	12.490	12.490	409.840	833	on to Mansilla.
MANSILLA DE LAS MULAS	6.167	18.657	416.007	799	
PUENTE VILLARENTE	5.782	24.440	421.790	800	Inexplicably there are no Pilgrims' Route
HILL (Crossing to Golpesar)	7.416	31.856	429.206	890	signs to follow. We carry on
LEÓN (Cathedral)	4.884	36.740	434.090	823	along the road to León.

EL BURGO RANEROS - LEÓN 36.740 m

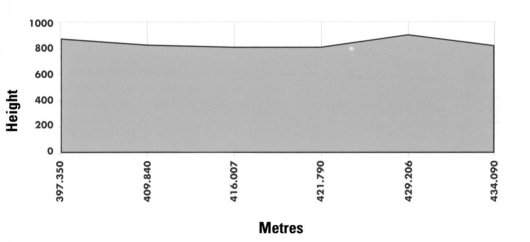

Metres

LEÓN - RABANAL DEL CAMINO

ROUTE	PART	STAGE	TOTAL	HGT.	REMARKS
LEÓN (Cathedral)			434.090	823	We cover these sections by road
TROBAJO DEL CAMINO	4.601	4.601	438.691	853	using paths to gain acces to
VIRGEN DEL CAMINO	2.707	7.308	441.398	905	villages.
VALVERDE DE LA VIRGEN	3.737	11.045	445.135	881	We avoid the left-hand path so as
SAN MIGUEL DEL CAMINO	3.092	14.137	448.227	905	not to have to cross the road.
SAN MARTÍN DEL CAMINO	10.153	24.290	458.380	870	The Route runs parallel to the road.
ÓRBIGO (Roman bridge)	6.910	31.200	465.289	820	
HOSPITAL DE ÓRBIGO	413	31.612	465.702	819	
CRUCERO STO. TORIBIO	10.338	41.950	476.040	905	We leave the road and carry on along
ASTORGA (Cathedral)	5.331	47.281	481.370	873	a path on the right, but very soon
CROSSROADS (Near Castrillo)	6.686	53.966	488.056	963	rejoin the road.
SANTA CATALINA DE SOMOZA	1.924	55.890	489.980	1.012	Good paths and roads lead us up
EL GANSO	4.298	60.188	494.277	1.030	an even but steadily rising slope.
RABANAL DEL CAMINO (S. José Herm.)	6.662	66.850	500.940	1.140	Sharply climbing road.
RABANAL DEL CAMINO (Church)	176	67.026	501.115	1.156	

LEÓN - RABANAL DEL CAMINO 67.026 m.

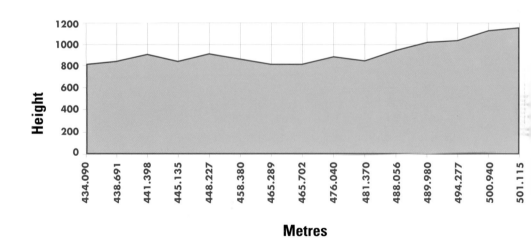

RABANAL DEL CAMINO - CACABELOS

OUTE	PART	STAGE	TOTAL	HGT.	REMARKS
ABANAL DEL CAMINO (Church)			501.115	1.156	Stony village interior.
RUCE DE CARRETERA	1.200	1.200	502.316	1.198	Good path.
ONCEBADÓN (Church)	4.480	5.680	506.796	1.440	Very stony village centre.
RUZ DE FERRO (Iron Cross)	1.882	7.562	508.678	1.505	Good, steadily rising road.
ANJARÍN	2.391	9.953	511.069	1.440	
ILITARY BASE CROSSING	2.122	12.076	513.191	1.497	Good road.
ROSS (Highest point)	1.204	13.280	514.395	1.515	
ACEBO	3.596	16.876	517.991	1.156	Very dangerous path full of
EGO DE AMBRÓS	3.287	20.162	521.278	950	undergrowth.
EXAGONAL HOUSE	1.575	21.737	522.852	865	We continue our descent down
OLINASECA (Church)	2.900	24.637	525.753	620	narrow very dangerous paths.
AMPO	4.638	29.275	530.391	550	Very broad earth track.
ONFERRADA (Templar's Castle)	3.151	32.426	533.542	541	
RBANIZACIÓN ENDESA (Church)	3.009	35.435	536.550	560	Road crosses series of streets.
OLUMBRIANOS (Church)	2.174	37.609	538.725	535	Road.
UENTESNUEVAS (Church)	2.794	40.403	541.519	530	Tracks in very good condition, well
AMPONARAYA (Church)	1.741	42.144	543.260	505	signposted up to Cacabelos.
ACABELOS (Sta. María)	5.779	47.923	549.039	486	

RABANAL DEL CAMINO - CACABELOS 47.923

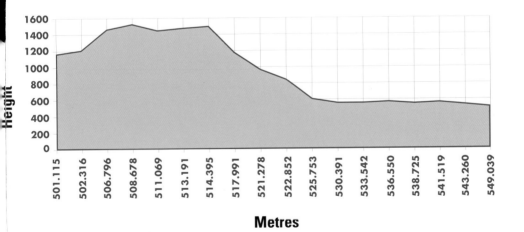

CACABELOS - O CEBREIRO

ROUTE	PART	STAGE	TOTAL	HGT.	REMARKS
CACABELOS (Sta. María)			549.039	486	Road up to crossing for Valtuilli Arriba,
HILL (Before Villafranca)	6.181	6.181	555.220	590	then a path on the right.
VILLAFRANCA (River Burbia bridge)	1.876	8.057	557.096	511	Village streets.
PEREJE (Church)	4.628	12.685	561.724	550	The route diverts fron the N-VI to
TRABADELO (Fountain)	4.454	17.139	566.178	585	take in villages, then follows the
VEGA DE VALCARCE	7.106	24.245	573.284	630	old N-VI to Herrerías.
HERRERÍAS (Old N-VI crossing)	3.035	27.280	576.319	702	
RIVER VALCARCE BRIDGE	1.598	28.878	577.917	707	We begin the hard climb to La Faba,
LA FABA (Fountain)	2.195	31.073	580.111	917	certain sections have to be covered
LAGUNA DE CASTILLA	2.361	33.434	582.472	1.148	largely on foot.
CAST. AND LEÓN - GALICIA BORDER	1.245	34.679	583.717	1.245	The path improves but continues
O CEBREIRO (Path/road crossing)	1.039	35.718	584.756	1.300	to rise. We are in GALICIA.

CACABELOS - O CEBREIRO 35.718 m.

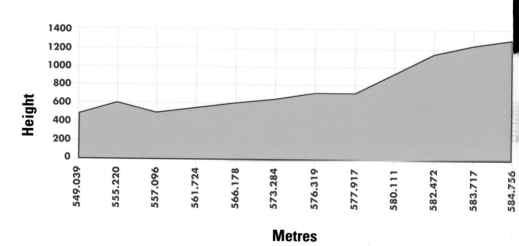

O CEBREIRO - PORTOMARÍN

UTE	PART	STAGE	TOTAL	HGT.	REMARKS
CEBREIRO (Path/road crossing)			584.756	1.300	
IARES (Church)	3.319	3.319	588.075	1.264	Road and, running parallel to it,
SPITAL DA CONDESA	2.568	5.887	590.643	1.270	a path in good condition.
ADORNELO (Church)	2.217	8.104	592.860	1.295	Good path.
TO DO POIO	463	8.567	593.323	1.313	Steep climb to crown the Hill.
NFRÍA (Church)	3.481	12.047	596.803	1.290	
OUEDO (S. Pedro Hermitage)	2.352	14.400	599.156	1.200	Excellent path, some road sections.
LOVAL (Crossing)	3.167	17.566	602.322	960	
S PASANTES (Chapel)	1.585	19.151	603.907	805	
IACASTELA	2.264	21.415	606.171	665	
TO CASA SAN XIL	3.474	24.889	609.645	865	Hard climb up as good path amidst
OCABO HILL	1.684	26.573	611.329	905	luxuriant vegetation.
JRELA (Chapel)	5.169	31.741	616.497	670	Once over the top of the Hill we
GUIADA (Chapel)	2.965	34.706	619.462	515	continue to the right along a clear
ARRIA (Plaza Galicia)	3.981	38.687	623.443	440	path. Alternating paths and roads.
ARRIA (Castle hill)	1.192	39.879	624.635	453	
LEI	3.208	43.087	627.843	515	Stony paths, difficult for those
IORGADE (Chapel)	8.442	51.529	636.285	655	on bikes. Numerous «corredoiras».
ORTOMARÍN (At foot of steps)	9.951	61.479	646.235	350	

O CEBREIRO - PORTOMARÍN 61.479 m.

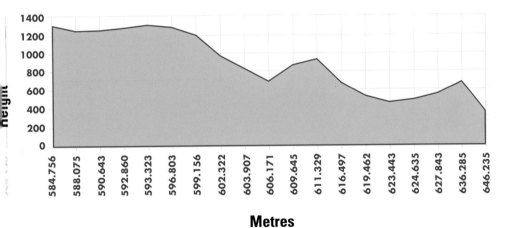

Metres

PORTOMARÍN - ARZÚA

ROUTE	PART	STAGE	TOTAL	HGT.	REMARKS
PORTOMARÍN (At foot of steps)			646.235	350	Crossing the river over the iron bridg
SAN ANTÓN HILL	1.721	1.721	647.956	450	we climb very steeply up a good pat
CROSSROADS (Ceramics factory)	806	2.527	648.763	467	New path running parallel to the roa
GONZAR	5.085	7.612	653.848	558	
CASTROMAIOR	1.212	8.825	655.060	590	Very good paths leads us on to
CASTROMAIOR HILL	732	9.556	655.792	650	palas de Rei.
HOSPITAL	1.686	11.242	657.477	675	
VENTAS DE NARÓN (Chapel)	1.582	12.824	659.060	700	
SIERRA LIGONDE HILL	1.077	13.901	660.136	717	
LIGONDE (Cross)	2.204	16.104	662.340	625	
EIREXE	962	17.066	663.302	630	
CROSSROADS (Portos-Monterroso)	950	18.016	664.252	650	
ROSARIO	4.939	22.956	669.191	635	
PALAS DE REI (Refuge)	583	23.539	669.774	605	
PALAS DE REI (Church)	882	24.421	670.656	565	
SAN XULIÁN (Stone cross)	3.537	27.958	674.194	465	Beautiful paths lined by old trees.
CASANOVA (Refuge)	2.321	30.279	676.514	485	
COTO (Provincial border)	2.559	32.838	679.074	505	
LEBOREIRO	796	33.634	679.870	485	Good tree-lined path.
FURELOS (Church)	3.969	37.603	683.838	415	
MELIDE (Cemetery)	1.871	39.474	685.709	454	
BOENTE DE ABAIXO	5.454	44.928	691.163	425	
RÍO (Milestone - km 42)	2.908	47.836	694.072	415	Good, typically Galician paths,
RIBADISO DE ABAIXO	2.392	50.228	696.464	320	with continuous climbs and descents.
ARZÚA (Rectory)	3.176	53.405	699.640	385	

PORTOMARÍN - ARZÚA 53.405 m.

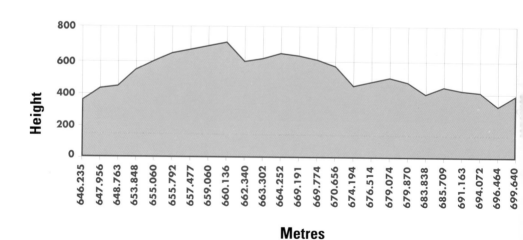

ARZÚA - SANTIAGO

ROUTE	PART	STAGE	TOTAL	HGT.	REMARKS
ARZÚA (Rectory)			699.640	385	Good paths and asphalted traks.
ABERNAVELLA	5.055	5.055	704.695	395	
ALLE	2.634	7.689	707.329	345	
ALCEDA	3.300	10.989	710.629	360	Good paths through trees, some
MPALME	4.173	15.162	714.802	405	sections along roads.
RCA (Football pitch)	4.307	19.468	719.108	290	
AIRPORT (Crossing Curtis Road)	5.383	24.851	724.491	355	Steep climb from Amenal.
SAN PAIO CHURCH	1.474	26.325	725.965	335	Path skirting the airport.
LAVACOLLA (Church)	2.124	28.449	728.089	300	Asphalted tracks, steep climb
MONTE DO GOZO (San Marcos Church)	5.360	33.809	733.449	370	on leaving Lavacolla.
ANTIAGO - PUERTA SANTA	4.588	38.397	738.037	260	

ARZÚA - SANTIAGO 38.397 m.

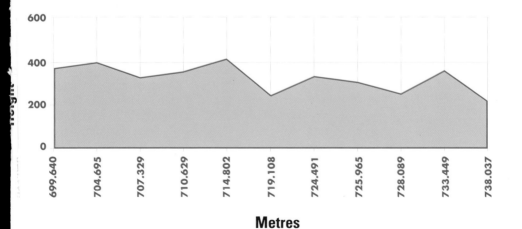

Metres

NOTES

NOTES

CAPITULUM *hujus Almae Apostolicae et Metropolitanae Ecclesiae Compostellanae sigilli Altaris Beati Jacobi Apostoli custos, ut omnibus Fidelibus et Peregrinis ex toto terrarum Orbe, devotionis affectu vel voti causa, ad limina Apostoli Nostri Hispaniarum Patroni ac Tutelaris* **SANCTI JACOBI** *convenientibus, authenticas visitationis litteras expediat, omnibus et singulis praesentes inspecturis, notum facio:*..............................

....

hoc sacratissimun Templum pietatis causa devote visitasse. In quorum fidem praesentes litteras, sigilo ejusdem Sanctae Ecclesiae munitas ei confero.

Datum Compostellae die ....*mensis* ....
anno Dni ....

Secretarius Capitularis

THE 'COMPOSTELA'

This is the certificate which, since the 14th century, is traditionally awarded to all those who can prove that they have covered a certain number of kilometres (about 150) of the pilgrims' way. Nowadays, they are issued by the 'Oficina de Acogida del Peregrino' attached to Santiago cathedral, at Rúa del Villar nº 1 (Dean's House) in Santiago de Compostela.